PATRICK ANDERSON

REWRITING THE TROUBLES

War and Propaganda
Ireland and Algeria

GREENISLAND PRESS

First published in 2022
Greenisland Press, Belfast

An imprint of Elsinor Verlag (Elsinor Press), Coesfeld, Germany

.

Cover design: Seán Misteíl
Printed: Germany

ISBN: 978-3-949573-02-6

DEDICATION

For my parents, Josephine and Arthur, who, like many, endured
the dark days of the 'Troubles'

CONTENTS

GLOSSARY

Algeria

ALN	Armée de Libération Nationale (1954-62)
AML	Association des Amis du Manifeste et de la Liberté (1944-5)
CCE	Comité de Coordination et d' Éxécution (1956-8)
CNRA	Conseil National de la Révolution Algérienne (1956-62)
CRUA	Comité Révolutionnaire pour l'Unité et l'Action (1954)
ENA	Étoile Nord Africaine (1926-37)
FAF	Front de l'Algérie Française (1960-1)
FIS	Front Islamique du Salut (1989-92)
FLN	Front de Libération National (1954-)
GPRA	Gouvernement Provisoire de la République Algérienne (1954-62)
MNA	Mouvement National Algérien (1954-62)
MTLD	Mouvement pour le Triomphe des Libertés Démocratiques (1946-54)
OAS	Organisation de l'Armée Secrète (1961-2)
OCC	Organisation Clandestine du Contingent
OS	Organistion Spéciale (1947-51)
PCA	Parti Communiste Algérien (1936-66)
PCF	Parti Communiste Français (1920-)
PPA	Parti du Peuple Algérien (1937-55)
SAS	Section Administrative Spécialisé
SFIO	Section Française de l'Internationale Ouvrière (1905-69)
UDMA	Union Démocratique de Manifest Algérien

Ireland

CLMC	Combined Loyalist Military Command
DUP	Democratic Unionist Party
ECHR	European Commission of Human Rights
ECrtHR	European Court of Human Rights
FRU	Force Research Unit
MI5	British Security Service (domestic)
INLA	Irish National Liberation Army
IRA	Irish Republican Army
LVF	Loyalist Volunteer Force
NICRA	Northern Ireland Civil Rights Association
NIO	Northern Ireland Office
OIRA	Official IRA
OO	Orange Order
PIRA	Provisional IRA
PUP	Progressive Unionist Party
RHC	Red Hand Commando
RIR	Royal Irish Regiment
RUC	Royal Ulster Constabulary
SAS	Special Air Service
SDLP	Social Democratic and Labour Party
SF	Sinn Féin
SOSNI	Secretary of State for Northern Ireland
UDA	Ulster Defence Association
UDP	Ulster Democratic Party
UDR	British Army Ulster Defence Regiment
UFF	Ulster Freedom Fighters (UDA)
UR	Ulster Resistance
UUP	Ulster Unionist Party
UVF	Ulster Volunteer Force
WP	Workers' Party

CHRONOLOGY OF EVENTS

Algeria

148 BC: Romans destroy Carthage
683:       Arab invasions introduce Islam
1830:   French invade Algeria
1832:   Abd el- Kader jihad, admiration for his respect for human rights
1848:   Algeria becomes integral part of France
1871:   El Mokrani revolt/jihad
1926:   Etoile Nord-Africaine promotes Algerian independence
1931:   Association of Algerian Muslim Ulema, Ben Badis
1936:   Blum-Viollette, small extension of reforms fails
1937:   PPA formed by Messali Hadj
1938:   Ferhat Abbas forms UPA
1945:   May 8, Setif uprising and severe repression
1947:   Statute of Algeria, MTLD win municipal elections, OS military wing of MTLD
1948:   Fraud overturns Muslim electoral victory
1949:   OS post office raid
1954:   November 1, FLN attacks across Algeria
1955:   20 August, Philippeville massacre of Europeans
1956:   6 February, journee des tomates, Mollet bombarded by vegetables in Algiers

16 March, special powers voted through French National Assembly,

18 May, 21 conscripts killed and mutilated at Palestro

19 June, Ahmed Zabane and Abdel Kader Ferradj guillotined

20-24 June, ALN shoot 49 French civilians, killing 10 in 21 separate attacks

10 August ORAF 'counter-terrorist' bombing rue de Thebes, 70 Muslims killed

20 August Soummam conference, CCE decides on random terror against civilians

30 September Battle of Algiers, Milk Bar, Cafeteria bomb, bomb at Air France fails to explode

2 October, 9 Muslims dead bomb on bus

28 December, 4 churches bombed, Amedee Froger assassinated by Ali le Pointe,

1957: Jan – Feb., ALN civilian bomb attacks, Massu police powers

29 March, Melouza massacre

3 June Algiers bombs kill 8

9 June bomb at Casino kills 9

23 September Yacef Saadi caught

8 October Ali le Pointe killed by paratroopers

27 December Abbane Ramdane liquidated by militarists of FLN

1958: 8 February, French bomb Sakiet Tunisia

13 May Committee of Public Safety

4 June De Gaulle, Algiers, 'je vous ai compris' speech

28 September new constitution

1959: Challe offensive

1960: 24-29 January, Barricades Week

9-13 December De Gaulle in Algeria

1961: January OAS founded,

20-26 April, Army putsch fails

1962: 5 March 120 OAS explosions across Algiers

7-18 March Evian agreement

23 March-6 April, Battle of Bab el Oued

26 March Rue d'Isly massacre of *pieds-noirs* by army, officially 54 dead

3 July, De Gaulle recognises Algerian independence

1992: Cancellation of elections in Algiers, FIS had won

1993: Army-Islamist guerrilla violence

2001: Berber party withdraws from government following unrest

2012: Fiftieth anniversary of independence

Ireland

1171:   Henry II invades Ireland, beginning of Anglo-Norman rule
1594:   Ulster rebellion against Elizabeth I
1609:   Plantation of Ulster
1641:   Northern rebellion against Scottish and English settlers
1798:   United Irishmen rebellion, French land
1801:   Act of Union
1914:   Curragh Mutiny, UVF gunrunning followed by Irish Volunteers gunrunning

Third Home Rule bill passed, Royal assent suspended WW1
1916:   Easter Rising
1918:   Sinn Féin win election
1919-21: War of Independence
1921:   Northern Ireland and Dáil Éireann
1949:   Ireland becomes a republic
1966:   Fifty-year anniversary of Easter Rising, UVF declares war on IRA, embarks on false-flag bombings and sectarian killings
1968:   October, Derry, RUC attack civil rights demonstrators, worldwide TV images
1969:   January, loyalists and B-Specials assault civil rights demonstrators, Burntollet Bridge, Battle of the Bogside, August, loyalists burn 1500 Catholic homes
1970:   Provisional IRA defend St Matthews, Falls Curfew, Catholics reject British army
1971:   August Internment without trial, torture of detainees, Ballymurphy massacre, UVF bombs McGurks bomb kills 15 Catholic civilians
1972:   30 January, Bloody Sunday, British Army shoots 27 civilians, killing 14

24 March Stormont prorogued, direct rule from London

21 July, Bloody Friday, IRA bomb Belfast, kills 5 civilians, 3 security forces, 1 UDA

31 July, Operation Motorman, 30,000 troops re-take Free Derry

1 December, UVF bomb Dublin, kills 2 civilians, successfully provokes clampdown on IRA
1973:   9 December, Sunningdale Agreement

1974:	15-28 May, UWC Strike/Rebellion
	17 May 3 UVF bombs Dublin, Monaghan, 34 civilians killed, including an unborn child
1975:	Miami Showband UVF-UDR false flag bombing
1976:	4 January, Reavey and O'Dowd families killed by Glenanne gang, UVF/UDR/RUC
	5 January, Kingsmills, republican reprisal, 11 Protestant civilians killed
1978:	IRA La Mon Bomb, 12 Protestants killed
1979:	IRA kill 19 paratroopers, Warrenpoint, and assassinate Lord Mountbatten, Sligo
1981:	10 IRA-INLA prisoners die on seven-month long hunger strike for political status
1984:	IRA Brighton bomb, PM Thatcher narrowly escapes death
1985:	Anglo-Irish Agreement
1987:	Enniskillen IRA bomb against UDR kills 12 Protestant civilians
1989:	Gerry Adams, Sinn Féin seek: 'a non-armed political movement to work for self-determination' in Ireland
1990:	Peter Brooke responded, Britain has no 'strategic or economic interest'
1991:	IRA mortars 10 Downing St
1992:	17 January, IRA Teebane bomb attack on workers constructing army installations kills 7 Protestant workers and one soldier
	10 April, Baltic Exchange bomb, £800 million damage, more than all previous bombs
1993:	24 April, Bishopsgate Bomb, City of London, between £350 million – £1 billion damage, jeopardising the insurance industry, requiring the government becoming 're-insurer of last resort'
	23 October, IRA attack on UDA leadership, Shankill Rd kills 8 Protestants
1994:	INLA kill 3 senior UVF; UVF kill six Catholics
1996:	6 February IRA ceasefire collapses with Docklands bombing in financial district, British resume negotiations
	15 June IRA Manchester bomb, biggest in Britain since WWII, £700 million damage to city's infrastructure, (equivalent to £1.4 billion in 2022)
1998:	Belfast Good Friday Agreement

1830 French seize Algeria and coastal communities

Algiers

1945 Setif Uprising

1954 FLN attacks across Algeria

1960 Barricades Week

1961 OAS founded

1962 de Gaulle recognises Algerian independence

MALI

NIGER

BURKINA FASO

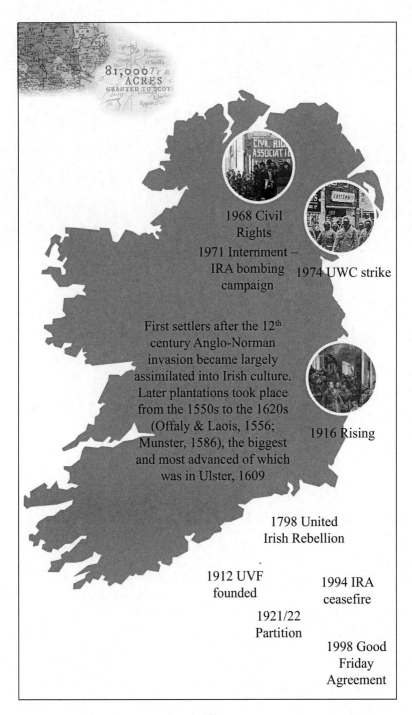

81,000 Tr u
ACRES
GRANTED TO SCOTS

1968 Civil
Rights

1971 Internment –
IRA bombing 1974 UWC strike
campaign

First settlers after the 12th
century Anglo-Norman
invasion became largely
assimilated into Irish culture.
Later plantations took place
from the 1550s to the 1620s
(Offaly & Laois, 1556;
Munster, 1586), the biggest
and most advanced of which
was in Ulster, 1609

1916 Rising

1798 United
Irish Rebellion

1912 UVF
founded

1994 IRA
ceasefire

1921/22
Partition

1998 Good
Friday
Agreement

13

INTRODUCTION

Political violence in Northern Ireland ended with the 1998 Belfast/Good Friday Agreement (GFA). But reconciliation has been slow. One reason for this is the difficulty in coming to terms with what it was all about. The politics of remembering means there is no agreed narrative but a network of contested public discourses. For Ulster unionists the conflict was about a democracy beset by terrorism, finally defeated by the forces of law and order and the securing of the union. For Irish republicans the conflict was one of resistance to British repression, and the IRA made it necessary for the binding international agreement which redresses Britain's long denial of Ireland's right to self-determination. When the British army called an end to its longest ever campaign, *Operation Banner*, officially it had checked the terrorists long enough to permit a political settlement.

This study examines the British media's role in the contested re-writing of the 'Troubles' by comparing its reportage of the 'Troubles' and the remarkably similar conflict in Algeria. The media portrayal of Ireland was always dominated by the British government's version. This now competes with an alternative narrative. Edward S. Herman and Noam Chomsky's propaganda model explains how the government versions came to dominate. The government had help. The bulk of the British press is conservative and emphatically patriotic. The broadcast media proclaimed fidelity to the government and the remnants of public-service broadcasting are not truly independent.[1] Thus any

---

1   Until 1990 one third of BBC staff was vetted by MI5. BBC denied this and MI5 even asked BBC not to make so many requests, Christopher Andrew, *Defence of the Realm* (London, Penguin, 2010) p. 396. One producer recalled BBC Northern Ireland had been penetrated by agents of the intelligence community, Martin Dillon, *God and the Gun* (London, Orion 1997), p. 198. Between 1962 and 1967, Northern Ireland's representative on the BBC board of governors was Sir Richard Pim, ex-RUC inspector general. The BBC participated in the MI6/CIA plot to overthrow Iran's elected government, M. Curtis, *Web of Deceit,* (London, Vintage, 2003), p. 310.

competing interpretation may only be found in the liberal press. For the periods under study this means the *Guardian* and *Observer*.[2] The model, used in this study, has a record of successfully demonstrating how the [US] media come to follow the [US] government line on a political conflict.

The official view of Britain as umpire harmonises with the widespread belief of a peaceful retreat from empire. This overlooks the bloody retreat from Kenya, the full horror of which has only recently become public. The revelations of army atrocities during the Kenyan 'Emergency' were so enormous that Bernard Porter, professor emeritus of British imperial history, was moved to ask: 'How did they get away with it?'[3] In France, renewed revelations of torture and extrajudicial killings in Algeria reopened a public debate that questioned France's own self-image as benign coloniser and generous de-coloniser.

Whether or not the Kenyan revelations force a similar British re-evaluation, the increasing space gained by the Irish republican narrative has produced a new controversy. Government officials had always taken care not to use the word 'war' but with the IRA ceasefire its prior existence was recognised. Unionist politicians took note. Former First Minister Peter Robinson and his successor Arlene Foster declared they opposed a 'rewriting of history'. Journalists, too, have urged a similar resistance.[4] The Democratic Unionist Party (DUP) encouraged vigilance: 'whether it be coroners' inquests, inquiry documents or historic cabinet papers there needs to be a constant repetition of the need for no re-writing of the past.'[5] Their concern is that each succeeding inquiry, official or otherwise, casts British security forces as a participant rather than peacekeeper. The unionist *News Letter* highlighted the danger: 'If the legacy structures make IRA and state seem equally at fault it will be the final moral collapse.'[6] Unionist academics, too, have identified a 'remarkable IRA achievement', the republican view 'threatens to become the dominant narrative of the causes of political violence during the troubles … '[7] From May to

---

2   The *Guardian* and *Observer* are sister papers, and were of liberal, left-wing opinion in the period under discussion, and owned by the Scott Trust, designed to ensure editorial independence free from commercial or political interference.

3   B. Porter, 'How Did They Get Away with It?' *LRB,* vol. 25, no. 5 (3 March 2003).

4   'We shouldn't let Gerry Kelly write the history of the Troubles', *Belfast Telegraph* 23 August 2013.

5   http://www.mydup.com/news/article/building-the-future-rather-than-re-writing-the-past-campbell DUP New Year Message, 2017, accessed 5 June 2018.

6   Ben Lowry, *News Letter*, 12 May 2018.

7   H. Patterson, *Ireland's Violent Frontier,* (Palgrave Macmillan, 2016), p. 230.

October 2018, the *News Letter* ran a 'Stop the Legacy Scandal' series, accusing Britain of 'near insanity', the 'greatest scandal since WWII.'[8]

The conflict now is over whose meanings and definitions will dominate.

Three publications are central to this study. Herman and Chomsky's *Manufacturing Consent* uses a 'propaganda model' to demonstrate how media output reflects the priorities of power. Their method is to rigorously compare the media portrayals of 'matched historic pairs'. Ian Lustick's *State Building Failure in British Ireland and French Algeria* establishes French Algeria and British Ireland as such a 'matched pair'. The official narrative is evaluated against David McKittrick et al.'s *Lost Lives*. This pitiful compilation of all deaths of the 'Troubles', including perpetrators and context, is the most widely accepted record.

The study is divided into four parts. Part One (Chapters One, Two and Three) explains how this investigation proceeds. Chapter One outlines the methods of the 'propaganda model' and its adaptation in respect to Ireland. Chapter Two explains how settler colonialism created the conditions for conflict. Chapter Three outlines a short history of each conflict, identifying and contextualising the many paired events for comparison. Part Two (Chapters Four to Seven) compares the conduct of the respective armies with how these were reported in the liberal press. Part Three (chapters eight to ten) makes the same investigation of the terrorists/insurgents of the ALN (*Armée de Libération Nationale*) and the IRA. Part Four (Chapters Eleven to Thirteen) similarly compares the counter-terrorists/loyalists of UVF-UDA paramilitaries and the OAS (*Organisation de l'Armée Secrète*). The study contains a detailed classification and categorisation of the complete *Guardian-Observer* output for 1954–62 (Algerian War) and 1969–74 (the bloodiest period of the 'Troubles'). All matched historic events were found there.

The official British narrative benefitted from a culture within the media that propagates one dominant concept: Britain's basic benevolence.[9] The British public is largely unaware of the army's conduct in Ireland. Officially, the army was on the side of the angels, and any suggestion otherwise is frequently met with: 'our boys would never …' But the evidence reveals otherwise. Army officers, their political masters and members of the judiciary acted to deceive the

---

8   Ben Lowry, *News Letter*, 18 July 2018.

9   See M. Curtis, *Web of Deceit: Britain's Real Role in The World* (London: Vintage, 2003).

public, to justify, deny, cover up and minimise army killings and abuses. Journalists seldom deviated from the official line. More often, serving soldiers lifted the façade. When army brutality or killings could not be brushed aside, it was framed as a breakdown in discipline due to extreme provocation. Much of the public believed 'our boys' fight with 'one arm tied behind their backs'.

A part of this army directed and manipulated death squads against their (Catholic) fellow citizens. The difficulty of absorbing the 'restrained' British executing Kenyans at twice the rate of the 'ruthless' French in contemporaneous Algeria pales when compared to the effort required to absorb the British army running death squads in Ireland. The very idea of British death squads is virtually beyond the bounds of the expressible, despite the use of 'friendly forces' as a standard tactic throughout the empire. The same soldiers who pacified Kenya carried their methods to Ireland. An elitist conception of democracy kept the public ignorant. 'Bugger the public's right to know. The game is protection of the state,' as Margaret Thatcher's press secretary Bernard Ingham would say.[10] The British public, it seems, was unreliable. The majority wanted the troops brought home, and many believed the solution lay with a reunited Ireland.

Almost all comment on foreign policy in the British media, with Northern Ireland lying somewhere between foreign and domestic, refers to the consensus among major political parties. The British army's Irish campaign is a prime example of this 'all-party approach'. It has a remarkable longevity. This consensus framed the debate. To answer Porter, this is how 'they get away with it'. The official view was a dutiful Britain acting as umpire. The troops were selflessly separating two religious tribes until they reached a political agreement. Violence was never justified because Northern Ireland was legitimate and the UK a democracy. The competing interpretation has an IRA insurgency confronted by a British army and its loyalist paramilitary adjuncts. Despite the British army's almost exclusive experience in counterinsurgency (two world wars were exceptions) and of Britain's long imperial history, the government version was successfully propagated internationally. Successive Irish governments came to repeat it. Dublin advocated more for Algeria's right to self-determination than for Ireland's.

Any 'mistakes' the army might have 'stumbled' into, Bloody Sunday or torturing detainees, were unfortunate, isolated incidents shamelessly

10   Ibid., p. 297.

18

exploited by a sophisticated Irish republican propaganda machine. However, Lt. Col. Maurice Tugwell, British Army Information Policy Unit, doubted: 'if there has ever been an armed force so well informed about the media.'[11] General Julian Thompson believed media training made the army 'very good at dealing with the media.'[12] In fact, British intelligence was/is so successful that clever propaganda stories manufactured during the 1920s' Irish campaign would even turn up in modern Irish journalism and history texts.[13] Sir Michael Howard, of the Institute for Strategic Studies, was so certain of this British sophistication that he lectured the US military on how 'to conduct covert operations and keep them covert.'[14] In 1999 the House of Commons Defence Committee noted, with approval, that Britain is recognised internationally as better managing the media on US and British military interventions. The goal of this management was 'capturing the imagination' of the public.[15]

The axiom of British restraint (Ireland) and French ruthlessness (Algeria) is proposed by the most liberal voices. 'Find me another country that behaved so well,' is a familiar refrain. The belief is widespread, but this study shatters any such evaluation. Alistair Horne repeats it in his famous *Savage War of Peace*. He does not even mention the British army's appalling conduct in contemporaneous Kenya. British restraint, in the face of IRA atrocities, is repeatedly contrasted with the ruthless French in Algeria. Certainly, the French response to the FLN was brutal and shameful. But Britain did not face the same ferocity. The religious dimension in Algeria has been underestimated while Horne explained that the 'trouble [in Ireland] was caused largely by priests.'[16]

Of course, France did great wrong by colonising Algeria, and de Gaulle's 'retreat from Algeria' resulted in the pitiful exodus of the *pieds noirs* (the French settlers in Algeria). Ulster unionists have fared better, spared an abrupt British withdrawal but not the insurgency. Hundreds of Protestant civilians lost their lives; more died in the armed defence of the state. They have been forced into an accommodation with Irish republicanism. Their pride has been hurt and they have suffered a loss

11   D. Charters and M. Tugwell, *Armies in Low Intensity Conflicts* (London, Brasseys, 1989) p. 234. Tugwell propagated the Bloody Sunday dead as IRA.

12   *News Letter*, 10 September 2018.

13   B. Murphy, *The Origins and Organisation of British Propaganda in Ireland, 1920* (Cork: Aubane, 2006).

14   Sir Michael Howard, 'Mistake to Declare this a War', *RUSI,* December 2001, p. 1.

15   Curtis, *Web of Deceit*, pp. 21, 23.

16   G. Kamiya, 'Bush's Favorite Historian', *Salon*, 8 May 2007.

of prestige in their institutions and culture. Orange culture has been singled out for its bigotry, and the discriminatory practices of the Stormont parliament condemned internationally. 'Their' police and security forces have been accused of prolonging the conflict. However, the insurgent communities suffered more. Muslims suffered appallingly at the hands of the French and the FLN (*Front de Libération National*/National Liberation Front). Catholic nationalists bore the greatest loss in proportionate and absolute terms. The great majority of Catholic dead was civilian, mostly the result of loyalist and security forces' activities and to a lesser extent, republicans.

The Algerian war was typically portrayed as a classic anti-colonial struggle. But recent access to government archives in Algiers, together with the reawakening of Western interest in violent political Islam, suggests a re-evaluation is necessary. While the leadership was secular, Algeria's largely rural insurgents, according to their own testimonies, were engaged in a jihad against the infidel rather than an anti-imperial struggle. The FLN was and is dominated by a military elite rather than liberators of the nation. The conflict in Ireland was portrayed as a democracy beset by irrational religious terrorists. But religion identified rather than created the antagonists. The IRA's campaign against Britain, according to their own testimonies, was motivated to remove the remnants of the colonial legacy and towards Irish self-determination rather than any religious impulse. Contrary to the British liberal press, religion was more important in Algeria than was reported, while in Ireland the colonial legacy was more important than was acknowledged.

The politics of remembering plays out now with loyalists' flag protests, contentious Orange marches and republican commemorations. Unionist academics pursue the religious explanation and reject a colonial analysis. The reason is clear: if religion was/is the cause of the conflict, then Irish republicanism is sectarian rather than a movement to reverse the injustice of partition. But if the conflict is the legacy of colonialism, then the focus will be on unionism and the policies of London. This explains why unionism bristles at any comparison with the French Algerian colon or use of the term settler. The self-appellation of planter or settler was previously an honorific but any recognition now of a colonial explanation could eventually mean decolonising and 'to decolonise is logically to deplore one's own past and present, and regret one's very existence' in Ireland.[17] The conquest and colonisation

---

17 'Let us hope that cancel culture does not now target the Planter', *News Letter,* 8 June 2022.

of Ireland rests uneasily with the Protestant psyche. Unionists criticised US Congressman Richard Neal's use of 'planter' in 2022 as insinuating they had no right to be in Northern Ireland. It reflects a long recognised settler fear and insecurity.

The compromise of the GFA means Protestants need have no such fears but has resulted in greater parity between the two communities' aspirations and an attendant increased space for the republican narrative. This has prompted unionism's constant vigilance against the 're-writing of history'. If, as unionism claims, republicans wanted to clear out British Protestants, then they have failed. But if, as republicans claim, 'Brits out' meant Britain recognising Ireland's right to self-determination, then they have achieved a qualified form of it. The new Northern Ireland has the mechanisms to ensure that no community will dominate. Unionism must now accept that its brand of British identity can only coexist on an equal basis with the Irish identity. The increasing space for the republican narrative also means a new focus on unionism as a source of the conflict. Unionists complain they are unfairly being asked to take the blame while republicans get everything they want. Since even the liberal press conformed to the official version of a religious squabble, it is hardly surprising that Ulster unionists now view Irish republicans as rewriting history.

.

PART ONE

CHAPTER ONE

The Propaganda Model

This chapter outlines Herman and Chomsky's propaganda model which examines how media output functions in the interest of power.

The model explains the characteristics of news stories and media campaigns and is concerned with the extent to which journalistic output is open or closed to dissenting or alternative voices. The model is built on the hypothesis of the (US) media applying a *dichotomous* treatment to conflict situations according to the political context: ally or enemy involvement. Premised on a political-economy framework, the model assumes powerful national elites will use the media attempting to manipulate public opinion in the pursuit of the 'national interest'. The model proposes five news filters:

1. Size and concentrated ownership
2. Advertising as a primary source of income
3. Reliance on official sources and approved experts
4. Disciplining the media
5. Anti-communism as a national religion

These filters fix the premises of discourse and interpretation and explain the basis and operations of what are, essentially, propaganda campaigns. Stories hurtful to government and power die out quickly, useful stories enjoy a long and vigorous life. The model does not address the success or otherwise of propaganda campaigns and rejects conspiracy theories. The focus is on media behaviour and performance, not on media effects.[18] The model bears no serious refutation.[19] The fifth filter, a prevailing (US) anti-communism, is replaced here with *Anti-Irish prejudice as an enduring trait of British culture.*

1. Size and concentrated ownership

A radical press emerged in Britain early in the nineteenth century. Various efforts – libel laws, prosecution, taxation – failed to destroy it. However, by the end of the nineteenth century the market was able to 'enforce responsibility'. By 1991, five men controlled newspapers with national sales of over ninety-two per cent. They all acknowledged intervening on editorial policy. The newspaper industry, almost exclusively in the hands of large capitalist organisations, was unsurprisingly pro-establishment.

These partisan press barons offered a monolithic vision. Those who bucked the system suffered the ultimate newspaper punishment, by-line deprivation. Memoirs of journalists portray a debased professional culture. To survive and prosper, journalists pandered to the political prejudices of their paymasters.[20] This bred a herd instinct and conformity, inhibiting investigation.[21]

2. Advertising as a de facto licence

Britain lost its social-democratic press in the mid-twentieth century with the closing of the *News Chronicle, Daily Herald* and *Sunday Citizen.* They were squeezed out of the advertising schedules not because they appealed to too few but because they appealed to the wrong people. The *Daily Herald* closed with a readership double the combined readership of *The Times, Financial Times* and *Guardian.* The *News Chronicle* closed in 1960 with a circulation six times that of the *Guardian.* This requires some explanation. Newspapers are believed to have a commercial incentive to reflect the interests of people at large. However, while minorities, with high spending power, find themselves excellently catered for, minorities, who are less important to advertisers, find there is no newspaper catering to them. The closing of the *Herald*

---

18   An example of mobilising support would be the *Daily Telegraph* generating two million letters which overturned the conviction (three times) of paratrooper Lee Cleeg for murdering teenager Karen O'Reilly, Nick Cohen, *Independent,* 29 January 1995; Paul Vallely, *Independent,* 5 July 1995; McKittrick et al., *Lost Lives,* pp 1207-1210.

19   ES Herman, 'The Propaganda Model: a retrospective', *Journalism Studies,* vol. 1, no. 1 (2000), pp. 101–12.

20   B. McNair, *The Sociology of Journalism,* (London: Arnold, 1989), p. 104.

21   See R. Snoddy, *The Good, the Bad and the Unacceptable* (London: Faber, 1992); and H. Porter, *Lies, Damned Lies and Some Exclusives* (London: Chatto & Windus, 1984).

and the *Chronicle* contrasts with keeping *The Times* and *London Evening Standard* (conservative newspapers) operating, even when sustaining heavy losses.

The 1971 McGregor Commission found journalists cited advertisers, above all else, as an undesirable influence on their work. The loss of revenue suffered by the *Observer* following its criticism over Suez is a good example of advertisers' power. Advertising fell off from companies with patriotic chairmen of military background and from Jewish-owned companies. The defence contractor English Electric refused to advertise with the *Observer* for ten years. David Astor, *Observer* editor, admitted that competition for readers, pleasing to advertisers, forced him to shed some integrity. Advertisers ensured a gradual change. His policy was to try to preserve the integrity of political and foreign affairs coverage, while popularising the rest. Britain's loss of the social-democratic press resulted in a decline in coverage of current affairs, with a corresponding increase in entertainment, human-interest stories, travel, cooking etc. Coverage of Ireland also suffered from de-contextualised and ahistorical reporting.

3. Official sources and approved experts
The media's need for a steady, reliable flow of material results in a symbiotic relationship with powerful sources of information. Economics dictated they concentrate resources where information was available. Information from official sources (army or government) reduces expense while material from sources not prima facie credible or which will elicit criticism, threat or non-cooperation, requires costly checking.[22] Alternative sources can make an impact but are limited by resourcing and credibility problems as well as by official attempts of intimidation. From 1972 to 1977, the BBC interviewed IRA leader Dáithí Ó Conaill twice. In contrast, the British army's experience in fifty-three counterinsurgencies between 1945 and 1969 meant that it was quickly able to gear up its public relations operation. Its PR office worked twenty-four hours a day, 'getting their version in first'.[23] This phrase appears frequently. Simon Hoggart noted that when a journalist is not on the ground of some event, it is 'a ninety-nine per cent certainty

---

22   See the furore over Roger Bolton's documentary 'Death on the Rock' or Jeremy Paxman's filming an IRA roadblock, L Curtis, *Ireland and the Propaganda War*, (London, Pluto,1984), pp. 165-72. See also D. Elstein, '"Death on the Rock" 21 Years Later and Still the Official Version Lives On', *Open Democracy*, 23 November 2009.

23   Simon Hoggart, 'The Army PR Men', *New Society*, 11 October 1973, p. 204.

that the story that is printed is the army's'.[24] By 1976 the army had forty press officers and one hundred support staff. The government had another twenty civil servants for media contacts. Hundreds of police officers and thousands of army officers received media training.[25] The British government has now acknowledged that the task of the IPU (Information Policy Unit) was propaganda and disinformation.[26] In 1970, sociologist Frank Burton was conducting ethnographic research in Ardoyne, Belfast. He explained that journalists rarely witnessed events but had to reconstruct them. They came to depend on a hierarchy of credible witnesses.[27] The British army's view typically prevailed over the residents', except occasionally when a resident happened to be English or an ex-serviceman.[28] Repentant republican terrorists were also credible sources.[29]

Two important experts were John Cole and Conor Cruise O'Brien. Belfast-born Cole hailed from a unionist background and before becoming deputy editor of the *Guardian* had worked as reporter and industrial correspondent of the *Belfast Telegraph* in the 1950s, and for a time its political correspondent at Stormont. Heralded as a 'liberal', he was the paper's in-house expert on Ireland, largely shaping the editorial line.[30] Cole is widely believed to have written the editorial after Bloody Sunday which exculpated the army and clashed with its own reporter, Simon Winchester, who witnessed the killings.[31] But it was written by Alastair Hetherington, editor since 1956, who acknowledged it was mostly 'John's thinking.'[32] He remembers Cole as 'a powerful influence on me and on *Guardian* policy'. They differed only once, 'over internment.'[33] Hetherington admits to some doubt: 'for some

24 Ibid., p. 205.

25 Two hundred and sixty-two civilian and police, and 1,858 army officers received media training in 1972, *The Leveller*, June 1978.

26 See 'Britain's Propaganda War During the Troubles', BBC Radio 4, 22 March 2010, http://news.bbc.co.uk/1/hi/8577087.stm, accessed 10 May 2018.

27 F. Burton, *The Politics of Legitimacy* (Routledge & Kegan Paul Books, 1978), pp. 135–55.

28 See *Guardian*, 9 September 1972 for English interviewees and Shankill Road residents as more convincing than nationalists. See also the *Guardian* of 28 July 1973, a 'young executive' more believable than 'propaganda allegations'.

29 See Sean O'Callaghan, ex-IRA, repentant or fantasist, *Irish Times*, 2 September 2017 and Shane O'Doherty, *The Volunteer* (Harper-Collins, 1993).

30 *Guardian* 150th anniversary booklet, May 1971, p. 8.

31 L. Curtis, *Ireland the Propaganda War – The British Media and the 'battle for Hearts and Minds'* (Pluto, 1984), pp. 40-44.

32 A. Hetherington, *Guardian Years* (Chatto & Windus, 1981) p.309.

33 Ibid., p. 294.

months after Bloody Sunday I took over most of the Irish leader writing …'[34] Joe Haines, Harold Wilson's press secretary, was so troubled by Hetherington's 'near total reliance on Cole' that he privately advised the Irish government to invite Hetherington to Dublin 'on his own', hoping this might wean Hetherington away from Cole's unionism.[35] British Prime Minister Jim Callaghan, Home Secretary Maudling and Secretaries of State Whitelaw and Rees all consulted and trusted Cole's judgement.[36] Cole opposed the 1985 Anglo-Irish Agreement and was unable to update his views during the peace process.[37] His colleagues remembered him as 'un-mistakenly a Protestant son of Belfast … [and] were dismayed when he committed the paper to supporting internment'.[38]

Cole rebuked Catholic farmers who voted for a student radical (Bernadette Devlin) rather than the unionist candidate and Orangeman, Captain Terence O'Neill, 'in spite of all the pious talk of ending sectarianism'.[39] A curious rebuke from a 'left-leaning' newspaper. *Guardian* journalist Ian Aitken recalled Cole distrusted fellow reporter John O'Callaghan as too sympathetic to Irish nationalism.[40] O'Callaghan eventually resigned over the paper's coverage.[41] Cole also espoused the counter-insurgency view that pacification should precede political reforms.[42] From his credited articles we learn:

- Prime Minister Brookeborough and unionism embarked on a more enlightened policy towards Catholics. (But Brookeborough's obituary described him as an unyielding believer in Protestant Ascendancy)[43]
- Catholic schools are the biggest source of division and promote republicanism

34   Ibid.
35   P. Deveney, *Callaghan's Journey to Downing Street* (Palgrave, 2010), pp. 115-7.
36   Hetherington, op. cit., p. 294.
37   Michael White, *Guardian* 8 November 2013.
38   *Guardian* obituary, 8 November 2013.
39   T. O'Neill's *Ulster at the Crossroads*, (London: Faber, 1969), p. 28.
40   Interview, Ian Aiken, (London) July 1998.
41   T. P. Coogan, *The Troubles* (St Martin's Griffin, 2002), p. 317.
42   R. Clutterbuck, John Cole's Security Constraints, in D Watts, *The Constitution of Northern Ireland*, (London, Heineman, 1981), p. 140.
43   *Times* 20 August 1973.

- Partition is not the issue; investment and jobs were more important than civil rights
- Catholics refusing to vote for unionist candidates allowed Ian Paisley to humiliate and nearly defeat Stormont Prime Minister Terence O'Neill who stood down in April 1969
- The Cardinal [Conway] could quell Catholic rioting but the Catholic hierarchy was the least likely source of progress
- Respect unionist rule as self-determination
- Civil Rights activists are as bad as the Orange Order
- Bernadette Devlin is a figure of murdering hate
- IRA are terrorists while loyalist paramilitaries are 'guerrillas'
- The UDA and UWC did not bring down Sunningdale, the IRA did
- When paratroopers were killing teenagers, the army knew fifteen-year-olds were killing soldiers
- Loyalist paramilitaries helped defeat the IRA.[44]

Conor Cruise O'Brien was born into one branch of Ireland's political and cultural elite and married into another. His wife was the daughter of Sean MacEntee, veteran of the 1916 Rising and an Irish government minister. His own family expected to be part of the new Irish political elite following Home Rule. This 'Redmondite' tradition was supplanted by the IRA's and Sinn Féin's securing of British withdrawal from twenty-six of Ireland's thirty-two counties in 1922. He complained to his wife: 'Your people pushed my people aside'.[45] He never denied that his fierce opposition to Irish republicanism stemmed, in part, from his loss of expected birth-right.[46] Interestingly, early in his career, he had worked for the Irish government, writing in opposition to the partition of Ireland.[47] This would change.

David Astor was impressed by O'Brien's lecture explaining that the conflict was the result of Irish, not British, imperialism. Astor believed O'Brien's *States of Ireland* was the 'best he has ever written'. He offered O'Brien a position as editor in chief at the *Observer*: 'I've heard

---

44 See *Guardian*: 3, 4, April 1957, 5, 14, 19, 25 February, 30 April, 3 May, 10, 21 September of 1969; 29 June, 15 October of 1970; 11 February, 20, 22 March, 10 June, 20 August, 15 September, 21 December of 1971; 11 February, 18 October of 1972; 18 June, 3 September of 1973 and 3 June 1974.

45 Bryan Fanning, *Histories of the Irish Future*, (London, Bloomsbury, 2015), p.187.

46 Brendan O'Leary 'Lost Nun and Closet Extremist', *Times Higher Education*, 9 April 1999, p. 4.

47 For O'Brien's propaganda skills, see Tom Paulin, *Ireland and the English Crisis*, (Newcastle, Bloodaxe, 1984), pp. 23-38, and D. H. Akenson, *Conor,* (Cornell University Press, 1994), pp.136-8, 143 and 537.

it said, in Irish academic circles, that it's the only book that actually changed people's opinion.'[48] O'Brien infamously pulped Mary Holland's reportage arguing she had been conned by Irish Catholics: 'the most expert conmen and con-women in the world'. Regarding Irish republicans, particularly their 'killing strain' with the mother usually the 'carrier', he 'inclined to the view' that these mothers had something to do with the actions and beliefs of their sons.[49] He portrayed the Irish as superstitious, ignorant and fond of alcohol. Of the relationship between Ireland and Britain: 'It seems she [Mother Ireland] had some sort of affair with her next-door neighbour. The facts are hard to make out. He seems to have acted rather possessively and, according to her, he used to beat her and often let her go hungry.'[50] O'Brien portrayed the conflict as religious and Irish Catholics were unconsciously imperialistic. He was a leading exponent of a school of historical writing that argued Ireland's political violence stems from the 1916 Rising. The 1912 military mobilisation of unionism with attendant threats of violence, leading to Northern Ireland's creation, however, was entirely rational and legitimate. This revisionist school gained much space in the British media.[51] In contrast, he was 'fanatically sympathetic to Algerian nationalism'.[52] As an Irish government minister, he secretly supported police brutality against republicans and vigorously pursued censorship.[53] He preferred transmitting BBC into Ireland rather than enlarging Ireland's own RTÉ network. He opposed the peace process. From his journalism we learn:

- The problem is: religion, the IRA, an Irish one, the desire for unity
- Dublin politicians encourage violence
- The Irish glory in 'sacred' violence
- The British army typically only retaliates

48   Interview, David Astor (London) July 1998.

49   Coogan *The Troubles,* p. 318.

50   O. Edwards, *O'Brien Introduces Ireland,* (Harper-Collins, 1969), p. 14.

51   S. Deane, Wherever Green is Red, in Brady, C. (ed.) *Interpreting Irish History: Debate on Historical Revisionism,* (Dublin: Irish Academic Press), pp. 234-5. C. Gillissen, 'Ireland, France and the question of Algeria at the UN, 1955–1962', *Irish Studies in International Affairs,* vol. (2008), p. 155, and P. Joannon, *De Gaulle and Ireland,* (Dublin, Public Administration, 1991) p. 74.

52   C. Gillissen, 'Ireland, France and the question of Algeria at the UN, 1955–1962', *Irish Studies in International Affairs,* vol. (2008), p. 155, and P. Joannon, *De Gaulle and Ireland,* (Dublin, Public Administration, 1991) p.74

53   O'Brien wanted to prosecute editors who published letters he disapproved of, Coogan, *Troubles, p. 323.*

- Negotiating with the IRA encourages violence
- Britain will make reforms, the army will behave, the Irish will misbehave [54]

4. Disciplining the media

Government intimidation takes many forms: letters, telegrams, phone calls, petitions, lawsuits, speeches, bills before parliament, complaints and threatening with the Official Secrets Act. It may be organised centrally or locally or consist of independent actions. This is costly, inhibiting and is related to power. Harold Evans, *Sunday Times* editor, recalled an evening reception where the 'Home Secretary Reginald Maudling assailed him: "here comes the editor of the IRA Gazette."' [55]

RUC Chief Constable Hugh Annesley would allow no criticism of his men to go unanswered: 'You have to smile sometimes at how far he goes, to be honest'.[56] Jeremy Paxman, a prominent British journalist, remembers RUC harassment and attempts to recruit him as an agent.[57] Fionnuala O'Connor reported a 1984 unionist conference where the audience was reproached about the number of Catholics who had 'crept into the BBC'.[58] Delegates were encouraged to complain. A television journalist contacted her, explaining his name was on this list of Catholic (unreliable) BBC personnel. His broadcast of the police killing a protestor resulted in enormous pressure: 'Every night I'm subject to calls ... the abuse was amazing.'[59] His broadcast had been minimal, not an investigation or even a commentary. He stopped reporting Ireland.

John Pilger, another prominent investigative journalist, would not even go to Ireland, believing he would be forced to contribute to a distorted coverage. Journalists Simon Winchester and Simon Hoggart recall being harassed and frozen out from information.[60] Television producer Peter Gill complained of more cooperation from the Iraqi army than the British army.[61] Robert Fisk was threatened with legal

54 *Observer*: 12 September, 24 October, 11 November, 12 December of 1971; 26 March, 23 July, 8 August, 24 September, 15 October, 5, 26 November, 3 December of 1972; 4 February 1973; 14 April, 9 June of 1974.
55 Evans, *Paper Chase* p. 470.
56 Parker, *May the Lord* p. 203.
57 Paxman, quoted in *Sunday Life*, 25 October 1998.
58 O'Connor, *In Search of a State* (Blackstaff, 1993), p. 179.
59 Ibid.
60 Winchester was denied entry to the launch of the Widgery Report. Brigadier Thompson (*Daily Telegraph)* emerged beaming: 'the army shot well, didn't they?', Coogan, *The Troubles* p. 135.
61 A. Hooper, *The Military and Media*, (Aldershot, 1982), p. 143.

action for reports that challenged army versions.[62] Bernard Falk was imprisoned for four days under contempt legislation; Duncan Campbell was tried for treason under the Official Secrets Act.[63] Jo Thomas, of the *New York Times,* was initially favoured with weekly briefings in Downing Street and dinner at the best places. When she began investigating forty-seven controversial army and police shootings, the good favour of her colleagues and British public-relations people abruptly ended. A senior editor told her to 'stay out of Northern Ireland.' Then 'a high-ranking British official who, in the past, had links to the intelligence community' took her to lunch and suggested she lay off. Her mail arrived opened. Then 'I was abruptly ordered home.' A senior editor explained: she 'had been paying too much attention to Northern Ireland.'[64] American journalist Mark Hosenball, who covered Ireland, was expelled from the UK.[65] Journalist Anne McHardy's telephone was bugged.[66]

Increasingly, the press was legally restrained, and the fear of libel became deeply ingrained in the professional culture of the British journalist.[67] For the duration of the conflict there was no British Freedom of Information Act. Journalists had only a limited right to protect sources. This did not extend to cases of public disorder or national security. Further, the Zircon affair of secret spy satellites escaping the financial scrutiny of the Public Accounts Committee revealed the British government as one of the most secret states in the Western world.[68] The Official Secrets Act is so wide that since 1912 the D-Notice committee helped interpret it for editors. Windsor Clarke of the D-Notice committee wrote that the D-Notice is voluntary and provided this revealing evaluation: 'that editors do not publish is a tribute to their sense of responsibility.'[69] For a long time, D-Notices

---

62   A.P. Schmidt and J. de Graaf, *Violence as Communication,* (London, Sage), p. 94.

63   B. Rolston and D. Miller, *War and Words,* (Beyond the Pale, 1996), p. 238.

64   Jo Thomas, 'Bloody Ireland', *Columbia Journalism Review*, vol. 27, no. 1 (May–June 1988), pp. 31-7.

65   'Britain refuses to disclose', NY Times 19 November 1976.

66   McHardy, *Guardian* 9 June 2004. Tommy Roberts, UDR Colonel and Roy Mason's press secretary, boasted of 'listening to the tapes.' All journalists were taped, *Guardian,* 6 February 2008.

67   K. May and A. Rowan, *Inside Information,* (London, Constable, 1982), pp. 81, 89 for a culture of secrecy.

68   *New Statesman*, 30 September 1988.

69   *The Times*, 8 August 1973.

were completely unknown to the public. This 'voluntary' system points to a history of 'responsible' editors and a culture of subservient self-censorship. Arthur Christiansen, editor of the *Daily Express*, never mentioned a D-Notice in the paper. He was ashamed to let readers know he was a willing party to censorship.[70]

Journalists Keith Kyle, Jonathan Dimbleby and Peter Taylor complained that when it came to Ireland the pressure was constant, not just the standard letters of protest from government but personal meetings between the chairman of the Broadcasting Authority and the secretary of state and RUC chief constable. These discussions were confidential, but their results gradually filtered down, suggesting that more 'responsible' coverage would be welcome or that ITV's *This Week* might lay off Ireland for a while or that another reporter might cover it. 'There was little talk of censorship, government and broadcasting authorities are usually far too adept.'[71] When Andrew Stephen joined the *Daily Telegraph*, the Northern Ireland Office rang his editor and explained that Stephen was irresponsible, unhelpful and misguided, and that perhaps he should be put on other stories.[72] By the 1980s, *Times* journalist James Adams was writing of a journalist's duty to self-censor.[73]

When the government introduced the ban on broadcasting republican spokespeople, ITN (Independent Television News) editor David Nicholas complained they were already acting responsibly. He accepted the official version and wanted to give republicans a hard time.[74] Following the revelations of army torture during Operation Demetrius (the British army operation in August 1971 which involved the mass arrest and internment of hundreds of nationalists and the torture of selected detainees), eighty Conservative backbenchers met with Home Secretary Reginald Maudling. The delegation, including Colonel 'Mad Mitch' Mitchell (of Aden notoriety), urged Maudling to advocate patriotic censorship. Maudling acted with uncharacteristic decisiveness, immediately contacting the chairmen of both the BBC and ITV. There would be no impartiality between the detainees' and army versions. In addition to the stick, the government also holds the

---

70   Smith, *The British Press,* (Vancouver 1974), p. 177. Most editors approved of D-Notices, May and Rowan, *Inside Information*, p. 81.

71   Taylor in P. Madden (ed.), *The British Media and Ireland* (London: Free Speech on Ireland, 1979), p. 43. R. Dimbleby, *New Statesman*, 31 December 1971, K. Kyle, *The Listener*, 10 March 1977.

72   Madden, *British Media*, p. 27.

73   May and Rowan, *Inside Information*, p. 31.

74   See B. McNair, *The Sociology of Journalism* (London: Arnold, 1998), pp. 70, 96.

carrot. Favoured journalists received knighthoods, for example, Sir David English, a political ally of Margaret Thatcher's, and right-wing press baron Lord Rothermere. Sir Larry Lamb received his knighthood by a thankful Margaret Thatcher one year after her election.

There are others carrying a stick. For articles claiming IRA leaders were embezzling funds, Chris Ryder, of the *Sunday Times*, was threatened with having 'his head blown off'. Ryder was in danger from the army and the IRA. He was a victim of a clever army intelligence operation planting disinformation to sow dissent among the IRA.[75] Martin O'Hagan was held by the IRA and interrogated about a republican informer believed to be his source. After twelve hours he was released, shaken but not physically harmed.[76] O'Hagan was later murdered by the loyalist LVF for exposing their drug dealing.[77] Jim Campbell was shot five times for offending the UVF.[78] Other journalists were deliberately shot with, sometimes lethal, plastic bullets, arrested, beaten up and intimidated by soldiers and police.[79] Baton-wielding soldiers threatened Oistin Mac Bride to prevent his photographing the large number of their spent cartridges.[80] Loyalists threatened to 'cut the throat' of 'Fenian cunt' Allison Morris.[81]

5. Anti-Irish prejudice as an enduring trait of British culture
Anti-Irish prejudice, in popular culture or religious and intellectual tradition, has a long history in Britain. Racism may be the more appropriate term. Certainly, only the term 'racism' adequately implies the viciousness of the stereotype and the mixture of contempt and hatred historically directed towards the Irish. Since the GFA there has been a noticeable decline. Brexit revealed it had not gone away. Bruce Arnold scoffed: 'Bought by Brussels, little Ireland's ridiculous leaders have landed it in a Brexit crisis'.[82] Nicholas Watt, BBC political editor, reported a former Conservative minister sidled up to tell him: 'The Irish really should know their place.'[83]

75   See L. Curtis, *Ireland and the Propaganda War* (Pluto, 1984), pp. 236-7, 271 and M. Dillon, *Dirty War,* (Arrow, 1990), pp. 55-63.

76   Dillon, *Dirty War,* pp. 329-330.

77   *Guardian*, 2 October 2001.

78   *Belfast Telegraph*, 6 July 2015.

79   D. Miller, *Don't Mention the War,* (London, Pluto, 1994), pp. 274-57.

80   Oistin MacBride, *An Irish Photobiography,* (Beyond the Pale, 2001), pp. 68-69.

81   *Guardian*, 4 March 2014.

82   Bruce Arnold, *The Telegraph*, 31 July 2019.

83   https://www.bbc.co.uk/news/uk-politics-46528952 accessed 7 Dec 2019.

Historians and intellectuals

Edmund Spenser, a writer so important he was buried at Westminster Abbey, was contemptuous of the Irish. His sixteenth-century *View of the Present State of Ireland* advocated compelling the Irish to submit to English law. The pronounced assumption continuing through the centuries was that conflict in Ireland is a battle between English civilisation and Irish barbarism. Religion intensified Irish barbarism by fostering sloth, ignorance and support for hostile papal conspiracies. David Hume's eighteenth-century *History of England* explained that the Irish from the beginning of time had been 'buried in the most profound barbarism and ignorance', and, never conquered by the Romans, continued in 'the most rude state of society.'[84] The text went through thirty editions.

Spenser, Hume and Macauley all built upon the work of Giraldus Cambrensis, whose view of the barbarous Irish survived virtually unchallenged for seven centuries. Thomas Carlyle considered Ireland 'a human swinery' and 'a black howling Babel of superstition.' The Irish were the 'sorest evil this country has to strive with.'[85] In 1955, prolific historian A.L. Rowse could write: 'murder never seems to have been rated very high in the Irish catalogue of crimes … Celts are still apt to be unwashed … time had rather stood still for Ireland, as it is apt to do for Celts.'[86] Paul Johnson, right-wing journalist and popular historian, was an advisor to Margaret Thatcher. An English Catholic, his writings exhibited an anti-Irish vitriol. He favoured Spenser's prophecy of Ireland: 'Almighty God hath not yet appointed the time of her Reformation, but reserveth her in this unquiet state still for some secret scourge, which shall by her come into England.'[87] He would quote Gladstone on Ireland: 'the resources of civilisation against its enemies are not yet exhausted.'[88] The *Sunday Times* urged eternal vigilance against Irish barbarians: 'The notorious problem is how a civilised country can overpower uncivilised people without becoming less civilised in the process.'[89] Cambrensis endures.

---

84   N. Lebow, 'British Historians and Irish History', *Éire-Ireland*, vol. 8, no. 4 (1973), p. 196.
85   F. Campbell, *The Orange Card,* (London, Connolly, 1979), p. 12.
86   L. Curtis, *Nothing but the Same Old Story*, (Information on Ireland, 1985) p. 75.
87   P. Johnson, *Ireland,* p. 194.
88   Johnson, *New Statesman,* 31 October 1975.
89   *Sunday Times* editorial, 13 March 1977.

Religion

Protestant Britain was forged in defensive unity through recurrent and protracted conflict with the Catholic 'other'. There is, too, an ample library of anti-Catholic literature explaining how the debased Irish were incapable of embracing Protestantism or 'English Catholicism'. The sixteenth-century massacre of Huguenots received almost daily mention in the nineteenth-century's plentiful religious journalism. It belongs to a tradition of English anti-Catholicism with a widespread appeal and long life among all classes.[90] British anti-Catholicism (French and Irish) was peculiarly related to the common beliefs of the ends and nature of the British state.[91] Protestant distrust of the political claims of Rome meant Catholics were potential (in Ireland, actual) subversives regarding the Protestant Constitution. Catholicism was opposed to the enlightened modern state. Anti-Catholicism fused with anti-Irish prejudice. Even Gladstone, a previous opponent of the popular clamour, wrote that papal obligations opposed Catholics to modern government, and made them subversives to the enlightened state. The oaths of office described Catholicism as idolatrous and damnable.

Of course, anti-Catholicism has abated. It has not disappeared. In May 2018, Germaine Grèer noted 'this country is very anti-Catholic.'[92] An effigy of the pope is burned every year during a large anti-Catholic procession in the town of Lewes, Sussex, with British army participation until 1980. A British army major, learned at his new employment with the *Observer* that the *Guardian* led the anti-Catholic crusade.[93] During the 1950s, the Scott Trust, which owns both papers, would employ neither Catholics nor Jews. In the 1970s Fr F.X. Harriott pondered the Irish 'reputation for violence ... and why old people [in Ireland] are treated with so little compassion ... is it something in the blood or does it stem from a consistently taught version of the Catholic faith?'[94] He concluded that violence was fostered by Irish Catholic schools, families and parishes. Fr Harriott was worried that the loyalty of English Catholics would once again be called into question. He may have had reason.[95] Orwell's writing, too, maintains an obsessive anti-

---

90   L. Perry Curtis, Anglo-Saxons and Celts: A Study of Anti-Irish Prejudices, (NYU Press, 1968); J. Gillingham, 'The Beginnings of English Imperialism', Journal of Historical Sociology 5, no.4, pp.392-409.

91   L. Colley, *Britons: Forging the Nation, 1707-1837* (Yale University Press, 1992).

92   BBC R4, Woman's Hour, 15 May 2018.

93   See P. O'Donovan, *A Journalist's Odyssey* (London: Esmonde, 1985).

94   *The Month*, April 1974.

95   'Britain's Catholics Still Face Prejudice', *Guardian*, 2 November 2017.

Catholic tone.[96]

In 2010 the *London Evening Standard* protested that Pope Benedict's visit to Britain was antagonistic and being shoved down people's throats. The anti-Catholic abuse was 'so shrill that soon only the dogs would be able to hear it.'[97] Cherie Blair, the wife of Prime Minister Tony Blair, was moved to say that Catholics should not have to apologise for being Catholic.[98] The opposition to Benedict's visit contrasts with muted protest against the visits of Chinese Premier Hu Jintao and Saudi Arabia's King Abdullah.[99] Government minister Michael Gove argued that Prime Minister Theresa May's 'Anglo-Catholic beliefs pose a risk to our post-Brexit future.'[100]

Popular culture
Anti-Irish prejudice reaches back to Shakespeare's 'stage Irishman', the foolish Captain MacMorris in *Henry V*. For the next three hundred years, playwrights portrayed the Irish as ingratiating rogues (lazy, cunning, often drunk) or as braggarts, often ex-soldiers boasting of imaginary exploits. The pseudo-science of nineteenth century Social Darwinism was used to support the popular belief of the inferior Irish. Victorian cartoon images depicted the Irish as savage and barbarous, and the image of the 'white Negro' or 'simian Celt' lasted well into the twentieth century. The cartoon images of the stupid, drunken, violent Irishman continued into the 1970s and 1980s with Michael Cummings' illustrations in the *Daily Mail* and 'Jak' in the *London Evening Standard*.

Between 1977 and 1979 Futura publishing sold half a million copies of the *Official Irish Joke Book*[s]. The prototype Irishman is not so much a figure of fun as an object of contempt and deep hostility. This prejudice/racism spans the political spectrum, from imperialist Kipling: 'that damn pernicious little bitch of a country,' to the left's Beatrice and Sidney Webb: 'Home Rule is an absolute necessity to depopulate the country of this detestable race.'[101] *Sunday Express* editor John Junor considered President Reagan's Irish visit: 'I would infinitely prefer to spend three days in June looking for worms in a dung heap.'[102] Bernard

96   *The Spectator*, 11 June 2011.
97   Brendan O'Neill, no Catholic devotee but a radical humanist, http://www.spiked-online.com/newsite/article/9495#.VYLXvEYm_tI, (accessed 3 July 2015).
98   *Daily Telegraph*, 17 September 2010. See also S. Glover, *Daily Mail*, 11 September 2010; 'Bagehot's Notebook', *The Economist*, 16 September 2010.
99   BBC Radio 4, Woman's Hour, 15 May 2018.
100 *The Times* 9 March 2017.
101 Curtis, *Nothing but the Same,* pp. 66, 57.
102 *Sunday Express*, 29 January 1984, in Curtis, *Nothing but the Same,* p. 79.

Levin described the Irish 'patriots ... their minds locked and barred, mouths gaping wide to extrude the very last morsel of folly and consumed with a wild terror at the prospect that sense may one day prevail.'[103] It was impossible, said Conservative Party chairman Edward du Cann, for the English to understand the Irish who 'speak with such a total lack of logic ... There's no reality in Ireland. It's a land of fairies, pixies and leprechauns.'[104]

Labour MP Robert Kilroy-Silk thought Ireland was peopled by peasants, pixies and priests. Edwina Curie, a government minister, remembered 'when I first met an Irish accountant. I laughed. I mean ... an Irish accountant.'[105] Lord Arran wrote in the *London Evening Standard*: 'I always have hated the Irish. I always will ... I loathe and detest the miserable bastards. They are savage murderous thugs. All of them.'[106] He believed he spoke for most people and had no fear of prosecution. The novelist John Walsh, of Irish background, grew up in 1970s London. He remembers Jak in the *London Evening Standard* as a special offender: 'But then the *Standard* seemed to nurse a special animus against the London Irish.'[107] Angela Ince and Lord Arran regularly wondered aloud about the dark side of the Irish. They were all 'mad Paddies'.[108]

The point here is not to compile a list of people with anti-Irish prejudices but to highlight how prominent and otherwise sophisticated public figures feel free to perpetuate such negative stereotypes without fear of any opprobrium. In 1997 Manchester Airport was obliged to remove an 'Irish clock' showing time moving backwards.

The language of politics in Britain in relation to Ireland was/is dominated by the putative division between barbarism and civilisation. The classic barbarian, is, first, Irish, then Catholic, and, if not Catholic, an extreme Protestant, a Dissenter of the old, troublesome Calvinist or Ranter type. In addition, he is working class and unemployed (unemployable). Finally, 'he' is sometimes 'she'. Seamus Deane summed it up: 'Of all the blighting distinctions which govern our responses and limit our imagination at the moment, none is more potent

---

103   *The Times*, 23 September 1977, in Curtis, *Nothing but the Same*, p. 79.
104   *Vanity Fair*, January 1996.
105   *Belfast Telegraph*, 17 December 1996.
106   *London Evening Standard*, 24 May 1974.
107   J. Walsh, *Falling Angels*, p. 218.
108   Ibid., 222.

than the 400-year-old distinction between barbarians and civilians.'[109] The *New Left Review*, a British magazine of the radical intelligentsia, did not publish one article about Ireland's conflict between 1969-1994.[110]

A propaganda system at work?

These filters narrow the range of news fit to print, and sharply limit what can become sustained campaigns. But newspapers are not simply ciphers of a hidden agenda based on a pro-capitalist ideology revealing itself in the reporting of events. It is more a guided market system. The guidance is provided by government, media owners, executives, approved commentators and experts. Further, the British political consensus on Ireland has been remarkable in its uniformity and longevity. The received wisdom is that Britain undertook the umpire role with the best intentions, reacting only to provocation, sometimes unwisely, because of personal failures, the complexity of history or a failure to fully appreciate the evil nature of its enemies. Dissent from this framework earns the accusation of terrorist apologist. The general dichotomisation produces 'worthy' and 'unworthy' victims. Journalists may be critical within accepted parameters but departures from orthodoxy are rare. Newspapers actively compete, and formal censorship, is mostly absent. It is not readily apparent that a propaganda system is at work.

Critics of the propaganda model reject the idea that institutional factors can result in hundreds of independent journalists jointly disseminating false propaganda. Such a conclusion must assume a conspiracy. I do not discount the idea of British Intelligence working to manipulate the media.[111] We now know that British Prime Minister Ted Heath 'piled on the pressure' for 'massive' and 'unattributable propaganda'.[112] I recognise too that Sir Martin Furnival-Jones, MI5, informed Heath that the best thing the intelligence services could do was 'define the problem'.[113]

109 Deane, 'Wherever Green is Read', p. 14.
110 See S. Porter and D. O'Hearn, 'New Left Podsnappery', *New Left Review*, no. 212 (July–August 1995), and replies from Patterson and Blackburn, same issue. See also 'The Other 1968', *Guardian*- 23 April 2008.
111 See British Intelligence in the media, *Washington Post* 22 February 1975. *Izvestia's* December 1968 listing names of journalist-spies was dismissed as propaganda until historians confirmed MI6 embedded agents in the British press. Alistair Horne, for example, worked for MI6 and *Daily Telegraph*, 'Secret Agents' of the UK Press, BBC Radio 4, 4 March 2013. Astor played down his MI6 links, Ben McIntyre *A Spy Among Friends: Kim Philby and the Great Betrayal* (London, Bloomsbury) p.14.
112 *Belfast Telegraph*, 26 May 2018; see too Rory Cormac, *Disrupt and Deny* (OUP 2018).
113 Andrew, *Defence of the Realm*, 2010, p. 618.

But, to be clear, this study does not depend on any such conspiracy.

The resulting propaganda is the result of market forces operating to meet the needs of the day. It can be illustrated by the school chemistry experiment used to explain the extraordinary behaviour of snowflakes and crystalline structures forming perfectly symmetrical shapes, seemingly without design. The experiment involves pouring a stream of balls over a flat box framework. Inevitably, the balls produce an almost perfect pyramid since the most stable resting position in the structure is always one that contributes to the pyramid. Any ball that settles securely inevitably builds, while others in less stable positions either bounce out or are moved to more secure positions. The pyramid is simply the inevitable result of spheres falling onto a square frame. Consider the frame as representing the five filters. By 'pouring' news and information into the framework, a narrative helpful to power will inevitably build. Supportive editors and journalists, lauded as responsible and balanced, find a place in the pyramid. Unsupportive journalists, deemed extremist or irrational, will bounce out or be moved (reassigned).

In criticising newspaper priorities, this study draws upon the newspapers themselves for facts. Is this a classic non sequitur – proof that the criticism is self-refuting? That the press provides some contrasting information, however, proves little about the adequacy or accuracy of the coverage. More important is the attention given to a fact and its placement, tone, repetition and the analytical framework within which it is written. While certain facts may be found by the diligent reader, the absence of bias and de facto suppression is not demonstrated. A further criticism of the propaganda model is that it fails to uncover journalists' intentions. But these cannot be measured. An extended, quantitative analysis is a better line of inquiry. Some journalists may internalise a propaganda narrative and others may know it is false.

I interviewed ten journalists, all with experience of Ireland and Algeria: Clare Hollingworth, David Astor, Neal Ascherson, Bill Millinship, Ian Aitken, Herb Greer (all *Guardian/Observer)*; Robert Kee (BBC), Alan Williams (*Daily Express*) Ronnie Payne (*Daily Telegraph*) and Tom Pocock (*London Evening Standard*). Nine were eyewitnesses. Their words help explain how the 'news fit to print' bends to the official narrative. Their first-hand accounts permit an insight into their internalised (frequently mistaken) beliefs. They also demonstrate a sensitivity when these beliefs are challenged. This was sensitive ground. More than once, I was advised not to take the Algerian analogy too far. Their words also provide background on government disciplining and demonstrate a hierarchy of credible sources. Almost all had elite education, eight were British veterans (usually conscripted). They sympathised with the 'squaddie' who was only doing his job. Tom Pocock lunched with Colonel John MacMillan, they 'talked of old friends … Col Mitchell who commanded the Argylls with such dash.' Wearing army uniform, Pocock accompanied soldiers on patrol: 'friendly and smiling corporals who had to put up with the obscenities of Belfast housewives.'[114] All were happy to speak on Algeria but less so about Ireland. In Algeria they had relied on French, FLN and OAS sources. In Ireland, only the American-born journalist, Herb Greer, acknowledged an IRA source, and he was solidly anti-republican. Most afforded greater credibility to official British sources than to official French sources. Some had internalised the counter-insurgency analysis of Ireland. On French misconduct they spoke freely. They professed to know less about Ireland. It was a far-away country of which they knew little. It was too long ago. This is curious for such a well-educated group and Ireland having been a news story for thirty years. Algeria, of course, was even further away in time. If there was any misconduct, their responses focussed more on the RUC than the British army. There was a general agreement Britain was restrained and the French were ruthless; usually supported by citing specific events (often incorrectly). On Algeria, there was considerable sympathy for the ALN against the ruthless French and a general dislike of the French settlers. The interviews reveal many common perspectives. Coupled with media policing and a widespread deference to official sources, these shared worldviews resulted in journalists professing their independence while working within a propaganda system.

---

114   T. Pocock, *East and West of Suez: The Retreat from Empire* (Bodley Head, 1986), p. 186.

41

CHAPTER TWO

The Analogy in the Room
– Settler Colonialism in Ireland and Algeria

This chapter reviews and evaluates the competing analyses explaining the historic roots of the Northern Ireland (NI) conflict. It has typically been explained as a religious conflict, less often as the legacy of colonialism. The north of Ireland has been compared with the Israeli–Palestinian conflict, apartheid South Africa, the United States during the 1960s' civil rights movement, the partition of India, and Rhodesian settlers opposing indigenous Zimbabwean rule. The many and obvious similarities to French Algeria are frequently overlooked.

To label a situation 'colonial' implies two things: it was illegitimate and unlikely to last. Whyte concludes that the colonial analogy of Algeria and Ireland is partly and undoubtedly true.[115] English and Scottish settlers came over to Ireland in the seventeenth century in much the same manner as their compatriots did in America. No one calls the American settlements anything other than colonies. Some of the same individuals were involved. In Ireland, the result was to produce an enduring division of the population, as occurred in other settler colonies, such as South Africa, Rhodesia and Algeria. The fact that Northern Ireland in legal terms is not a colony but a part of the United Kingdom does not destroy the analogy. France's all-embracing, colonial-myth system similarly contained the legal fiction that Algeria was not a colony but a province and an integral part of France. This did not stop Paris from eventually treating that outlying state territory as expendable. In Britain, too, opinion polls generally indicate a majority in favour of

---

115   See J. Whyte, *Interpreting NI* (Oxford: Clarendon, 1991).

withdrawal, suggesting the British don't really believe the North of Ireland is an integral part of the nation. Still, most analysts in Northern Ireland do not accept the analogy. Typically, they do not tell us why, but simply remain silent on the subject, and do not argue the case against employing it. This is intriguing since international opinion generally favours the colonial analogy and views the conflict as a legacy of British imperialism.

Before the white man saw off the buffalo
Those commentators prepared to tender their views offer little that is convincing. ATQ Stewart, a historian credited with a special insight into the unionist psyche, argued: 'white Algerians are settlers in a sense that Ulstermen are not.'[116] He did not elaborate. Bruce rejects the analogy because the 'planting' took place so long ago. Protestants in Ulster have been there since before the 'white man saw off the American buffalo'.[117] This explains little.

Padraig O'Malley rejects the analogy for three reasons: Protestants have been there longer; the racial/ethnic/religious differences were greater in Algeria; and the British army remained loyal.[118] But the British army was of dubious loyalty. The regular or 'green army' differed from the intelligence services and Harold Wilson believed MI5 plotted against him.[119] His press secretary Joe Haines also believed part of the army was working against the government. The army's inaction during the crisis period of the 1974 Ulster Workers' Council (UWC) strike has never been completely explained, and senior officers frustrated potential British-IRA agreements.[120] The limitations of O'Malley's 'greater differences' are revealed in the following event in Algeria.[121] A Muslim Special Branch officer shot an OAS gunman but was surprised to discover he was a friend from the soccer team of his youth. This would be almost impossible in Northern Ireland where children of the two traditions rarely played on the same teams. The possibility of RUC Special Branch, especially the exotic specimen of a Catholic one, shooting a loyalist engaged in random sectarian murder was literally zero. In addition, Alastair Horne, analysing the violence

116   A.T.Q. Stewart, *The Narrow Ground*, (London, Faber and Faber), p.161.
117   S. Bruce, *Edge of the Union, (OUP)*, p. 130.
118   P. O'Malley, *Uncivil Wars,* (Blackstaff, 1983), p. 299.
119   The Plot against Harold Wilson, BBC 2, broadcast 16 March 2006.
120   Newsinger *British Counterinsurgency*, (Palgrave 2015), pp 176-7, Dillon, *Enemy Within*, (Doubleday, 1994), p. 115.
121   P. Henissart, *Wolves in the City,* (London, Rupert 1970), p. 224.

of December 1960 in Algiers, noted in the impoverished neighbourhood of Belcourt that 'for the past six years of war the two working-class communities had coexisted in a state of uneasy peace.'[122] Indeed, Muslims continued to live in the working-class French Algerian neighbourhood (and OAS stronghold) of Bab el Oued as late as March 1962, almost the end of the war.

In contrast, as early as 1970, Ian Paisley called for the forced removal of Catholics.[123] He lobbied Reginald Maudling to move Catholics from Unity Flats which bordered the loyalist Shankill. Catholics living openly in working-class loyalist neighbourhoods is, even now, still highly unlikely. In the early 1970s, the Reverend William Beattie of Ian Paisley's Democratic Unionist Party (DUP), 'invited the entire Catholic population to move across the border [and] even offered to foot the transport bill to get the recalcitrant "Taigs" over the border.'[124]

When comparing divided societies, much care is necessary when pronouncing on the extent of the differences between ethnic communities. O'Malley's first point, the period of settlement, is, again, insufficient to reject the analogy, as this chapter will show. O'Malley argues Irish republicans favour the analogy because they hope for a similar defeat of the *colons* (French settlers, *the pieds noirs*). This is a misreading. Irish republicans sought the overthrow of the colonial legacy, *not* the expulsion of the settlers' descendants.

Conor Cruise O'Brien rejected the Algerian analogy for three reasons: Protestants were a larger minority in Ireland (twenty-five per cent) than the French were in Algeria (ten per cent); Irish Catholic solidarity, North and South, is less than Algerian Muslim solidarity; and, again, Protestants had been in Ireland longer than the French were in Algeria.[125] But O'Brien has overlooked the *harkis*, the French army auxiliaries. Including their families, they amounted to 1.5 million pro-French Muslims in a total population of 9 million, seventeen per cent.[126] He also overlooked the lack of solidarity between Berbers and Arabs, evident during and even after the war, as in the Berber Spring of 1980 and the movement for autonomy in Kabylia. The FLN, during the war and still yet, conceive their task as forging widely disparate peoples into

---

122 Horne, *A Savage War of Peace*, p. 432.
123 Deutsch and Magowan, *NI*, p. 78.
124 *Guardian* 5 January 2003.
125 C. C. O'Brien, 'Violence in Ireland: Another Algeria?', *NYRB*, September 1971, pp. 17–19.
126 M. S. Alexander, *Algerian War*, (Palgrave-MacMillan, 2002), p.123.

a nation. They perpetrated extensive surgery attempting to transform the wide cultural diversity of Algeria. [127] Lastly, the period of residence of the settler/migrants is not as important as whether the social relationship of dominance remains or not. David Astor recalls one thought that dominated O'Brien's thinking:

> 'They [Unionists] won't go quietly ... Britain couldn't get out because of what Sinn Féin would do, what Dublin would not be able to do and the capacity for killing that would break out from unionists ... This was very much government thinking at the time. Conor Cruise was the only one who said this ... '[128]

Wright views Algeria and the American South as examples of settler colonialism but considers 'Ulster' as an ethnic conflict on the national frontier.[129] He, too, cites the longer period of Protestant settlement. His second distinction is US and Algerian super-exploitation. In fact, political and cultural advantage mattered more to unionists than material advantages, demonstrated by the DUP over Brexit. They opposed EU proposals offering local economic advantage over a potential loss to their symbolic attachment to Britain. Further, the Algerian population grew rapidly under the French, while the Irish experienced a population disaster under British economic policy. There are writers who will not permit Ireland the status even of 'postcolonial'. Liam Kennedy's evaluation of comparative standard-of-living measures (infant mortality, literacy, GDP per person etc.) shows newly independent Ireland to be much ahead of his categories of truly colonised. But his own data reveal Algeria as second to Ireland and much ahead of his 'truly colonised'.[130]

Henry Patterson rejects the republicans' 'internationally appealing version' of their struggle, which equates the IRA with the ANC (African National Congress) and identifies the reaction of the Protestant community with privileged *colon* reaction in Algeria, Israel and South Africa. The ANC took a different view. Sinn Féin President Gerry Adams was guard of honour at Nelson Mandela's funeral. Senior British

---

127   H. Roberts, *The Battlefield: Algeria,* (London, Verso, 2003), pp. 16–18.
128   Interview, David Astor, 22 July 1998.
129   F. Wright, *NI,* (Dublin: Gill & Macmillan, 1987).
130   L. Kennedy, *Colonialism, Religion and Nationalism,* (Belfast, Irish Studies, 1996), pp. 167–81.

politicians, soldiers and policemen all described unionists as 'rather like the Boers of South Africa.'[131] Sir Ronald Storrs, governor of Jerusalem (1920-48), considered the Balfour Declaration and the partition of Palestine was to set up 'a little loyal Jewish Ulster in a sea of potential hostile Arabism.'[132] Algerians also recognise the analogy. In 1947 Hocine Ait Ahmed, one of the FLN's historic nine leaders, presented a report to the PPA (*Parti du Peuple Algerien*) congress. Ireland was the main precedent to Algeria: '... a heavily settled colony just across the water from the imperial metropole, Ireland had liberated itself through confrontational politics, diplomacy and armed struggle.'[133] Even loyalist paramilitaries see the analogy. Noel Little, Ulster Resistance, explained the purpose of their weapons: '... the eventuality of the British ... doing an Algeria.'[134]

A legacy of British imperial history

John McGarry and Brendan O'Leary argue that there is considerable merit in the Marxist explanation of the origins of the conflict in the English and Scottish colonial settlements. They note, however, that the analogy has caused some tensions for 'green Marxists' because it suggests settler/Protestant resistance to native/Catholic nationalism is deep-rooted and not nurtured by the metropolis.[135] Green Marxists would have a more coherent case if they argued that decolonisation is the best solution and if they declared that 'Brits out' meant the expropriation and, if necessary, expulsion of the descendants of the Plantation settlers. Republicans reject this.[136] McGarry and O'Leary also note that unionists reject the colony analogy, even pre-1921, maintaining the legal fictions embodied in the Act of Union that Ireland was an integral part of the UK, and that 1921 was secession, not decolonisation.

131 M. Urban, *Big Boys Rules*, (London, Faber, 1992) p.18, Robert Mark, *In the Office of the Constable* (Collins, 1978), p. 106, Merlyn Rees *NI* (London, Methuen, 1985) p.316.

132 Miller, *Britain, Palestine and Empire,* (NY, Routledge 2016), p. 174, Lewis, *Semites and Anti-Semites,* p. 177.

133 Byrne, *Mecca of Revolution*, (OUP), p. 32.

134 Northern Ireland Shootings, *Guardian*, 15 October 2012.

135 McGarry and O'Leary, *Explaining NI*, pp. 62–91. Edward Carson complained the Tories had used Ulster, T. Paulin, *Ireland and the English*, pp. 118–25.

136 Sinn Féin maintains 'Brits out' meant ending British government involvement and not Protestant expulsion; Smith, *Fighting for Ireland*, p. 222.

McGarry and O'Leary also examine 'Red Marxists', who explain the conflict was due to the 'narrow nationalism' of Irish Catholics.[137] Protestant settlers who arrived in Ireland in the seventeenth century were portrayed by the British and Irish Communist Organisation (BICO) as the democratic vanguard of an enlightened Scottish peasantry who succeeded in throwing off the authoritarian yoke of the Roman Church. Accordingly, Ulster's economic development and historical progress, manners and civilisation, all result from the Plantation. Algeria's Communist Party likewise viewed the nationalism of the Muslims as backward and reactionary. The imperialism of Islam was more worrying. The party initially opposed the FLN with the doctrinaire explanation that wars of liberation belong to industrial working-class societies. In similar fashion, the 'backward politics' of Irish nationalists was as nothing compared to the Workers' Party's socialist revolution. This overlooks the difficulties of espousing radical politics in the vigilant unionist communities, much like progressives experienced in Algeria's settler communities.[138] Patterson describes republican politics as primitive and illusory. His analysis approves of a description of Catholics as old Roman plebs.[139] BICO, too, was very sensitive about describing Northern Ireland as a settler society.

Irish republicans argue the North is the remnant of Britain's first colony, and it had never been a serious candidate for integration, citing Cromwell's attempts at ethnic cleansing as evidence. The Famine of 1845–50 and Britain's response demonstrates that Ireland was a colony, not an equal part of the nation. Indeed, the preservation of the distance between Britain and NI may be the single consistent strand in British policy throughout the conflict. David Astor pointed out: '… the French didn't see Algeria as a colony but as a part of France. They really believed that but we never said that … we didn't fight a long battle to stay.'[140] *Operation Banner* did last thirty-eight years.

---

137 McGarry and O'Leary, *Explaining NI*, pp. 138–70. See also S. Hutton and P. Stewart (eds), *Ireland's Histories*, (London: Routledge, 1991), pp. 164 for Bew and Patterson consistently overlooking the exclusionary history of the Protestant working class and exaggerating working-class Irish nationalist politics as reactionary and narrowly Catholic.

138 See Ruth Moore, 'Kissing King Billy Goodbye', *New Internationalist*, May 1994. Henri Alleg, 'Political Violence in Algeria', in Darby et al, *Political Violence,* p. 137 acknowledges similar difficulties for radicals in French Algeria. See also R. Tlemcani, *State and Revolution in Algeria* (London: Zed, 1986) for Communist Party efforts to crush Algerian nationalism, comparable to BICO's efforts.

139 B. O'Leary, 'The weight of the dead generations', *Fortnight*, May 1989.

140 Interview with David Astor, London, 22 July 1998.

Further, the international consensus on the determination of self-determination defines the 'self' as the territorial majority at the time of decolonisation. The partition of the decolonised entities, as happened in Ireland in 1921, is frowned upon.[141] International opinion generally, but especially in America and the newly independent nations, views the conflict as a legacy of British imperialism, and, until the GFA, considered Northern Ireland as something less than fully legitimate. The overwhelming weight of international opinion favours reuniting Ireland. Opinion polls also consistently show that at least half the British public believes the North should leave the UK. Neal Ascherson, of the *Observer*, explains the difference between Britain and France: 'Take Algeria: people had lived for a hundred years, as it were, in somebody else's country. That's true in the case of NI. They lived there for 300 years. But the British or English perception of that settlement as an integral part of England/Britain was a bit shaky, and the tendency was to regard it as Irish.'[142]

Regular slips by members of the British elite, referenced below, indicate they, too, regard Northern Ireland in a foreign or colonial context.[143] Thus, Home Secretary Reginald Maudling cautioned that when Ireland was the case in point, the British Constitution did not export easily. Peter Brooke, the Secretary of State for NI (1989-92), concluded that Cyprus taught them that one should 'never say never' regarding political possibilities. The Secretary of State Merlyn Rees (1974-76) cautioned his colleagues against thinking that because Ulster was near, it was somehow British. Foreign Minister Douglas Hurd warned the EU that military intervention in Bosnia might lead to a protracted commitment like Northern Ireland, suggesting external intervention in Bosnia was somehow similar to Britain's internal problem.

There is also the peculiar constitutional position of the region designated Northern Ireland. It proceeded from full integration in 1800, via a sudden extensive measure of self-government that unionism had not called for in 1921, to a gradual approximation under direct rule of its earlier position, and then to an intermediate position (post GFA) where the constitutional question has been parked. The exclusion clauses in the Prevention of Terrorism Act applying only to Irish people

---

141 McGarry and O'Leary, *Explaining NI*, p. 493n, see also Harry Beran, 'Who should be entitled to self-determination referenda?', in M. Werner and R. Crisp (eds), *Terrorism, Protest and Power* (Aldershot: Edward Edgar, 1990).

142 Interview, Neal Ascherson, London, 28 July 1998.

143 All examples, Todd and Ruane, *Dynamics of the Conflict,* (Cambridge University Press, 1996), p. 264.

and the unwillingness of the Labour Party or Liberal Democrats to compete in NI elections, or of the Conservative Party to organise enthusiastically, further reveals it as a place apart.

Nation-building failures
Lustick outlines two detailed comparisons of Ireland and Algeria.[144] His explanation of settler colony Ireland differs from Irish republican explanations (which emphasise the primacy of imperial Britain), shifting emphasis from British imperialism towards a focus on the agency of the settler community. Settlers and their descendants rapidly see their interests as diverging from and different from the metropolis. Lustick emphasises a rigid structure of separation created by the settlers and their associated privileges. In Lustick's explanation native violence is the result of settler repression. Violence was embedded in the settler colonial structure, which resisted full-scale democratic transformations. Violence was neither irrational nor due to Irish Catholic or Algerian Muslim cultural pathology. He underlines settler responsibility for these exaggerated accounts of native disloyalty to maintain and underscore their privileges.

State-building (always in process) accomplished elsewhere by the English/British and French states were attempted, but not accomplished, in Ireland or Algeria. When Ireland was at last formally integrated, in 1800, into the significantly named United Kingdom of Great Britain and Ireland, it was still governed differently from the rest of the putative unitary state. Efforts of the central states to incorporate/integrate Algeria and Ireland on a permanent basis failed because the large settler populations, in a privileged relationship to the central authority, were numerically weak compared to the native population. According to state-building theory, the co-option of local elites, and the eventual extension of political participation rights to the natives, is an important process in the redirection of loyalty to the new central authorities and in fully incorporating the outlying area.

In Ireland and Algeria, the settlers were sufficiently numerous to use core support to achieve and maintain dominance, their hubris interrupting this process. But the settlers were too weak in the event of potential native mobilisation to cut ties with the metropolitan power and preserve their ascendancy alone. Out of this combination of

---

144 Lustick, *State Building Failures,* (University of California, 1985), Lustick, *Unsettled States (*Cornell University Press, 1993*).*

advantage and vulnerability flow two contradictory imperatives: preservation of the ties to the core, and consolidation and maintenance of settler privilege.

Settlers in Ireland

In 1612 John Davies published *A Discoverie of the True Causes Why Ireland Was Never Entirely Subdued*. It lists all the failed attempts, from the twelfth century onwards, by the English monarchs to extend 'the protection' of their laws to the Gaelic Irish. Davies absolves the Crown and blames the 'Old English' settlers and their descendants for treating the Irish as enemies or aliens rather than as subjects. Irish leaders had repeatedly presented themselves as cooperative before the central authorities. They were responding to the 'new departure' and to the 'surrender and re-grant' policies of Henry VIII, Elizabeth and the Stuarts following the Treaty of Limerick, and, finally, to Pitt's promises in 1800 of Catholic representation at Westminster. These offers would have softened any opposition to British rule in Ireland and helped legitimise and stabilise British state-building efforts. But British initiatives were frustrated by the settlers bent on blocking native participation for fear of losing their own pre-eminence. Settlers highlighted the disloyalty of the natives in contrast to their own indisputable loyalty. Nor was it in the settlers' interest to convert the disloyal to loyalty. They took more pains in making the land turn Protestant rather than the people. Preaching the Reformation in English, rather than Gaelic, reflects a clear lack of will.

Even after the French invasion during the United Irish rebellion of 1798, when England sought Irish Catholic loyalty, key Anglo-Irish Protestant leaders only accepted union with Britain on condition that it precluded Catholic emancipation. In 1801 Britain failed to keep its promise of emancipation. The long delay in granting political participation to Catholic elites and the grudging manner it was finally conceded pushed Catholics towards separatism. Daniel O'Connell declared, 'if the people of Ireland were well governed, then they are ready to become a kind of West Britain, if made so in benefits and justice, but if not, we are Irishmen again.'[145] Irish Catholics were eventually incorporated into the British political system, and their slow successes in it finally compelled Protestants to abandon formerly

---

145   McGarry and O'Leary, *Explaining Northern Ireland*, p. 84.

sacrosanct political positions. Land reforms were conceded, the Anglican Church was disestablished, and opposition to Irish Home Rule was eventually redirected to Ulster's exclusion.

Settlers in Algeria

France invaded Algeria in 1830. In response, Sheikh Abdel Khader pursued an initially successful jihad. But by 1847 the scorched-earth tactics of Marchal Bugeaud (who became governor-general of Algeria) forced Khader's surrender. Bugeaud established the Arab Bureau, staffed by army officers, which acted as intermediary between the military and the indigenous population. The *colons* soon accused the Arab Bureau and army of favouring the natives. The army, too, became increasingly frustrated with having to rescue settlers when their actions provoked local revolt. From 1863 to 1867 Emperor Napoleon III applied himself personally to the task of suppressing *colon* influence and reconciling native Algerians to French rule. A July 1865 *Senatus Consultus,* an Act of the French senate, embodied his wish to see Algerians as French subjects, with rights to participate in local elections and afforded the opportunity to become French citizens.[146] As support for the Second Empire eroded in France and the emperor became distracted from Algerian affairs, the *colon* position gained strength in the senate and undermined the reforms.

In 1871 Sheikh Mohammed Moqrani led another jihad against the extension of settler authority over the Berber autonomous confederation. It was brutally suppressed. Explaining the need 'to erase all hope of shaking our domination from the minds of the Muslims', the Superior Government Council of Algeria justified land expropriations as: 'a punishment capable of leaving a permanent trace.'[147] In 1870 the *Cremieux* Decree extended French citizenship *en masse* to the Jews of Algeria, with reluctant *colon* acceptance due to the necessity of military assistance. From 1871 to 1891 the ascendancy of the European population in Algeria was as secure as ever it would be. A new sentiment, *Algérie libre,* favouring autonomy from France began to gain ground. After twenty years of native prostration, *colon* fears had subsided and the increase in the European population to twenty per cent by 1896 raised settler confidence of dominating without metropolitan aid. In response to muted *colon* threats of secession, new arrangements were made for the administration of Algeria that moved

---

146 Conditional upon renouncing their Muslim status, allegiance to Islamic law and polygamy.

the territory as close to autonomy from France, under settler rule, as it was ever to come.

Délégations Financières (budgetary councils) were created in 1898, and two years later Algeria was accorded special constitutional status, with a budget formally separate from metropolitan France. This local hegemony was possible as long as the *colons* felt secure. In 1901, however, at the village of Marguerite disaffected natives killed five French settlers. It was like a thunderclap, raising fears of a larger religious rising. In 1916, conscription provoked a more serious rising in the Aures. *Algérie libre* faded away.

By the second decade of the twentieth century, two imperatives pushed Paris to attempt reforms again. First, the spectre of Algerian Arab nationalism had appeared at the Congress of Nationalities in Lausanne in 1916. Second, and more importantly, the threat of a massive German offensive in the spring of 1918 underlay requirements for Arab manpower in the factories and trenches. Prime Minister Clemenceau pointedly ignored *colon* objections, and proposed reforms explicitly designed to increase the loyalty of Algerian natives. But post-war France watered down the reforms, again capitulating to *colon* opposition. The Blum-Viollette reform bill of 1936 may have been the last meaningful opportunity to build Algeria into the French state. The Muslim elite began to stir. At the 1936 Muslim Congress in Algiers, 5,000 delegates supported metropolitan reforms. In response French Algerians formed armed militias and threatened civil war. The Daladier government was unwilling to pursue reforms in the face of determined settler resistance.

Comparing Ireland and Algeria

States are shaped by political processes, constrained or encouraged by geographical and cultural factors and strategies that exploit or overcome them. There is no reason to believe that the integration of any outlying territory into the domain of a central state, once accomplished, must be permanent. Acquiring territory is one thing, retaining it another. Legitimacy resides in the minds of the governed. The mere existence of separatist movements, Scottish, Welsh, Breton, Corsican reflects the general point that state building is never over.

Lustick identifies four parallels between France and Britain:

1. both successfully legitimised their role in several heterogeneous peripheral areas and failed to do the same in another culturally distinct territory

2. the core state is governed according to the norms of parliamentary democracy
3. the unincorporated territory was colonised by settlers whose purpose was to support and consolidate the extension of the metropolitan state authority
4. settlers were substantially outnumbered by the native population[148]

These key corresponding elements make systematic comparison of the two cases possible. But it is the differences between them – combined with a hypothesis that the state-building failure in both cases can be explained by the disruptive effects of settlers – that makes the comparison worthwhile. Lustick evaluates the major differences and identifies settler political activity as crucial to understanding state-building failure. One difference is the prevalence of nationalist political formulae in France for most of the period of French rule over Algeria, 1830–1962, as opposed to Britain's rule over Ireland when for centuries feudal, religious and dynastic ideologies prevailed. Hannah Arendt's point, of exclusive nationalism making incorporation more difficult, means the parallel failures are even more striking.[149]

A second difference is the supposedly wider cultural gap between France and Algeria. In Ireland, cultural differences between the settlers and the natives were accentuated and depicted as civilisation versus barbarism. English perceptions of the Irish focused on the same cultural, racial, social and economic traits that allegedly distinguished the Arabs from the French: tribal organisation, feudal authority structures, transhumance and uncivilised sexual practices. In the English view, every Christian country was civilised. The Irish, deemed uncivilised, must be un-Christian, too. The Irish were regarded as primitive, just as the Muslims were viewed by the French.

Remembering Hennissart's account of Muslim (French) police shooting an OAS gunman, we need to be very careful when describing how comparatively different are two sets of two groups.[150] A third difference is the period of contact. Ireland and England were in relatively intimate contact for 300 years, while for France and Algeria it was 130 years. But the differences in political participation patterns

---

147   Lustick, *Unsettled States*, p. 58.
148   Lustick, *State Building Failures*, pp. 43-44.
149   Ibid., p. 91.
150   On resettling in France, *pieds noirs* tended to live close to Arabs, for example, Toulon. In *Bab el Oued* there was de facto integration.

for the two metropoles are important. The French Third Republic was a thoroughly republican, mass-participating democracy, while for hundreds of years the integrative policies towards Ireland were fashioned by a slowly expanding, oligarchic elite. Thus, the question of equality of political rights in the outlying territory was important for a greater portion of the French-Algerian contact than for the British-Irish contact. More important than the period of contact is why efforts to extend political participation to Muslims and Catholics failed. France made serious attempts to cultivate the loyalty of the native population through reforms but was always undermined by successful settler opposition and campaigns to expropriate Arab land. The similarity with the actions and motivations of settlers in Ireland is striking.

Four reasons for settler success:

1. settlers acted as a conduit for information about the outlying area
2. settlers acted as a recruitment pool for the local bureaucracy
3. through single-issue tactics, reforms were often abandoned in exchange for settler support on more immediate metropolitan concerns
4. maintenance of their privileges provided the basis for settler ideological expediency

Consider Major Frederick Crawford who loyally served in the British Army during the Boer War but organised illegal importing of arms to oppose the British government in Ulster. Speaking in Bangor on 29 April 1912, he declared: 'if they were put out of the union ... he would infinitely prefer to change his allegiance right over to the emperor of Germany or anyone else who had got a proper and stable government.'[151] During the Suez crisis when British Prime Minister Anthony Eden depended on twelve unionist votes, Brookeborough ruthlessly applied his leverage.[152] The Ulsterman's conditional loyalty resonates with the alternating defiance and ultra-patriotism of French Algerians.[153]

When settlers believed the native threat had receded (early eighteenth-century Ireland, late nineteenth-century Algeria), they sought

---

151 Horgan, *Complete Grammar of Anarchy,* (Dublin, Mansel, 1918), p. 7.
152 Patterson, *Ireland's Violent Frontier*, p. 8.
153 D. Miller, *Queen's Rebels* (Dublin: Gill-Macmillan, 1978) for unionism's conditional loyalty. For *pieds noirs* similar oscillations, Murray and Wengraf, 'The Algerian Revolution', *NLR*, no. 22 (1963), p.17n.

to increase their autonomy. Following the alienation of the natives from the centre, the increasingly frustrated, metropolitan elite came to see disengagement (not closer integration) as the key to reducing the strain of ruling in these areas. Always, the settlers barred the way to reform.

'The settlers,' says Lustick, 'by preventing stable incorporation of Ireland and Algeria, helped create conditions that eventually broke the ideological consensus that included Ireland within the United Kingdom and Algeria within the indivisible French republic.'[154] Unionists, while not wishing to live in a Home-Rule Ireland, did not seek their own parliament. Northern Ireland was thrust upon them. Brexit would painfully remind unionists the British people were not bound to them.[155]

The children of wrath

Richard Rose documents the sectarianism of the Northern Ireland state, but does not establish that the two communities, distinguished by religion, are fighting about religion. Religion identifies the antagonistic communities that colonialism created. Religious affiliation, said Conor Cruise O'Brien, is the rule of thumb by which one can distinguish between the native Irish stock (Catholics) and those of settler stock (Scottish/English Protestants). Religion identifies the real, but otherwise unidentifiable, adversary. But O'Brien backs off from a colonial interpretation, maintaining that religion, inseparably intertwined with political allegiance, kept the differences alive over the centuries. While acknowledging the still-dominant character of the colonial settlement, he is unclear when precisely the colonial relationship stopped dividing the communities.

The problem, according to Michael MacDonald, is that Ireland has been ruled for many centuries by British settlers, and not by British administrators. Colonial administrators generally strive to serve the interests of the mother country, while settlers want to turn the colony to their own purposes. Administrators generally try to root their power in existing native institutions in the hope of minimising any dislocation, while settlers develop their own stake in what they come to regard as their permanent home. Settlers demand their superiority be maintained even at the cost of instability. Rather than co-opting traditional native authorities to control the natives the settlers attack and undermine these authorities because they fear more their potential to rally native resistance.

---

154   Lustick, *Unsettled States*, p. 84.
155   'Brexit more important than NI, shock poll', *Express* 26 March 2018.

Settlers undermine the independence of native authorities because they threaten settler hegemony, not because they impede the extension of settler culture. Instead of trying to minimise disruption, the logic of settler colonialism accentuates it. Thus, in Northern Ireland after 1921, as in Ireland after 1603 and 1800, Protestants had a vested interest in sustaining Catholic disloyalty because, first, it legitimised Protestant privileges; second, it accentuated the salience of Protestant loyalty to Britain; third, it provided the threat that maintained Protestant solidarity. Unionist leader James Molyneaux famously warned the 1994 IRA ceasefire 'represented the most destabalising event to the union since partition.'[156] But Protestant loyalty is problematic. In return for their devotion, Protestants expected certain privileges, such as the freedom to handle the Catholic threat in their own way. When so favoured, their loyalty is boundless. But when Britain refused, they threatened rebellion, civil war and a unilateral declaration of independence. But unionist loyalty is unrequited now. Although originally British surrogates, Protestant hegemony has become superfluous to, even incompatible with, long-term British interests. Political stability can only come through reforms, resulting in Catholic gains. But the logic of settler colonialism dictated that Protestant privileges must be maintained even at the cost of instability. This explains the extraordinary behaviour of unionism during the 1974 Ulster Workers' Council (UWC) strike/rebellion that brought down the first power-sharing executive. This was the very institutional reform designed to weaken the IRA, confirm the rights of unionists and secure recognition from the Irish Republic.

Northern Ireland: a suitable case for Gaullism?

Hugh Roberts in his 1986 book sets out directly to refute the Algerian analogy. He differentiates loyalist paramilitary 'counter-terrorism' from OAS terrorism: 'If Protestant gunmen actually were machine-gunning Catholics at bus stops from speeding cars ... and planting plastic explosives ... there would be some point in the comparison.'[157] Even a cursory look through McKittrick's *Lost Lives*, shows Roberts to be obviously mistaken.[158] By 1986, the date of Roberts' publication,

---

156 *Irish Times*, 30 August 2014.

157 Roberts, *Northern Ireland and Algeria: A Suitable Case for Gaullism?* (Belfast, Athol, 1986), p.32

158 Loyalist random killings of Catholics began with victim numbers 1 and 2 (June 1966), hundreds more can be found in McKittrick et al, *Lost Lives*.

loyalists were responsible for 27% of all conflict deaths at that time and the majority of civilian deaths.[159] Loyalists were actually much greater killers than the OAS whose killings amounted to 0.56% of Algerian conflict deaths.[160] Roberts' claims, after almost twenty years of a loyalist campaign, reflects the *pieds-noirs* blindness to Muslim victims.[161] He also rejects any comparison of Irish republicans with ALN veterans. The Muslims were the overwhelming majority, and the FLN resorted to violence after decades of constitutional activity and rigged elections. None of the arising analogies, according to Roberts, applies to Northern Ireland. This is clearly a particular view of the history of Britain in Ireland.

Roberts also rejects Irish reunification, arguing that Ireland was not a political unit or sovereign state before British rule, and argues that Algeria, north of the Sahara, was unified by Turkish rule between 1516 and 1830. He wrote later that Algeria was not a nation before the French invasion, that the patchwork of disparate tribes was irredeemably refractory and incapable of formulating a national political project.[162] He also argues that the ideological core of anti-British nationalism in Ireland was undoubtedly furnished by Catholicism. He accepts only a qualified role for Islam in the Algerian nationalist movement, and claims Irish politicians are shepherded by the Catholic Church while in Algeria the religious leaders are shepherded by the state. But he exaggerates the influence of the Catholic Church in Ireland, while downplaying Islam's influence in Algeria. Ireland displays a growing secularism and is a pioneer in sexual equality rights, while the independent Algerian state capitulated to the demands of *Al Qiyan* (The Values), making concessions to conservative religious rituals and restrictions to female dress code. He is certainly aware that in 1982 the Algerian state bowed to Islamist demands and implemented a family code based on Shariah law. He also maintains that Catholicism is fundamentally more intolerant than Islam, and rebukes metropolitan intellectuals for their complacency: 'England won its battle against the papacy so long ago that its intelligentsia appears to have no memory of it.'[163] He condemns '*bien pensant* English intellectuals, who deride the Ulster Protestants' dark mutterings about "Rome Rule" and *convince*

---

159   Ibid., p. 1476.
160   Evans, *Algeria*, p. 338.
161   For blindness to Muslim suffering see Harrison, *Challenging de Gaulle*, pp. 17–52 and Memmi's *The Coloniser*.
162   Roberts, *The Battlefield: Algeria*, (London, Verso, 2003), pp. 26–7.
163   Roberts, *Gaullism?* p. 46.

themselves that there is nothing in it.'[164] Imperial manipulations emanating from Rome are more usually found in Ian Paisley's preaching.

Roberts claims the settlement of Ireland was the work of voluntary emigrants, the most robustly independent and ideologically advanced elements of the metropolitan society, who had chosen to make a new life for themselves in Ireland to live by their own lights. A contemporaneous Protestant minister saw it differently:

> And from Scotland came many, and from England not a few, yet all of them generally the scum of both nations who, for debt, or breaking and fleeing from justice, or seeking shelter, came hither, hoping to be without fear of man's justice … for their carriage made them to be abhorred at home in their native land.[165]

Roberts allows the settlers of Algeria should be seen in this light. They were social and national flotsam and jetsam, paupers, or other truculent elements who were 'shovelled out' by the thousands, especially the defeated Parisian republican workers of the abortive 1848 rising. If there was a bigoted, reactionary class, he writes, it was the Anglo-Irish of Southern Ireland. The Scottish Presbyterians of the North have repeatedly given their full support to the cause of democratic reform in the interests of the (Catholic) community. He claims Protestant Ulster was to 'the forefront of the democratic movement and it supported every demand for progressive democratic reform in the Catholic interest from the 1770s to 1920.'[166] This is simply irreconcilable with the history of the Orange Order and the nineteenth-century Presbyterian fanaticism of clerics such as Reverend Hanna and Reverend Cooke. Finally, he admonishes any 'British intellectuals who *take to heart* the evidence of discrimination against the Catholic community …'[167] This denial of discrimination is usually found among the most intransigent unionism. Roberts' work is the one determined attempt to refute the Algerian analogy. It is seriously flawed.[168]

---

164 Ibid., my emphasis.
165 Stewart, *Narrow Ground*, p. 81.
166 Roberts, *Gaullism?* p. 64.
167 Ibid.,
168 Roberts, in *The Battlefield: Algeria*, contradicts his earlier writing: '[President] Boumedienne was Algeria's Cromwell', p. 25, the FLN was correct to view Algerian classes as impediments to the development of a national society, p. 27.

Ulster Protestants as settlers?

Paul Bew and Richard English explain the conflict in Ireland as religious in origin rather than as a legacy of colonialism. Bew exhibits a pained reaction to any colonial comparison, the 'so-called' Algerian analogy was 'glib' and 'deeply unserious.'[169] For its refutation he recommends Hugh Roberts. Bew endorses Roberts as a great scholar of Algeria whose work is powerful and impressive. John Wilson Foster also claims Roberts 'demolishes the analogy between Algeria and Ulster' and 'correctly confutes the simple anti-colonialist and anti-imperialist analysis of Sinn Féin.'[170] Robert McCartney, leader of the UK Unionist Party, also endorsed Roberts' analysis and lauded its accuracy. Something is at work here. The repeated rejection of the Algerian analogy as pejorative/superficial/unserious, with no reference to Lustick's meticulous documentation and the powerful arguments of McDonald and Pamela Clayton, is telling. To recommend Roberts and ignore Lustick is to refuse the analogy without refuting.[171]

English maintains the conflict in Ireland should not be conceived in settler-native terms. Irish history would have been different if the Catholics had been converted. The Reformation was unsuccessful because of a lack of will and insufficient Protestant guile. It was a great mistake that the reformers had preached in English rather than the native Gaelic. He argues religious differences 'demolishes any neat sense that Irish nationalism-versus-unionism involved a native-settler division.'[172] He repeats a familiar refrain: 'Can people born in a country and possessing ancestors there who date back many years, really be delegitimized as inauthentic settlers?'[173] Thus, the Irish failure to embrace the Reformation means nationalism and republicanism should be the focus of the historical problem. However, so many 'mistakes' by so many intelligent people points to a policy.[174]

English and Bew avoid Lustick's analyses which illuminate an important distinction. Settler colonialism is not the same thing as

---

169   O'Leary, 'A Long March', *DRB*, no. 5 (Spring 2008).

170   Foster, *Colonial Consequences* (Dublin, Lilliput, 1991), pp. 263-78.

171   Bew recommends Roberts, who recommends Clifford, who claimed Catholicism fostered republicanism; Roberts, *Battlefield*, pp. 25–6. Clifford has since performed a volte-face.

172   English, *Irish Freedom,* (London, Macmillan, 2006), p. 64.

173   Ibid., p. 95.

174   O'Leary, 'Cuttlefish, Cholesterol and Saoirse', *Field Day Review*, no. 3 (March-April 2007).

colonialism. It is a process where people migrate with the express purpose of territorial occupation and the formation of a new community rather than the extraction of labour or resources. In Ireland this meant making the *land* turn Protestant rather than the previous landholders turning Protestant. Empires may be short, but settlers stay, except in the rare case of evacuation. Invasion in the settler colonial context then is not a specific event but, rather, a structure. And it is resilient. There is, then, no such thing as post-settler colonialism or neo-settler colonialism. It is of the present as well as of the past.[175]

Unionists, in rejecting the colonial analogy, specifically deny they are *colons* in the sense of the French in Algeria. This is highly significant. French Algerians also steadfastly rejected the *colon* label and like unionists declared the label to be pejorative. Yet academics and British journalists do not hesitate to refer to French Algerians as settlers or as the settler problem. For French Algerian and British Ulstermen, the natives had no history before the settlement. There was, in the unionist view, no pre-Plantation Irish state. In similar fashion, Algeria was never a nation. Consider Jean Lareguy's French officer in exchange with captured FLN leader, Larbi Ben M'Hidi: 'If we left you to your own devices, you'd be at each other's throats. You are not a nation.' M'Hidi replies: 'I know ... I've looked for Algeria in books and cemeteries and I never found her. But since then, you've filled our cemeteries sufficiently to create a history for us.'[176] This tension of disputed legitimacy is the central theme of Camus' *L'Etranger.*

Mersault, the main character, exposed French Algeria's failure to recognise its own sins. The *pieds noirs,* in general, were as unconscious as Mersault and wished to remain so. Camus, from humble circumstances, could not (as working-class loyalists cannot) consider himself the inheritor of a colonial oppression. He, too, had been humiliated and exploited.[177] Thus the poorest of the French Algerians, the *petits blancs,* were not settlers but served as scapegoats for the bad conscience of the metropolitan French. In similar fashion, senior unionist Ken Maginnis noted the 'British were burdened by a legacy of guilt ... about an Irish debt to be paid ... [they] eased their consciences by transferring the guilt to Ulster unionists.'[178] The complexity of the

---

175 The past and present were one and the same fight, Dewar, *Orangeism: A New Historical Perspective,* (Grand Orange Lodge, 1969).

176 Lartéguy, *Centurions,* (London, Heinemann, 1961), p. 444.

177 Messud, Camus and Algeria: The Moral Question, *NYRB,* 7 November 2013.

178 Boyce and O'Day, *Defenders of the Union,* p. 274.

relationship of the contemporary Protestant and the colonisation of Ulster, the 'elephant in the room', is difficult for any unionist self-identifying as liberal and progressive to contemplate.[179] In addition, there are potent reasons for playing down settler origins. Any redistribution of land to its original inhabitants, were it ever considered, would almost eradicate Protestant farmers.[180] (Regardless of a variety of notions of when ownership becomes legitimate the longevity of their presence makes them natives of the land and this their homeland – well recognised by Irish republicans.) Fear of losing the land, the 'mother of all fears', in any united Ireland also motivates the present rejection of the settler analysis.[181] More to the point of this study, it would mean explaining the conflict with a focus on Britain rather than nationalism.

If the conflict is the legacy of colonialism the focus will be on unionism and London. But if the conflict is religious, then Irish republicans are motivated by sectarian bigotry. However, while republicans do not propose Protestant dispossession, Newton Emerson claims even academic analysis of the North as a colony is dangerous.[182] Unionists argue the colonial analysis is pejorative and hence the outrage when Congressman Richard Neal referred to the 'Planters.'[183] This resembles Israeli government labelling any criticism of Zionism as anti-Semitic. Unionists now seek the status of victims, reputedly mystified that some unruly policemen and possible discrimination could have produced such a conflict.[184] Arthur Aughey implies the settler interpretation is now redundant because of partition and the decline of the British Empire.[185] But the settler mentality shows much greater durability. Unionist newspaper editors and letter-writers used the self-appellation of 'settler' as late as 1968. Whether by direct reference to their settler origins or by declaring affinity with the British Empire and with other states of settler origin, unionist ideologists identified themselves in a proud tradition of British settlement throughout the world.[186] For example, former unionist leader and prime minister

179 Reid, The Elephant in the Room, Colonialism, Postcolonialism and Northern Ireland, *Geography* 30 December 2014.
180 Clayton, *Enemies and Passing Friends* (London: Pluto, 1996), pp. 32-3.
181 *Guardian* 18 July 2019, Protestant fear Zimbabwe style land grab.
182 *Irish Times* 23 September 2021.
183 *Irish News*, 27 May, 2022.
184 74% of unionists denied discrimination existed, Whyte, *Interpreting NI*, p. 6; Mulholland, *NI,* pp. 10, 38–66.
185 Aughey, Recent Perceptions of Unionism, Political Quarterly, 61 (2) 1990, pp. 188-99, new unionism the best prospect.
186 Clayton, *Enemies and Passing Friends*, pp. 46, 1-23.

Terence O'Neill once nonchalantly told British Prime Minister Harold Wilson, 'I do not intend to be the Garfield Todd of Northern Ireland.'[187] Todd was the prime minister of Rhodesia forced from office by his own party for pursuing modest reforms.

A 1969 Orange Order publication described unionists as 'unconquerable colonists', proud of their 'planter' roots.[188] Ian Paisley lauded the work ethic of his Ballymena constituents and attributed it to their settler origins. His ancestors brought civilisation when the ancestors of Taoiseach Charles Haughey were living in caves.[189] Certainly, the oft-repeated refrain that 'the Protestants are not going to be driven into the sea nor will they conveniently disappear' suggests that settler origins remain a vivid part of Protestant consciousness.[190] The Orange marching season, of 3,500 parades with jingoistic military music, slogans and banners bearing the names of lodges, images of empire and native receipt of civilisation, is an affirmation of the settler experience of siege and victory. If Ireland was reunited First Minister Arlene Foster, in her own words, 'would probably have to move.'[191]

There is yet one difficulty. The conquest that began the history of the colony is a clear act of usurpation. Settlers seek to transform the usurpation into legitimacy. John Foster allows Ulster has a semi-colonial past and acknowledges that acceptance of this usurpation sits uneasily on some shelf of the Protestant psyche. The Ulster Protestant represses his guilt over his treatment of Catholics and has for some time lived with a sense of his own unattractiveness in the eyes of the world. He, too, identifies the Anglican settlers of southern Ireland as the real colonisers. He has a different reading of Albert Memmi's insecure *colon*:

> The Ulster Protestant feeling the perpetual threat of being taken over, already experiences in some sense, and exhibits the symptoms of *the condition of being colonised* … the people of Ulster are estranged from their own image. Is this not a condition of the colonised?[192]

187   *History Ireland,* Issue 3, Vol. 4, Autumn 1996.
188   Dewar, *Orangeism,* cited in B. O'Brien, *The Long War,* (O'Brien, Dublin 1999), pp. 82–3.
189   *Sunday Press*, 23 January 1994.
190   Clayton, *Enemies,* p. 47.
191   *Irish News,* 5 April 2018.
192   Foster, *Colonial Consequences,* pp. 277–8, original emphasis.

The history of settler colonialism is not the only explanation for the Irish conflict, and unionists may ignore it or deny it. John Wilson Foster goes further; he wants the Ulster Protestant designated as the colonised. Richard English continues in the same vein: 'Irish irridentism, especially in its violent republican incarnation, presented as great a threat to Ulster Protestants, as French imperialism posed to native Algerians.'[193] Perri Giovannucci, too, has noted that the settler longs to take the place of the native.[194] Finally, Clayton explains that as long as migrants/settlers constitute a group that was/is seen to be distinct and which maintained status closure and a relatively powerful position vis-à-vis the indigenous people, who represented at least a latent threat to this supremacy, then the settler society remains in place, *however old the settlement*. Undoubtedly, there were conversions, intermarriage and illicit sex but discrete categories were maintained despite changing participation and membership in the course of individual life histories. Northern Ireland, then, is the remnant of the original colony. Six northern counties were held back from decolonisation by British unionists (the descendants of settlers, if not always by blood, then by social position) to give us a colonial situation with a twist: the settlers as the majority.[195] This is now eroding.

Conclusion

This chapter pointed out the weakness of the religious explanation. Notably, the Algerian analogy is rejected without addressing it. Explaining the difference between colonialism and settler colonialism revealed the analogy as an important one. While it is more exact before 1921, the northern state then established is the remnant of the original settler colony. De Gaulle also considered partition but rejected it. He would not work with the OAS. It would have meant France, having granted Algerian 'independence' while keeping the most developed part, could have had referenda galore with repeated massive majorities in favour of continuing integration with France. Nothing would have been resolved. Algerians would have remained second-class citizens and would have continued to resist. The Algerian analogy is strikingly close and bears no serious refutation.

---

193   English and Skelly (eds), *Ideas Matter*, p. 20.
194   P Giovannucci, *Literature and Development in North Africa,* (New York, Routledge) 2008.
195   Clayton, *Enemies and Passing Friends*, pp. xiii, 3–34.

CHAPTER THREE

Holy War or Anti-Colonial Insurgency

This chapter summarises the conflicts in Algeria (1954-62) and Northern Ireland (1968-98). They unfolded with remarkable similarity. Many 'matched pairs' were identified: governments prioritising reform or military solution; legitimacy of insurgents' cause, and their tactics regarding civilians; counter-terrorists opposing reforms; random killing of 'disloyal' civilians; and rebellions against governments to which they professed loyalty.

Writing from Algiers in 1959, Henry Tanner described a scene familiar to Belfast shoppers: 'Women automatically open their bags. Men stop and lift their arms ... all through September and October bombs were discovered in cafes, public squares and on school grounds.' The French army was everywhere, even guarding schoolchildren at play. Tanner spoke with 'average Muslims'. They were nationalists, not rebels, and all their talk had a central theme: dignity. French-Algerians would deny them parity until forced to by Paris or the ALN. Recent gains in voting rights, jobs and improvements in infrastructure, were due exclusively to the rebellion.[196]

The media drama

The French and British armies pursued an undeclared 'dirty war', including psy-ops (psychological operations), double agents, extrajudicial killing and torture. The ALN and IRA engaged in guerrilla and/or terror tactics, combining combat attrition and economic

196   *New York Times*, 25 October 1959.

sabotage. The OAS and UDA-UVF pursued a campaign of random murder against 'disloyal' civilians. These paramilitary adjuncts colluded, officially or otherwise, with military intelligence, MI5/MI6 or SDECE (*Service de Documentation Exterieure et de Contre-Espionnage)* and with elements of the locally recruited security forces, Algeria's *Unités Territoriales* and gendarmes or with the UDR/RIR and RUC in Northern Ireland.

Government responses to the insurgency seriously compromised the principles of the liberal democratic state. By March 1956 Algeria had acquired a Special Powers Act. NI had its Special Powers Act since 1922. Still, French soldiers complained of having to knock before searching a house or having to account before the law for shooting rebels. In fact, very few soldiers, British or French, were prosecuted for illegal killings. The partisan gendarmes and RUC were reformed. The B-Specials and the *Unités Territoriales* were disbanded. The UDR was amalgamated with the Royal Irish Rangers to form the Royal Irish Regiment, and the RUC into the PSNI. The Stormont Assembly and *L'Assemblée Algérienne* were both suspended, resulting in direct rule from Paris or London. Both armies perpetrated a notorious massacre of civilians: Bloody Sunday and rue d'Isly. Initially, neither government would accord POW status to the rebels. The ALN were *fellagha*, bandits. Margaret Thatcher was clear on IRA activity: 'crime is crime is crime.' The Irish criminals, however, were convicted under special legislation, and suspects were tortured by soldiers and police.[197] Both the IRA and ALN resorted to hunger strikes seeking political status. France granted it. Britain did, too, thought again, and thereafter pursued a policy of 'criminalisation'.

By 1958 the French army had almost completely defeated the ALN. The price was a considerable loss of prestige internationally. While the British army used methods perfected in the colonial wars of Aden, Kenya and Malaya, British prestige never suffered to the same extent. Still, Britain could never completely defeat the IRA, operating within the constraints of the EU and an urban setting saturated with foreign television crews. French-Algerian *ultras* and Ulster loyalists provide a close match. Claiming they took 'the war to the terrorists', they

---

197 The Compton Report, HMSO November 1971, found no brutality but some ill treatment. It was widely regarded as a whitewash. The Parker Report, HMSO March 1972, recommended continued use of the methods. The European Commission on Human Rights, 2 September 1976, Ireland v United Kingdom, Case 5310/71, ruled Britain guilty of torture. The European Court of Human Rights, Strasbourg, 18 January 1978, Ireland v United Kingdom, 5310/71, dropped the word torture but maintained inhuman and degrading treatment was an administrative practice. Belfast High Court and the Supreme Court in London, have since ruled the methods as torture.

indiscriminately murdered 'disloyal' civilians. Both had friends in the security forces. Few OAS leaders died in combat. Two members of UVF death squads and no UDA sectarian killers met their deaths at the hands of the British army.[198] French administrators were charmed by Algeria's Kabyle people (a Berber ethnic group in the north of Algeria) and dismayed by French-Algerians. Westminster politicians socialised well with Irish nationalists but saw Ulstermen as dour Calvinists. Both 'loyal' communities rebelled: Algiers' Barricades Week, January 1960 and the UWC Strike/Rebellion of May 1974.

Most of Algeria's fighting was in the east. The west was quiet for months on end. The Sahara saw more oil prospectors than guerrillas. At other times, Algiers, like Belfast, resembled a battlefield. Algeria was French, but you needed a special permit to travel there. NI was British, but you could be exiled there and banned from the 'mainland' under Exclusion Orders. Algeria's troubles were *evenements* (events), the Croix de Guerre was not awarded, and army operations were to maintain order.[199] France finally acknowledged it as a war in 1999. Although in Ireland *Operation Banner* lasted thirty-eight years and was the British army's longest ever campaign, Britain does not recognise the conflict as a war. However, relative to population size, the number of deaths in NI's conflict is one quarter to one third of total British dead of WWII. Civilians suffered death more often in the 'Troubles' than British civilians in WWII.[200]

Algeria, 1945–62

Algeria's war erupted on 1 November 1954. There were shootings throughout the remote Aures and Kabylia. Two sentries were killed at Batna; a farm was burnt in Oran. A bomb exploded harmlessly on Algiers docks. The toll was seven dead: three soldiers, two policemen, a *caid* (a Muslim government official) and Guy Monnerot, a French teacher who died after he and his wife were shot on a mountain road.[201]

---

198 McKittrick et al, *Lost Lives,* (Edinburgh University Press, 1999), #1352, #3053. UDA/UVF shot in street disturbances, #419, #1013, #1021, #985. UDA run over by army #645-6.

199 A new medal had to be struck, *le medal de la Valeur*.

200 In NI, 3636 died in a 1994 population of 1,640,000 … a ratio of 1:450. The Commonwealth Graves Commission (2014-15, p. 38) has total UK WWII dead of 450,900, in a 1945 population of 49,190,000 … a ratio of 1:109. The Times Atlas of WWII (1978, pp 204-5) has total UK war dead of 383,786, in a 1945 population of 49,190,000 … a ratio of: 1:128. NI's civilian dead of 2037 produces a death ratio of 1:714. The UK's 66,375 civilian dead (CWGC) of WWII produces a 1:741 ratio. Times Atlas of WWII has 62,000 UK civilian dead producing a ratio of 1:793.

201 Orders not to kill civilians were immediately disregarded, Hutchinson, *Revolutionary Terrorism,* (Stanford, 1978), p. 160.

The poorly equipped and badly organised fighters amounted to between 300 and 3,000 mujahideen.[202] It was an inauspicious start, the work of twenty-two men who had met secretly in the rue de Chatres, Algiers, the previous spring. The attacks failed to rouse the masses. The decision to act was based on a common agreement that the legal nationalist movement had failed, and that violence was the only way to destroy the colonial system. There was no programme or underlying revolutionary ideology. They were military men.

Setif, 1945

All Saints' Night 1954 was the culmination of long years of anguish. Algerian nationalism crystallised following the French massacres in Guelma and Setif on 8 May 1945. The day was to have been one of celebrations for the Allied victory in Europe. The demonstrators had police permission, conditional upon the non-displaying of provocative banners. But in eleven separate locations demonstrators with Algerian flags chanted, 'Vive Messali!' Messali Hadj was the political leader who had long preached independence. Other banners read: 'Down with colonialism.' Graffiti appeared warning the French they would be massacred.[203] French-Algerians saw a prearranged plan. The police shot dead twenty-year-old Bouziz Salah. This killing and police removing the flags and banners was the catalyst for the murder of 103 Europeans, accompanied by horrific mutilations and the rape of many women. Chanting 'Holy War in the name of Allah' and 'Allahu Akbar', the enraged demonstrators indiscriminately cut throats, slashed breasts and disembowelled French-Algerians.[204] The official response was terrible and completely lacking in discrimination. The Foreign Legion and Senegalese troops, joined by settler vigilantes, questioned Algerians in the street and shot them at will. The number of dead ranged between a French figure of 1,500 and a Muslim 15,000-45,000.[205] Those arrested testified they had been told of a general uprising and were encouraged to exterminate the French in pursuit of the jihad. An unspeakable provocation was followed by an unpardonable massacre. Algeria was made peaceful but sullen. The OS (Organisation Spéciale), forerunner

202 Entelis, *Algeria: Revolution Institutionalised,* (Boulder, Westview, 1986), p. 51. Ben Bella claimed the rebellion began with 350 weapons, Horne, *Savage War of Peace,* (London, Macmillan, 1977). p. 84.

203 Clark, *Algeria in Turmoil,* (NY, Grosset, 1960), pp. 29-37, Evans, *Algeria: France's Undeclared War,* (OUP, 2012), pp. 85-8.

204 Evans, *Algeria, France's Undeclared*, p. 86, Horne, *Savage War of Peace*, (London, Macmillan, 1977), p. 26.

205 Evans, *Algeria, France's Undeclared*, p. 91.

to the FLN, was formed in 1947. The 350 members of this *maquis* (resistance) cut down telegraph poles and assassinated an occasional *caid*. Its last action was the 1950 Oran post office raid when most of the organisation was captured. After Setif, General Duval warned he had given French-Algerians ten years of peace. He overestimated by a year.

Une drole de rebellion

The twenty-two men of the CRUA (*Comité Révolutionnaire pour l'Unité et l'Action*) emerged from the OS and launched its rebellion with a manifesto announcing the birth of a revolutionary movement, the FLN (*Front de Libération Nationale*). Its military organisation, the ALN (*Armée de Libération Nationale*), was organised in six military regions (*wilayas*). Considering its limitations in human and material resources, the CRUA's proclamation was single-mindedly audacious: to fight on, without ceasefire, until full independence. Secular and Western in its tone, it did not call for a jihad but exploited the common Islamic heritage of Arab and Berber. Secular ideas of social revolution, imperialism and socialism were foreign to these rural people.

The manifesto also made it clear it was the duty of every Muslim to rally to the FLN. French-Algerians now took seriously the offer of '*la valise ou le cerceuil*', the suitcase or the coffin. Initial French incoherence gave way to decisive action. Paratroopers arrived from France and quickly reduced the ALN to a few hundred. On the first day of the insurrection, the second in command of *wilaya* 5 (Oran) was killed. *Wilaya* 4's organisation was cracked in ten days. By the following spring, its commander, Rabah Bitat, and his deputy were both in prison. The commander of *wilaya* 2, Mourad Didouche, was killed in January 1955. By February, Ben Boulaid, commander of *wilaya* 1, was in prison. The winter of 1954–55 was the coldest on record, and the ALN, pursued into the mountains, could only manage an occasional act of sabotage. As far as French-Algerians were concerned, the war was between the army (often German Foreign Legionnaires) and the Muslims. Badly battered that first winter, the ALN emerged from the mountains in the spring. Its depleted ranks were soon filled with young recruits energised by the mass arrests and collective punishments of the French army. This *drole de rebellion* would soon change.

Drole de rebellion to savage war

A major turning point occurred with the Philippeville massacres of August 1955. Youssef Zighout, new commander of *wilaya* 2, and his deputy, Lakhdar Ben Tobbal, embarked on a bloody strategy calculated to accelerate the process of mass mobilisation. They ordered attacks on twenty-six localities in the Constantinois region, brutally murdering 123 French civilians without regard to age or sex, from a 73-year-old grandmother to a five-day-old baby. The scenes of such revolting savagery – dismembered limbs, disembowelments and the terrible mutilation of a four-year-old girl – converted Jacques Soustelle, the liberal governor general, into an ardent supporter of *Algérie Française*. The predictable and merciless French riposte swelled the ranks of the ALN. The gulf between the two communities widened. Muslim deputies of the Algerian assembly issued a 'Declaration of the Sixty-One' rejecting integration with France and supporting independence.

Throughout 1955 the ALN targeted Muslims loyal to France. Legitimate targets expanded from *caids* to elected municipal officers, tax collectors, those who paid tax, and the families of Muslims serving in the French army. Lips and noses were severed for disobeying instructions. In time, whole communities were wiped out for refusing to cooperate. In the village of Melouza the ALN burned, mutilated and systematically slaughtered 303 men and boys for continuing to support their nationalist rivals, Messali Hadj's MNA (*Mouvement National Algérien*).[206] The *drole de rebellion* was turning into a savage war. Kidnapping and ritual murders were common, including French civilians of any age or gender, suspected collaborators and 'reluctant' Muslims. A favoured method was the 'Kabyle smile', a euphemism for a slit throat. For the first two years, the ALN killed six Muslims to every French person.

By 1956 the MNA was the only political movement still resisting the FLN's call for unity. Ferhat Abbas, leader of the moderate UDMA (*Union Démocratique du Manifeste Algérien*) went over in April. When the Algerian Communist Party voted itself out of existence in July, the FLN had the field to itself after only twenty-one months' existence. But the military battle had turned in France's favour. Reinforcements resulted in replacing occasional flying columns with *quadrillage* (the grid map population control/surveillance system). Towns and communications centres were held in strength while paratroopers and legionnaires probed the countryside. In response, the ALN embarked on urban terror. And all through August and September, rebel leaders met secretly to clarify the objectives of the rising. Fifteen military delegates attended this Soummam Conference; the sixteenth was the political secretary, Ramdane Abane. He dominated the conference,

---

206   Evans, *Algeria, France's Undeclared,* (OUP, 2012), pp. 217-220.

which affirmed the primacy of the political over the military and the internal over the external. The FLN was never a mass-based party. If anything, they looked down on the people who had to be liberated by a dedicated band of revolutionaries.[207] Externals' such as Ben Bella, who never reached Soummam, were denounced for failing to procure weapons. On 6 February 1956, Prime Minister Guy Mollet arrived in Algiers. Enraged French-Algerians pelted him with rotten vegetables. This *journée des tomates* led to a hardening of French policy. The Palestro massacre of twenty-one conscript reservists on 18 May added to the French public's growing disquiet.

The Battle of Algiers

In 1956, the army began to supplement its grid system by regrouping the people of ALN-active regions. The FLN's response was twofold: an eight-day general strike to demonstrate their authority to the UN, and a transfer of the battle to the city. On 30 September three young, middle-class Muslim women placed bombs at the Milk Bar, the Cafeteria (a student dance venue) and the downtown Air France centre. Three Europeans were killed with scores seriously wounded. Yacef Saadi, the ALN's Kasbah commander, targeted civilians for more than a year. The Milk Bar bombing, which catered for mothers and children, enraged *pieds noirs*. In January 1957, General Jacques Massu's elite 10th Paratroopers arrived, directly from Suez. Massu quickly broke the strike, herded strikers back to work and forced open shuttered businesses. The army slowly made progress. Systematic torture prevailed and suspects just disappeared.[208] By 24 September Saadi was in custody. Two weeks later his deputy, Ali la Pointe, was blasted from his hideout, killing him, his companions and civilians. The Battle of Algiers was over. Massu's overwhelming, multifaceted repression completely shattered the FLN's already fragile network. But the bombs and torture allegations brought television cameras, riveting domestic and world attention on Algeria. The Nobel Laureate François Mauriac and 357 eminent French figures publicly condemned the army. The new Dreyfuss affair, said Mauraic.

The battle moved to the frontiers. By late 1957 sophisticated physical barriers were erected at the Moroccan and Tunisian borders. The Morice Line, 300-kilometre barbed-wire fences, running south from the coast along the Tunisian border, was electrified and mined;

---

207 Stora, *Algeria,* (Cornell, 2001), pp. 60-1, Evans, *Algeria: Anger of the Dispossessed,* (Yale, 2007), pp. 64-5.

208 Paul Delouvier claimed 3024, Godard rejected this, Horne, *Savage War,* p. 202.

ten kilometres wide it could not be crossed in a single night. Army trucks patrolled twenty-four hours a day. The fighters of the interior were now isolated. Eventually the external 'border army' would dominate Algerian nationalism. In December 1957 the FLN secretly murdered the political Ramdane Abane and reversed Soummam (the conference which affirmed the primacy of the political over the military). The 'military' would dominate the 'political.'[209]

13 May, Charles de Gaulle and the GPRA
Throughout 1958, with the borders effectively sealed, the French army attacked each *wilaya* separately, destroying communications and reducing the ALN to small attacks reminiscent of the early days. But Algeria was destabilising the French political system. The single-minded French-Algerians had always gotten their way, but Paris now faced an equally determined Algerian nationalism, a disillusioned domestic public opinion and mounting international pressure. The increasing toll of young conscripts was bringing the war home and the public were becoming ever more aware of torture allegations. Further complicating the picture was the wounded and unhealed French army, still smarting from humiliations stretching from the debacle of surrendering to Germany in 1940, through to defeat by the Vietnamese at Dien Bien Phu and continuing with Suez. The crisis came to a head on 13 May 1958 when the ALN executed three soldiers following France's guillotining of three rebels. A huge crowd stormed the palace of the Governor-General and proclaimed a Committee of Public Safety, with a reluctant Massu as president.

Gaullist agents hijacked the committee, and de Gaulle, cleverly playing the crisis, accepted President Coty's invitation to form a government. Pitched as de Gaulle or anarchy, it was approved by Parliament on 1 June. He moved quickly. Arriving in Algiers on 4 June, he declared to enthralled and expectant crowds his famously ambiguous *'Je vous ai compris'* ('I have understood you.') Bill Millinship recalled: 'I was there ... The applause was definitely muted.'[210] Robert Kee reported the speech for the BBC: 'There was a definite silence for a few seconds ... and then a less than full applause.'[211]

In September, Algeria's newly enfranchised Muslims defied an FLN boycott and voted overwhelmingly to endorse de Gaulle's new

---

209 Algeria's army/state holds the FLN, rather than the party holding the army, Stora, *Algeria*, pp. 66-7, 129-43.
210 Interview, Bill Millinship, London, 18 July 1998.
211 Interview, Robert Kee, London, 20 July 1998.

constitution. On 3 October de Gaulle returned to Algeria and unveiled his ambitious Constantine Plan of economic development and reform. Fearing they were being outmanoeuvred, the FLN launched a three-part offensive which included: (1) A campaign of violence in metropolitan France, resulting in eighty deaths between August and September 1958; (2) The creation of the GPRA (*Gouvernement Provisoire de la République Algérienne*) in Cairo, on 19 September; and (3) A major flow of arms from China.

Barricades Week and the generals' putsch

By 1959 General Challe's offensive had almost entirely defeated the ALN and *wilayas* 2, 3 and 4 were in thorough disarray, a product of astute manipulation by French intelligence. In August 1959, while visiting Challe's headquarters, de Gaulle insisted military success had not solved the problem. Finally, on 16 September 1959 he uttered the words 'self-determination'. A boost to FLN morale, soldiers wondered why they should die for a country that Paris would leave. For French-Algerians it meant loss of their birth-right.

The alliance of ultra-patriots and soldiers, first manifested during the May 1958 crisis and which triggered de Gaulle's return to power, began to re-form. Activist officers of the revolutionary-warfare school assured the FNF (*Front National Français*) of their support. Using the pretext of the disciplinary recall to France of their beloved Massu, the FNF called a general strike on 24 January 1960.[212] They barricaded downtown Algiers, government buildings, the university and demanded a new government. Twenty-four gendarmes were killed attempting to remove these barricades. The army, inexplicably, arrived too late. A week of disorder and open collusion prevailed between French-Algerians and elements of the 10th Paratroopers. This 'patriots uprising' only ended with de Gaulle's stirring broadcast reminding the army of its duty. The 10th paratroopers were replaced by the more forceful 25th who placed a cordon all around the *camp retranché*.[213] Many patriot-rebels slipped away. The diehards surrendered. Their leaders were imprisoned; the ranks were offered prison or a chance to fight the ALN in the desert. The whole point was to force the army to take sides. The *ultras* hoped the army's unwillingness to move against fellow patriots would snowball into full-scale opposition to de Gaulle. For the first time, Paris refused their demands.

212 Massu, a loyal Gaullist, was recalled to Paris after a journalist possibly misquoted him; Kettle, *De Gaulle*, pp. 568–9.

213 Horne, *Savage War,* pp. 360-1; Harrison, *Challenging de Gaulle,* (NY, Praeger, 1989), p. 9.

For the next two years, *pieds-noirs* intransigence and the army's dubious loyalty impeded de Gaulle's coming to terms with the FLN. FLN division also slowed progress. GPRA President Ferhat Abbas declared he, too, had his colonels. On 14 June 1960, de Gaulle broadcast an invitation to the GPRA to discuss a ceasefire. These Melun talks broke down, but he had now extended de facto recognition. The FLN restored a small network in Algiers, and another campaign of no-warning bombs was again unleashed on civilians, increasing pressure for a solution. In a famous address on 4 November 1960, de Gaulle spoke of *Algérie Algérienne* and of an Algerian republic. In December he toured Algeria promoting his referendum on self-determination. Countless green-and-white nationalist flags appeared in Algiers on 11 December with thousands demonstrating and chanting '*Vive l'Algérie Musulmane'.*[214] Not *Algérie Arabe* or *Algérie Algérienne*. The *ultras* of Barricades Week began to reconstitute as the *Front de l'Algérie Française* (FAF). They succeeded in attracting more support from middle-level officers. In April 1961, de Gaulle faced down the last serious disloyalty in the army when generals Salan, Challe, Johaud and Zeller staged their hopeless putsch. After yet another stirring speech, enough officers vacillated while the conscripts backed him and sabotaged the activist officers. The navy and air force remained loyal, as did the army in France and in Germany. In a few weeks the attempted coup was over. The final fury and despair of French-Algerians would revolve around the OAS.

Evian and the OAS
The FLN's policy of fighting on until independence finally yielded some movement. On 20 May 1961, the two sides sat down at Evian. The French, hoping for some FLN response, ordered a unilateral ceasefire and released thousands of prisoners. The talks took place against a background of OAS murder of Muslim civilians. The ALN mostly remained disciplined. Ben Bella and other prisoners were on hunger strike, international pressure was unbearable, and the French people wanted a solution. Agreement was reached on 18 March 1962. Algeria would be independent. On 8 October 1962 it was welcomed to the UN with a comparison of its struggle for freedom to Ireland's.[215]

The OAS grew out of the many vigilante groups that had engaged in 'counterterrorism' since 1955. They embarked on a scorched-earth policy intending to hand back Algeria in the state in which France had

214   Gordon, *Passing of French Algeria,* (OUP 1966), pp. 61–2.
215   Evans, *Algeria, France's Undeclared,* p. 340.

found it in 1830. They played no part at Evian. They represented the intransigent settlers whose repeated blocking of reforms had made the conflict inevitable. Throughout the autumn of 1961 urban Algeria collapsed into bloody anarchy. At their peak, the OAS killed scores of Muslims every week claiming they were liquidating ALN terrorists. In fact, their victims were random Muslims, taxi drivers and deliverymen. When the OAS killed a party of French conscripts on 23 March 1962, the army responded. In this Battle of Bab-el-Oued the *petits blancs* were disabused of the myth that the army would not fire on them. On 26 March 1962, a protest demonstration of *Algerois* ended with the army shooting fifty-four demonstrators dead in the rue d'Isly massacre.

French Algeria died badly. The Evian agreements contained specific arrangements for them to stay, including protection for their property. The FLN agreed this, not least because of their technical and administrative skills. But OAS atrocities compounded *pieds-noirs* fear of the ALN's serious reasons for revenge. The French decision to open the borders to the 'army of the frontier' added to the general panic. By the end of 1962, one million had left.

Northern Ireland, 1968–94
The 1968 street demonstrations of the Northern Ireland Civil Rights Association (NICRA), and the inability of the state to respond to reasonable demands to be treated as *British* citizens, mark the start of the conflict. These social activists, liberal Protestants, middle-class Catholics, students and republicans, sought full rights as British citizens and pressed for an end to anti-Catholic discrimination and the gerrymandering of local government. Unionists deny it but there is little doubt that Stormont institutionalised a constant and irrefutable pattern of discrimination.

Clarifying the battlelines
On 21 May 1966, the UVF declared war on the IRA and embarked on sectarian murders and false-flag bombings designed to implicate republicans. Unionist vigilance had been heightened by the fiftieth-anniversary celebrations of the 1916 Easter Rising. Within Ian Paisley's jittery Ulster Protestant Volunteers (UPV) there existed a counterpart to his Ulster Constitution Defence Committee. This 'highly clandestine cellular group' of UVF members was 'a force within a force' and formed the nucleus of 'a conspiracy [running] through the veins of

Protestant Ulster.'[216] Protestant fears included high profile meetings between the Queen, the Archbishop Canterbury and the Pope and memories of the 1950s IRA border campaign.[217] Unionist extremists, seeking to expose civil rights' agitation for full British rights as republican subversion, conspired to provoke a sectarian confrontation and clarification.

The civil rights demonstrations and Paisley's counterdemonstrations progressively raised tensions. The brutal police attacks on civil right demonstrations in October 1968 was particularly motivating for Derry's nationalists. On 1 January 1969, the People's Democracy, a student organisation, embarked on a Belfast-to-Derry march, purposefully modelled on Martin Luther King's Selma-to-Montgomery march. They were attacked at Burntollet Bridge by loyalists, police and one hundred off-duty B-Specials. Coincidentally, Paisley had been in America when King was assassinated, where he learned that civil rights agitation was designed to destroy Protestant Churches and bring about a godless America. He viewed Catholics, republicans and the dangers of ecumenism through this lens. The attack on the students dramatically exposed the sectarian dimension of the 'Orange' state. John McKeague, commander of the Shankill Defence Force, fomented violence throughout the summer of 1969, indicating that there was direction behind what appeared spontaneous.[218] Unionist MP John McQuade was often in the thick of these disturbances. Seeking to clarify the battle lines, loyalists invaded and firebombed Catholic neighbourhoods in Belfast in August 1969.

Civil rights protests to internment
On 12 August 1969 the Apprentice Boys, another 'loyal order' association, paraded around the nationalist city of Derry to celebrate, said the *Sunday Times*, their continued political hegemony: 'if Catholics take the insult lying down, all is well; if they do not, it is necessary to make them lie down.'[219] In August 1969, after nearly ten months of intense political excitement, the residents of Derry's Bogside were not prepared to lie down. Nationalist youths threw stones at police, who, assisted by loyalists, laid siege to their neighbourhood for three days.

---

216 Edwards, *UVF: Behinds the Mask*, (Merrion, 2017), p. 17; Bruce, *Red Hand*, (OUP, 1992), pp. xiii, 19-23.

217 Garland, *Gusty Spence*, (Blackstaff, 2001) p.46.

218 Mulholland, *Longest War,* (OUP, 2002), pp. 67-74. McKeague was a member of Paisley's UPV and a founding or early member of various loyalist paramilitaries including Tara, Taylor, *Loyalists*, (Bloomsbury, 2000), p. 77.

219 Sunday Times Insight, *Ulster* (Penguin, 1972), p. 115.

After two previous RUC incursions in January and April, resulting in police killing one civilian, and with memories of October 1968 still fresh, the residents were well prepared with stones and petrol bombs. The violence spread to Armagh, where seventeen B-Specials unjustifiably opened fire, following no order and shooting from the hip, killing John Gallagher, an uninvolved bystander.

Earlier, aiming to relieve the pressure on Derry, 200 protestors attempted to hand in a letter of complaint about police brutality to the RUC barracks in Hastings Street in west Belfast. A crowd of teenagers threw stones and petrol bombs. The police sped out in Shorland armoured personnel carriers, fitted with machine-gun turrets designed for border security. The police indiscriminately fired these heavy machine guns on the nationalist Falls Road. B-Specials and sections of the RUC participated or acquiesced with loyalists in burning down whole streets of Catholic homes in north and west Belfast. Hundreds of homes were destroyed, eighty-five per cent in nationalist areas. Six people died, one Protestant and five Catholics. The British army arrived just in time to avert further escalation while 6,000 Catholic refugees streamed across the border into the Republic.

A British inquiry led by Lord Scarman found the RUC seriously at fault but not complicit. The B-Specials fired recklessly and sided with loyalists. Firebombed and shot-up nationalists saw it differently: 'People truly feared that a massacre was about to take place and that the aim of those invading Catholic Ardoyne was about to end its existence.'[220] The report concluded the IRA, while involved, did not start or plan the riots but were taken by surprise. An un-named unionist senator betrayed the *settlers'* eternal vigilance: 'If only the bloody British Army hadn't come in, we would have shot 10,000 of them by dawn.'[221] Loyalists spoke wistfully of '48 hours.' Had the army been a little later, 'Belfast would have been cleared entirely of Catholics.'[222] The British army, however, which was mandated to aid the civil power, was soon shoring up the crumbling Orange-unionist supremacy.

The IRA, with few guns and few members, could not protect the Catholic community.[223] They embarked on a frantic search for weapons.

---

220   *Ardoyne: The Untold Truth,* p. 23.

221   Insight Team, *Ulster,* p. 142.

222   Mulholland, *Longest War,* p.73, from the popular loyalist song 'The night we burned Ardoyne'.

223   Malachi O'Doherty considers the possibility whether, 'police and loyalist mobs would have attacked the Falls Road had hundreds of people there not been organized by republicans into overrunning the police' and concluded 'it seems unlikely.' He argues the 1969 pogrom is another nationalist myth; the police made stupid decisions. *The Trouble with Guns,* (Belfast, Blackstaff, 1998), p. 38 and p. 33-47.

Cathal Goulding of IRA HQ in Dublin had refused to send any guns north. The Dublin-based IRA, focused on uniting the working classes, sought solidarity with northern Protestants. Belfast Catholics saw loyalist bigots (who were, like them, working class) burning their homes with the help of state forces. Out of this trauma the Provisional IRA was born in December 1969, marking a decisive split in republicanism. The Provisionals concentrated on the military option. Until the summer of 1970, army records show they hardly made a single aggressive move. On 27 June 1970, the new Provisional IRA repelled a loyalist attack on the small nationalist enclave, Ballymacarett in east Belfast, in what became known as the 'Battle of St Matthews'. With the army failing to intervene, the IRA regained the mantle of defenders.[224]

The unionist establishment, bent on confronting what it regarded as a republican insurgency, demanded the British army remove the barricades, erected to defend Catholic neighbourhoods. One week after the IRA's improved status, soldiers invaded the Falls Road, enforcing a three-day curfew. They killed four civilians and wounded sixty-four others. The British and the IRA engaged in running gunfights, with fifteen soldiers wounded. The soldiers recovered thirty rifles and fifty-five pistols. The terror of this operation, including gassing the civilian community from helicopters, marked a dramatic deterioration in Army-Catholic relations. Catholics saw the army propping up the detested Stormont regime, especially after facilitating two gloating unionist MPs drive through the area in an army jeep.

Counter-insurgency writers argue that republicans manipulated events so that the IRA now had its war. But as early as June 1970 the new Conservative government had already decided on the military suppression of the Catholics. The inexcusable neglect of Home Secretary Reginald Maudling meant that the army was effectively in charge, and the army decided it would be easier to push strutting Orange marches through sullen Catholic neighbourhoods (that late June weekend) rather than confront enraged loyalists. One senior British official lamented the failure to ban Orange marches, the imposition of the curfew and the massive arms searches which marked 'the turning point of our policy in Ulster.'[225] In 1969 Catholics had initially welcomed the army as protectors, but now they turned to the IRA. Following the curfew republicans bombed some electricity pylons and transformers but expanded this into a campaign of bombing commercial

---

224 *Sunday Times* Insight, *Ulster*, pp. 196-7. See also Smith, *Fighting for Ireland*, (London, Routledge, 1995), pp. 92-5 and Mulholland, *Longest War*, pp. 90-2.
225 Insight Team, *Ulster* p. 205.

targets aimed at destabilising the economy. From the beginning of 1971 until the summer, the IRA exploded an average of two bombs per day, with twenty exploding in one day alone in July. The bombs injured many but at this point, caused no civilian deaths.

The first British soldier to be killed in action in Ireland since the War of Independence (1919-21), Gunner Robert Curtis, was shot dead by the IRA in February 1971. In response, the unionists demanded the introduction of internment without trial for republicans.

Rise of the Provisionals to Loyalist Rebellion

On 9 August 1971 Belfast resounded to the overhead clatter of army helicopters ferrying suspects to interrogation centres. All but one of the 342 men interned without trial were Catholic. John McGuffin, the Protestant civil rights activist, was the exception. Unionist demands for repression made a bad situation worse. Late-night searches resembled life in a military dictatorship. The huge numbers of random arrests, the daily harassment in Catholic neighbourhoods, and brutality during interrogation transformed the conflict. Internment was also a security disaster leading to a massive increase in violence. Forty-one state forces and seventy-one civilians died in the next four months. Counter-insurgency expert J. Bowyer Bell concluded that widespread repression, harassment and brutal interrogations were permitted because of an unacknowledged anti-Irish prejudice: '… much unpleasant news from Ireland was filtered out, not simply by the awful jingo papers … but by the British in general.'[226] Ian Aitken, of the 'liberal' *Guardian*, in an early comparison with Algeria, pondered, if 'the French had been as brutal as the Russians, they'd have stopped it [Algerian uprising] in its tracks … and if we'd adopted French tactics we might have stopped it in its tracks, too.'[227]

By early 1972, NI was on the verge of anarchy. Parliamentary democracy, such as it was, had broken down, civil disobedience was rampant, soldiers died in IRA ambushes, loyalist paramilitaries tortured random Catholics to death, and Protestant and Catholic civilians, unintentionally or not, died on the streets as the towns rocked to the increasing tempo of IRA bombs. On 30 January 1972, paratroopers shot twenty-seven civil rights demonstrators in Derry, killing fourteen, in what became known as Bloody Sunday. Stormont was suspended and direct rule from London began. Many nationalists thought this was the

---

226 Bowyer Bell, *The Irish Troubles* (St. Martin's 1993), p. 230.
227 Interview, Ian Aitken, London, 27 July 1998.

time the IRA could have ceased its campaign.

In 1973 the British and Irish governments, the Ulster Unionist Party (UUP), the Social Democratic and Labour Party (SDLP) and the Alliance Party signed the Sunningdale Agreement. However, sharing power with Catholics was deeply unpopular with many unionists. The proposal for a Council of Ireland (involving Stormont and Leinster House, seat of the Irish government) was an anathema. The Ulster Workers' Council (UWC) assembled to oppose it. This hybrid body of the UDA, UVF, unionist politicians and loyalist trade unionists, organised a General Strike/Rebellion in May 1974. Initially using intimidation, it gained widespread Protestant support in the wake of army and police inaction. Neal Ascherson recalled the army, 'let it be known in Downing Street that nobody should contemplate using them …'[228] One officer boasted to the right-wing Monday Club: 'the army decided that it was right and that it knew best and the politicians had better toe the line.'[229] General Frank King, the general officer commanding, was not prepared to confront loyalists. There was no British de Gaulle prepared to push a reluctant army to its duty. And so, the power-sharing initiative collapsed.

On 17 May 1974, thirty-four lives were taken in no-warning bombings in Dublin and Monaghan – a message to the South not to interfere in the North. Much later the UVF claimed sole responsibility for the attack but increasing evidence points also to the involvement of British intelligence.[230] Justin Keating, Irish government minister, publicly accused the British.[231]

Long war to the Belfast (Good Friday) Agreement
The British side-lined the search for a political solution and returned to the military option but increasingly placed in the firing line local soldiers (the UDR) and police (the RUC) who would increasingly bear the brunt of fatalities, as opposed to British soldiers. This policy of 'Ulsterisation' allowed the British to depict the conflict as between two warring religious communities. The drop in number of British army fatalities also reduced any potential in Britain for a troops out movement and also meant less interest or scrutiny from the mainstream media. In 1975 the IRA was severely weakened and potentially came close to military defeat when it agreed to a prolonged ceasefire with false hopes

228 Interview, Neal Ascherson (at the *Observer*, London), July 1998.
229 Farrell, *Orange State,* (Pluto, 1976), p. 320.
230 See Cadwallader, *Lethal Allies*, *British Collusion* (Mercier 2013).
231 *Irish Times,* 29 December 2003.

of withdrawal. The Secretary of State Merlyn Rees later boasted: 'We set out to con them and we did ... my aim was to weaken the IRA. The longer the ceasefire, the harder it was for the IRA to re-start.'[232]

In response, the IRA at GHQ gave greater autonomy to a new Northern Command, which was controlled by younger members. They set out to reorganise IRA units into cells which were more difficult for the intelligence agencies to monitor or penetrate.

The 1970s and 1980s was one long period of bloody attrition, with republicans more convinced of British perfidy.[233] Roy Mason, the new British secretary, pursued an aggressive military policy, presiding over an increased use of covert operations and brutal interrogations. The British Gardiner Report of 1975 recommended the removal of special (political) status for IRA prisoners as part of a criminalisation policy. Mason boasted he was 'squeezing the IRA like a tube of toothpaste'. But a secret military document, the Glover Report, written in 1978, contradicted his depiction of the IRA as criminals on the verge of defeat. The IRA published the document in April 1979, its interception adding to its propaganda victory. Amnesty International and the 1979 Bennett Report revealed continuing brutality during interrogation.

Covert military squads colluded with loyalist paramilitaries in the random killing of Catholic civilians.[234] They operated under various names: Military Reconnaissance Force, sometimes styled Military Reaction Force, Mobile Reaction Force, Mobile Reconnaissance Force and the Force Research Unit. The IRA remained largely, but not totally, disciplined, and focused on attacking the state, occasionally making internationalist headlines which reminded the world that the conflict remained unresolved. On 27 August 1979, the IRA assassinated Lord Mountbatten, Queen Elizabeth's cousin. On the same day, eighteen paratroopers died in an IRA ambush, the regiment's greatest single day loss since Arnhem.

While British journalists propagated an image of the IRA as being nothing but a criminal gang, British officers wanted the conflict recognised as war.[235] The policy of criminalisation was finally shattered

---

232 Rees, *Northern Ireland, Personal Perspective*, (London, Metheun, 1985), pp. 223, 224.

233 Secretary of State Patrick Mayhew was 'very explicit' that Whitelaw's talks in 1972 designed to 'trap' Sinn Féin, 'were a mistake and did enormous damage ...', Langdon, *Mo Mowlam*, (Little, Brown, 2000), p. 273.

234 The evidence continues to grow. See D. Finn, NI's Deep State, *Le Monde Diplomatic*, December 2019, https://mondediplo.com/2019/12/07northern-ireland, accessed 6 December 2020, and C. Hogan, How British Forces colluded in Sectarian Violence, *New Statesman*, 7 March 2019.

235 'Each of them [army officers] said they would rather the IRA was depicted as a serious enemy, because it was a war', Dillon, *Enemy Within*, (London, Doubleday, 1994), p. 156.

by the hunger strikes of 1981, beginning with the election of Bobby Sands as an MP and the deaths of his nine comrades. The political convulsions within the nationalist community led directly to the advancement of Sinn Féin, the beginning of its electoral rise to future dominance on the national stage. The British and Irish governments scrambled to counter Sinn Féin's electoral success. Taoiseach Garret FitzGerald stated that the Anglo-Irish Agreement of 1985 (which gave the South an advisory role on the North) was the result of the IRA's performance in the hunger strikes.[236] Nationalists and unionists alike also felt that British minds had been focused by the Brighton bomb in October 1984, when the IRA narrowly missed killing the entire British Cabinet. In the 1990s massive bombs caused extensive damage in central London, threatening its survival as a financial capital. In February 1991, IRA mortars again narrowly missed wiping out the British Cabinet, one exploding in the back garden of 10 Downing Street. The IRA and the British army fought each other to a standstill, and through it all the British (including the Thatcher government) maintained secret contacts. Eventually, the Hume-Adams talks, with US help, bore fruit and in August 1994 the IRA cease fired. This eventually led to negotiations and to the Belfast (Good Friday) Agreement of 1998. This time the agreement included the British and Irish governments and most of the main parties, including Sinn Féin and representatives of loyalism. The DUP refused to participate until 2007.

Loyalist paramilitaries
Throughout the main IRA-British army engagement, there was a third participant, loyalist paramilitaries. Their role, self-appointed and/or a tool of military intelligence, was to carry out attacks and killings beyond the remit of an army ostensibly engaged in peacekeeping. Many were serving or former soldiers or policemen.[237] They attacked Catholic civilians and, only very rarely, republicans, according to their strategy for maintaining the union. Any proposed changes in the constitutional position would be paid for in civilian (Catholic) blood. They were manipulated and used, willingly or otherwise, by military intelligence, as prescribed by Kitson's counter-insurgency tactics. Rivalries between MI5 and MI6 and a fall-out between loyalists and military intelligence exposed this prolonged collusion. Loyalist killings benefitted the British

---

236   O'Malley, *Biting at the Grave,* (Boston, Beacon, 1990), p. 221.
237   Bruce, *Red Hand,* pp. 199-201.

campaign in two ways. Firstly, it required the IRA to deploy some resources against loyalist attacks. Though never a priority, it deflected the IRA from its main strategy of economic sabotage and British combat attrition. Secondly, and more importantly, it allowed the British government to portray the army as a referee separating two warring tribes. This is one of the more impressive British achievements and essential to appreciate for a fuller understanding of the media representation of the conflict. Britain, with help from Dublin, propagated this narrative internationally. Many were/are convinced.

The vast majority (eighty-five per cent) of loyalist victims were civilians – randomly selected Catholics or Protestants mistaken for Catholics. The remaining fifteen per cent were Protestants who had fallen foul of fellow loyalists and a very small number of IRA activists.[238] Loyalists, allied with Paisleyism, brought down the mildly reformist O'Neill government in 1968 and the power-sharing Executive in 1974. Their violence was/is often inaccurately portrayed as a reaction to the IRA. But the pattern is clear. When they sensed a British betrayal or impending reforms, there was increased killing of Catholic civilians.

Exploding Some Myths
Army loyalty

The story of the mutinous French army is well known, but overblown. In May 1958, when the army played a decisive role in the fall of the stumbling Fourth Republic, it did not seek power. General Massu, always a faithful Gaullist, was a reluctant member of the Committee for Public Safety. When ordered, he immediately stepped down. Neither should Barricades Week mislead us. The acquiescing 10th paratroopers were partly recruited from Algiers and based there for three years. The forceful 25th paratroopers, who replaced them, were furious at having to abandon their operations in the *bled* to deal with supposed patriots. When the putsch did come, it was made by a minority. Most officers vacillated, others remained loyal, as did the conscripts, who actively sabotaged the rebellious colonels. When it came to policy, Paris prevailed.

The dubious loyalty of the British army has received less attention. Three times during the twentieth century the army made it clear it would not obey certain orders. In the 1914 Curragh Mutiny, the army refused 'to coerce Ulster'. In 1965 the army would not coerce settlers during the Rhodesian 'kith and kin' episode. Army inaction during the 1974

---

238   CAIN index of deaths, www.ulst.ac.uk/sutton accessed 8 June 2018.

UWC Strike/Rebellion has never been fully explained.[239] An MI5 agent inside the UDA claimed MI5 encouraged the UWC to undermine the British Labour Prime Minister Harold Wilson, suspected as Moscow's agent.[240] The 'Clockwork Orange plot', as it became known, revealed the intelligence services actively undermining Wilson. The army's infamous Heathrow Airport exercise was carried out without his permission.[241] When Wilson did seek an accommodation with Irish republicans, the army did not support him. British intelligence famously misled Secretary of State Merlyn Rees when the army refused to move against the UWC.[242] At least one member of the UWC executive was a serving soldier in the UDR, and there was also an RUC 'For Ulster' group, rumoured to be ready to disobey if called to move against unionists.[243] In 1997 seventy RIR soldiers threatened to disobey in solidarity with the Orangemen of Drumcree.

Dillon revealed that the army refused to follow Secretary of State Whitelaw's policy, and deliberately wrecked the 1972 IRA truce. When the Cabinet Committee of GEN 42 contemplated a negotiated settlement, it did so in the absence of General Officer Commanding Tuzo, 'some of the military leaders would disapprove of negotiations with the IRA.'[244] More importantly, British political elites are less divided than their French counterparts. Senior British soldiers enjoy a close relationship with their political masters. An Irish Taoiseach explained: 'The army is a kind of sacred thing in British society. If the army says something is an operational necessity, then that's it.'[245] It is acceptable for army officers to brief the leader of the opposition and make political representations. He explained it as the old-boys network. Taoiseach Garret FitzGerald stated the morale of the army was paramount with British politicians.[246]

239   Newsinger, *British Counterinsurgency,* (Palgrave, 2015), pp 176-7, Wilkinson, *Terrorism and the Liberal State,* (London, Macmillan 1977), pp 158-9, Rolston & Miller, *War and Words,* pp. 183-5 and David Blundy, *Sunday Times,* 13 March 1977.

240   *Sunday Times,* 22 March 1987.

241   Baroness Falkender, Wilson's private secretary, *Sunday Times* (31 March 1981). BBC journalists Roger Penrose and Roger Courtier recorded Wilson's fears, Wilson Plot: Secret Tapes, http://news.bbc.co.uk/1/hi/uk_politics/4789060.stm, accessed 7 January 2015.

242   Coogan, *The Troubles,* (St Martin's, 2002), p. 242. General Tuzo wanted no second front, Sanders & Woods, *Times of Troubles,* (Edinburgh University, 2012), p. 76. The army sought to generate calls for 'an all-out effort for military victory', Coogan, op. cit., p. 251 and Bloch & Fitzgerald, *British Intelligence and Covert Action* (Dingle, Brandon, 1983), pp. 265–6.

243   Farrell, *Orange State,* p.319.

244   Dillon, *Enemy Within,* p. 115.

245   Coogan, *Troubles,* p. 107.

246   *Insight,* UTV, 30 January 2000.

Torture

The French army tortured and justified it as a response to ALN no-warning bombings against civilians. British army/RUC torture was more sophisticated. Their centralised approach led to less widespread abuses. But in Ireland there was no corresponding justificatory 'ticking bomb' scenario. The IRA and agencies it contacted had recognised codewords for genuine bomb warnings. The non-selective nature and geographic dispersion of those chosen for torture was aimed at intimidating the Irish nationalist community generally. ALN leader Si Azzedine explained that French torture, too, was meant to intimidate the wider Muslim community. Kitson's analysis borrowed directly from Trinquier's prescriptions – the state should attack first to separate the water from the fish.

There were differences. Paris granted full legal authority to the army and tacit verbal approval. This resulted in an orgy of brutality in dispersed interrogation centres. But the initial timidity of the Wuillaume Report was replaced with prosecutions. French soldiers were punished, fined and imprisoned. No doubt others escaped justice. The Ministry of Justice fought a losing battle with the military tribunals in Algeria. In Ireland, Lords Compton and Parker's official reports covered up and justified army brutality. Lord Justice McGonigal even ruled that emergency legislation permits an 'interviewer [*sic*] ... to use a moderate degree of physical maltreatment for the purpose of inducing a person to make a statement.'[247] This virtual 'torturer's charter' had consequences. No British soldier and only one policeman was ever prosecuted for brutality, in spite of the findings of the European Court and Amnesty International, thousands of official complaints and millions of pounds paid in compensation. The British approach was designed for political acceptability as well as technical effectiveness, high local impact and low public visibility generally.

Counterinsurgency or peacekeeping?

Operation Banner explained that the British army's role was to put down an IRA insurrection.[248] It did not move decisively against loyalist paramilitaries, and military intelligence used them when required. There was also a peacekeeping role in containing communal riots. The French army did the same. The *Compagnies Républicaines de Sécurité* (CRS) even held back soldiers during the December 1960 demonstrations to

---

247   D. Reed, *Ireland: Key to the British Revolution* (London: Larkin, 1984), p. 251.
248   *Operation Banner,* (London: MoD, 2006), pp. 1-3, 1-4, 2-10, 3-2, 4-9, 8-1, 2, 3, 4, 13.

protect Muslims chanting pro-FLN slogans. Paratroopers recently returned from desert fighting failed to distinguish between the ALN and pro-FLN demonstrators. The CRS forcefully dissuaded them from entering the Kasbah. British paratroopers, intent on teaching Derry teenagers a lesson, encountered no similar dissuasion from the RUC. France's *mission civilisatrice* meant the army was, in ways, pro-Muslim and anti-*colon*. To compete with the FLN, it behaved almost as a political party, paternalist and progressive as in Massu advocating socialism to combat rural poverty.[249] Many Muslims welcomed the army assuming full powers as the FLN ruthlessly enforced their will on 'recalcitrant' Muslims. The army did eventually move decisively against the OAS. Catholics also initially welcomed the British army but too much has been made of this. For both Irish and Algerian, the metropolitan army was preferable to security in the hands of the settlers or their descendants.

A comparison of troop numbers is also revealing. Estimates of ALN size range from 20,000 to 50,000. The deployment of 450,000 French soldiers follows the counter-insurgency ratio of ten soldiers to every insurgent. On a pro-rata basis of the insurgent communities, a British deployment of 35,000 in Ireland corresponds to a figure exceeding 600,000.[250] The number of British soldiers in Ireland surpassed the number of British soldiers that invaded Iraq in 2003. In addition, the French were thinly dispersed over Algeria's huge and remote countryside. Massu's 9,000 soldiers for Algiers (population, one million) corresponds to less than half the British deployment of 35,000 for an urban population of 1.5 million, five British soldiers for every two French soldiers. The 27,000 British soldiers of Operation Motorman in Derry's Bogside (population 30,000), in relative terms, is six times the soldiers available to Massu for subduing the Kasbah (population 70,000). Some estimates have the British-army-to-IRA ratio as high as sixty to one.[251]

Recent scholarship estimates Algerian war dead between 250,000 and 300,000.[252] Relative to population size, the Algerian War was a ten-times bloodier affair. More directly relevant, for this study, was the approximately 4,000 deaths in Algeria's towns and cities, which attracted the attention of the press. Casualties in the remote *bled* received much less media space.

---

249   Jean Daniel, *L'Express*, 11 February 1960.
250   Evans, *Algeria, France's Undeclared,* pp. 325, 337-8, Horne, *Savage War,* pp. 96, 113, 124, www.cain.ac.uk (accessed 15 July 2015).
251   Toolis, *Rebel Hearts,* (NY, St. Martin's 1995), p. 23.
252   Evans, *Algeria, France's Undeclared,* p. 338.

ALN and IRA

Alistair Horne considered the summer of 1958, when, between 24 August and 28 September the FLN took the war to France. He concluded the IRA was more indiscriminate than the ALN: 'there was not one act of promiscuous bombing against civilians such as had been commonplace in Algiers and was to become so on a larger scale in Britain under the scourge of the IRA.'[253] His assertion is contradicted by official figures which show that less than one per cent of IRA bombs caused civilian deaths.[254] The British press regularly declared: miraculously no one had been killed. But there were no miracles as Yacef Saadi explained once to Germaine Tillion. The French press had recently rejoiced after a spate of explosions: 'Thank God no-one was killed.' Saadi countered: 'It is not God you should thank but me ... I had taken every precaution.'[255] Saadi was correct on this occasion, but it was untypical of the ALN. Horne missed the obvious point that, unlike the ALN, IRA warnings were routine. IRA operations did not follow the ALN's policy of deliberately choosing peak periods to maximise civilian casualties.[256] Bowyer Bell, counter-insurgency expert and no friend of terrorism, concluded: 'the IRA killed civilians by error, through callous incompetence, by outrageous neglect but not by intent.'[257] While offering little comfort to the bereaved Bell is more accurate than Horne.

Horne wrote that Mohamed Lebjaoui was sent to France to 'heat up the war'. Lebjaoui remembers his orders were to kill French civilians indiscriminately: 'I was charged with "bringing the war home to France" ... For each Algerian killed, a French civilian would be.'[258] His mission was to sensitise French opinion to the reality of the war, and to make the French public understand that they were responsible for what was done in their name. By continuing to close their eyes, they would suffer the consequences. 'We must have blood in the headlines of all the newspapers, Abane told me as a goodbye.'[259] Lebjaoui was captured before he could bloody the headlines. Horne ignores Abane's

253 Horne, *Savage War,* p. 318.
254 See M. Sutton, *Bear in Mind These Dead* and Bew & Gillespie, *NI of the Troubles, 1968-1993,* (Dublin: Gill, 1993).
255 G. Tillion, *France and Algeria,* (NY, Knopf, 1960), p. 46.
256 Zohra Drif's chosen café favoured mothers and children, *Inside the Battle of Algiers,* (Just World, 2017), pp. 110-12, 129.
257 Bowyer Bell, *Irish Troubles,* p. 677.
258 Hutchinson, *Revolutionary Terrorism,* p. 94.
259 Ibid., p. 94.

instructions, and quotes Lebjaoui's personal intention of destroying metros and bus stations to 'make the Parisians go on foot, without killing a single person.'[260] Horne inaccurately portrays the ALN as more careful towards civilians than the IRA. Thousands of Algerian workers were killed in France simply for failing to support the FLN. The 'Café Wars' cost 4,000 lives in a struggle for the leadership of Algerian nationalism in metropolitan France.[261] In the four-week period Horne cites, he missed one death and six civilians wounded by a bomb on the ferry *Président de Cazalet*, two workers killed and twenty wounded by another bomb at a tyre factory near Paris, grenades thrown into a café in Marseilles, three civilians injured by a bomb in the Marseilles prefecture, and five French civilians shot dead. The ALN also attempted to blow up the Eiffel Tower and Mourepiane oil refinery in Marseille with what would have resulted in unimaginable casualties. Whole neighbourhoods were evacuated, firefighter Jean Peri was killed, nineteen were wounded including the mayor, Gaston Defferre, who supported Algerian independence.[262] This was only in France. In Algeria, the ALN continued to kill civilians relentlessly, French and Muslim. Horne omits these casualties and outlines Lebjaoui's post-war assertion rather than FLN policy. Shortly after these attacks, on 10 October 1958 FLN leader Belkacem Krim publicly stated that the leadership had not yet resolved its position on attacking civilian targets.[263] I found no similar statement by Irish republicans.[264]

Horne also calls for a quantitative comparison of ALN bombs and IRA bombs, predicting it would reveal the IRA's greater ruthlessness. But in neither absolute nor proportional terms does the IRA come close to the ALN's killing of civilians.[265] Possibly, for Horne, IRA attacks against his homeland loomed larger than ALN attacks in France. In 2013 he acknowledged, when working as a journalist, his patriotism motivated him to simultaneously work for MI6.[266]

---

260   Horne, *Savage War*, p. 237.

261   Evans, *Algeria, France's Undeclared*, p. 277.

262   Evans, *Algeria, France's Undeclared*, p. 243, Hutchinson, *Revolutionary Terrorism*, p. 496, Ali Haroun, *La 7e Wilaya* (Paris: Seuil, 1986), and Albert Lentin, *Historia Magazine*, no. 265 (27 November 1972). See also the timeline www.marxists.org/history/algeria/1958, accessed 10 July 2015.

263   Hutchinson, *Revolutionary Terrorism*, p. 97.

264   The FLN targeted *pieds noirs* as the enemy, review of Drif's *Inside the Battle of Algiers, The Nation*, 2 February 2018.

265   See Chapter Nine for a detailed comparison of ALN and IRA actions.

266   'He had to follow the patriotic drum'; BBC Radio, *Documents*, 4 March 2013.

Loyalist paramilitaries and French Algerian ultras

Albert Memmi probed the mentality generated by the relentless reciprocity of the coloniser–colonised relationship. He portrays the French Algerian ostentatiously singing the 'Marseillaise' to proclaim his loyalty. But it was profoundly conditional. Although a faithful keeper of true French values he maintains a mixed love/resentment relationship with the motherland. Paris is constantly reminded of his war sacrifices. If the mother country is faithless, he will secede. His frequent parades and demonstrations are as much to reassure himself as impress the native. Yet no permanent reassurance is possible. He calls endlessly for more soldiers, more guns. When the native does give his consent, the settler is suspicious.[267] But the 'coloniser who refuses' must leave or knock on the door of the colonised.[268] The 'coloniser who accepts' legitimises his position by extolling his eminent virtues while pointing out the natives' obvious flaws. He denies or justifies discrimination and accepts no responsibility for the current upheaval. He has done no wrong. He lives by the law. His advantages, symbolic and economic, are demonstrated every day: his police, his traditions, his flag. The small coloniser is often an obstinate defender of colonial privileges. To protect his own interests, he protects 'other infinitely more important ones, of which he is, incidentally, the victim. But, though dupe and victim, he also gets his share.'[269] Racial boundaries are rigidly maintained and lay the foundation for the immutability of colonial life.

Unionists deny a general discrimination against Catholics.[270] Many profess bewilderment as to what they have supposedly done wrong and are resolved to exculpate their political tradition of any responsibility for the conflict. There is especially one privilege the dominant community was determined to preserve: the knowledge that 'the law is our law'.[271] Unionism was offended by Chris Patten's large-scale reforming of the RUC. Britain had publicly redirected blame. Following the GFA, loyalists have frequently complained of loss, a sense that 'their

---

267 Memmi, *The Coloniser and the Colonised* (Boston: Beacon, 2016), pp. xii, xxviii, 11-13, 33, 62-65.

268 For Protestant republicans and IRA members, see M. Hyndman, *Journeys from a Protestant Past* (Beyond the Pale, 1996).

269 Memmi, *The Coloniser*, p. 7.

270 Mulholland, *Longest War,* p. 10, and Whyte, *Interpreting Northern Ireland* (Oxford: Clarendon, 1991), p. 66.

271 Wright, *Northern Ireland,* (Dublin: Gill & Macmillan, 1992), p. 124.

country' has gone. They are offended by Catholics 'getting in everywhere', acting like they own the place.[272] In 2022 Baroness Hoey complained the law and journalism in Northern Ireland, 'have become dominated by those of nationalist persuasion.'[273] Memmi's portrait of the *colon* is remarkably familiar in Northern Ireland.

Conclusion

This chapter challenges the view of a ruthless, mutinous French army and a smaller deployment of a restrained British army doing its duty. In relative terms, British deployment was larger. On torture, the French army had full police powers and tortured as they thought necessary. British forces tortured in a system administered by the MoD. When four French generals rebelled against government policy they were imprisoned. When senior British officers refused to support government policy, London conceded. In addition, Britain did not face the same ferocity as France. The IRA's ruthless intensity did not match the ALN's cold savagery. OAS and loyalist paramilitaries are a closer match. Both claimed they were assisting the state by eliminating terrorists. In fact, these self-styled 'counter-terrorists' killed civilians from the 'other' community.

272 O'Connor, *In Search of a State: Catholics in Northern Ireland* (Belfast: Blackstaff, 1993), p.178.
273 *Irish Times* 10 January 2022.

PART TWO

CHAPTER FOUR

Trinquier, Kitson and the Role of the Army

This chapter explores the soldiers' motives found in the published accounts and memoirs of those who served. How they understood the conflict permits a comparison of each army's perception of its role, its political masters, and the insurgent and loyal communities. These accounts and the historic record facilitate the evaluation of the comparative press coverages. An important comparison is who dictated policy – soldiers or politicians? The French army included the traditional officer class of Saint-Cyr, large numbers of unhappy conscripts, and the activist officers who understood the conflict through Colonel Roger Trinquier's la guerre révolutionnaire. *These 'dirty warriors' believed they were liberating Algerians (Muslim and French) from the clutches of the FLN, frustrating the designs of Egyptian President Gamal Nasser and the hidden hand of the Soviet Union. The British army is a professional army. British army accounts point to the prescriptions of Brigadier Frank Kitson who had adapted Trinquier's methods. The French army claimed to protect the Muslims from the FLN. The British army failed to distinguish between Irish Catholics and the IRA.*

French Army
Centurions, communists and conscripts
The French army obediently withdrew from Tunisia, Morocco, Madagascar and all French possessions in Africa, but not Algeria. For the professional soldiers, pursuit of the ALN resembled war just enough to whet their appetite for a triumph after years without victory. The post-WWII army had not quite lost its inferiority complex which began with the humiliation of 1940 followed by the trauma of Indo-China. For eight

years the Legion and the pride of Saint-Cyr, the French military academy, had spilled their blood in distant jungles and rice fields against a background of general indifference at home, where politicians refused to send conscripts to a dirty war. The army, fighting continuously since 1939, emerged from Indo-China as an alienated band of brothers, contemptuous of the politicians of the Fourth Republic. During one WWII commemoration, several officers in civilian clothes, publicly and with impunity, slapped, kicked and manhandled two government ministers. One general said: 'They dished us in Indochina, they dished us in Tunisia, they dished us in Morocco. They'll never dish us in Algeria. I swear it and you can tell Paris.'[274]

Arriving in Algeria directly from Indo-China, these elite warriors would rescue everyone from the rebels and, if necessary, from Paris. They would take Algerians in hand and lift them up to the standards of France.

Jean Lartéguy, war correspondent and decorated soldier, captures their sense of betrayal in *The Centurions,* a sympathetic portrayal of noble warriors compelled to get their hands dirty defending French and Western civilisation. The officers are composites, veterans of Indo-China where they learned the 'communist' method, torture. Lartéguy begins with a quotation from Marcus Flavinius, centurion of the Augusta Legion, to his cousin Tertullus in ancient Rome. These legionnaires sought reassurance that their fellow citizens supported and understood their actions in defence of civilisation. 'If it should be otherwise, if we should have to leave our bleached bones on these desert sands in vain, then beware of the anger of the Legions.'[275] These modern warriors knew well how communist agitators manipulated the population. They would nip these outrages in the bud. Captain Boisfeuras meets with the local police inspector, an old friend from Saigon days. The inspector already knew all the FLN leaders and their hideouts, but French law prevented the paratroopers doing what was forbidden to the police. Larteguy's officers intended to expunge the memory of defeat, humiliation and withdrawal even against a treacherous Paris.

Other soldiers had more immediate motivations. Simon Murray remembers how he and his fellow Legionnaires enjoyed chasing rebels through the mountains. Paratrooper Pierre Leulliette's memoirs relate

274   J. Kraft, *The Struggle for Algeria* (NY, Doubleday, 1961), p. 98.
275   J. Lartéguy, *The Centurions* (London: Heinemann, 1961), no pagination.

the same exhilaration. The army provided everything: their equipment, food and wine, the prostitutes who followed behind and, when necessary, padres to bury them. The army also contained *les soldats perdus*, the 'lost soldiers', more loyal to the army than France. The traditional officer class wanted to send a clear message to Paris. No-one would deny them their victory. Talented activist officers were an obvious force within the army, conducting themselves with a certain élan. The conscripts, however, were totally uncommitted to any concept of *Algérie Française*. They tried to give a good impression of France to Muslim villagers but knew this was undermined by the combat units. The conscripts loathed French Algerians for blocking reforms. American journalist Herb Greer remembered: 'Everybody hated the *colon* ... They possessed *une certain idee de la France* ... It's the centre of their being ... It's like those guys at Drumcree, it's all they have left.'[276]

La guerre révolutionnaire

The Fourth Republic was weak and lacked authoritative political leadership. Left to its own devices, the army defined policy.[277] Their doctrine of *la guerre révolutionnaire* was based on the belief of a worldwide communist threat. Nuclear stalemate meant the most likely form of war the West would fight, indeed, was already fighting, was a subversive revolutionary one. This permanent and universal threat had as its primary object, not defeat of an enemy but, the physical and moral conquest of the population. Accordingly, the best army in the world was worthless unless backed by political action. Traditional weapons should be supplemented with special techniques for mobilising the masses and manipulating opinion: propaganda, indoctrination and organisation. National liberation struggles were not generated by imperial domination but were the product of manipulation. Theorists such as Colonel Lacheroy and Colonel Trinquier were obsessed with these new methods. Since the masses were manipulated by the rebels, an adept propaganda campaign, *action psychologique,* was necessary to imbue the insurgent community with proper thinking. Supplemented by a repressive apparatus, this would pre-empt subversion. By 1958 the army was already suspicious of *pieds-noirs ultras* who blocked political reforms which the army supported. The army would deprive the FLN of grievances and attendant propaganda.

---

276   Interview, Herb Greer (Manchester), 21 July 1998.
277   E. Behr, *The Algerian Problem* (London: Hodder & Stoughton, 1961), pp. 138-40.

Jules Roy, army veteran and Algerian-born, believed in France's proclamation of the rights of man. His *War in Algeria* sold 100,000 copies, provoking as much astonishment as if a 'Texan veteran of the Alamo had written "Pity the poor Mexican."'[278] Roy sought out the soldiers' motives. They were fighting to raise Algerian living standards, to redistribute the land, and to keep them linked materially and spiritually to France. This social role had been part of the curriculum of Saint-Cyr since the mid-nineteenth century. The officers' calling was literally conceived in religious terms and regarded as the fulfilment of a sacerdotal function. The self-image of the French colonial soldier was that of heroic leader and a civilising missionary. For the traditional officer class, this was certainly true. General De Bollardière publicly condemned the army for falling short of this ideal. The army competed with the FLN for the hearts and minds of impoverished and fatalistic Muslim villagers. General Massu did not hesitate to condemn their living conditions which prevented them from being fully French. He was proud of the *Sections Administratives Spécialisées* (SAS), with its record of improving Muslim lives with increased food supplies, health, housing and schools. Once the army got the terrorists off the backs of the ordinary Muslims, it intended bestowing on them all the benefits of French civilisation. The great colonial administrator General Hubert Lyautey had developed this *mission civilisatrice* in early twentieth century Madagascar and Morocco. Pacification should be followed by social and economic development, turning former insurgents towards cooperation.

British Army
Numerous campaigns against irregulars along the fringes of the empire
The professional British army never saw itself as a cadre for a national army that would fight a major war. Its almost exclusive experience was in fighting 'minor battles and major campaigns in out-of-the-way places, usually against primitive opponents.'[279] Conventional wars, including the two world wars, were exceptions. In 1969, the British army, much experienced in counterinsurgency, arrived on Belfast streets with its uniforms, equipment, attitudes and methods geared to their recent pacification of Aden (Yemen). At least one banner unfurled before a bemused Belfast crowd was written in Arabic.[280]

278   J. Roy, *War in Algeria* (NY, Grove, 1961), p. 9.
279   Charters and Tugwell, *Armies in Low Intensity Conflict*, (London, Brassey, 1989), p. 176.
280   Taylor, *Brits,* (London, Bloomsbury), p. 32.

From 1870 until the turn of the twentieth century, the British army had conducted numerous campaigns against irregulars along the fringes of the empire. Scorched-earth tactics were openly advocated and practised. Further experience was gained in the Boer War (1899–1902) and in Ireland (1918–1921). From 1945 to 1968 the British army conducted a total of *fifty-three* counter-insurgency campaigns throughout the world. There have also been more covert operations, Oman (1970) the best now known.[281] Historically speaking, the British army has not been prepared for 'peacekeeping in a democratic society'. Rather, the counter-insurgency lessons learned in an earlier campaign in Ireland have often been applied elsewhere in the empire. In 1946 the former Inspector General of the RUC, Sir Charles Wickham, and RUC County Inspector Moffat, went out to advise the [British mandate] Palestine Police. Wickham was uniquely qualified for the role.[282] He recommended action against *terrorism*, as against all forms of crime, had to be based on information. Bowyer Bell surveyed the history of rebellions against Britain. He concluded the British response to this latest insurrection in Ireland coincided remarkably well with its response to post-WWII imperial dissolution.[283]

Keeping the peace – the queen's peace
British troops were not summoned onto the streets in 1969 to act as umpire between Protestants and Catholics. Previously dormant Irish nationalism, having been murderously awakened, now opposed the forces of the Protestant unionist government. The troops were sent to aid the civil power. Catholics initially welcomed British soldiers, believing they would be less partisan than the local Protestant-dominated security forces. The army's methods would, however, soon provoke an insurgency, the potential of which, would always be limited by one million loyal Protestants. This aided the government in its determination to deny the conflict was an insurgency. The political usefulness of denouncing all republican action as terrorism proved too

---

281   Woodies, *Armies and Politics* (London: Lawrence & Wishart, 1977), pp. 278-9.

282   After WWII British intelligence needed to integrate Greek security battalions (Nazi collaborators) into a new police force. They found Wickham, who had fought Boers and Bolsheviks for the British Empire. RUC Inspector General, from 1922–45, he recruited UVF members into the new police. He armed Hitler's collaborators to shoot down Greeks who had fought the Germans. In 1999 Chris Patten, however, who led the Independent Commission on Policing, recommended the overhaul of policing and the establishment of the Police Service of Northern Ireland.
https://www.opendemocracy.net/en/can-europe-make-it/british-perfidy-in-greece-story-worth-remembering/ accessed 10 July 2015.

283   JB Bell, *On Revolt,* (Harvard, 1976), p. 205.

great a temptation, even when the action was patently military, attacking patrols and military barracks. Soldiers certainly did not regard themselves as terrorised.

The army's *Land Operations Volume III* identified its role as 'counter-revolutionary'. Its job was to put down a republican insurrection. According to army manuals, ambushes categorised as 'setting four' were to be used in a counter-insurgency campaign verging on limited war in which the security forces had lost control of certain areas. However, no state of emergency was declared, except indirectly via Britain's derogation from Article Five of the European Convention on Human Rights on the grounds of an emergency threatening the life of the nation. Colonel Robin Evelegh described the situation as disguised military rule rather than overt military rule. The generals increasingly felt free to act without the restraint of politicians. Each battalion did its own thing, within or without the law. All were tolerated. General Tuzo recommended a return to 'the methods of the colonies'.[284] In the early 1970s the British government's search for a political solution ran in tandem with or competed with the army's desire for military success. From the collapse of power-sharing in May 1974 until the Anglo-Irish Agreement of 1985, the government was more occupied with a military defeat of the IRA than a search for a political solution. Evelegh's account permits an insight into the army's frustrations with its political masters: 'orders to operate in low profile could only mean orders not to enforce the law'.[285] He felt the government was 'indulging' republicans. Tolerating Derry's no-go areas, 'relieves the perpetrators of a crime from the legal consequences.'[286] The army's dictating policy on the ground, demonstrated by its lack of support for the Sunningdale Agreement, prolonged the conflict.

Low intensity operations and la guerre révolutionnaire
There is yet a widespread belief that British counterinsurgency is subject to the guiding principle of minimum force. The *Guardian's* Ian Aitken explained: 'There is a very large gap between what the French did and we did ... an SAS unit ... could have put a stop to it.'[287] However, minimum force carries little influence in British military

---

284 Edward Burke (2015): Counterinsurgency against 'Kith and Kin'? The British Army in Northern Ireland, 1970–76, *Journal of Imperial and Commonwealth History*, Vol 43, issue 4, p. 29.

285 Evelegh, *Peacekeeping in a Democratic Society* (London, Hurst, 1978), p. 17.

286 Ibid., p. 18.

287 Interview, Ian Aitken (London), July 1998.

training. Any success in Kenya was not the result of any supposed 'British way' of counterinsurgency but due to extreme coercive methods.[288] In Ireland, the army followed Kitson's prescriptions. He was 'the sun around which the planets revolved and he very much set the tone for the operational style.'[289] Kitson's views on subversion and dissent caused quite a stir in the early 1970s. He reminded his readers that suppression of the Irish and defence of the Protestant religion were two of the main reasons the regular army was raised in the first place. His work drew on his own experience of suppressing the Kikuyu in Kenya. He acknowledged the profound influence of Trinquier's Algerian prescriptions, *la guerre révolutionnaire*.[290]

General Michael Carver decided to implement Kitson's 'punchy methods'. Colonel 'Brian', of the Gloucestershire regiment, relished his mission statement from Kitson's 39th Brigade: 'kill them'. Brian was not labouring under any restraint and admitted to hating nationalists: 'with a kind of hatred I never thought could get into me ... some of the things I did then I'm not ashamed of doing really but I do wish I hadn't done them sometimes ... [we] fuelled the IRA for the next ten years.'[291] According to Kitson, an insurgency is most vulnerable before it gains popular support. And so, Carver authorised mass arrests, large-scale searches and increased stop-and-search measures. The data on British security policy is not readily available, but Hillyard estimates between 1971 and 1986 one in every four Catholic males (16-44 years) was arrested at least once.[292] During the same period, 338,803 houses were searched, amounting to seventy-five per cent of all houses in Northern Ireland; 250,000 of the searches took place between 1972 and 1976. These house searches were concentrated on the 170,000 Catholic homes in north and west Belfast, which were subject to multiple searches.[293] Trinquier's large-scale screening was improved by the use of computers.

The methods of Algiers became standard British practice. The emphasis was on intelligence: defeating the enemy means finding him.

---

288 Curtis, *Web of Deceit, Britain's Real Role in the World,* (London, Vintage 2003), Porch, *Counterinsurgency: Exposing the Myth of the New Way of War* (Cambridge University Press, 2013).

289 M. Jackson, *Soldier, (Transworld, 2007),* p. 82.

290 F. Kitson, *Low Intensity Operations* (London, Faber, 1971).

291 Taylor, *Brits*, pp. 140-1.

292 Hillyard, in Hennings, *Justice Under Fire*, (Pluto, 1988), p. 197.

293 See J. Hughes, 'State Violence in the Origins of Nationalism', in J.A. Hall and S. Malesevic, *Nationalism and War* (Cambridge University Press, 2013), pp. 111–15.

Civil–military coordination was essential, including psychological operations and propaganda in the campaign for hearts and minds. Trinquier recommended torture, 'the particular bane of the terrorist'.[294] It was just another necessary weapon in this new type of war and was believed to have stopped the ALN cold. Kitson was no maverick: he represented the prevailing mood in the army. Special forces were never subject to any restraint. Like guerrillas, they were to avoid anything resembling a fair fight. The role of special forces was to ambush and discredit the enemy and organise friendly forces against a common enemy. Collusion with loyalist death squads became part of British military methods.[295]

According to its former Director-General, MI5's 'assist ... led to considerable soul searching ... a gruesome business ... which kept him awake at nights.'[296]

The Liberal Press
France's flaw: military repression delays political settlement
The *Guardian-Observer* accused Paris of allowing military repression to precede and side-line political reforms. The British liberal press denounced any French political initiatives, designed to accommodate both communities, as a denial of Algerian self-determination. De Gaulle's Constantine Plan was portrayed as a bribe aimed at repudiating Algerian national aspirations. The consistent theme was the French had it the wrong way round. Instead of pursuing a policy of pacification followed by reforms, they should start reforming and peace would inevitably follow.[297] French initiatives began in 1956 with PM Guy Mollet offering the FLN a process of: ceasefire, elections, negotiations, reform. The *Guardian* argued that Mollet's policy 'puts off until after a ceasefire the political offer which might bring about a ceasefire.'[298] Darsie Gillie's featured article criticised Mollet for allowing army reprisals to overshadow the political problem and for his stance of refusing to 'negotiate with murder'.[299] Editorials condemned the

---

294 R Maran, *Torture* (NY, Prager, 1989), p. 99.

295 Porch, *Counterinsurgency,* pp. 268-88.

296 B Porter review, Defence of the Realm, *LRB,* Vol 31, no 22, 19 November 2009.

297 The *Guardian* accused the French of seeking pacification first: 19, 23 (editorial), 29, 30 (editorial) October 1956; 1 January, 15, 17, February, 11, 29 March, 11 September, 1 October (editorial) 1957; 19 (editorial), 27 March, 31 August, 30 September (editorial), 4 October (editorial) 1958; 15 (editorial), 17 March, 9 June (editorial), 3 July, 18 August, 17, 18 September 1959; 18 January, 1, 28, August 1961.

298 Ibid., 30 October 1956 (editorial).

299 Ibid., 17 February 1957.

military option: 'The war in Algeria is not the continuation of policy by other means, it is a hideous substitute for a policy.'[300] The *Guardian* featured J.H. Huizinga's response to de Gaulle's famous 'peace of the brave' speech offering ceasefire and elections followed by negotiations. This Dutch historian argued that de Gaulle had offered negotiations not with the FLN but with the representatives of the Algerian people elected after the former had abandoned the fight: 'Who has ever heard of a nationalist movement after four years of the bloodiest war ... agreeing to surrender its arms and submit its dispute with the colonial ruler to a popular verdict organized under the latter's auspices?'[301] This could have been written by dissident republicans who rejected the British organising the referendum on the GFA. The *Observer's* Nora Beloff also rejected Mollet's initiative: 'Mollet is still offering free elections under international supervision only after a ceasefire – in other words after the Algerians have called off the rebellion.'[302] She also rejected de Gaulle's peace offer because this would preclude the FLN as 'qualified representatives' of the Algerian nation and would deem them 'erring citizens of France who would be received back into the body politic by the good graces of the French Government.'[303]

Alistair Hetherington, *Guardian* editor, rejected the initiative on two grounds: 'First, the French demand that the rebels, but not the French forces, should lay down their arms in advance of any political negotiation.' Second, although the general accepts self-determination for Algeria, 'he insists the choice should be exercised not under impartial international auspices, but under French army control.'[304] In contrast, any mention of the UN or any international 'interference' in Ireland provoked outrage. There were no editorials demanding the British army lay down its arms before negotiations in Ireland.[305]

Maintaining no French military solution was possible, the *Observer* recommended Paris begin negotiating.[306] De Gaulle's Constantine Plan, with its massive programme of improvements in housing and education,

300 Ibid., 1 March 1958 (editorial).

301 Ibid., 17 March 1959.

302 *Observer*, 10 March 1957.

303 Ibid., 26 October 1958.

304 Ibid., 11 September (editorial).

305 Britain rejects Irish [UN] offer, *Guardian* 16 Aug 1969 or Britain ready to veto call for UN force, *Guardian* 19 Aug 1969 and 'Jack Lynch tossed his own petrol bomb with his demand for UN troops', *Observer* 17 August 1969.

306 French policy as the wrong way round, see: *Observer*, 27 May 1956, 10 March, 2, 9, 30 June, 17 November 1957; 5 January, 13, 20 April,11 May, 8 June, 26 October 1958; 23 August, 2, 9 September, 6 December 1959; 7 February, 3, 24 April, 19, 26 June, 11 September, 13 November 1960; 23 July 1961.

also failed to impress. Nora Beloff argued he was trying to buy off Muslims by offering them 'better living conditions, more educational facilities and more liberal forms of local administration on condition that they agree to stay French – in other words repudiate their nationalist aims.'[307] *Observer* editorials repeated this. Of course, the Algerians wanted a better life, but 'like other people in the twentieth century they want independence still more.'[308] Hetherington's editorials agreed. De Gaulle's economic package 'can never satisfy the idealism which lies at the basis of the FLN.'[309]

In contrast, the sentiments behind John Hume's 'you can't eat a flag' were often used to repudiate Irish republican 'delusions'.[310] Brexit overturned this dictum too, at least with respect to English nationalism.

Paris did propose several political initiatives aimed at accommodating the conflicting demands of French and Muslim communities. The *Guardian-Observer* rejected any and all if they fell short of the FLN's full demands.[311] De Gaulle's obstinacy was portrayed as holding up talks. In fact, the FLN refused to talk unless France conceded their right to independence in advance. On 21 March 1957 Algeria's Resident Minister Robert Lacoste proposed Swiss canton-style reforms of local self-government and internal federalism, a living mosaic of self-governing communities. This creative attempt to solve a difficult problem did not impress, with the *Guardian* declaring it would fail to 'stop the course of history' and deemed decentralisation as an attempt to 'divide and rule'.[312] A *Guardian* editorial held: 'decentralization or federation seems unlikely to win over those leaders who can sweep the people along with them.'[313] *Observer* editorials also rejected federation, arguing that the Algerian tragedy 'cannot now be stopped by the introduction of some complicated scheme for local self-government: only the granting of the principle of Algerian independence

---

307   *Observer*, 14 September 1958.

308   *Observer*, 5 October 1958 (editorial).

309   *Guardian*, 13 December 1958 (editorial).

310   PJ McLaughlin, *John Hume and the Revision of Irish Nationalism*, (Manchester University Press, 2013), p. 7. As far back as 19 October 1959 a *Guardian* article explained: 'Modern household appliances will overcome the border feud', see also *Guardian*, 13 December 1956, *Observer* editorial 4 December 1955. 'Unemployment' was frequently cited after 1969.

311   For criticism of French initiatives, see *Guardian*, 6 December 1956, 10, 16 January, 15, 17 February, 22, 29 March, 19 June, 20 July, 16, 22 August 1957; 1, 17 (editorial), 19, 27 April, 23, 29 May 1958; 17, 18, 30 September 1959; 12 April, 18, 29 July, 1, 28 August 1961, and *Observer*, 9 June, 25 August, 22 September, 1 December 1957, 1 January, 20 April, 14 September, 5, 26 October 1958; 11 January, 1 February, 23 August, 20 September 1959; 5 November 1961.

312   *Guardian*, 22 August 1957.

313   Ibid., 11 September 1957 (editorial).

... offers any hope.'[314]

The prevailing theme was that all French initiatives were designed to prevent French Algerians being outvoted. Both newspapers called for UN involvement because de Gaulle and the French Algerians were holding up a settlement. As the Battle of Algiers wound down, Tanya Zinkin reflected sadly on Algeria: 'how wise the British have been in their willingness to devolve power quickly.'[315] The same page carried reports of gunfights between British security forces and an earlier IRA. This blind-spot on Ireland makes a regular appearance, with partition endorsed for Ireland and rejected for Algeria.[316]

British wisdom: total repression to ensure constructive political discussion

Hugh Hanning summarised the overwhelming portrayal of British policy: 'The case over Ulster is not hard to make. Both the political strategy and the military tactics of the UK Government are eminently reasonable.'[317] From the very beginning, during the civil rights phase, before even the IRA resurgence, editorials called for total repression: the violence of Ulster was 'organized, cynical, politically motivated and deserving of total repression by the security forces ... [it] is devoted to destroying what exists for the same revolutionary reasons as the Viet Cong destroy what exists.'[318] This early portrait of politically motivated republicans soon disappeared. Critical journalists like Paul Foot rebuked the *Guardian* for endorsing a policy of repression. Hetherington responded: 'To restore calm and order is the first priority. To initiate constructive political discussion and to devise new forms of economic support come next.'[319] 'Constructive' meant no mention of the Constitution, the heart of the problem. The same editorial claimed that IRA attacks justified the focus on security and the internment policy. At the time of this editorial (31 August 1971) the security forces had killed twice as many civilians as had the IRA.[320]

314 *Observer*, 25 August 1957 (editorial).
315 *Guardian*, 30 September 1957.
316 Just two weeks earlier, the *Guardian* was urging a completely different 'course of history' in Ireland. See Cardinal D'Alton's proposals for uniting Ireland under the Commonwealth, *Guardian*, 4, 5 March 1957. It might usefully be compared to the issue of 22 March 1957 in relation to Algeria, where in one case the paper argues against partition (Algeria) and in another endorses partition (Ireland).
317 Ibid., 26 April 1971.
318 Ibid., 14 July 1970 (editorial). Cole favored continued repression, but Hetherington changed, *Guardian Years*, pp. 294-322.
319 Ibid., 13 August 1971 (editorial).
320 41 & 20 respectively, McKittrick et al, *Lost Lives,* https://cain.ulster.ac.uk/cgi-bin/tab3.pl accessed 10 December 2021.

Long after many voices, not just those of Irish nationalists, had concluded that the internment policy only increased the violence, *Guardian* editorials repeatedly called for its continuation.[321] 'Does anyone believe that if the internees are released, they will all abstain from further violence? ... a great deal of cant is being talked.'[322] The ruthless French, however, would periodically release hundreds of internees in an effort to win Algerians over to new political initiatives, even in the wake of appalling ALN massacres and in the face of enraged *pieds noirs* opinion. In the aftermath of the huge upsurge in violence following internment in August 1971, Hetherington-Cole's editorials called for increased military efforts: 'A measure of military defeat for the IRA greater than has so far been achieved is a necessary preliminary to a political settlement.'[323] A few weeks later, they again urged military repression, claiming security operations would be rendered impossible by 'confining the army to a so-called "peace-keeping role."' [324] With the breakdown of the IRA ceasefire in the summer of 1972, they ditched the peace-keeping role ('so called', in his/their words) and enlarged the constituency of those in need of repression: 'Catholics would be wise to cooperate with the army ... Limited curfews may be necessary, confining the whole population [of defined areas] to their homes at night ... but if that [civil disobedience] took place it would leave little doubt as to whether there is any substantial body of moderate opinion in these areas.'[325] Two weeks later, the editor directly warned Catholics: army discipline will depend on 'whether people shield the IRA and obstruct soldiers. Women and children banging dustbin lids, sitting in front of army vehicles and abusing patrols in the street are directly helping the Provisionals.'[326] Still, if the Catholics persisted with their protests, editorials warned of an even more ominous eventuality: the British will 'begin to question whether any distinction can be drawn between the Catholic community and the IRA.'[327] Protesting about army abuses was labelled as assisting the IRA. General Officer Commanding Frank King believed: 'the inhabitants were to blame, they knew who the gunmen

---

321 Hetherington wrote they only ever had one disagreement ... over internment, Cole wanted it maintained, *Guardian Years*, pp. 294-322. The same pages detail Simon Winchester hearing from his officer-friend, who happened to be serving in Ardoyne, telling him to be wary of the army explanation of the Bernard Watt killing, *Guardian* 3 Feb 1971.

322 *Guardian*, 29 November 1971 (editorial).

323 Ibid., 4 January 1972 (editorial).

324 Ibid., 16 March 1972 (editorial).

325 Ibid., 15 July 1972 (editorial).

326 Ibid., 29 July 1972 (editorial).

327 Ibid.

were and could have thrown them out.'[328] The view of the 'liberal' *Guardian* and the general coincided with the justification of loyalist paramilitaries for their random killings of Catholic civilians. On the first anniversary of internment, Hetherington-Cole again endorsed the security policy: '"bin lid bashing" has been ordered by the so-called Civil Rights Association' (note 'so-called' again). They accused Catholics of 'spitting on the [Britain's] olive branch' and held that 'no political negotiations can have much meaning or reality while the IRA remains active or while women and children give it cover and support.'[329] In the *Guardian's* view there was no moderate Catholic opinion.

Hetherington-Cole clearly invested a great deal of confidence in army briefings and warned Catholics of even more dire consequences: 'Those who assist the Provisionals [are] ... jeopardizing their own future ... The ultimate alternative to [British Secretary] Mr. Whitelaw's policy is a mass movement of population.'[330] This solution is what we now call ethnic cleansing. After another full year of this disastrous policy, the editorial line had not changed: 'the role of the army remains decisive; that must never be forgotten.'[331] There are twenty-nine such editorials for the period under study, calling for a defeat of IRA gunmen first, and then reforms that exclude the constitutional issue, coupled with dire warnings to Catholic women and children, and even the suggestion of their forced movement.[332]

During the worst violence, following internment, *Observer* editorials held to the same approach: 'Before there can be a settlement there will have to be talks. Before there can be talks the gunmen must be neutralized.'[333] However, international condemnation of Bloody Sunday moved the editor, if only a little. It would be understandable for the

---

328 General Officer Commanding (GOC) Frank King, writing to Bishop Edward Daly, 25 May 1974, in Edward Burke (2015): Counterinsurgency, *Journal of Imperial and Commonwealth History*, Vol 43, issue 4.

329 Ibid., 9 August 1972 (editorial).

330 Ibid.

331 Ibid., 2 July 1973 (editorial).

332 *Guardian* editorials advocating the security-first policy: 5 May, 14 July 1970; 13, 14, 26 August, 6 September, 25 October, 3, 15, 22, 26, 29 November, 3, 20 December 1971; 4 January, 16, 23 March, 15, 24, 29 July, 1, 9 August, 18 October 1972; 8 February, 9 March, 16 April, 2 July, 14 September, 23 November 1973. *Guardian* articles advocating the same: 10 August 1970, 25 October, 22 November, 3, 21 December 1971, 20 January, 3, 13 March, 10 April 1972, 8 April, 6 June 1974. Though not as heavily as the *Guardian*, the weight of the *Observer* coverage is ultimately on the security-first option; see 15 August, 5 September, 12 December 1971, 6, 27 February, 12, 26 March 1972, 25 March 1973.

333 *Observer*, 15 August 1971 (editorial).

British to 'persist in the policy of seeking first a military solution before resuming the search for a political settlement ... [but] there is no future in just going grimly on ... if internment and security were dealt with ... the scene would be nearly set for a serious constitutional advance in the North.'[334] The paper soon returned to the security-first option. Nora Beloff grew resigned: 'the very real desire to dump Ulster is outweighed by the recognition that Britain cannot get out until peace is restored.'[335] This is the direct opposite of her writing from Algiers. Although not so heavily as the *Guardian*, the weight of *Observer* coverage is ultimately on the military option. Both papers also called for improvements in the Catholic treatment, conditional in the *Guardian*'s case on Catholics treading lightly around the constitutional issue.

Day-to-day reports in both newspapers also show British troops were almost exclusively deployed in Catholic neighbourhoods. Consider, for example, the arrest of members of the SDLP, opponents of the IRA. Surrounded by soldiers pointing rifles at him, the future Nobel Peace Prize winner, John Hume was informed he was wanted for questioning. 'Just obeying orders,' said the arresting officer. Unionist politicians did not endure a similar experience. While refusing to talk with [IRA] murderers, the government contemporaneously held talks with the 'defensive' UDA. Incredibly, the UDA was only declared illegal on 10 August 1992. The UVF even expressed surprise at its relative freedom to operate. The regular army, unlike army intelligence, was not much interested in loyalist paramilitaries.[336] This is curious for an army 'standing in the middle.'

Conclusion

Soldiers on the ground often dictated policy. The French army needed a military victory and would not allow Paris to deny it to them. They would liberate loyal Muslims from the FLN and from treacherous politicians. British soldiers were not liberating Irish Catholics from the IRA. Too often they were incapable of distinguishing them. According to British army manuals, they were conducting a counterinsurgency campaign, not a peacekeeping mission.[337] General Michael Carver

---

334 Bloody Sunday moved the *Observer* a little, see editorials: 6 February 1972 and 27 February 1972.

335 *Observer*, 25 March 1973.

336 British soldiers identified Catholics as the insurgent community, *Guardian*, 16 August, 25 October 1971, 16 May, 18 September, 13, 19 October, 30 November, 15 December 1972, 28 August 1973, 13 April 1974. For UVF surprise at how little army attention it received, see *Guardian*, 9 September, 11, 30 November, 4, 12, 15 December 1972, 2 February, 18 October, 23 November 1973, and *Observer*, 11, 25 November 1973.

337 Urban, *Big Boys Rules*, (London, Faber, 1992), pp. 19, 162, 264.

wanted to 'declare a state of emergency in Northern Ireland and resort to the same measures that a government would be prepared to do in war.' Confident they could deliver a military victory senior British officers were furious about government contacts with republicans. The comparative reportages reveal a pronounced dichotomy. The voice of British liberal opinion urged the French government to reform and negotiate with the FLN. Peace would follow. This was reversed for Ireland. The British government should pursue military pacification before there could be any talk of reform.

De Gaulle's withdrawal from Algeria permitted the FLN's 'sweeping the people along', as proscribed by the *Guardian*. Perhaps negotiations with the elected representatives of the Algerian people, as Paris had proposed and the British liberal press rejected, might have spared all Algerians much pain and delivered some good. We shall never know which way the newly enfranchised Algerians would have voted. Certainly, the broom-wielding colonels have denied them democracy ever since. In contrast, IRA commander Martin McGuinness, turned Deputy/Joint First Minister, was chosen by Ulster unionists and Irish nationalists as their most respected politician. The contest now revolves around responsibility for prolonging the conflict. While the liberal press endorsed repression in Ireland, it is now clear the compromise of the 1990s was already possible in the 1970s.

CHAPTER FIVE

The Ruthless French and the Restrained British

This chapter compares the methods used by the security forces with soldiers' memoirs elaborating on the historic record. French accounts display a desire for 'real soldiering' in the remote bled, *and much distaste for the policeman's role in Algiers. They are often self-critical and, at times, express feelings of shame. There are, too, some examples of racial hatred. British soldiers' accounts reveal that a clear separation of ethnic and cultural identity existed between the Irish and 'us'. Too often, not always, they reveal a deep-rooted anti-Irish racism, a culture of violence, and a joy in killing.[338] The liberal-press coverage of the respective security forces is evaluated against the record and these testimonies of serving soldiers.*

French Army
Legionnaires and commandos de chasse
Early in the war, small skirmishes took place almost daily along the borders with Morocco and Tunisia. Joseph Kraft, of the *New York Times,* covered a typical engagement between a company of paratroopers and a twelve-man ALN unit. The soldiers converged towards the foot of the hollow where they found two dead. These operations in the remote mountains of the Aures and Nementchas required the recall to duty of reservists, including Jean-Jacques Servan-Schreiber, a liberal journalist. His desert patrol attempted to win 'hearts and minds'. He detailed French atrocities and is credited with turning public opinion against the war. Soldiers complained of fighting with their hands tied. An ALN member caught with a smoking gun would

---

338   See A.F.N. Clarke, *Contact* (London: Secker & Warburg, 1989).

appear in court, where he would take refuge in the '*maquis* of procedure.'[339] The honorific of *maquis* (resistance) would always be denied to the ALN. Soldiers complained about judicial inquiries where they could be compelled to answer for their conduct in the field.

Ted Morgan, a conscript, remembered it was ALN policy to mutilate French dead to lower morale. But Herb Greer recalled that French trucks deliberately ran over ALN dead to demoralise the rebels. Servan-Schreiber remembers soldiers' respect for ALN dead. General Paul Aussaresses maintained ALN dead were buried facing Mecca. Paratrooper Pierre Leulliette was surprised that village elders would refuse to bury ALN in their cemeteries but only where they fell. Simon Murray and his fellow legionnaires were happiest when chasing rebels but were fully aware that de Gaulle would not permit savage methods. Servan-Schreiber recalled officers would only give qualified assurances of soldiers' accounts of shootings being accepted at inquiries, warning they better produce evidence.

Morgan discounted any legionnaire discipline: 'beneath the veneer of panache they were rapacious brutes, trained to kill …'[340] Pierre Clostermann's reconnaissance missions in old, slow-moving aircraft put him within ALN rifle-range. He had two objectives: free-firing in restricted zones and rocket-fire on ALN-held villages. Shooting up villages troubled him because children would have no shelter in winter. But it was essential to save his fellow countrymen. Any respect for ALN courage was erased by their atrocities. He fought for all Algerians, Muslim and French. He detested the locally recruited settlers' defence regiment.

Missionary soldiers: hearts and minds

For most soldiers, pacification meant little or no action. Conscripts' letters home testify to the mildness of their service: 'Our regiment never went on operations, but guarded farms, warehouses and transformers … and escort civilian transport'; or, 'I paint when I have time off, surrounded by wondrous children'; or, 'It is especially the *colons* … who are most responsible for this rebellion.'[341] Morgan also remembers protecting remote farms, keeping roads open and power lines operating. A popular image of the Algerian War is Pontecorvo's *Battle of Algiers*. Morgan broadens the canvas to the vast *bled*. Conscripts were

---

339   Soustelle's memorable phrase, Clark, *Algeria in Turmoil* (NY, Grosset, 1960), p. 132.
340   Morgan, *My Battle of Algiers*, (NY, Harper-Collins 2005), p. 122.
341   Kraft, *The Struggle for Algeria* (NY, Doubleday, 1961), pp. 95-6.

frequently bored, usually only legionnaires and paratroopers engaged in small, remotely dispersed, firefights.

Gradually, the army extended *quadrillage* to the whole countryside. This forced relocation into protective camps, drove many towards the ALN but others were won over. Many camps had electricity, running water, a school and a nurse. Paris particularly wanted Muslim women to participate in public life, while the army wanted to wean away the invisible female support so vital to the ALN. Algerian writer Mouloud Feraoun remembers many villages, including his own, siding with France. Some 700 SAS (*Sections Administratives Specialisées*) installations were scattered throughout the country, commanded by a French officer with a squad of Muslim auxiliaries (*harkis*). ALN members were frequently turned and became village militias. The SAS ran the transport and food supply, provided work, built schools and rebuilt them after ALN destruction. They constructed roads and clinics, settled local disputes, ran the postal service, published a weekly newssheet and managed elections. Feraoun recalls a Lieutenant Jacoste who won the respect of the villagers of Oudhias. Always travelling without a weapon or escort, the ALN killed him in the village. Most camps took the social role seriously. Others became centres for gathering intelligence. The writer Jules Roy felt compelled by the death of his friend Albert Camus to return to their Algerian homeland. He visited the village of Toudja where locals, prior to the arrival of the SAS, had never seen a Frenchman. France had only come to Toudja in 1956 to put down the rebellion and legionnaires undermined any SAS advances. Every family in Toudja had suffered the death of a family member.[342] Summary execution had become common enough for soldiers to coin the euphemism *corvée de bois* (wood-collection duty). Not all villages would side with France.

The dirty police job in Algiers
The city of Algiers was more complicated with its population of 900,000, half European and half Muslim. In the spring of 1955, the ALN took the war to the city. The daily attacks on civilians forced soldiers to become policemen. French law prevented night searches and they complained loudly for six months before the introduction of the *measures d'exception*. There was no similar restraint in Northern Ireland where 'Special Powers' had been continuously available since 1922. Orders not to search veiled women facilitated ALN Kasbah

342   Roy, *The War in Algeria* (NY, Grove, 1961), p. 47.

commander Saadi's female bombers, an overlooked French restraint.[343] General Massu, however, ordered extreme measures. While an advocate for the SAS, his first priority was to stop the murders of Europeans and Muslims who bore the heaviest burden including financial contributions. They suffered assassination, mutilations, were burned alive and had their throats slit. He implemented an information-gathering network (*ilot*), a chain of linkages from army headquarters to block 'captains', street 'captains' and down into every Muslim family. Low level intelligence moved upwards straight to army HQ, enabling Massu to trace and destroy ALN members. French officers went out alone, night after night, with patrols entirely made up of turned ALN members. Leuillette also found the police job distasteful. To break the 1957 general strike, they were on a war footing, urban setting or not. They smashed in doors and suspects had to dress immediately 'without even time to drink their coffee'.[344] At first the sick were exempted, but later '… medical certificates or not they all had to go to work'.[345] The Philippeville atrocity and attacks on schools, buses and restaurants convinced General Paul Aussaresses that torture and executions were necessary. Grenade attacks against the public were occurring at three or four per day.[346] Colonel Godard rejected torture. Suspects could choose information or execution. Back home on leave, Leuillette's fellow citizens could not believe their army was guilty of misconduct.

British Army
The right angle to the story
Generations of counter-insurgency experience taught the British army that an effective campaign for the hearts and minds of the population was key. But even its sophisticated PR department had limitations. If Ireland had been a distant colony, then a team of psy-warriors might have found ways of 'persuading Irish nationalists there was no legitimacy to the republican struggle.'[347] The flip side of winning hearts and minds is collective punishment and Kitson recommended: 'if the fish cannot be destroyed … it may be necessary to do something about the water.'[348] Collective punishment included saturation use of CS gas and the random nature of those chosen for interrogation and torture.

343 O'Ballance, *The Algerian Insurrection* (London, Faber, 1967), pp. 215-6.
344 Leulliette, *St Michael and the Dragon*, (London, Heinemann, 1964), p. 239.
345 Ibid.
346 Aussaresses, *Battle of the Casbah*, (NY, Enigma, 2006), p. 65.
347 Charters and Tugwell, *Armies in Low Intensity Conflict* (London, Brassey's, 1989), pp. 178-9.
348 Kitson, *Low Intensity Operations* (London, Faber, 1971), p. 49.

Civilians shot dead as 'gunmen' left few doubts. Random torture-murders by loyalists, facilitated by army intelligence, were the ultimate collective punishments.

Rather than playing catch-up to sophisticated republican propaganda, the British were pioneers in propaganda. The Irish Public Information Department (1920), led by Sir Basil Clarke, specialised in 'propaganda by news'. News as opposed to views to make it more credible. To make propaganda believable it must be dissolved in some fluid that the 'patient' will readily assimilate, it must have an air of truth. Their propaganda was/is so powerful that unsuspecting (or sympathetic) journalists and historians have reproduced these old concoctions as primary sources.[349] They provided information to the press before the insurgents, ensuring the 'right angle to the story'. This phrase would make frequent appearances.

The army's media campaign began almost immediately in 1969. By 1972 some 262 civilians and police and 1,858 army officers had received media training.[350] Former paratrooper Geraghty claimed the army could 'plant any rumour ... without the risk of rebuttal.'[351] The army could 'shape popular perceptions of events to suit a military strategy.'[352] Officers ridiculed journalists about that 'mythical commodity you call truth' and mocked the RUC when exposed producing false stories.[353] The army was also ultimately exposed as the 'Lisburn Lie Machine.'[354] Journalists Cusack and McDonald described these manipulations as 'eccentric ... some were taken in and now laugh about it.'[355]

Remarkable restraint despite extreme provocation
Colonel Dewar claimed the army demonstrated 'a remarkable degree of restraint despite extreme provocation.'[356] This phrase also enjoyed much media space. Journalist Kevin Myers agreed: 'the forbearance and good cheer of the average squaddie despite the direct provocation were extraordinary.'[357] Dewar admits to only one episode of heavy-

---

349   See B. Murphy, *The Origins and Organisation of British Propaganda in Ireland,* (Aubane Historical, 2016).
350   Madden (ed.) *The British Media and Ireland* (London, Free Speech, 1979), p. 79.
351   Geraghty, *The Irish War*, (John Hopkins, 2000), p. 122.
352   ibid., p. 132.
353   Urban, *Big Boys Rules,* (London, Faber, 1992), p. 159.
354   Cusack and MacDonald, *UVF* (Dublin: Poolbeg, 1997), p. 149.
355   ibid., p. 149.
356   Dewar, *The British Army in Northern Ireland,* (London, Armoury, 1985), p. 9.
357   Saunders & Wood, *Times of Troubles,* (Edinburgh University Press), p. 176.

handedness. The company was 'angry at our loss and with the people whose complicity [?] made it possible.'[358] Dewar contradicts his British restraint analysis when enthusing about 1 PARA.

Seasoned by gun battles with the Belfast IRA, they were very well suited to arresting teenaged stone-throwers in Derry. This 'seasoning' included the killing, without sanction, of eleven civilians in the 'Ballymurphy Massacre', five months before Bloody Sunday.[359] Dewar portrays teenagers provoking Britain's toughest battalion on Bloody Sunday. He continues with a fabrication about 'nails bombs and machine-guns.'[360] After thirty-eight years, the Saville Report exonerated the twenty-seven victims, and blamed the soldiers, who were never in any danger. Dewar's account, frequently repeated in the media, is now officially discredited fiction. His musings reveal a nostalgia for the post-war campaigns, far enough away, where the press could be more easily misled than in Ireland.

Getting our version out first

Brigadier Peter Morton's *Emergency Tour* unintentionally destroys the image of an army supposedly unsophisticated in dealing with the media. His own log undermines the image of British restraint: 'the Company Commander evidently enjoyed himself, because his patrol fired 250 rounds in response to the 80 fired at them.'[361] These soldiers went on to capture IRA leader Peter Cleary at an isolated farmhouse. He was shot 'attempting to escape.' Morton, himself, was keenly aware of propaganda and boasted: 'as the IRA disinformation machine … version was out much later than ours, it was ours which was accepted by all except the most partisan.'[362] His paratroopers also killed a twelve-year-old girl. He backed her killer, an 'unfortunate Private', to the hilt. His concoction was exposed as untrue and '3 PARA was castigated by the press, partly for killing Majella O'Hare but more for producing conflicting versions of events.'[363] His sympathies are reserved for the unfortunate soldier and himself – none for the girl or her family. In April 2011, after a legal ordeal lasting thirty-five years, the British government formally apologised for unjustifiably killing this twelve

---

358 Ibid., p. 196, see too D Hamill, *Pig in the Middle* (London, Methuen 1985) who joins in this reflex assignment of guilt.

359 *Guardian*, 26 June 2014.

360 Dewar, *The British Army*, p. 58.

361 Morton, *Emergency Tour, Paras South Armagh*, (Northamptonshire: William Kimber, 1989), p. 81.

362 Ibid., p. 61.

363 Ibid., p. 213.

year-old child. The police could not, however, bring her identified murderer to trial. Tasked once with monitoring the anniversary of internment, Morton could not exactly recall 'the natives beating their tom toms but …'[364] The Irish were 'bog wogs', lived with their large families in primitive squalor, drew welfare benefits from the benevolent British, kept no food at home but made frequent trips to the pub. They 'have no standards and live like animals.'[365] Other accounts augment Morton's anti-Irish racism.[366] General Tuzo concluded: 'the time had come to cease operating in a civilised way against an uncivilised enemy.'[367]

A few kills would be nice
Clarke's *Contact,* an account of the same tour, supplements Morton's prejudices. He writes not a word about the killing of civilians, including Majella O'Hare, and only briefly touches on interrogation methods. He abhors the use of violence as a political tool but believes 'a couple of kills' would improve soldiers' morale.[368] The Irish are uncivilised, live in the Dark Ages, are natural killers, thieves and barbarians. However, his soldiers, charged with maintaining English civilisation, experience a high from the violence and were exhilarated whenever an Irishman [note not an IRA man] hits the ground.[369] Clarke loathes 'Paddy Irishman', his filthy dwellings and slimy, unwashed dishes, and bedroom floors awash with the contents of chamber pots and even an afterbirth.[370] These 'afterbirth' tales were serialised to great acclaim over five days in the *Daily Mirror* and made into a popular TV show. Clarke enthuses about his friend biting off someone's nose.[371] Recruits who were not thugs to begin with were made into thugs. Their successful production of bloodlust was evident from the 'emotional disconnect found in the absent glare of their eyes.'[372] His soldiers prayed for an opportunity to shoot anything and watch the blood flow. Anyone arrested was well-aware that the slightest excuse would result in their being beaten or shot. All soldiers preferred to shoot.[373] He remembers

364   Ibid., p. 207.
365   Ibid., pp. 49-68.
366   Kennedy, *Soldier 'I' SAS* (London: Bloomsbury, 1989), p. 147.
367   Burke (2015): Counterinsurgency against 'Kith and Kin'? *Journal of Imperial and Commonwealth History*, Vol 43, issue 4, p. 31.
368   Clarke, *Contact,* p. 43.
369   ibid., p. 63.
370   *Ibid.,* p. 3.
371   ibid., p. 55.
372   ibid., p. 153.
373   ibid., p. 152.

cheering on Bloody Sunday and yearning for stories of felled gunmen.[374] David Reynolds and Peter Harclerode, in separate accounts of Bloody Sunday, also fabricated outlandish tales of gun-battles, acid bombs and secret IRA burials.[375] Michael Asher's *Shoot to Kill* admits the soldiers' brutality: 'We were fire-eating berserkers ... unreligious, apolitical and remorseless, a caste of warriors-janizaries who worshipped at the high altar of violence.'[376] O'Mahony also acknowledges their brutality. They were petty thieves and hooligans, their criminal records for violence known to the army.[377] The judges had offered them a choice: the army or prison. These convict-recruits, excused their custodial punishment, went on to 'keep the peace', carrying high-powered rifles on Irish streets. He also remembers his commanding officer promising a 'crate of beer for the first one to kill a Paddy.'[378] Ken Wharton's books are sympathetic interviews of soldiers who served in Ireland. They also contain many episodes that reflect badly on the army: 'we picked up a couple of boys. At least three of them were searching for their testicles in the street afterwards.'[379] One corporal remembered, 'if they hadn't been IRA sympathisers before, they were after ...'[380] Graham Wiggs recalled an 'amusing incident' at Musgrave Park Hospital when a soldier 'with a big smile on his face' secretly switched off the power to a wounded republican.[381] Geraghty's book contains four references to the 'cull' of young Irishmen.[382] Paratrooper Henry Gow recalls: 'I was the original natural born killer ... I was killing for the love of it ... I loved violence ...'[383] Of course, there were other soldiers who behaved better.[384]

374 Clarke, *Contact*, pp. 48, 53.

375 Reynolds, *The Paras,* (London, Express Newspapers, 1990), Harclerode, *PARA,* (London, Armoury, 1992).

376 Asher, *Shoot to Kill* (London, Viking, 1990), p. 120.

377 O'Mahony, *Soldier of the Queen*, (Dingle, Brandon, 2000), pp. 98–101.

378 Ibid, p. 121.

379 Wharton, *A Long Long War.* (Solihull, Helion, 2010), p. 175.

380 Ibid., pp. 202-3.

381 Wharton, *Wasted Years, Wasted Lives,* (Solihull, Hellion, 2013), pp. 49-50.

382 Geraghty, *The Irish War*, pp. 75, 126, 127, 354.

383 *Independent*, 26 April 1995.

384 In March 1976 a young man, imprisoned for weapons possession, was freed on appeal. A paratrooper recanted his earlier testimony: 'I lied. I was ordered to say he was armed though I knew he was not', McKittrick, *Lost Lives*, p. 351.

The Liberal Press
French repression and Gestapo methods

French ruthlessness and British restraint was a template in reporting and in editorials: 'Neither the British nor the American peoples would endorse the policy of repression which successive French Governments have ferociously practised in Algeria.'[385] Rawle Knox conceded soldiers may have lost their temper in Cyprus, but if Britain remained, 'it will have to be absolutely ruthless, as the French in Algeria.'[386] French methods, 'would be difficult to apply in democratic European countries.'[387] This is a recurring framework of British journalists. Tom Pocock remembers the French were 'so brutal' because of 'the humiliation of defeat and collaboration during the war, then defeat in Indo China ... [but British soldiers] conducted searches without knocking people about particularly and with a bit of throwaway humour ... we won the war and could afford to be magnanimous.'[388] Explaining a recent spate of unexplained explosions, the *Guardian* had no doubts: 'French intelligence agents seem to have been at their murderous tricks again.'[389]

Simon Hoggart knowingly pondered how the Irish 'would react to the arrival of the French CRS.'[390] Robert Kee urged me to be cautious: 'Be careful of the Algerian analogy. Look at the ruthlessness of the rue d'Isly ... the French are most unlike us in their ruthlessness.'[391] The rue d'Isly killings are a favourite reference to demonstrate French ruthlessness. But they are mistaken. In addition, Kee was a rare exception – a journalist knowledgeable of, and interested in Ireland. Harold Jackman sympathised with the army's almost impossible brief in Ireland, and complained that, 'it cannot use its advantage of firepower except to a limited degree.'[392] With direct reference to rue d'Isly, Jackman explains it was different for the French army, which 'let loose once in Algiers killing about 80 French settlers.'[393] He warns Catholics

---

385 *Guardian*, 10 March 1958 (editorial). This continues yet, see Michael White, *Guardian* 16 Nov 2015, 'France and Britain: the differences in their struggle with extremism ... You could argue that Ireland is Britain's Algeria, a deep poison arising from failed incorporation of a nearby people. Yet by way of contrast, Derry's Bloody Sunday has been endlessly investigated as part of the long reconciliation.' He overlooked Widgery's whitewash and the many obstacles from the MoD to thwart and subvert inquiries and inquests.

386 *Observer*, 12 October 1958.

387 Ibid., 7 June 1959.

388 Interview, Tom Pocock, London, July 1998.

389 *Guardian*, 18 April 1959 (editorial).

390 Simon Hoggart (of *Guardian)*, in *New Society*, 11 October 1973.

390 Interview, Robert Kee, London, 20 July 1998.

392 Harold Jackson, *Guardian*, 12 March 1971.

393 Ibid.

that the community from which 'the IRA killers come cannot escape at least moral responsibility ... their inaction amounts to support.'[394] This again harmonises with loyalist justifications for the random murder of Catholics. Wishing to break with 'traditional British restraint', Jackman recommended 'a firm crackdown by the army'. The resulting benefits would include an 'increased flow of information from the locals.'[395]

This popular trope does not bear much scrutiny. The rue d'Isly shootings were a less sinister but more deadly affair than Bloody Sunday.[396] One line of French soldiers, a total of nine Muslim *Spahis*, opened fire on a procession of *pieds noirs* and continued firing for seven minutes. These nine soldiers panicked and produced a massacre. On that day, General Ailleret ordered that soldiers could not be used for police duty. Senior officers had also refused to supervise. Such was the mood within the French army that distrust of government policy meant an order had become a matter for debate. There was, by all accounts, no more to it than that. The fifty-four dead were all French. Ian Aitken, an eyewitness, remembered: 'The local Arab troops were very jumpy, undisciplined, they panicked and without any orders began shooting all over the place ... you could see their officers trying to stop them ... we never found any other explanation except ill-discipline and the claim of shooting from the rooftops.'[397] Tom Pocock, another eyewitness, also recalled 'the futile attempt of their officers to stop the shooting by nervous soldiers ... '[398] On Bloody Sunday, British soldiers fired for much longer than seven minutes, and in a controlled, selective and deliberate manner. The Saville Report has soldiers shooting for forty-five minutes. Significantly, British soldiers were encouraged by their superiors, Colonel Wilford and General Ford: 'Go on paras, go and get them ...'[399] In Algiers, the junior lieutenants in command, the only officers on the ground, slapped soldiers' faces and screamed at them to stop.

However, with the template firmly fixed, the liberal press maintained a critical focus on the ruthless French. Official French figures for the Algerian War list 25,000 French soldiers and 141,000 ALN dead, a figure confirmed by the Algerian government.[400] This represents a

394   Ibid.
395   Ibid.
396   See *Keesings Contemporary Archives*, vol. xiii (1962–63), p. 19149 for a contemporary account of rue d'Isly. See also www.piedsnoirs-aujourdhui.com (accessed 10 July 2015).
397   Interview, Ian Aitken (London), 27 July 1998.
398   Interview, Tom Pocock (London), 29 July 1998.
399   *New York Times*, 30 November 2015.
400   Evans, *Algeria: France's Undeclared War* (OUP, 2012), pp. 337– 8 for casualties.

French kill ratio of six ALN for every French soldier. Recent scholarship and demographic analyses produce a total Algerian war dead of 250-300,000.[401] Taking a compromise figure of 275,000 and subtracting 30,000 Algerians killed by the FLN, the French may be responsible for almost 250,000 Algerian dead (ALN and civilians). This generates a French kill ratio of approximately ten to one, which falls below five to one when we include the 30,000 *harkis* murdered by the FLN after hostilities had supposedly ceased. Some estimate *harki* deaths as high as 150,000. Consider now Britain's contemporaneous 'Kenyan Emergency' of 1952-60 and, unlike Ireland, far enough away to (in Dewar's words) *easily mislead*. The official British figures list 12,000 Kenyan dead and 200 British security forces dead (sixty-three soldiers, the remainder comprised of local Kenyans of the British Home Guard and police sent out from Britain).

According to their own compilation, the British killed at a ratio of sixty Kenyans for every British death, or ten times the French ratio of six to one.[402] The French ratio of five to one, as established by more recent scholarship, may be the more accurate figure. This would mean the British killed at twelve times the French rate. David Anderson's figure of 20,000 Kenyan dead produces a British killing ratio of a hundred to one, or a killing rate twenty times the French rate.[403] John Black calculates the Kenyan dead at 50,000, resulting in a killing ratio of 250 to one, or fifty times the French rate.[404] Carolyn Elkins calculates that more than 100,000 Kenyans died at British hands, producing a ratio of 500 to one, or 100 times the French rate. By all estimates, the 'restrained' British killed at many times the rate of the 'ruthless' French. In Kenya, where Britain faced nothing like the ALN, the British executed 1,090 people – more than twice the number the French executed in Algeria.

Despite these startling figures, the image of British restraint prevails. Coverage of Algeria typically included phrases such as: 'the authorities often turn a blind eye', 'paratroops on the rampage', 'all Arabs are the

401 Evans, *Algeria*, pp. 336-8.
402 See A. Clayton, *Counterinsurgency in Kenya, 1952-60,* (Sunflower University Press, 1984) for official British casualty figures and Barnet & Njama, *Mau Mau from Within* (London: MacGibbon & Kee, 1966) for unofficial figures. See also Caroline Elkins, *Britain's Gulag: The Brutal end of Empire in Kenya* (London: Jonathan Cape, 2005), and David Anderson, *Histories of the Hanged: Britain's Dirty War in Kenya and the End of Empire* (London: Weidenfeld & Nicolson, 2005).
403 Anderson, *Histories,* pp. 4–5; Elkin, *Britain's Gulag*, p. 366; Porter, 'Cannabis and Empire', *LRB*, March 2005.
404 See J. Black, 'The Demography of Mau Mau: fertility and mortality in Kenya in the 1950s: a demographer's viewpoint', *African Affairs*, vol. 106, no. 423 (April 2007).

enemy' and 'Gestapo methods'.[405] Official French sources were treated with a healthy skepticism, and reports were qualified with, 'if the French version is confirmed' or 'there's little credit to recent French claims.'[406] But a close reading of the newspapers' own brief daily reports reveals French peacekeeping as well as ruthlessness.[407] Certainly the French conducted a brutal counter-insurgency, but the overwhelming media portrayal of the French as typically only engaged in ruthless repression is too narrow. Consider, for example, this report of the ALN killing two policemen. A third policeman then overpowered the gunman only to see the gathering crowd attempt to lynch the killer. 'The policeman found his obligations reversed. He did his best to defend the Algerian. He was alive when police drove him to hospital ... '[408]

Journalists also provide contrasting eyewitness testimony. Ian Aitken remembered: 'When the CRS arrived there was a general strike of the white settlers. All the Arabs were delighted to see them banging the white fellows on the head.'[409] Bill Millinship recalled: 'the CRS kept the paratroopers out of the Kasbah ... no disorder on their patch'.[410] French soldiers also engaged in fist fighting to keep Muslims and *pieds noirs* apart.[411] French veteran associations even called for greater punishments for soldiers who engaged in brutality. Philip Williams remembers: 'The cities were amazingly normal ... a great many soldiers about, but not one in a hundred was armed.'[412] A fuller picture includes repression and peacekeeping.

405   For critical focus on the French army, see *Guardian*, 12, 30 October 1956, 5 January, 2 February, 30 March, 5 April, 8 August, 19 September, 3 October 1957, 3 March, 7 June, 9 September, 10, 12 October, 2 November 1958, 8 April, 2, 9, October 1959, 13 December 1960, 15 October, 13 December 1961, 2 April 1962, and *Observer*, 8 August 1957, 9 March, 4 April, 9 September, 2 November 1958, 7 June 1959, 21 February 1960, 15 October 1961.

406   For a healthy skepticism of the official French view of army conduct, exclusive of torture, see *Guardian*, 18, 31 August, 13 November 1956, 1 January, 1 March, 31 May, 2, 3, 4, 14 September, 10 October 1957, 11 April, 5 May, 6 June 1958, 6 April 1960, 2 April 1962, and *Observer*, 18 August 1957, 2 March 1958, 1 February, 6 June 1959, 24 July 1960.

407   The following examples were not reported as peacekeeping, but it is possible to find acknowledgements of French impartiality: *Guardian*, 5, 7 January, 13 February, 6, 10, 12, 13 June, 19 September, 13 December, 1957, 28 April, 13 May 1959, 1 January, 17 February, 12, 14, 16 November, 7, 12, 13 December 1960, 27 March, 7 April, 3, 24 May, 29 December 1961, 20 January, 22 February, 2, 3, 5, 13 March, 5, 14, 24 May 1962, and *Observer*, 11 October 1959, 24 January, 18 December 1960.

408   *Guardian*, 2 February 1960.

409   Interview, Ian Aitken, London, July 1998.

410   Interview, Bill Millinship, London, July 1998.

411   See P. Henissart, *Wolves in the City,* (London: Rupert Hart-Davis, 1970), p. 405 for the army protecting Muslims. Trinquier advised his men to avoid the CRS.

412   *Observer*, 11 October 1959, my emphasis.

There is also evidence of too much zeal in portraying French ruthlessness. Both newspapers had to make retractions.[413] The 1958 discovery of a second grave containing 400 Muslims recalled the ALN's earlier Melouza massacre. It prompted a *Guardian* editorial explaining the 'exceptional ruthlessness' of the ALN's leaders: 'some of them, at least, appear to have been NCOs in the French army with all the limitations that implies.'[414] Germaine Tillion, ethnologist, *maquisard* and Holocaust survivor, was convinced Melouza was the work of the ALN for which they had previously avoided responsibility. She famously confronted Yacef Saadi. Her views on Melouza were never printed in the *Guardian* although she was a frequent source for French army abuses. The *Observer* also had to retract its claims about Melouza.[415]

Remarkable British restraint despite extreme provocation
It is possible to find a report where the behaviour of British troops falls short of the angels. A paratrooper explained: 'you are going to have a chance to shoot some bastard through the head ... we terrified people, really ... After every shooting incident we would order 1500 house searches, 1500...'[416] But this is rare. Between the residents' and the army's version, invariably the press concluded that the troops had been provoked. Even before civil rights demonstrations were replaced by armed conflict, the role of provocateur had already been assigned. From the beginning, Hetherington and Cole had already assigned roles: 'People in Derry or elsewhere ought not to provoke them [soldiers and police] foolishly.'[417] But during that year, 1969, the police had perpetuated almost all deaths, and the Scarman Report had already condemned RUC sectarian conduct.

At the same time, an *Observer* editorial also decided, again in advance, the army's future behaviour. 'It only needs a small but fanatical minority to make life impossible even for an overwhelming military force that behaves with civilized restraint.'[418] The pattern is persistent: the Catholic residents are, even 'will be', to blame. Hetherington-Cole display an open hostility to any other version. 'In Belfast the army is facing an intolerable situation with restraint; and

---

413 On 13 March 1958 the *Guardian*'s report on torture had to be retracted following a complaint from the Foreign Press Association.
414 *Guardian*, 24 September 1958 (editorial).
415 *Observer*, 9 June 1957.
416 *Guardian*, 13 July 1973.
417 Ibid., 15 August 1969 (editorial).
418 *Observer*, 17 August 1969 (editorial).

those who choose the bullet rather than the ballot can hardly cry foul if the other side accepts their choice of weapon.'[419] However, if the IRA continued to kill soldiers, even the indulgent British may find it difficult not to exact revenge, with the *Guardian* warning once again: 'lesser armies would long since have taken revenge on innocent people.'[420] The template of a restrained British compared to a lesser army remained fixed.[421]

Guardian editorials sympathised with the army's appalling burden. There may have been 'regrettable misjudgements but amazingly there have been so few. The restraint of soldiers … is superhuman.'[422] This remarkable editorial was written one day after soldiers had killed twelve unarmed civilians in Belfast, including a priest waving a white flag attempting to reach one victim, two fifty-year-old housewives, one in her own home and one searching for her children and four teenagers. In another part of the city soldiers killed a teenage boy, lifted him overhead and displayed his limp body to traumatised residents.[423] The template of British restraint and Irish provocation remained fixed.[424]

Simon Winchester described an 'angry mob' of women and children protesting about the army saturating their neighbourhood with CS gas for three consecutive days. The soldiers were 'goaded mercilessly to a point where one private in a regrettable and embarrassing, yet highly understandable, incident hit the girl to the ground.'[425] The merciless goading from a young girl shook the soldiers, who had been hoping for a much-needed night of peace. The effect on the girl and the 'mob' of

---

419   Ibid., 5 February 1971 (editorial).

420   Ibid., 27 May 1971.

421   Vincent Browne witnessed the Soviet invasion of Prague: 'The contrast was striking between those troops and the behaviour of the British army I was later to witness in Northern Ireland', I. Kenny, *Talking to Ourselves* (Galway: Kenny's, 1994), p. 109. See also Erich Ruby, 'Ein Lehrgang in Hoffnung', *Suddeutsche Zeitung*, September 1968: 'On August in Prague people spat at the tank crews. They splashed them with paint. The soldiers looked like clowns as they climbed down from their burning tanks. And yet they did not shoot.' See also Neal Ascherson, *Guardian*, 20 January 2008 for his recollections of the Soviet invasion: 'many soldiers grew tired of suffering Czech abuse in silence and leaned down from their tanks to explain'.

422   *Guardian*, 10 August 1971 (editorial).

423   McKittrick et al, *Lost Lives,* pp. 81–6.

424   For Catholic provocation and British restraint, see *Guardian*, 15 August 1969 (editorial), 29 June (editorial), 11 July, 3, 4 August, 12 October, 11 November 1970, 5 February (editorial), 11, 12 March (editorial), 12, 26 April, 22, 27 May, 9 July, 7, 10 (editorial), 12 (editorial), 14, 19 (editorial), 25 August, 10 September, 9, 18, 23 October, 2 November (editorial), 25 December 1971, 16 May, 15, 29 July, 1, 19 August, 11, 19 October 1972, 9 February 1973, and *Observer*, 17 (editorial), 24 August, 14 September 1969, 5 July (editorial), 14 March (editorial), 18 July, 22 August, 9 September 1971, 6 February 1972 (editorial).

425   *Guardian*, 3 August 1971.

women and children was not recorded. But medical evidence tells us that CS gas can cause severe pulmonary damage and can significantly damage the heart and liver. British police are aware of this. It has been used very rarely in Britain.[426] However, three consecutive nights of saturation gassing was not recorded as goading the residents. Nor was there any report on whether they hoped for a night of peace. Writing before an approaching civil rights demonstration, Winchester explained how the mechanics of a riot 'make certain that some rubber bullets will smash through the windows of an elderly woman's house and some soldiers will use a baton harshly on a young and harmless seeming Catholic girl'.[427] His perceptual framework once again exonerates the troops in advance. British soldiers were particularly vulnerable to the taunts of 'harmless seeming' young girls.[428]

The *Guardian*'s 'frightening illustration of what the forces are up against' turned out to be a priest outraged by the soldiers' brutality: 'they are savages nothing more than lying savages. I hate to say this to an Englishman, but it is true.'[429] Could the reproach of (even) a Belfast priest be so frightening? Mary Holland, *Observer,* provided further proof of the unique local talent: 'In Belfast soldiers have had to suffer abuse from a people particularly eloquent in obscenity.'[430] Her editor agreed: 'Their task has been to stand as a human barrier separating crowds whose frenzy even the Congo could hardly rival.'[431] In addition, soldiers killed in IRA attacks were not soldiers but cooks, school-crossing guards, musicians, dog-handlers, laundrymen and bandsmen.[432] The *Observer* despaired: 'How could the IRA kill an innocent young soldier?'[433] The overall tone is typified by Simon Winchester endorsing the army's desire to show the world the outrages committed against them 'by the Irish'; once again merging the water and fish. All the

426 Ackroyd et al, pp. 217-221, *Lancet,* 18 July 1998, *Guardian* 8 July 1999.

427 Ibid., 8 August 1972.

428 For Irish girls provoking troops, see *Guardian,* 8 August 1970, 5 May, 12, 20 August, 13 September 1971, 4, 8 August 1972., see also S. Winchester, *In Holy Terror,* (Faber. 1975), p. 124.

428 *Guardian,* 14 August 1971.

430 *Observer,* 14 September 1969.

431 Ibid., 5 July 1970 (editorial).

432 For sympathetic coverage of troops, see *Guardian,* 4 August 1969, 4, 7, 10, 11, 13 July, 4, 8, 11 August, 18 September, 31 October, 1970, 4, 5, 6, 8, 27 February, 12 March, 26 April, 25, 27 May, 11, 12,14 August, 18, 25 September, 2, 10 October 1971, 21 January, 20 November, 20 December 1972, 29 May, 18 June, 10 July, 28 August, 26 November 1973, 20 March, 11, 19 April, 5, 15 May, 7 June 1974, and *Observer,* 28 August, 14 September 1969, 28 June, 5 July 1970, 5 September, 10, 17, 31 October, 12 December 1971, 6 February, 1 April 1972.

433 *Observer,* 10 October 1971.

gunmen wanted was for the army to retaliate: 'just as they were accused of having done in Famagusta, Palestine and Amritsar ... [this] possibly governs the almost unbelievable leniency with which it deals with Belfast terrorism.'[434] After sixty years the liberal press still skirted around the unpalatable truth of British massacres.

All of the familiar phrases used in Ireland – of 'lesser armies' and 'extreme provocation' – can also be found in earlier coverage of British counter-insurgency in Cyprus.[435] The record, however, does not support an unbelievable leniency. In 1971, soldiers killed more than five civilians for every IRA member they killed. For the five-year period under study, the army killed ninety-nine civilians and forty-six IRA members. Of the ninety-nine civilians just one was armed.[436] I was able to identify eighty four of these ninety-nine in the reportage. Eighteen were killed at home or near home. In seventy-one of the eighty-four cases, the *Guardian* uncritically prints the army version of gunmen, bombers, petrol bombers, certain snipers, rioters or civilian victims of the IRA. *Every one of these seventy-one reports is untrue.*[437]

---

434   *Guardian*, 27 May 1971.

435   For sympathetic portraits of British army conduct in Cyprus, see *Guardian*, 19 February, 11, 20, 24, 31 October 1957, 5 December 1958, 13, 19 May 1960, and *Observer*, 6, 13 July, 5, 12 October, 16 November 1958. The phrases are familiar: 'no-one would believe the British deliberately ...', 'few, if any armies, would be so restrained under such provocation', 'our boys would never ...'.

436   For context see McKittrick·et al., *Lost Lives*. In three civilian killings (William Bell, John Ward and Elizabeth McGregor) the army admitted a mistake. There are two further cases of William Ferris and Anthony Mitchell which are tragic misfortunes where the army account is not disputed. For the rest of the civilians killed by the army, not every case is reported. Of the forty-six IRA dead, twenty were definitely armed, fifteen were definitely unarmed, and eleven are disputed.

437   The list below contains those killed by the army and identified in the *Guardian*. In all cases the *Guardian* used the army version. Compared against McKittrick et al., *Lost Lives*, they were all falsely reported as carrying guns, bombs, grenades, shot as snipers, rioters or in crossfire, or by the IRA, or as sectarian murders: C. O'Neill, T. Burns, P. Uglik, P. Elliman, D. O'Hagan, B. Watt, W.M. Halligan, S. Cusack, D. Beattie, N. Watson, S. Worthington, L. McGuigan, J. Beattie, F. Quinn, H. Mullan, F. McGuinness, D. Heatley, J. Connolly, D. Taggart, N. Philips, J. Murphy, J. Haverty, W. McKavanagh, H. Herron, E. McDevitt, A. McGavigan, W. M. McGreanery, P. Daly, D. Thompson, E. Copeland, C. Quinn, K. Thompson, J. Parker, M. McShane, J. Maugham, M. Connors, T. McIlroy, P. Magee, P. Donaghy, F. Rowntree, R. McMullan, M. Deery, N. McGrath, J. Bonnar, A. Fionda, P. Butler, N. Fitzpatrick, M. Gargan, D. McCafferty, T. Burns, T. Toolan, F. McKeown, D. Hegarty, R. McKinnie, R. Johnson, D. Rooney, M. Hays, M. Nann, A. Murray, E. McGregor, A. Hardy, B. Maguire, J. Loughran, H. Connolly, K. Heatly, E. Sharpe, S. Martin, R. McGuinness, A. Howe. The reports on these victims, while not untrue, are innocuous or of dubious justification (robber, ringleader): S. Ruddy, J. McLaughlin, R. Anderson, P. McVeigh, J. Pedlow, A. Moorehead, L. McDowell, T. Friel, D. Burke, W. McDonald. M. McLarnon, killed in his own doorway, was simply reported as dying in 'a shooting incident'. A former lieutenant in the Green Howards later wrote to his family asking forgiveness. He admitted seeking revenge but had now taken Jesus as his saviour.

This pattern of publishing the army version for such a prolonged period requires some explanation. Whether through naivety, complicity, laziness, deference or a shared world view, the cover-up of state killings may be the more appropriate explanation. The remaining nine cases are recorded simply as 'shooting incidents.' The case of twelve-year-old Anthony Dowell illustrates the *Guardian*'s preference. He was killed during a gun battle between the IRA and paratroopers; a military-calibre bullet took his life.

Hetherington-Cole wrote admiringly of the paratroopers' military instincts, and explained they were victims of the IRA's most 'conspicuous talent, which, apart from murder, was propaganda.'[438] There was not a word of sympathy for a twelve-year-old boy who had lost his life or for his family. Nor was there any for the family of their neighbour Edward Sharp, a civilian killed by the same paratroopers at his home a few days earlier.[439]

In fact, Hetherington-Cole had already offered, again, in advance, a blanket justification of army killings of boys: 'recent incidents in which soldiers and policemen were killed would have been impossible without the organized help of crowds of youths who threw stones … where IRA snipers could work.'[440] This belief in a common purpose between the IRA and stone-throwing youths is contradicted by anthropological studies of Belfast youths.[441] The IRA viewed stone-throwing youths as a nuisance whose presence frustrated the ambushes they had spent so much time preparing. In addition, one soldier recalls he and his fellow soldiers deliberately used chocolates to try to keep youngsters close to gain protection. Using civilians as cover was a routine army practise for some. Brigadier Peter Morton admitted: 'I used to do things like trail the school bus or I would always be very close to the car in front so that the IRA chap on the hill couldn't separate me from the other vehicle.'[442] The cover of AFN Clarke's *Contact* shows an army base literally sandwiched between terraced houses.

More damaging was the absence of guns on the dead 'gunmen'. The *Guardian* routinely and uncritically printed army claims of secret burials and IRA colleagues spiriting away the body or the gun.[443] These

438 *Guardian*, 24 April 1973 (editorial).
439 Ibid., 13 March 1973.
440 Ibid., 12 March 1971 (editorial).
441 For IRA frustration with, and anger at, youths whose proximity to soldiers compromised their ambushes, see J.A. Sluka, *Hearts and Minds,* (London: JAI Press, 1989).
442 T Harnden, *Bandit Country,* (London: Coronet, 1999), p. 178.
443 Examples of secret burials or disappearing gun or body in the *Guardian:* 8, 12 February, 28 September, 10, 18 October, 8 November, 22 December 1971, 2, 4 February, 11 November 1972, and *Observer*, 14 February, October 1971.

intrepid 'clean-up' operations presumably relied on the superhuman British restraint when bullets were flying. Simon Winchester again: 'It may be some days before the deaths column in the Belfast daily newspaper, the *Irish News* – "Suddenly at home" – will allow an accurate balance sheet [army vs IRA deaths] to be drawn up.'[444] Believing municipal cemeteries, in British-administered Ireland, permit burials without a proper death certificate clearly invests too much credibility in army sources. It also undermines their own frequent portrayal of the Irish seeking after martyrdom. In addition, the army's propensity to set up bases attached to schools, hospitals, sports stadia, in the middle of terraced houses and on top of council flats, went unremarked and unreported.

A number of high-profile killings are often cited as reasons for the early growth of the IRA. Two weeks before Bloody Sunday, the *Guardian* quoted a senior officer explaining that the 'battle for Belfast' was almost over. He continued with these prescient words: 'there will still be the Bogside to flush out and that could be a very bloody operation.'[445] One week before Bloody Sunday, Simon Winchester also predicted the future with surprising accuracy, accusing civil rights leaders of seeking violence during the approaching Sunday's procession.[446] Extracts from Hetherington's editorial, the day after the killings, are remarkable.[447] The march was illegal and 'a warning had been given ... The army has an intolerably difficult task ... The presence of snipers in the later stages of the march must have added a murderous dimension.' More disturbing is Hetherington's recommendation of tougher methods: 'Hot pursuit and other Israeli techniques might be called for.' The headline of the same edition describes the procession as a riot. There are photographs of sheltering soldiers but no photographs of the dead. In the following days, blame was laid on the Civil Rights Association, the dead were labelled IRA members, and there was a glowing portrait of the impartiality of Lord Widgery. Six of the dead were reported as armed. 'If there had been no march 13 people would be alive this morning.'[448] Following Bloody Sunday, NICRA announced it still intended to protest in Newry the following week. A *Guardian* cartoon, 2 February 1972, portrayed the protestors, in advance, as carrying petrol bombs.

---

444   *Guardian*, 18 October 1971.
445   *Guardian*, 17 January 1972.
446   Ibid., 25 January 1972.
447   Ibid., 31 January 1972 (editorial).
448   *Guardian*, 17, 24, 25, 26, 31 January, 1, 2, 4, 5, 7, 21, 22, 24 February, 3 March 1972.
      See the heading on page five of March: 'Six victims [of Bloody Sunday] "may have held guns"'.

An editorial following the Sharpeville Massacre read, 'no one can deny that their protest was legitimate'. The *Guardian* could see plainly in Africa what it could not see in Ireland. The South African government was condemned and advised that the use of force could not 'repress further acts of defiance. It must remove the reason for the defiance.'[449] Its coverage of Ireland urged the opposite on a 'restrained' Westminster. Just days after Bloody Sunday, Simon Hoggart reported that an unnamed woman had informed the army of the IRA acquiring British uniforms for the demonstration in Newry. Consequently, the army feared 'the uniforms could be used by men shooting at the crowd to discredit the army.'[450] Hoggart, we have already seen, would not afford any credence to such a claim from the French. One month after Bloody Sunday, Alun Chalfont wrote that stone-throwers are 'reasonably safe in the knowledge that, as they are in Londonderry and not in Prague or Birmingham, Alabama, it is unlikely that anyone will get his head blown off.'[451] This points to some deep-seated lacuna among journalists, an inability to acknowledge any possibility of British army wrongdoing. Winchester even exculpated the army: 'There is no clear-cut boundary between Catholics and the IRA and they merge and blur into one at times like Bloody Sunday and only appear as separate entities at infrequent intervals.'[452] Once again, the justifications from loyalist death squads, for the random murder of Catholics, and the *Guardian's* portrayal, are disturbingly similar.

The *Observer* also blamed Bloody Sunday on the IRA, sympathised with the soldiers, was also somehow aware in advance that the 'civil disobedience marchers' intended to provoke a bloodbath, and supported Widgery's inquiry.[453] The Widgery Report 'has about it a ring of honesty and hard sense that compels respect.'[454] Until Saville overturned it, Widgery's exoneration remained Britain's public position in spite of the army's inability to produce a single corroborating civilian witness. An *Observer* cartoon, 23 April 1972, about Bloody Sunday, makes very light of civilians unjustifiably killed by the state. But even Widgery's

449 Ibid., 22 March 1960 (editorial).
450 Ibid., 5 February 1972.
451 Ibid., 6 March 1972.
452 Ibid., 24 July 1972.
453 See *Observer*, 23, 30 January, 6, 13, 20, 27 February, 23 April 1972, 16 September 1973. See 6 February 1972, where a feature box surrounded a highlighted sentence taken from Mary Holland's report: 'a wounded IRA gunman in hiding who admits to firing on a British soldier in Londonderry last Sunday'. The following week's edition contained a short letter from Mary Holland pointing out that 'the marksman I quoted says he fired his shot at 5 p.m., after the confrontation with the British army had taken place and more than a mile away from where it occurred'.
454 *Observer*, 23 April 1972 (editorial).

mild criticism prompted Prime Minister Heath's irritation: 'the "low-key" approach could not go to the stage where it allowed the Provisional IRA to establish control of an area.'[455] Home Secretary Reginald Maudling's response was to reject calls for a new political initiative as 'surrender'.

Many other cases reveal the *Guardian* in the same light. The army's killings of two civilians, Seamus Cusack and Desmond Beattie, increased IRA support in Derry, but the *Guardian* reported: 'despite considerable provocation the army were restrained.'[456] The ensuing coverage evolved from the army's version of 'gunmen and bombers' to 'alleged rioters' and finally to a report, without comment, of an independent inquiry that found the army to have exacted revenge on unarmed civilians.[457] *Guardian* editorials also justified killings of civilians even while stating clearly that the newspaper was relying on army sources: 'For three nights ... a crowd which threw ghastly missiles also sheltered men who, the army says, fired sixty shots at them.'[458] The editor sympathised, not with the traumatised nationalist residents but, with unionist demands for more repression, and with reference to nationalist demands for an inquiry recommended unionists swallow their 'irritation at the negative tactics of Catholic politicians.'[459] The *Guardian*'s last editorial on the killings blamed Catholic political demands for holding up reforms.[460] The, *Observer,* in a rare break from the template, suggested the army may have had a 'breakdown in restraint'.[461]

In 1969 Samuel Devenney died following a savage beating by nine RUC members in his own home. The police refused to cooperate with inquiries. There were no internal disciplinary charges. The *Guardian* coverage ranged from accusing nationalists of seeking martyrs through to an editorial seeking to assure the Protestant community that the RUC was still patrolling the neighbourhood where Devenney was assaulted.

455 Ibid.

456 *Guardian*, 9 July 1971.

457 For the killings of Cusack and Beattie, see *Guardian*, 7, 10, 12, 13 (editorial), 14, 17 July (editorial), 12 (editorial), 14 (editorial), 21 August (editorial), 8 September, 11, 19 November 1971, 7, 8 February (editorial), 16 March 1972. The SDLP were extremists holding out for an inquiry (ibid., 8 September 1971). Demanding an inquiry is also described as 'blocking government initiatives' and 'Roman Catholic preconditions' (ibid., 7 February 1972).

458 Ibid., 13 July 1971 (editorial).

459 Ibid., 12 August 1971 (editorial).

460 Ibid., 21 August 1971 (editorial).

461 *Observer*, 11, 18 July 1971.

The *Guardian*'s final editorial makes no reference to bringing police killers to justice, and even excused the police conspiracy of silence.[462] The sympathetic coverage of the RUC's refusal to hand over photographs is in stark contrast to its condemnation of French General Ailleret's refusal to hand over photographs in Djamila Boupacha case.[463] In 2014, forty-five years after his death, the police stated the Devenney file would remain secret for eight more years. The files remain sealed.

Francis McCloskey, a sixty-six-year-old pensioner, also died following a police beating. The *Guardian* claimed he had been in the IRA in his youth and Catholic violence had brought it on. Peter Jenkins suggested he had really died in a cycling accident.[464] The coverage of the Watt, Thornton and Rooney deaths at the hands of the army illustrated a similar partiality.[465] In the case of two sisters killed by the army, Simon Winchester wondered whom to believe: 'Certainly the army does seem less prey to insidious propaganda pressures than the opposing forces [residents].'[466] The *Guardian* adopted the army line completely, the *Observer* less so.[467] The next day Hetherington-Cole's editorial issued another warning to Catholics: 'Stay off the streets at night.'[468] But both newspapers were wrong. The two sisters were unarmed. No shots had been fired at soldiers.[469] Reliance on army sources was the norm although Winchester and Hetherington already knew army PR produced false accounts.[470]

Coverage of the breakdown of the 1972 IRA ceasefire reveals the *Guardian*, especially Hetherington-Cole, once again following the government line.[471] Frank Steele of MI6 remembers it differently. He thought the 1972 ceasefire would fail because unionists, police and

462 For Samuel Devenney see *Guardian:* 9 August 1969, 30 January (editorial), 20 March, 24 September (editorial), 19 November 1970 (editorial), 2 August 1972, 26 February 1973, and *Observer*, 1 February, 22, 29 March 1970.

463 *Guardian*, 10 February 1962.

464 For sympathetic portrayal of the RUC, see the McCloskey case, *Guardian*, 17 July 1969 and 13 July 1970.

465 For the Thornton case, see *Guardian*, 9, 14 August, 29 October 1971 ('open verdict'). For the Rooney case, see *Guardian*, 8, 16 (editorial), August, October ('killed in riot'). For the Watts case, see *Guardian*, 2, 9, February 1971, and *Observer*, 7 February 1971 ('rioter and agitator').

466 *Guardian*, 25 October 1971.

467 Coverage of the killing of the Maguire sisters: *Guardian*, 25, 26 October 1971, and in the *Observer*, 24 October 1971.

468 *Guardian*, 26 October 1971 (editorial).

469 McKittrick et al., *Lost Lives*, pp. 107–8.

470 Hetherington, *Guardian Years,* pp. 303-5.

471 See *Guardian*, 10 (editorial), 11 (editorial), 12, 13, 15, 18, 29 July 1972. There is a divergence between Cole's editorials and Harold Jackson's and Simon Hoggart's reportage. Early editorials claimed 'the IRA deliberately sabotaged the ceasefire'. Later coverage came close to accusing the army.

loyalists did not want it, and part of the army and hardliners in the IRA also did not want it. In 2012 the Public Record Office released an internal memo (marked 'secret') between William Whitelaw and the General Officer Commanding. Dated 10 July 1972, one day after the breakdown of the ceasefire, the memo shows that Whitelaw would publicly reveal the secret British-IRA talks and put the blame for the breakdown squarely on the IRA. Whitelaw urges the army to pursue the war against the IRA with the 'utmost vigour', and reassured soldiers they would 'be suitably indemnified' against any possible court proceedings.[472] In 1972 an amnesty had been drawn up to cover any future problems.

In April 1973 army intelligence spread a story of IRA members stealing IRA funds. Simon Hoggart denied any army source: 'the army did no inventing and the reports are based almost entirely on work by reporters.'[473] However, Dillon details how this whole episode of 'investigative journalism' was a clever sting by army intelligence to portray the IRA as criminals rather than insurgents.[474] When the army's involvement became known, questions arose over whether journalists had been tricked or had colluded with the army.

You would think that we might reasonably have expected less credibility afforded to army sources thereafter.

However, there are numerous examples where the *Guardian* printed the army version subsequently shown to be untrue.[475] Residents of Catholic neighbourhoods frequently accused the soldiers of brutality. Hetherington-Cole rejected 'the clap trap that is talked about the

---

472   *Derry Journal*, 19 June 2012.

473   *Guardian*, 12 April 1973.

474   For the embezzlement story, see *Guardian*, 9, 12 April, 12, 14 May 1973. See also Kevin Myers in the *Observer*, 8 April 1973. See Dillon, *Dirty War*, pp. 60-68 for army manipulation of journalists who 'uncovered' this embezzlement.

475   For numerous examples of following army sources, see *Guardian*, 9 September, 10, 20, 25 October, 11, 19 November, 20 December 1971, 10 March, 16 May, 15, 17, 18, 22 July, 8, 26, 29 August, 23 September, 11, 19, 22 October, 18, 20, 22, 30 December 1972, 29 January, 9 February, 10, 13, 14, 15, 25 March, 14, 16 May, 16 June, 23 August 1973, 3, 19 April 1974. For fifteen-year-old gunmen and bombers, see *Guardian*, 16 September, 11 November 1971, 18 June, 5 September 1973, 3, 11 April 1974. For the counter-insurgency view, see *Guardian*, 3 November 1970 (editorial), 9 February, 29 June 1971, 1, 15, 18 July, 1, 8, 17 August (editorial), 12, 14 May 1973, 7 June 1974, and *Observer*, 5 July 1970, 17 October, 12 December 1971, 26 March 1973. For skepticism of brutality during house searches, see *Guardian*, 4, 6, 7, 10 July, 11 November 1970, 25, 27 May 1971, 15 (editorial), 24 (editorial), 1, 9 September, 31 October 1972, 8 February (editorial), 4, 15, 16, May, 4, 15, 16, 27 August 1973, 20 March 1974. Very few reject army line, *Guardian,* 29 September 1969 (editorial), 22 January, 10 October 1972. For a slightly critical approach to the RUC and B-Specials, see *Guardian*, 6, 7 October, 4 December 1968, 23 August, 24 October (editorial), 28 March 1970, and *Observer*, 6 October 1968, 20 April 1969, 12 May 1974.

army.'[476] During the three-day Falls Curfew, the army killed four civilians, illegally confined the population and ransacked hundreds of homes. Roy Hattersley MP opined: 'Had General Freeland been St. Michael and his soldiers been angels or archangels, someone would have complained that Lucifer was ejected from Heaven with more force than was absolutely necessary.'[477] Hattersley, in British terms, was on the left. His analogy of soldiers as angels and the Irish as devils is particularly revealing. The angelic lens continued: 'The restraint and self-discipline of the army and police are in marked contrast to the conduct of security forces elsewhere.'[478] But by chance the curfew trapped an Italian film crew. Franco Biancicci had also been in the Algiers Kasbah immediately after paratroopers ransacked it: 'it was the same thing exactly. Doors kicked in, furniture smashed, floorboards pulled up, wall plaster ripped off, holy pictures stamped underfoot or thrust down lavatories ...'[479] Nicky Curtis, an eye-witness soldier, remembered 'crucifixes snapped, kids crying, crunching the Pope's picture ... this is when I did feel like we had invaded.'[480] The upper-class-accented commands from megaphones in helicopters clattering loudly over rooftops ordering people into their homes soon to be invaded by 3,000 soldiers, including the anti-Catholic Scottish regiments, resulted in lifetime alienation from the British state.

Conclusion

Many French soldiers believed in France's *mission civilisatrice*. French SAS installations worked to improve impoverished villages but their 'hearts and minds' approach contrasted with commando raids in the *bled* and Algiers. British soldiers were conducting a counterinsurgency. Too often their accounts are self-serving myths. They did not distinguish Catholics and the IRA. Liberal-press coverage was framed by French ruthlessness and British restraint. The French used Gestapo methods. The British maintained a remarkable restraint despite extreme provocation. Allegations of British brutality were propaganda. Much evidence was presented of an over-reliance on British army sources. Army PR was not playing catch-up to clever republican propaganda

---

476 See *Guardian*, 8 February 197 (editorial), also 'sadly stories are manufactured', *Guardian*, 15 July 1972 (editorial), or 'it is easy for propagandists to fabricate stories', *Guardian*, 24 July 1972 (editorial).

477 *Guardian*, 11 July 1970.

478 *Guardian*, 20 October 1971.

479 Coogan, *Troubles*, pp. 128-9.

480 Saunders and Wood, *Times of Troubles*, p. 130.

and the possibility of the British army conducting itself with anything less than superhuman restraint rarely made it to print. The coverage, routinely following the official narrative, has a lasting imprint for dealing with the past. Increasingly challenged or demonstrated as false or misleading, unionists view this as an assault on their protectors and reject it as 'rewriting history'.

CHAPTER SIX

The Method that Dared Not Speak its Name

This chapter investigates justifications for or denunciation of torture in the memoirs and published accounts of soldiers. The portrayal of brutal interrogations in the liberal press is held up against these accounts and the historic record, including the documentation in Darius Rejali's seminal work.[481] Dictatorships have tortured more, but democracies, particularly France and Britain, pioneered and exported the modern techniques of torture, especially torture that leaves no marks. As democracy and human rights spread after WWII, 'clean techniques', using electricity, water, noise and stress positions, spread too. When victims are scarred, the iniquity of the authorities is exposed. Democracies did not eliminate torture, they hid it better, making it more difficult to identify and document.

French Soldiers
Deux gifles: from protection to torture
By the spring of 1955 French success in the countryside led to increased ALN activity in the cities, including the random shooting of French civilians and the targeted killing of Muslim 'traitors.' Bomb attacks on urban centres took the lives of Muslim and French civilians alike. For the army, the Muslim population was not only an object of protection but a source of information. Joseph Kraft recorded a paratrooper explaining how one company proceeded. A fifteen-year-old boy had denied any knowledge of the *fellaghas* (bandits). 'That cost him a couple of smacks ... but he did not talk ... After two other smacks the

481   D. Rejali, *Torture and Democracy* (Princeton University Press, 2007).

kid promised to tell the truth.'[482] The phrase *deux gifles*, a 'couple of smacks', was a popular phrase covering a wide range of more savage treatment. The army was well versed in these techniques, stretching back to Indo-China and Morocco. Brutal and prolonged beatings, electric shocks from a field-telephone's modified hand generator, sexual degradation, burning with cigarettes and holding suspects under water all became regular procedure. Men were bitten by fierce dogs and were beaten on the soles of their feet, followed by immersion in cold water. Women were raped or had objects thrust into their vaginas.

Massu's paratroopers made earnest use of these techniques. Proceeding directly from Suez, they were to assist Algiers' 1,500 police. Granted police authority, Massu embarked on a complete census, issuing every man, woman and child with a personal identity card. This information-gathering network (*îlot*) was a chain linking his headquarters to every Muslim family. A special centre was established at the main gate connecting the Kasbah to the city and manned by *turned* ALN members. Mobile units patrolled the city. Day and night, they conducted *rattisages* (raking operations), searching for suspects or weapons. Long lines of Muslims held at checkpoints became a common sight. By September 1957 the army had won the Battle of Algiers. The ALN network, responsible for the civilian bomb attacks of 1956–57, was completely broken up, but at a terrible price. Between thirty to forty per cent of the active male population of the Kasbah was arrested at one time or another. Questioning often meant brutality. Hundreds, possibly thousands, just disappeared, and bodies began to wash up on beaches. Death flights out over the Mediterranean were common enough to produce the euphemism *crevettes Bigeard*, [Colonel] Bigeard's shrimps.

The method that dare not speak its name

In 1975 the UN defined torture as an act of a public official that intentionally inflicts pain or suffering for the purpose of obtaining information or a confession or to punish or intimidate. Torture constituted an aggravated and deliberate form of cruel, inhuman or degrading treatment or punishment. The definition specifically noted physical or mental pain. During the Algerian War, prohibitions against torture had been codified but torture itself had not then been defined. Paris had to reconcile brutal interrogations with its self-image of the

---

482   J. Kraft, *The Struggle for Algeria* (NY, Doubleday, 1961), p. 104.

Rights of Man. They established a premise of such extreme danger to the republic that the derogation of non-derogable rights seemed the only recourse. France was defending Western values against barbarians of the East. Many in France still believed in their *mission civilisatrice:* "'We' were not doing that for "us", "we" were doing it for "them".'[483]

In 1955, the government could no longer ignore the mounting criticism. François Mitterrand commissioned the Wuillaume Report. The word 'torture' was not part of the terms of reference, but the report viewed it as excessive maltreatment or abuse. Initially sceptical, he concluded that violence had been used by the police including beatings and electric shocks from the field-telephone. He deemed electric shocks to be more psychological and not excessively cruel. Long and detailed inquiries may result in identifying serious perpetrators but would encounter grave difficulties. The Wuillaume Report did not overly censure perpetrators, thus allowing them to continue. Wuillaume also suggested torture be institutionalised so that it might be properly supervised, a forerunner of Alan Dersowitz's recommendation following the 9/11 attacks.

For the sake of France

Jean Lartéguy is credited with the first envisioning of the 'ticking bomb' scenario. He makes only oblique references to torture. Soldiers had to overcome their consciences in this new type of war. Officers agonised over how to proceed with suspected bomber, Si Millial. Eventually, Captain Boisfeuras, an Indo-China veteran, overcomes Colonel Raspéguy's concerns.[484] 'We've only twenty-four hours left, your letter box [address], Si Millial?' [485] Captain Glastigny becomes uneasy with this new side to Boisfeuras but is prevented from intervening: '… you're not too keen on what we've now got to do Glastigny, it's no good putting him behind glass.'[486] In the 'schoolroom' stood Min, the Vietnamese torturer. Boisfeuras asks again. Si Millial remains silent and Min steps forward. It had come to this, a ghastly new type of war. They had to shed outdated notions that made for the 'greatness of Western man but which simultaneously prevent him from protecting himself.'[487] The methods produce results. Min reconnects the field telephone. Colonel Raspéguy longs to escape into the mountains and leave this

---

483   R. Maran, *Torture* (NY, Praeger, 1989), p. 17, 'Exceptional circumstances'.
484   Boisfeuras is a composite of General Paul Aussaresses and Colonel Marcel Bigeard.
485   J. Lartéguy, *The Centurions* (London, Heinemann, 1961), p. 460.
486   Ibid.
487   Ibid., p. 461.

dirty job to others. The French are distanced from the greatest brutality. It is Min, the Vietnamese who used the electricity. They had been driven to this by ALN terror. Overcoming their civilised scruples was necessary to defeat terrorists who murdered French farmers and Muslim workers, raped women, mutilated children and burned farms. The word torture was not used. Called upon to be the Algiers policeman, Lartéguy's paratroopers were at war. They completely shattered the ALN bomb network, but when the international press arrived politicians distanced themselves. As they marched over the Némentcha mountains, the regiment learned of legal proceedings against them. Yet the politicians had given the nod: 'It's for the sake of France.'[488]

Jules Roy was shaken by the allegations against his beloved army. He investigated and honestly named it torture. Again, the ALN made them do it.[489] They killed Muslims for betraying the cause, threw grenades into schools, buses and cafés, bombed public plazas and machine-gunned passing motorists. They tortured their co-religionists for failing to pay their 'revolutionary assessments'. To protect the innocent, the army succumbed. Leulliette also justified army actions as a response to ALN atrocities. They were criminals who cut throats, killed women and children, and placed bombs in cinemas.[490] General Paul Aussaresses' 2006 memoires caused a sensation in France. He displayed no remorse, claiming torture was effective and tolerated by Paris. Col Yves Godard, Massu's chief of staff, always opposed torture as damaging to the army's reputation.

Massu later admitted the torture but regretted it and believed it was unnecessary. Rejali concluded Massu won the Battle of Algiers by force and not through intelligence gained by torture. The army obtained accurate information through informants and public cooperation. The residents of the Kasbah blamed the ALN for bringing army repression on their heads. This was a shock to the FLN which considered itself sole representative of the people. At the time, it suited the army and the FLN to claim torture stopped the ALN bombs.

British Soldiers
The interrogators had not enjoyed their work
On 9 August 1971, 342 suspects were detained in Belfast during internment swoops. The majority suffered assaults, cuts and bruises and

---

488   Ibid., p. 486.
489   J. Roy, *The War in Algeria* (NY, Grove, 1961), pp. 13, 65, 106.
490   P. Leulliette, *St Michael and the Dragon,* (London, Heinemann, 1964), p. 234.

humiliation. Others were brutally beaten and ran the gauntlet barefoot over broken glass and bricks between baton-wielding soldiers and fierce dogs. They suffered broken bones, burst eardrums, were urinated on and had blank cartridges fired into their mouths. They were burned with matches, cigarettes and electric fires. Others suffered electric shocks, were injected with drugs, or had instruments thrust in their anal passage. Russian roulette and threatening the lives of family members were common. Soldiers operated a modified form of Bigeard's death flights. After a thirty-to-sixty-minute flight detainees were threatened with and pushed out of helicopters. Unknown to the blindfolded detainees, they were hovering just feet above the ground. Fourteen were selected for further brutality: in-depth interrogations using sensory deprivation. Some suffered waterboarding.[491]

In-depth interrogation included spread-eagling for hours against a wall, weight on tiptoes and fingertips, the KGB *stoika* position. When exhaustion led to collapse, detainees were revived and beaten upright. For the next seven days they were naked except for a loose-fitting boiler suit and a hood covering the head. They were beaten repeatedly, splashed with buckets of cold water and held upright; anything to keep them awake. This sleep deprivation lasted two, even three days, and was accompanied by a persistent background hissing (white) noise and a starvation diet.

As news leaked out about the treatment of prisoners, referred to as the Hooded Men, there was a public outcry and the British government was forced to set up an inquiry under Sir Edmund Compton. The terms of this inquiry were to investigate physical brutality only. Mental torture and cruelty were specifically excluded. This limited definition did not go unnoticed.

While Lord Compton recognised some ill-treatment had occurred, he argued that cruelty implied 'a disposition to inflict suffering, coupled with indifference to, or pleasure in, the victim's pain … We do not think that happened here.'[492] This is a clear reiteration of Père Delarue's advice to Massu's paratroopers, to conduct interrogations 'without sadism but efficacious.'[493] French soldiers were to take no pleasure but, equally, to feel no shame.

Compton, like Kitson, was a student of French Algeria.

Remarkably, Compton concluded the *stoika* position, the hooding

---

491   British Army waterboarding, *Irish Times*, 26 June 2017.

492   D. Reed, *Ireland,* (London, Larkin, 1984), p. 167.

493   Maran, *Torture,* p. 98.

and white noise provided security for both detainees and soldiers. But independent British scientists concluded that just two days of this deprivation of sensory input resulted in hallucinations, paranoid fantasies and a state of psychosis and severe psychiatric disorder. A second inquiry under Lord Parker recommended *continued use of the methods* even while acknowledging that 'mental effects may persist for up to two months'.[494] The scientific evidence concluded that the techniques led to temporary insanity and severe, persisting personality disorders of many years' duration. Parker claimed that interrogations had resulted in 700 new IRA members being identified, as well as arms caches and safe houses. His claims were never substantiated. There was no mention of a 'ticking bomb'. Lord Carrington, who ordered this, justified it as all detainees were 'murderers and thugs'.[495] American psychologist Rona Fields documented the serious effects the torture had on the detainees and Northern Irish society in general. The government had her book withdrawn. The shredding of these 10,000 copies seems to have completely disappeared from public awareness.[496]

It was all rather harmless

Colonel Dewar regretted internment without trial in part of the UK in 1971. Unlike Massu, he admits to no brutality, much less torture. It was all rather harmless, involving disorientation, standing for periods at a wall, some sleep deprivation and a nagging noise. This was not brutality – because Lord Parker said so. Dewar dismissed the 1976 torture verdict of the European Commission on Human Rights as resulting from the rarefied atmosphere of the courtroom. He claimed Britain discontinued the methods. However, the Bennett Report and Amnesty International concluded that brutality during interrogation continued uninterrupted throughout the 1970s.[497] Dewar refused to accept even Compton's mild admission: 'the army had used highly sophisticated and clinical, though

---

494   C. Ackroyd et al, *Technology of Political Control* (London, Pluto, 1980), p. 35.

495   Reed, *Ireland*, p. 167.

496   R. M. Fields, *Northern Ireland: Society Under Siege* (New Brunswick, Transaction, 1980). Fields recalled her difficulties to Clare Spark of Pacific Radio, California. British authorities seized her briefcase, one chapter was removed before publishing and shredded. Enoch Powell threatened to sue and a D-Notice was placed on publication. Her next re-publishing, in the US, was delayed by one year when Temple University received a handwritten note from a Stephen Gregory listing '200 errors'. She traced Gregory to an address in Northern Ireland. Already returned to England, neighbours informed her he worked for the British government. See her *Against Violence against Women* (Palgrave Macmillan, 2013), p191, *Belfast Telegraph,* 12 July 2009 and https://archive.org/details/pacifica_radio_archives-KZ2652, Pacific Radio Archive, 3729 Chuenga Blvd. W., North Hollywood, CA 91604.

497   H. Bennett, *Report, Police Interrogation Northern Ireland,* (London: HMSO, 1979); *Northern Ireland: Report of an Amnesty International Mission* (London, 1978).

admittedly and intentionally very frightening, methods to get vital information from evil men.'[498] The vital information was Parker's same 700 evil men. Unlike Massu, Dewar concluded brutal interrogations were indispensable and pondered: 'whether their continued use would have changed the course of events ...'[499]

Kitson's recommendation of discreet tying-in of the legal system to the counterinsurgency produced the Diplock Courts (no jury, single judge). RUC Chief Constable Ken Newman organised Castlereagh interrogation barracks as the cutting edge of a criminalisation policy which would frame British propaganda until the 1981 hunger strike.[500] Convictions were based on 'confessions' alone. In 1978, the European Court of Human Rights (ECrtHR), after some finessing regarding the use of the word 'torture', ruled the interrogations were inhuman and degrading. The underlying rationale for distinguishing torture from inhuman treatment occupies one sentence of this most contentious ruling. The most horrendous interrogations worldwide – in Israeli interrogation centres; in Abu Ghraib – have relied on this precedent.[501] But notably, the court ruled the methods were an administrative practice organised by the MoD. General Michael Carver revealed that Prime Minister Ted Heath, Home Secretary Reginald Maudling and Minister of Defence Lord Carrington all knew about the methods.[502] The template of French ruthlessness and British restraint is, however, firmly fixed. Consider the *Guardian's* Ian Aitken: 'The French are fantastically brutal in a way the British are not ... in Ireland it was largely to do with who the chief inspector was in any given police station ... wearing them out, making them stand against walls ... but it wasn't sticking wine bottles up your thingy, which is what they did to Djamila Boupacha.'[503] In fact, brutality during interrogations, including electric shocks, continued right into the 1990s.[504] The British army tortured in eleven countries since WWII without public protest. Liam Holden and William Parker were waterboarded.[505]

---

498   Dewar, *The British Army, Northern Ireland,* (London, Armoury, 1985), p. 55.

499   Ibid.

500   Taylor, *Loyalists* (Bloomsbury 2000), p. 158, Carver & Handley, *Does Torture Work* (OUP 2017) p. 1997.

501   Trinity College Law Review, 13 June 2016, accessed 5 June 2018. http://trinitycollegelawreview.org/the-haunting-of-the-hooded-men/

502   M. Carver, *Out of Step,* (London: Hutchinson, 1989). Rees believed it was Carrington's decision, *Irish Times,* 5 June 2018 5 June 2014.

503   Interview, Ian Aitken, London, 27 July 1998.

504   See M. Dillon, *The Enemy Within,* (London, Doubleday, 1994).

505   *Guardian,* 21 June 2012. See also McGuffin, *Internment.*

Recent revelations have shown Britain withheld documents and lied to the ECrtHR.[506] In March 2018 the ECrtHR ruled that withholding information in the 1978 case would not have altered their decision. This was widely condemned as deciding on too narrow a definition. The important point the court did not decide on is whether the 'five techniques' would be named as torture by today's definition. The Supreme Court in London and Belfast High Court ruled the methods as torture.[507]

Some were interrogated by very dubious methods

Former ITN foreign correspondent Desmond Hamill interviewed British officers. One admitted: 'Some were interrogated by very dubious methods ... for very little return.'[508] Others pointed out the interrogators were not soldiers but RUC Special Branch and society has to protect itself. 'If there is horror and discomfort to be inflicted on a few, is this not preferable to the danger and horror being inflicted on perhaps a million people? ... the world has become a more talkative place than when we used these techniques in colonial situations.'[509] Many were irritated at the public outcry over 'IRA propaganda.' One officer justified the torture with interrogators having to operate on a shoestring budget and in appalling conditions. The pressure to get results drove 'experienced and otherwise humane interrogators into becoming brutal rogues out of sheer frustration.'[510]

Colonel Evelegh concluded the 'specialist' interrogations were a failure: 'there are always policemen and soldiers stupid enough to see the solution to their information problems in beating suspects.'[511] He recommended the production of willing informers who would provide information the army did not even know to ask for. Evelegh is yet another student of Algiers. Michael Asher, SAS, recalls beery Ulstermen, Special Branch from Castlereagh, the 'notorious interrogation centre'. Their 'techniques filled the SB's coffers with

506   The Torture Files, RTE broadcast 4 June 2004.

507   Trinity Law Review Dublin, Irish Minister of Foreign Affairs announced a new application 2 December 2014, see http://trinitycollegelawreview.org/the-haunting-of-the-hooded-men/ and *Independent,* 13 February 2015, http://www.independent.co.uk/voices/comment/if-amal-clooney-wins-the-hoodedman-case-the-embarrassment-for-the-uk-would-be-huge-10044980.html. In March 2018 the ECHR rejected referring the case to the Grand Chamber. Human rights lawyers accused the ECHR of hiding behind procedure because of the political ramifications, not least the US depending on the 1978 decision for Guantanamo's detention centre. See also 'Rees Memo' shows UK Cabinet approving torture, Hooded Men, *Irish Times,* 15 December 2021.

508   Hamill, *Pig in the Middle,* (London, Metheun, 1985), p. 6.

509   Ibid., p. 69.

510   Ibid., p. 104.

information, but it led to the ECHR.'[512] Again, there is a distancing, local Ulstermen sought this distasteful job. Asher remembers an RUC patrol laughingly informing one prisoner he was going straight to a particularly motivated interrogator: 'His [RUC] brother was killed in the Bessbrook explosion last week ... Just crying out to get revenge.'[513] But Asher changed: 'In those dark eyes I saw reflected a picture of myself, sitting here in the uniform of an oppressor. I had never sought to be an oppressor of others.'[514]

The Liberal Press
An established practice unrestricted by government lacking all conviction

In an evolving situation, where complaints had not been fully investigated, editors had to evaluate official sources and the accusers. This early *Guardian* editorial, titled 'France's Flaw', can be applauded: 'But it is no answer to say that ... the rebels' crimes are far worse.'[515] Throughout the Battle of Algiers, the *Guardian* refused to permit any justification. Following Massu's clearing the ALN from the Kasbah, the editor accused the army of justifying torture: 'The excuse has been the infamous mutilations and indiscriminate terrorism for which the other side has been responsible. The excuse is, however, an insult to France.'[516] There was no excuse for the torture of Henri Alleg, a *pied noir* journalist sympathetic to Algerian nationalism. It had not taken place in hot temper or under the strain of battle. Further editorials blamed France for turning 'torture into an established practice ... [by] civilian ministers lacking all conviction.'[517]

Official French denials also were not credible: 'It is one thing for police or military in Algeria to use torture in defiance of orders from Paris. It is quite another for the Head of Government to connive at such methods.'[518] This bold stand was laudable since the only independent evidence then available was the July 1957 report of the International Commission Against Concentration Camps which concluded that French authorities were serious about upholding human rights, there had never been much torture, and there was even less now. 'It must be

---

511   R. Evelegh, *Peacekeeping,* (London, Hurst, 1978), p. 136.
512   M. Asher, *Shoot to Kill,* (London, Viking, 1990), pp. 25, 143.
513   Ibid., p. 257.
514   Ibid., p. 267.
515   *Guardian*, 16 August 1957 (editorial).
516   Ibid., 30 October 1957 (editorial).
517   Ibid., 6 March 1958 (editorial).
518   Ibid., 29 June 1959 (editorial).

said that there are some doubts about the value of the delegation's belief that torture was not "generalized".'[519] Two days later, the *Guardian* condemned the commission's report as too mild and maintained torture prevailed. France might have avoided 'much shame' and Muslims might have avoided 'much suffering … if the contemptible Parliamentary Commission hadn't taken three months … and the majority of French editors had not allowed the quality of civic courage to become the prerogative of a very small number.'[520] Going further, the *Guardian* countered the apologists' cry of rebels being worse, and asserted that the French themselves were worse.[521] This critical stand against the French government narrative was maintained for the duration of the war.[522] This diligence continued even after the war, with a firm rebuttal of Massu's 1971 pre-repentant reaffirmation of the justifiers' excuse.[523]

The *Observer* was also sceptical: 'the reciprocal terrorism of the French and the FLN makes it virtually impossible for the real criminal to be discovered.'[524] However, Resident Minister Robert Lacoste was permitted space to point out that several investigations, including the Red Cross, found few acts of cruelty: 'In every proven case sanctions have been taken against the guilty.'[525] The editor remained unconvinced, and urged the FLN to be wary of de Gaulle's offers because 'torture persisted'.[526] He further asserted that 'army morale prevents punishment of the torturers.'[527] In contrast, British MP Maurice

519 Ibid., 13 August 1957.
520 Ibid., 15 August 1957.
521 The censoring of a film containing torture scenes was condemned: 'although they are used by the FLN … and not as is more usual the other way around', ibid., 14 September 1960.
522 Articles and editorials citing torture and critical of official sources, French denials can be found in the *Guardian*: 6, 8, 11, 12, 30 October 1956; 2, 19, 21 February, 6 April, 7 May, 25, 27 July, 14, 16 (ed.) August, 3, 30 (ed.) October 1957; 5, 6 (ed.), 13, 15 March, 8 August, 18, 25 (ed.) September, 2, 25 October 1958; 3, 7 (ed.) February, 4, 25 April, 20, 22, 24 (ed.), 25, 26, 27, 29 June, 9 July, 8 August, 1 (ed.), 9 October, 21 December 1959; 1 January, 2 February, 6, 8, 14, 16, 24, 25 June, 9 July, 9 August, 14 September, 21 October, 8 December 1960; 17 March, 4 April, 19 June, 28 August, 10 October, 8, 9 November 1961; 17, 18, 19, 20 January, 2 February, 3 March, 21 April, 23 June, 6 July, 30 November 1962. Minister Lacoste 'undoubtedly bears a responsibility … for having created a situation in which it is easier than it should be to belittle such acts and to cover it up', 6 October 1956.
523 *Guardian*, 11 November 1971.
524 *Observer*, 16 February 1958.
525 Ibid., 27 April 1958.
526 Ibid., 19 June 1960 (editorial).
527 Ibid., 31 December 1961 (editorial). The Irish complained of the British government's similar 'concern to protect the army regardless of what happened', Justin O'Brien, *Killing Finucane: Murder in Defence of the Realm* (Dublin: Gill & Macmillan, 2005), p. 92.

Edelman (a Russian Jewish refugee and human rights campaigner) provided details of the imprisoning of torturers. On 17 March 1958 he informed the House of Commons that 'French authorities, far from condoning this outrageous behaviour, have convicted and punished 363 French soldiers.'[528]

The *Observer* remained critical of French authorities throughout the war.[529] At war's end, the editor looked back on its cruelty and, making no reference to ALN torture, concluded: 'Frenchmen have come to take torture for granted and to tolerate atrocities by their own armed forces.'[530] Neal Ascherson, who reported from Algeria, recalled a small, stalwart group, the Friends of Liberty, 'who were prepared to protest. To do so, took a lot of courage, you were very unpopular ... The French were racist, this couldn't be true because Algeria is a department of France.'[531] But Pierre Vidal-Naquet, the activist historian who repeatedly exposed torture during the war, pointed out that, until the Vietnam War, no other country so-accused had allowed such a quantity of challenging information to appear.[532] There was a tide of articles in the French press condemning torture. During one November 11 remembrance, soldiers prevented Jean-Louis Charbonnier, an alleged torturer, from participating. Paul Teitgen, general secretary of the Algiers police, and General Pâris de Bollardière, both resigned. Sartre condemned army torture, Camus condemned both sides.

Investigators should talk to prisoners rather than focusing on officials

While official French denials were not credible, the accusations of French activists were often presented as fact. Henri Alleg's *La Question* and Bechir Boumaaza's *La Gangrene* charged France with torture. The *Guardian's* Alastair Hetherington wrote that their censoring 'can only

---

528 www.hansard.millbanksystems.com/commons/1958/mar/17/algeria accessed July 2015.

529 The French are well-known torturers, *Guardian*: 6, 8 June, 10, 12, 30 October 1956; 14 August 1957; 8 August, 9 September 1958; 7 February, 9 October, 21 December 1959; 14 September 1960; 4 April, 28 October, 13 December 1961; 14 March, 11 January 1962. For example, 'the French tortured long before the rising started in 1954', 11 January 1962. For criticism of French officials over torture, see the *Observer*: 1957: 25 August, 17 November, 9 June 1957; 1 January, 2 February, 6 April 1958; 24 April 1959; 21 February, 12, 19 June 1960; 15 October, 31 December 1961; 14 January 1962. For example, P.M. Bourges-Manoury is 'likely to intensify repression ... and draw support from the mood of chauvinism ... and racial hatred ...' 9 June 1957.

530 *Observer*, 25 March 1962 (editorial).

531 Interview, Neal Ascherson (at the *Observer*, London), July 1998.

532 See Pierre Vidal-Naquet, *Torture: Cancer of Democracy* (Harmondsworth: Penguin, 1974), p. 143.

confirm the allegations.'[533] However, the banning of John McGuffin's *The Guinea Pigs* and the shredding of Rona Fields' *Northern Ireland: Society Under Siege* did not similarly 'confirm the allegations'.[534] McGuffin had explained that the British army did not torture to get information but that it was an experiment. Ireland was not just a laboratory where 'craft' became a 'procedure based on science' but a significant threshold in the emergence of an international torture network that links the intelligence services of Britain, France, the US and Israel.[535] In addition, the accusations of the French clergy, especially progressive Catholics, were most impressive. There were sympathetic accounts of Djamila Bouhired and Djamila Boupacha but Bouhired, Boupacha and even Yacef Saadi had not been tortured.[536] Bouhired was interrogated by Captain Jean Graziani, who was already convinced there were better ways. He cleverly turned Bouhired, who gave up a bomb cache and her colleague Djamila Bouazza. Indeed, those who were tortured, Ben M'Hidi, Henri Alleg and Ali Boumandjel, revealed nothing. Suspects often had no information. Interestingly, Djamila Bouhired had escaped an earlier arrest. When roused during an early-morning raid, she protested so loudly the 'ruthless' French left her in bed.

At the height of the Battle of Algiers, the *Guardian* recommended 'investigators should talk to prisoners ... there is too much emphasis on officials.'[537] Three days later, it again supported the accusers and criticised, 'the inanity of the supposition made by [Prime Minister] Bourges-Maunoury that it is easy for any witness to make a declaration about [army malpractice].'[538] Hetherington remained sceptical: 'The statement made by the Director of Prosecutions that they [detainees] made no complaint to the examining magistrate is feeble enough in the absence of a proper investigation.'[539]

The soldiers are worse than the bombers

Fr. Robert Davezies was charged with assisting the ALN. His journey against the French state began with his publishing of torture allegations.

533 *Guardian*, 24 June 1959 (editorial).
534 See note 16 above.
535 D Lloyd, *Irish Culture and Colonial Modernity*, (Cambridge University Press 2011), p. 182.
536 Rejali, *Torture and Democracy*, p. 483.
537 *Guardian*, 8 October 1956.
538 Ibid., 11 October 1957.
539 Ibid., 24 June 1959 (editorial).

His trial definitively answered the *Observer's* question of whose violence was worse. The *Guardian* directed the reader to Pastor Cazalis, who explained there were situations where not taking sides meant passively supporting wrong. 'Fr. Davezies had chosen solidarity with the violence of the liberators against the violence of the oppressors.'[540] Conor Cruise O'Brien agreed and argued that the ALN, fighting the full power of the coloniser state, was justified in using its poorer resources with fewer moral restrictions.[541]

O'Brien would reverse from this endorsement when explaining torture in Ireland.

The *Guardian* outlined the 'double problem of conscience created first by the practice of torture, and secondly the refusal of the pre-rebellion administration to leave a peaceful path open to Algerian patriots.'[542]

The *Observer* sympathised with the Frenchman's dilemma when torture was used in his name. Cardinal Lienart and Pastor Beaumont explained: 'This trial is about the risks of Christian faith. Fr. Davezies' actions, in a spirit of justice, are preferred to passiveness and silence.'[543] The same edition devoted three separate reports to these risks: 'The Bible, which is a decidedly dangerous book, says many times that the cause of the oppressed precedes that of authority.'[544] The liberal press consistently afforded greater credibility to the accusations of Catholic clergy and left-wing intellectuals.[545] The record is now clear. The French tortured in Algeria. The evidence was not so clear at the time. The International Red Cross, on its eighth inspection, delivered a favourable account for the majority of camps. The *Guardian* was unmoved and rejected 'the army's resentment of all criticism.'[546] The liberal press

---

540 Ibid., 11 January 1962.

541 C.C. O'Brien, Review of *The Wretched of the Earth* by Franz Fanon, *Nation*, no. 200, (21 June 1965), p. 676.

542 *Guardian*, 13 January 1962.

543 *Observer*, 14 January 1962.

544 Ibid.

545 For sympathetic coverage of allegations and reprints of critiques from *Temoignage Chretien, La Question, La Gangrene, Les Editions du Minuit*, see the *Guardian* of: 11 October 1956; 15, 30 March, 13 August 1957; 3, 5, 6, 13 March, 2, 25 October 1958; 10, 25 April, 13 May, 20, 24 (ed.), 25, 27 June, 12 December 1959; 2 February, 6, 8, 14, 16, 24, 25 June, 7 July, 9 August, 21 October, 8 December 1960; 17 March, 4 April, 19 June, 25 August, 9 November, 21 December 1961; 11, 13, 17, 18, 19, 20 January, 10 February, 5 March, 21 April, 23 June, 30 November 1962. And the *Observer* of: 17 November 1957; 26 January, 9 March, 6 April 1958; 12 April 1959; 12, 19 June 1960; 15 October, 31 December 1961; 14 January 1962. For example: 'the chauvinism which has developed in Government circles about the Algerian war', *Observer* 17 November 1957.

546 *Guardian*, 5 January 1960.

gave more space and credibility to non-official sources for the duration of the conflict. This brave stand has been vindicated.

'The information obtained was undoubtedly responsible for saving lives'

When reporting British 'in-depth interrogations', all was reversed. Official sources were believable and the accusers lacked credibility. Unattributed stories portrayed the other side, the IRA, as worse. Just weeks after the first accusations, the *Guardian*, on its front page, revealed an eager willingness to accept official sources. Army claims of improved intelligence gained from their interrogations were substantiated by reference to a secret army document: 'Generally the claims of rapidly improving intelligence in Northern Ireland are greeted sceptically ... But the circumstances of its [document's] appearance suggest it was perfectly genuine.'[547] The reporter, Simon Winchester, did not elaborate upon these circumstances. The *Guardian* also accepted Home Secretary Reginald Maudling's justifications: 'The interrogation resulted in the obtaining by the security forces of a large measure of information ... People should know where these arms are and who these men are who are killing civilians.'[548] This should not have been difficult nor required extreme measures. At the time, the security forces were killing civilians twice as often as the IRA were.[549] The editor continued with his trust in official sources: 'The army and police have been surprised at the amount of information which men arrested in the past few weeks have given, some almost without being asked.'[550] Evil men, apparently, cannot wait to clear their conscience.

The deference to official sources continued: 'The latest arrests are further proof that the army's intelligence machine is becoming steadily more efficient.'[551] To accept army arrests as proof is surely revelatory. Hetherington-Cole claimed: 'the information obtained from the 14 men who were interrogated in depth was undoubtedly responsible for saving the lives of innocent civilians.'[552] These claims were never substantiated and the men were subsequently released, some almost immediately. As in Algeria, the objective of torture was not intelligence gathering but destroying the morale of the targeted civilian population. Torture

547 *Guardian*, 20 October 1971.
548 Ibid., 17 November 1971.
549 See McKittrick et al *Lost Lives*.
550 Guardian, 17 November 1971 (editorial).
551 Ibid., 24 November 1971.
552 Ibid., 3 March 1972 (editorial).

humiliated and reminded the rebellious community that the army was in control. The *Observer* initially rejected the justification of life-saving information: 'This was General Massu's claim in Algeria and has been the argument of torturers down the ages ... individual excesses are likely and are understandable.'[553] Individual excesses were understandable in Ireland but not in Algeria. In any event, this would soon change: 'But by the use of interrogation methods that were later criticized by the Compton Report ... the [British] army undoubtedly gained much valuable information.'[554] Unionist MP John Laird agreed: 'the amount of information that the interrogation operation and the interrogation sessions had brought in had made the whole thing worthwhile.'[555] But Colonel Robin Evelegh condemned the servicemen's justifications, in the heat of the moment, as stupidity. The stupidity of enraged soldiers is perhaps more understandable than the repeated use of these same justifications by 'liberal' journalists and politicians far removed from any danger. Indeed, British liberals had levelled this very accusation against French editors in the infamous torture of Henri Alleg. The consistent pattern of reporting in Ireland was that it was a necessary response to evil men that succeeded in thwarting their evil plans.

'The other side really is worse'
David Astor maintained the army had not tortured: 'the army had terrible methods but they were stopped ... in torture the IRA are a great deal worse ... Find me another country more restrained than the British.'[556] Robert Kee, likewise distanced the army from the worst excesses, and similarly evaluated British conduct: 'Well, you can say what you like about the RUC, they certainly behaved badly. But the French despised the Arabs, it is of a different order, the extent of the brutality. The French are much more brutal.'[557] Ian Aitken recalled: 'Well, there wasn't torture in Ireland on anything like Algeria. I mean the army had, sort of, third-degree methods: they beat people up but the French organised proper Gestapo stuff.'[558] He endorsed the argument of the other side (the IRA) being worse: 'the people concerned were,

553 *Observer*, 24 October 1971 (editorial).
554 Ibid., 26 March 1972.
555 *Guardian* 17 Nov 1971.
556 Interview, David Astor, London, 22 July 1998.
557 Interview, Robert Kee, London, 20 July 1998.
558 Interview, Ian Aitken (London), July 1998.

and are, engaged in a particularly nasty war and could not expect to be treated with "courtesy cup" techniques.'[559] Two days later, his editor actually advocated terrorism: 'the most effective method of fighting an urban guerrilla war is terror. The IRA have already demonstrated that, you shoot through the mouth those suspected of major offences.'[560]

The *Observer* joined in with the 'other side is worse' justification and expanded on IRA tortures: 'These IRA torture stories came to light through the diligence of reporters, rather than through a propaganda leak by the Army. It was pure coincidence that they were published on the same day as the Compton Report.'[561] The coincidence of publishing unattributed stories on the same day of a report (mildly) critical of the army surely stretches readers' credulity. 'A man was arrested by the police ... it was discovered that he had been severely burned – probably with a hot poker. At least one other man, also in police hands, is under treatment.'[562] The names of the men, to my knowledge, were never published. And although the military reportedly had pictures of these men, 'the Army is not making much of the incidents ... it was the ultimate in hypocrisy when the IRA complains about so-called brutality by the security forces'.[563] It is surely curious that the army was not making much of this, especially with its well-staffed PR department and the obvious propaganda value. The pictures, to my knowledge, were never printed. The *Observer* repeated the *Guardian*'s claim: 'IRA activity is well known ... punishment by shooting through the feet, the knees and (for ultimate crimes) through the mouth.'[564] I found no substantiated cases of the IRA shooting suspected informers through the mouth during this period. In any event, the supportive stand of both newspapers was undermined by Lord Gardiner's conclusion that the interrogation methods were illegal under the Geneva Convention. This forced a grudging about-turn by Hetherington-Cole: 'If a procedure is both illegal and morally wrong it must be stopped ... the methods used by the IRA to silence traitors or to punish those who have offended them make [British] interrogations seem like a pat on the back'.[565] The other side was still worse. The British were the lesser evil, as Ignatieff would say.[566]

559 *Guardian*, 15 November 1971.
560 Ibid., 17 November 1971 (editorial).
561 *Observer*, 21 November 1971.
562 Ibid.
563 Ibid., 21 November 1971.
564 Ibid.
565 *Guardian*, 3 March 1973 (editorial).
566 Ignatieff, *The Lesser Evil*, (Princetown, 2004).

'The allegations are neither credible nor proven'
The credibility afforded to army and police sources is in marked contrast to the scepticism displayed towards those making the allegations, especially the previously believable Catholic clergy (the French variety). The very first accusations, made by Irish Catholics, were generally suspect. The *Guardian* uncritically accepted the words of an (already) officially discredited police force. 'These fellows [detainees] are likely to allege absolutely anything.'[567]

Hetherington-Cole challenged Cardinal Conway's call for an independent investigation: 'It would, of course, be helpful if Cardinal Conway were to specify when, where, and to whom the ill-treatment took place.'[568] In addition, they turned the accusation back onto the Catholic community in general: Lord Cameron's report 'did not bring much comfort to the Roman Catholic community, which did not escape criticism.'[569] Within days of the allegations being made, they explained them away: 'The complaints of ill-treatment and the ease with which they spread probably spring from the general sense of anger and frustration.'[570] Hetherington-Cole are repeatedly hostile towards the accusers and the community making them but, in an interesting concession, note: 'Every war produces its atrocity stories, many of which are unfounded or exaggerated. Ireland has already produced its quota.'[571] The next day's edition carried the heading 'MPs refuse offer of torture charge inquiry.'[572] But this is misleading, as the text details politicians refusing a *private* hearing while continuing to demand a public inquiry. The reader might be forgiven for concluding the accusers have little belief in their charges. While the cardinal was challenged to come up with the evidence, the *Guardian* accepted, without comment, the army refutation of further allegations levelled by John Hume MP: 'But as there had been no formal complaints, no further information would be given.'[573] The editor's office had previously mocked French government protests of no formal complaints as a feeble excuse. In any case, on the same page the reader is directed to certain characteristics of the accusing lawyers: 'Sceptics might fairly point out that the Association for Legal Justice is an almost wholly Roman Catholic

567   *Guardian*, 12 August 1971.
568   Ibid., 16 August 1971.
569   Ibid.
570   Ibid. 16 August 1971 (editorial).
571   Ibid., 18 October 1971 (editorial).
572   Ibid., 19 October 1971.
573   Ibid., 18 August 1971.

body.'[574] Irish Catholics are less credible than French Catholics. Hetherington-Cole, on the following day, defended this scepticism, claiming they had many examples of the Irish predilection for making up allegations against soldiers, and pointing out that propaganda is integral to the 'war in Ulster'.[575] They did not supply any of the many examples, but the scepticism was reinforced with another unattributed story: 'One woman told a reporter that a soldier had picked up her small child and swung it round by the heels; our reporter was in a position where he could see that no soldier entered the house in question.'[576] Hetherington-Cole were keen to discredit any accusations of British torture.

While the accusations continued, the editorial position remained steadfast. 'The allegations are neither proved nor wholly credible … a public inquiry cannot be granted.'[577] But on 9 November 1971 Amnesty International published prima facie evidence of torture. Two days later the *Guardian* responded robustly. The following five extracts are from this source.[578] In contrast to its reproach of independent international bodies for being too mild in their investigations of the French, Amnesty was reproached for being too zealous in its investigation of the British. 'Brick-bats were hurled at Amnesty for departing from its clinical role.' Three aspects of Amnesty's tactics 'have raised eyebrows and sent people racing to the microphones.' The first eyebrow-raiser was that the report 'came out more quickly than usual, increasing the suspicion that Amnesty is becoming more political.' Clearly, it would be hard to avoid the political when dealing with human rights abuses. The second eyebrow-raiser was that 'it was published a week before the Compton Tribunal which has brought a charge of provocation.' It was never explained why Amnesty's efforts to highlight torture as soon as possible were provocative. The third eyebrow-raiser was a concern that 'allegations tend to become condensed into facts.' This, of course, can be directed at Hetherington-Cole and their unattributed stories. The whole pattern of coverage downgraded the credibility of the accusations.

'No one seems to have been seriously injured or even slightly injured'
Still the accusations continued. Detailed publications by human rights

574   Ibid.
575   Ibid., 19 August 1971 (editorial).
576   Ibid.19 August 1971.
577   Ibid., 20 October 1971 (editorial).
578   Ibid., 11 November 1971.

campaigners Fr Raymond Murray and Fr Denis Faul (both IRA critics) alleging torture, brutality and drugging of suspects were, said an army spokesman, 'on the face of it, incredible'.[579] In spite of thousands of official complaints and millions of pounds paid in compensation, army denials were accepted uncritically. The *Guardian* reported without comment the British government's view that the Compton Tribunal 'was itself a better way of taking the steam out of the propaganda campaign'.[580] This stated intention of protecting the army in an inquiry supposedly mandated to uncover the truth was completely ignored. In Algeria, the *Guardian* had reprinted, approvingly, large sections of the accusations made by the Catholic *Témoignage Chrétien* and the accusations of Sartre, Simone de Beauvoir, Henri Alleg, Jean-Jacques Servan-Schreiber, Pierre-Henri Simon and Jules Roy. In Ireland, the publications of Catholic clergy and lawyers were deemed IRA propaganda. Hetherington-Cole's editorials continued to defend the army: 'It could also be said in defence of the procedures that no-one seems to have been seriously injured or evenly slightly injured.'[581] For sentiments like this the *Guardian* had ridiculed General Massu.

There is a pattern to the downgrading. Consider the following seven extracts.[582] The detainees were: simply 'tired out', 'subject to noise', 'boredom was the worst part', 'if only they'd had little tasks to do', some were 'bounced about a little', some wounds were 'old boils or self-inflicted'. Peter Jenkins thought Conservative backbenchers 'probably suffered far worse methods of interrogation at their public schools.' Hetherington-Cole maintained the accusations were simply propaganda and that any 'discomfort' was insignificant compared with the lives it would save and recommended: 'vigorous and tough interrogation must go on.'[583] This echoed Prime Minister Edward Heath's response to the mild criticism of the Compton Report that the hooding would be discontinued but in-depth interrogation would continue. In fact, both hooding and torture continued.

Astor held to the template of a restrained British army: 'accidents and rumours of brutalities are inseparable from an operation of this kind ... The Army is, in fact, showing extraordinary restraint.'[584] The *Guardian* defended Compton's denial of torture, with Roy Hattersley

579 Ibid., 21 January 1972.
580 Ibid., 17 November 1971.
581 Ibid., 3 March 1972 (editorial).
582 Ibid., 8 August, 18, 19, 20 October, 17 November 1971, 21 January, 3 March, 6, 8 May, 10 August 1972.
583 Ibid., 17 November 1971 (editorial).
584 *Observer*, 22 August 1971 (editorial).

MP concluding that the report's justifications were 'remarkably frank'.[585] They were, in fact, ludicrous. Peter Jenkins wrote: 'internment and systematic interrogation are powerful and *legitimate weapons* where a military victory is obtainable.'[586] When evidence of mental damage became public, Hetherington-Cole would only acknowledge: 'There is reason to suppose that heavy mental pressure brought about in this way can aggravate for months or years afterwards any latent tendencies to depression.'[587] The overwhelming weight of the coverage supported the official narrative and downgraded the allegations as propaganda.[588]

Astor shifted some blame away from Britain: 'Nowhere does Compton establish who was responsible … it appears to have been [unionist Prime Minister] Mr. Faulkner … the interrogators were men of the Ulster Constabulary.'[589] Westminster remained clean. It was the settlers again. But we know now it was authorised by Lord Carrington, and Heath and Maudling both knew. The *Observer* also accepts uncritically what it never accepted in Algeria: 'the army says the intelligence gained is the ultimate justification for the interrogation in depth.'[590] More damning, British soldiers did not even seek the ticking bomb justification. The army's justification was that its methods were designed to uncover IRA organisational structure. These credulous and supportive stands were subsequently undermined, on 2 September 1976, when the ECHR ruled the five techniques as: 'not only of inhuman and degrading treatment but also of torture.'[591] British refinement of these techniques, as previously noted, provided the precedent for the Bush administration legalising torture in exceptional circumstances in Guantánamo Bay and Abu Ghraib.[592]

585 *Guardian*, 18 November 1971.

586 Ibid., 25 October 1971, my emphasis.

587 For examples of credibility afforded British officials and hostility to the accusers, see *Guardian*, 8, 12, 16 (editorial), 18, 19 (editorial), 21 August, 2 September, 18 (editorial), 19, 20, 25 October, 11, 13, 15, 17 (editorial), 18 (editorial), 22 (editorial), 24, 29 November (editorial), 10, 11, 15, 16, 20 December 1971, 1 January, 3 March, 6,8 May, 9 September 1972,13 March, 14 August, 24 November 1973.

588 Ibid., 29 November 1971 (editorial).

589 *Observer*, 21 November 1971 (editorial).

590 Ibid., 30 January 1972.

591 ECHR case 5310/71 Ireland v United Kingdom.

592 Following the coverage in late 1971, both newspapers rarely reported the issue. In response to the ECHR torture verdict, *Guardian* headlines of 3 September 1976 read: 'Dublin feels Rees' fury' and 'Why Ireland dragged Britain in the dock'. On 18 January 1978 the ECrtHR ruled the interrogations to be 'inhuman and degrading treatment'. The *Guardian* editorial of 19 January 1978 crowed under the heading 'The price of bidding too high'. The Bush administration used this distinction to justify its interrogation centres in Guantánamo Bay and Abu Ghraib; 'Nobody is talking', *Guardian*, 18 February 2005.

Conclusion

French officers condemned torture. Others justified it while distancing the army. ALN atrocities provoked the worst cases. They believed Paris winked at it but there was no explicit order. The methods were developed from the bottom up. It is not clear whether this relative honesty was due to concern for Arab human rights or the prestige of the army. British accounts are different. The systemic brutality of their interrogations, and the centralised and sophisticated approach organised by their superiors at the Ministry of Defence and ordered by government was justified or downplayed. British soldiers also distanced the army from the worst excesses. Official British inquiries justified the methods.

The respective portrayals once again reveal a stark dichotomy. The French have brought shame on themselves. The British have done nothing to be ashamed of. French interrogations were torture and not rough handling. Credibility was afforded to the accusers. Official French sources were treated with a healthy scepticism. Justificatory arguments were rejected. Accusations of British torture were rejected as IRA propaganda or unavoidable excesses, even schoolboy antics. Official British sources were accepted and defended. In Algeria, French Catholic accusations of torture were highlighted. In Ireland, accusations of torture were rejected because it was Catholics making them. The other side, the IRA, was indeed so much worse. Much later, former RUC interrogators admitted torture, saying it was: 'time to set the historical record straight.'[593] The RUC was rewriting the Troubles.

---

593   We got confessions by torture, *Guardian* 11 Oct 2010, Senior officers were especially concerned about leaving no marks. https://www.theguardian.com/uk/2010/oct/11/inside-castlereagh-confessions-torture accessed 9 September 2020.

CHAPTER SEVEN

Algerie, C'est La France; Ireland, a Nearby Country About Which we Know Nothing

This chapter measures public support for the army and any public opposition to army methods or government policies. The words and actions of religious leaders, political spokespersons, public figures and intellectuals are examined to assess the public mood. The activities of student associations and the pronouncements and demonstrations of organised labour help to broaden our understanding of how society viewed the conflict(s). The exchanges and public debates among soldiers and senior officers permit some insight into their own mood and how they perceived government policy and their own conduct. The comparative portrayals in the liberal press are then held up to the record and this testimony and commentary.

The French
The techniques recommended for fighting terrorism
Servan-Schreiber's semi-fictional *Lieutenant in Algeria* shows some officers justifying repression as French humiliation on losing Algeria would lead to fascism. Other soldiers were critical. Still, he does not use the word torture. 'Often, we all came close to the essence of the problem ... but we were careful to stop just short.'[594] One officer, Galland, went straight to the sensitive spot 'on the technique recommended for fighting terrorism ... shameful methods.'[595] To have used the word torture would have formalised the breach and set it down

---

594   Servan Schreiber, *Lieutenant in Algeria,* (Westport: Greenwood, 1977), p. 200.
595   ibid.

for history. Although critical, he sympathises with frontline soldiers as pawns in a political and historical context. He rejected any comparison with SS methods as communist propaganda. French journalist Roger Faligot reported the same reluctance to condemn completely: "'I can't let it be said," declared Col Simoneau, "that intelligence was obtained by massacring people ... I had attached police officers to supervise the legality of the interrogations.'"[596]

Gradually, the controversy over torture, the death of young conscripts and the cost of holding Algeria started to shatter the myth that Algeria was France. In regular columns in *Le Figaro* Raymond Aron questioned whether colonial possessions made economic sense. Raymond Cartier, in *Paris Match*, reminded the government that wealthy Switzerland never had a square metre overseas.

Henri Alleg's *La Question* had an enormous impact. His personal account of torture was published by Editions de Minuit, a publisher holding a special place in France since its secret establishment under Nazi occupation. The French people faced being implicated, as Germans were, by what the army and government did in their name. Alleg's book sold 150,000 copies even with the government ban. Pierre Vidal-Naquet established a committee to inquire into the disappearance of Maurice Audin, a *pieds-noirs* activist sympathetic to Algerian independence. Torture was disturbing France and extending to an international audience.

A war against terror and colonial privilege
Paratrooper Pierre Leulliette rationalised that official codes of conduct were phrased in such a way that everyone understood to read between the lines. Although remarkably frank about torture, he, too, distances the French and points to the German legionnaires in the Villa Sesini. It even developed into sport with no pretence of seeking information, sometimes just to humiliate prosperous Muslims. Leulliette tried discussing his Algerian experience when home on leave but it challenged their high opinion of France: 'Ignorance is another form of guilt.'[597]

Jules Roy, another veteran, was distressed by stories of atrocities. The French could understand anyone 'taking up arms against England ... but against "us", the first to free the slaves, the first to promulgate the equality of all before the law?'[598] He condemned army excesses but

---

596   R. Faligot, *La Piscine,* (Oxford, Blackwell, 1989), p. 123.
597   P. Leulliette, *St Michael and the Dragon,* (London: Heinemann, 1964), p. 242.
598   J. Roy, *The War in Algeria* (NY, Grove, 1961), p. 106.

warned the FLN that France did not understand what it was accused of or why its sons were being killed. France cannot be wrong because she is France. Respecting the ideals of the French Republic required condemnation of army units resorting to torture. He virtually conceded French responsibility and urged Muslims to remain 'linked to a rich old aunt who is paying for the follies of her youth.'[599] He saw no difference between French or FLN atrocities. Letters from conscripts detailed their disgust. The Comité Résistance Spirituelle (Catholic priests) published them in *Des Rappelés Témoignent* (Conscripts Testify). One legionnaire even compared army conduct to the infamous Nazi reprisals in the village of Oradour sur Glane, a particularly sensitive comparison in France. French farmers also protested vociferously against the legionnaires for killing agricultural workers: 'Even the *fellagha* respect the harvest. Vandals, murderers, is this how you pacify?'[600] There was also vigorous opposition within the French Socialist Party. Socialist Prime Minister Guy Mollet had initially favoured a ceasefire and negotiation, but had changed after the infamous *journée des tomates*, and began pursuing repression before reform. The governing socialists attempted to preserve party unity by claiming the war was against colonial privileges and terrorist outrages.

An interrogation without joy, but without shame
General Massu initially justified torture. But General Pâris de Bollardière, one of his highest-ranking officers, would not permit it and resigned his command. Massu wrote two autobiographical accounts of the war. The first, *La Vraie Bataille d'Alger*, he wrote to counter both Gillo Pontecorvo's docudrama *Battle of Algiers* and the publication of *Souvenirs de la Bataille d'Alger* by his FLN opponent and *bête noire* Yacef Saadi. He next wrote *Le Torrent et la Digue* to counter media portrayals of the army. Massu claimed torture was necessary to obtain life-saving information. The chaplain, Père Delarue, advised paratroopers that their conscience dictated they protect the innocent against assassins. The situation demanded unaccustomed but effective methods: 'an interrogation without sadism but efficacious ... without joy but also without shame.'[601] Massu later reconsidered, declaring torture was not indispensable and the military benefit was negligible.

---

599   Ibid., p. 127.
600   A. Horne, *A Savage War of Peace* (London: Macmillan, 1977), p. 115.
601   R. Maran, *Torture* (NY, Praeger, 1989), p. 98.

General de Bollardière wrote his *Bataille d'Alger, Bataille de L'homme* to counter the supposed necessity of torture in exceptional circumstances. Torture was a terrible deformation of France's mission, the propagating of the rights of man. He argued the government had abandoned its responsibility, traditions and honour. Refusing torture was his way of forcing the army to dialogue again with the local population. His resignation led to the establishment of a *Commission de Sauvegarde des Droits et des Libertés Individuelles*. Many French villages and towns, including Paris, honoured de Bollardière with a street name.

Colonel Roger Trinquier was central in confronting the ALN's civilian bombing. He publicly stated torture was justified. *Le Monde, L'Express, France Observateur* and especially the Catholic *Témoignage Chrétien* were outraged. The French press devoted more space to the issue of torture than firefights in the desert. Criticism of army methods came from the left (Claude Bourdet in *France Observateur*, Jean Paul Sartre in *Les Temps Moderne*) and the right (Raymond Aron in *Le Figaro*). Raymond Cartier in *Paris Match* and Catholic intellectuals such as François Mauriac in *L'Express* added to the pressure. But Michael Clark of the *New York Times* disapproved of 'armchair moralists', who put the law above all other considerations. It denied people their right to protection, often to life itself: 'Paris was swarming with such moralists.'[602] He was dismayed by Catholic intellectuals such as Mauriac, Robert Barratt and Louis Massignon, and a good sprinkling of French Protestants, who all argued the repression was worse than the rebellion. Critics of the army included cardinals in France and many bishops in Algeria. Paul Teitgen, the *prefecture* of Algiers, argued strongly for the punishing and imprisoning of soldiers. Camus, Vidal-Naquet and Germaine Tillion condemned the atrocities of both sides. Sartre and Conor Cruise O'Brien (at the Irish embassy in Paris) argued that the ALN, fighting the French coloniser state, was justified in using its weaker resources with fewer moral restrictions.[603] Sartre argued ALN atrocities were a reaction: 'for at first it is not *their* violence, it is ours.'[604] Such was the criticism of the army that the government censored more than 250 books, newspapers and films.[605]

---

602   M. Clark, *Algeria in Turmoil* (NY, Grosset, 1960), p. 327.

603   Fanon, *Wretched of the Earth*, (Penguin 2001), pp. 7-26.

604   Fanon, *Wretched*, p. 16.

605   *Le Monde Diplomatic*, April 2001, https://mondediplo.com/2001/04/04algeriatorture

The British

Perfectly legal to shoot anyone who was the 'Queen's enemy'

In Britain among the officer class, the Cabinet, senior politicians and judiciary, there was widespread support for the army's methods. General Mike Jackson attributed this to the influence of Brigadier Frank Kitson whose prescriptions borrowed heavily from Trinquier's experience in Algeria. Wars of liberation supposedly emanated from Moscow and the real battle would be fought at home. Conservative MP John Biggs-Davison opined: 'if we lose in Belfast we may have to fight in Brixton or Birmingham'.[606]

Publicly, the British government maintained it was not a war, but frequently the façade was breached. When the ECHR condemned Britain's excessive use of lethal force in the killing of unarmed IRA activists in Gibraltar, Defence Minister Michael Portillo boasted to a wildly enthusiastic Conservative Party conference that three letters send a chill down the spine of Britain's enemies: 'SAS ... Don't mess with Britain.'[607]. In contrast, Auberon Waugh, a journalist traditionally on the political right, mocked the 'poodles of the press', and wondered whether Mrs Thatcher believed she could now send 'murder gangs galloping across Europe.'[608] Mark Urban explained undercover soldiers did not believe it necessary to even pretend they issued warnings before opening fire. He quotes one soldier: 'I do not object to this policy of shooting without warning ... I just wish the government had the balls to admit it.'[609] Senior officers were of the same view. General Timothy Creasy arrived in Ireland in 1977 after a 'private contract' suppressing a rebellion in Oman. His whole experience had been of putting down small-scale colonial rebellions. He soon made his views known: 'stop messing around and take out the terrorists.'[610] In Oman he said, they just disappeared. He was reminded that bodies might disappear into Oman's endless desert, but in Belfast, he would have to dig through the tarmac. It would require careful public management.

And managed it was. In April 1974 soldiers arrived at Patrick McElhone's home and shot dead this innocent civilian in front of his parents. No one was held accountable, much to the anger of the Irish government, which despaired it would boost IRA recruitment.[611] The

606 Faligot, *Kitson Experiment*, p. 3.
607 Miller, *Re-thinking Northern Ireland*, (NY, Longmans, 1998), p. 104.
608 *Spectator*, September 1988, p. 24.
609 Urban, *Big Boys Rules*, (London, Faber, 1992), p. 76.
610 Hamill, *Pig in the Middle*, (London, Methuen, 1985), p. 221.
611 McKittrick, *Lost Lives*, (Edinburgh, Mainstream, 199), pp. 470-1.

McElhone killing became a landmark case when the judge ruled it legal for soldiers to shoot anyone provided they thought the target was a 'terrorist'. Kitson can help explain this. He elaborated two alternative uses of the law during counterinsurgency. In one 'The law is just another weapon in the government's arsenal ... a propaganda cover for the disposal of unwanted members of the public ... to be tied into the war effort in as discreet a way as possible.'[612] The alternative was for the law to act impartially. The army's killing of another civilian, William McGreanery, is again instructive. Police Chief Superintendent Frank Lagan called for the prosecution of the soldier. This was overruled by the unionist attorney general Basil Kelly. As early as December 1971 Kelly had initiated a policy of impunity when he ruled that no soldier could be prosecuted for murder or anything he did in the course of his duty. 'Soldier A whether he acted wrongly or not, was at all times acting in the course of his duty and I cannot see how the malice, necessary to constitute murder, could be applied to his conduct.' [613] This indemnity appeared just six weeks before Bloody Sunday.

Shortly after Bloody Sunday, PM Edward Heath explained to General Carver that 'it was perfectly legal for the army to shoot somebody whether or not they were being shot at because anybody who obstructed or got in the way of the armed forces of the Queen was, by that very act, the Queen's enemy.'[614] He assured Carver the government was acting on the advice of the Cabinet's legal luminary. This was Lord Hailsham, descended from one of the oldest elite settler families of the Ulster plantation. When *Irish Times* journalist Conor O'Clery asked him about Irish-American politicians questioning Britain, he exploded: 'Those Roman Catholic bastards! How dare they interfere?'[615] These attitudes, prevailing in the judiciary, government and senior officers, filtered down to the ranks. Kitson, known as 'killer' to his friends,[616] criticised Colonel Wilford for not going far enough on Bloody Sunday.[617]

---

612 Adapting the law to counterinsurgency, F. Kitson, *Low Intensity Operations* (London: Faber, 1971), p. 69.

613 *Derry Journal*, 4 June 2010. See also www.patfinucanecentre.org/cases/mcgreanl (accessed July 2015).

614 Coogan, *The Troubles,* (St. Martins, 2002), p. 135.

615 *Irish Times*, 27 August 2009.

616 *Guardian* 21 January 1972.

617 Jackson, *Soldier*, (Transworld, 2007), p. 101.

Prejudice, the blindspot and an impervious mess-hall culture

Alan Williams once regaled me with another of his many war correspondent experiences: 'We were all at Free Derry corner gathered round a very impressive officer. A German correspondent I knew from Algeria, goaded him: "Tell me, Colonel, does the Queen's writ still run in the Kasbah?" We all fell about laughing.'[618] Senior officers chaffed at this indignity of IRA 'no-go' areas cocking a snoop at them. According to Colonel Evelegh, government 'orders to operate in low profile meant orders not to enforce the law'.[619] He complained that ministers did not have an unlimited right of discretion as to when to enforce the law. Such indulgences relieve criminals of legal consequences. London, as well as Derry's teenage hooligans, needed reminding of the law. Evelegh need not have worried. The words of British Prime Minister Ted Heath, on accepting Widgery's mildly critical report of Bloody Sunday, revealed that he, too, favoured a loose rein on the army.

Hamill's interviews show that after an initial euphoria on Bloody Sunday, some doubt crept in. When the numbers of civilian dead increased and there were still no reports of army deaths or even injury, one officer warned: 'I wouldn't cheer so loudly. There is something very wrong here.'[620] While they all agreed that Derry's hooligans should get a 'good hiding', and a forceful General Ford was on the ground and determined to have a success, some officers felt the paratroopers had lost control. Although Widgery cleared the soldiers, many were upset the dead were found to be unarmed. In army mythology, RUC forensic teams were too slow and lost necessary evidence. But others saw locally recruited soldiers and police as unusually motivated. One soldier, serving alongside the RUC and UDR, was astonished by their virulent anti-Catholic bigotry. Loyalists, however, 'were always mentioned in terms of approval.'[621]

Senior officers habitually backed their soldiers no matter their conduct. In 1972 a patrol of the 1st Battalion Argyll and Sutherland Highlanders in Fermanagh slashed to death two Catholics – Michael Naan suffered seventeen stab wounds and had his throat cut; Andrew Murray was stabbed thirteen times. That regiment's figurehead was Lieutenant Colonel 'Mad Mitch' Mitchell of Yemen/Aden infamy. For

618 Interview, Alan Williams (London), July 1998.
619 Evelegh, *Peacekeeping in a Democratic Society,* (London, Hurst, 1978), p. 17.
620 Hamill, *Pig in the Middle,* p. 91.
621 O'Mahony, *Soldier of the Queen,* (Brandon, 2000), p. 125.

nine years and for 'the good of the regiment', Captain Andrew Snowball covered up the brutal 'pitchfork murders' of the two civilians. Snowball later received a suspended sentence. He still attends regimental dinners of the Argyll and Sutherland Highlanders.[622] For thirty years, Colonel Derek Wilford publicly maintained he had seen a rifleman on Bloody Sunday. At the Saville Inquiry, he admitted this was not true. He still holds his OBE for services rendered. In 2007 General Mike Jackson wrote he had no doubt that his soldiers had come under fire on Bloody Sunday. But three years earlier, the MoD had already accepted that none of the twenty-seven victims had been armed. After a severe mauling at the Saville Inquiry by Michael Mansfield QC, Jackson finally admitted that the victims were innocent. But General Peter de la Billière maintains yet the self-serving myths. In 1978 the SAS shot dead sixteen-year-old John Boyle. There was a court case. The judge ruled the youth was an unarmed civilian. The police, and even Ian Paisley, were furious with the army's ineptitude. Not so, wrote de la Billière; the youth was a member of the IRA who had pointed an automatic rifle at a squad of elite soldiers.[623] He did not explain how this youth had uncovered the SAS covert surveillance post. When Gerry Fitt MP tried to raise this he was shouted down in the House of Commons. Roy Mason MP backed the soldiers with Airey Neave MP nodding agreement.[624]

Army background papers also reveal a deep-rooted anti-Irish prejudice. These documents, produced for internal use, supposedly provided officers with a comprehensive picture of the Irish. Accordingly, it was not true to say that the Irish could not listen to reason because frequently the 'logical, reasonable argument used by an Englishman was a set of irrelevant platitudes to an Irishman.'[625] Once a soldier properly understood this (gibberish, essentially), Irish 'actions, words, thoughts and feelings are as understandable and predictable as are those of any other people.'[626] Doubtless, the Irish would be glad to be welcomed to the human race. These internal papers held further gems. Irish mothers had little concept of the right or wrong way to bring up a family; it was just something they did. Family feuds and squabbles were common but ranks always closed on outsiders. World events meant nothing to them, only the pope and the US provoked a mild

---

622 McKittrick et al, *Lost Lives,* pp. 286–7.
623 De la Billière, *Looking for Trouble* (London: Harper-Collins, 1994), pp. 315-316.
624 R Murray, *The SAS in Ireland,* (Mercier, 2004), p. 233.
625 Hamill, *Pig in the Middle,* p. 125.
626 Ibid.

interest. The Irish were not great respecters of persons. But people who got things done could command their attention. This included army officers and NCOs. 'There is always a great cry for the major', the highest rank they can expect access to.[627] These unselfconscious attitudes of prejudice and condescension permeated British army training manuals at the end of the twentieth century. Soldiers often acted as though they were in a colonial-type situation, and, indeed, many had experience of Aden, Kenya, Malaya and Oman.[628]

Former British Labour Party Cabinet minister Roy Hattersley, on national television, explained that torture could be justified, in some situations when it could help save 'hundreds of lives'.[629] The judiciary also helped. Only one of the Hooded Men, Paddy Joe McLean, a founding member of the Civil Rights Movement, was called to give evidence at the Compton inquiry. His lawyer was not allowed to cross-examine any of the state's witnesses – up to one hundred British soldiers and RUC. 'So perturbed by Compton's proceedings were the authorities in Northern Ireland that Liam Shannon and Davy Rodgers were arrested and subjected to hooded-men torture while Compton was [still] at work …'[630] Anti-torture campaigners like Fr Raymond Murray were 'a tiny minority' and from the Protestant Churches 'there was silence.'[631] The Catholic Church was not much better. In a statement mildly critical of torture the bishops apologised for having to mention internment at all: 'Many Protestants in Northern Ireland – good Christian people – will not like our mentioning these things.'[632] Joe Hendron, SDLP politician and a medical doctor, knew one in three prisoners endured brutal interrogations but did not want 'to give the Provos [any] propaganda, so I didn't go public.'[633]

Paul Rose, of the 1960s Campaign for Democracy in Ulster, was parliamentary secretary to Cabinet minister Barbara Castle. She had publicly criticised British army 'excesses' in Cyprus and Kenya and those of the French army in Algeria to the point of irking Alistair Horne: 'Mrs Barbara Castle explained pedantically that terrorism was the result

---

627 Ibid.

628 Kitson's *Gangs and Countergang i*s a product of his activities in Kenya. General Harry Tuzo, born in India served in Borneo and Kenya, General Timothy Creasey commissioned into (British) India Army, served in Aden, Oman and Kenya, General Peter de al Billière served in Egypt, Oman and Malaya.

629 Ackroyd et al, *Technology of Political Control,* pp. 230-1.

630 *Irish Times* 25 July 2015.

631 *The Irish Catholic* 14 November 2013.

632 McVeigh, *A Wounded Church,* (Cork, Mercier, 1998), p. 83.

633 Ross, *Smashing H-Block* (Liverpool University Press, 2011), p. 32.

of repression not its cause.'[634] However, Castle advised Rose to concentrate on Vietnam rather than Ireland. He remembers her as totally oblivious to what was going on in her own backyard. With exceptions such as Kevin McNamara, Paul Rose, James Wellbeloved, Gareth Pierce, Ken Livingstone, George Galloway, Chris Mullin, Michael Mansfield, Lord Gifford, Jane Winter, Paul Foot, Tony Benn, Jeremy Corbyn, and the Troops Out Movement, few in Britain defended human rights in Ireland. The British left ignored Ireland. Its leading journal, the *New Left Review*, barely mentioned the conflict between 1970 and 1994, finally breaking its silence with an article critical of Irish nationalism.

The Liberal Press
The French: informed and engaged, despite their restricted media
A front-page report in the *Guardian* highlighted government control of French radio that suppressed political discussion and made criticism of Algerian policy impossible. French broadcasting was not protected from government intervention by a charter like the BBC. The prime minister's office was always in contact with news departments: 'Algeria was the centre of the sacrosanct zone, protected by pressure on radio, self-censorship in most of the daily press and threats of police action against the recalcitrant.'[635] The French government intimidated any journalist who dared criticise its policy. Bill Millinship remembers: 'We always had minders from the Quai d'Orsay [Foreign Affairs] who read everything we wrote ... The army once excluded the *Observer* from one of de Gaulle's tours ... we were considered very pro-FLN.'[636] Both the *Guardian* and the *Observer* regularly reported examples of French government pressure and seizure [637] Interviews with FLN leaders were impossible. Operating under such constraints, the partisan French coverage created a great deal of Muslim bitterness: 'crimes committed

---

634 Horne, *Savage War*, p. 244. Horne rejects Britain tortured in Ireland but accepts US sensory deprivation and physical brutality, in Abu Ghraib, is torture.

635 *Guardian*, 8 December 1956, May (editorial).

636 Interview, Bill Millinship (London), July 1998.

637 Examples of government pressure and OAS intimidation of journalists and the seizure of *L'Express, L'Humanité, France-Observateur, Les Temps Modernes* can be found in the *Guardian*, 8 December 1956, 16, 19 March, 26 April, 23 May 1957, 28 February, 7, 10 March 1958, 1 October 1959, 22 April, 16 September 1960, 17, 18 February 4 May, 20 June, 18 August, 25 September 1961, 7, 16 February 1962, and in the *Observer*, 23 June, 11 August 1957, 16 March 1958, 2 October 1960. For example: the 'seizure of *L'Express* containing an interview with Ferhat Abbas', *Guardian*, 16 September 1960, or 'the OAS bomb on the Catholic *Témoignage Chrétien*', *Guardian*, 25 September 1961.

by rebels were given great publicity but any committed on the other side were hushed up.'[638] Hetherington highlighted an obvious French flaw: 'typically there was press silence or evasion on state killings or army misconduct'.[639] This might be compared with Chapter Five, which detailed his own newspaper's routine printing of the British army's false versions when it killed civilians. In spite of the restrictions under which the French media laboured, the reader of the British liberal press would learn that Algeria has somehow produced 'a deep disturbance in the moral conscience of the French people.'[640] The Abbe de Cosse Brissal wrote in *L'Express*: 'We are all torturers if by a collusive silence we allow it to happen.'[641] Contrasting with the editorial line, the reader can find many examples in both newspapers of active French opposition to government policy in Algeria, including the Jeanson Network. These metropolitan French, *porteurs de valises,* intended to uphold the ideals of the French Republic by opposing the colonial war. They smuggled arms, men, documents and money for the FLN. In the summer of 1960, a group of prominent French intellectuals ignited a huge public debate by publishing their 'Manifesto of 121'. They claimed conscripts had the right to desert, condemned army torture, and declared the Algerians were fighting a war of national liberation. FLN leaders, including Ben Bella, were so moved that they declared the manifesto demonstrated: 'greatness still existed in France ... the war was not the sum of the French people ... We admired them, we loved them.'[642]

In the pages of the liberal Catholic weekly *Témoignage Chrétien*, Catholic intellectuals such as François Mauriac and André Mandouze and journalists such as Robert Barrat waged a vigorous campaign for Algerian independence. They denounced abuses by both the army and the ALN. Its one thousandth issue included Ben Bella's best wishes: 'Algerians know the part played by real Christians in our liberation struggle.'[643] President Bourguiba of Tunisia wrote that *Témoignage Chrétien* rallied 'precious support for our cause, support which had hesitated to show itself.'[644] Ted Morgan recalled his war experience as

---

638 *Guardian*, 21 December 1956.

639 Examples of French-press silence or evasion regarding French wrongdoing can be found in the *Guardian*, 21 December 1956, 2 January, 14, 16 June (editorial), 24 October 1958, 1 October 1959, 18 January 1962, and in the *Observer*, 2 October 1960.

640 *Observer*, 6 June 1960.

641 *Guardian*, 9 July 1960; *Observer*, 26 June 1960.

642 J. Cooley, *Baal, Christ and Mohammed* (London, John Murray, 1965), p. 314.

643 *Témoignage Chrétien,* 5 September 1963.

644 ibid.

a staff writer on the army's weekly *Réalitiés Algériennes*. When not otherwise engaged in writing up the prowess of the paratroopers, staff writers secretly gave details of army excesses to *Témoignage Chrétien*. Pamphlets circulated among conscripts reminding them of their recent experience under the Nazis. The French army was posited as occupiers, and conscripts were urged not to fire on their Arab brothers.

Student organisations protested so much that the government withdrew state subsidies. Sartre and de Beauvoir wrote articles and organised petitions. Picasso produced works of art critical of government policy. Television journalists, French film stars and writers protested publicly. Catholic priests and Protestant ministers were arrested at demonstrations. The protestors included the resistance hero and government advisor Germaine Tillion. Professors cancelled classes and universities united in coordinated protests. On several occasions millions of workers downed tools in one-day strike actions to protest the war. Dock workers refused to load army supplies bound for Algeria.[645] On two occasions all French newspapers, from left to right, united in sympathy with the plight of Djamila Bouhired and Djamila Boupacha. Both were mistakenly believed to have been tortured.[646] 'News from Algeria that the government would have preferred to downplay was often highlighted in France and significant public debate followed.

The British: don't know and don't want to know, in spite of an 'unrestricted' media

Newspapers might be seized in Paris but not in Britain. The *Observer* seconded the *Guardian*'s gratitude for the BBC's charter. Attacking the French government's censure of intellectuals who called on soldiers to disobey orders, its 'Comment' column warned: 'the affair illustrates the danger of having radio and television services under direct state control.'[647] The British public was doubly blessed. In addition to the BBC, they had a second source of truth. Orwell himself had singled out the *Guardian* for its honesty. However, the iconic BBC had sat on

---

645 Examples of the French public's opposition to government policy or a military solution can be found in the *Guardian*, 19 November 1956, 18 March, 20 April 1957, 22. October 1958, 30 May, 6, 11, 13, 30 June, 11 July, 9, 27 September, 3 November 1960, 18 March, 7, 16 December 1961, 1, 13 January, 7, 15, 23 February, 23 April, 29 November 1962, and in the *Observer*, 5 August 1957, 19 January, 20 April 1958, 31 January, 29 May, 12, 16 June, 18 September, 9, 23 October 1960, 18 April 1962; for example, '11 million Frenchmen went on a symbolic one day strike in protest against the methods of terror being followed in Algeria', *Guardian*, 25 March 1962.

646 *Guardian*, 14 March 1958; *Observer*, 22 April 1962.

647 *Observer*, 2 October 1960.

evidence of British torture. The *Times* reported first. The BBC then followed with careful and somewhat antagonistic interviews of relatives of the brutalised internees.[648]

The British government had little need to worry. Criticism of its policy in Ireland by the British left amounted to the 'silence of the lambs', in Paddy Hillyard's memorable words.[649] Notably, British prime ministers Harold Macmillan and James Callaghan both praised the press for its discretion, understanding and knowing its limits. In 1972 General William Jackson thanked journalists at the Northern Command's annual press luncheon: 'soldiers in Ireland are encouraged by appreciative coverage of their work.'[650] The letters page of the *Guardian* provides further examples of self-congratulation of both the *Guardian* and British character: '... British compromise and sweet reason of the kind so graphically and nobly epitomized by the columns of your own newspaper.'[651] And the *Guardian* did not take kindly to any other view. When journalist Eamonn McCann criticised its reporting of Ireland, his analysis was not addressed at all. The 'rebuttal' amounted to an accusation that 'the touch of sulphur lingers' around McCann.[652]

Yet, in spite of a media free from the overt government pressure, the reader would learn that, of Ireland, the British public knows nothing. Further, it does not want to know.[653] An early *Observer* editorial, entitled 'Ulster: Britain's Alabama', pointed out 'the people of this country, for many of whom, sadly, Ulster is a far-away country about which they don't want to know.'[654] When the British do think of Ireland, they 'agonise at the blind sectarianism of the Irish'[655] or wonder at 'the fathomless perversity of the Irish'.[656] In 1972 Roy Hattersley wrote that the British were mystified as to whether there is not 'something inherent in the Irish themselves that national content has not been established.'[657]

---

648 *Guardian*, 7 October 1958, 23 November, 30 December 1971, 6 January 1972.
649 P Hillyard, The Silence of the Lambs, British academics and the Northern Ireland problem, paper for the biennial *British Association of Irish Studies Conference*, University of Sunderland, 1995.
650 *Guardian*, 20 December 1972.
651 Ibid., 4 September 1973. For examples of the British sense of their own perfection, see *Observer*, 11 August, 6 October 1968, 16 February 1969.
651 Ibid., 21 October 1971.
653 Examples of ignorance of Ireland or bored and tired of the Irish can be found in the *Guardian*, 26 April, 28 August 1971, 11 July, 4, 24 October, 17, 21 November 1972, 27 June 1973, 25 April, 14 May 1974, and in the *Observer*, 10 August 1969, 29 August 1971, 25 March, 1 July 1973.
654 *Observer*, 10 August 1969 (editorial).
655 *Guardian*, 13 August 1971.
656 Ibid., 14 July 1972.
657 Ibid., 5 January 1972.

This resembles Spenser's sixteenth-century assessment of Ireland's 'unquiet state'. Britain's basic benevolence is a constant. Simon Winchester's 'from a British or moderate point of view' reveals this as almost second nature.[658] Lord Stonham, a Home Office minister, encouraged a delegation of Irish politicians visiting London to voice their concerns over government policy: 'But you are British and to be British is the greatest heritage you could have.'[659] Their response was not recorded.

The *Observer* declared the British public would never 'stand for the methods of the French.'[660] But a doorstep poll in the *Guardian* revealed two stark choices proposed by the British public: Get out, or the 'Crater' treatment.[661] This was a reference to Colonel (Mad Mitch) Mitchell and the atrocities of the Argyll and Sutherland Regiment in Aden. The *Guardian* sympathetically profiled Colonel Mitchell, and praised his bravery in pacifying Crater, for which, it pointed out, he had not yet received a medal. This 'pacifier' of the Yemeni knew how to handle the Irish: 'Send round a list of say, 100 suspected terrorists ... By the time you've knocked off ten, the other ninety will be in Killarney.'[662] Mitchell was a member of the right-wing Monday Club, a supporter of white-minority rule in Rhodesia, and subsequently an adviser to the Contras in Nicaragua. It is curious that a reputedly liberal newspaper would lend any credibility to his views for resolving a difficult political conflict. Two weeks later the army shot twenty-seven civil rights demonstrators on Bloody Sunday. In the two days following, the House of Commons cheered when the home secretary praised the troops' use of 'minimum force'.[663] The *Observer* carried a 'man in the street' response, declaring it to be a representative poll: 'I'm proud of our boys. I think it's a miracle, the restraint they've shown. All credit to the Army. It could have been 300.' [664] But there was no credit to the army and ignorance of Ireland and the army's role has not been illuminated by the media. The public might understand a Frenchman calling for tougher action against Algerian 'cut-throats'. His ignorance, after all, was the result of an intimidated French media. In Britain, the liberal press proclaimed their freedoms, but, unlike France, there were no

658 Ibid., 2 July 1973.
659 *Observer*, 6 October 1968.
660 Ibid., 12 October 1958.
661 *Guardian*, 26 April 1971.
662 Ibid., 15 January 1972.
663 Ibid., 1, 2 February 1972.
664 *Observer*, 6 February 1972.

trade-union demonstrations against army brutality. There was little student protest, even awareness.[665] In contrast to Jeanson's view that every true son of the French Republic should engage in dismantling the legacy of empire, in Britain there was a marked reluctance on the part of politicians or the press to even acknowledge any British responsibility for the conflict. Labour MP E.L. Mallalien wrote: 'the situation is not of their [British] making.'[666] David Astor, too, was mystified:

> We were caught by the army's relationship to the Protestants, the officers at the Curragh. My recollection, I was born in 1912, we never said Ireland is England. The French said Algeria is France. It's close, it's almost the closest relationship you could think of, but it has this substantive difference. The English have never said Ulster is England, ever. The English got caught in the thing. They didn't arrange the plantation. It was Queen Elizabeth I ... nobody knew how the hell they got there ... it's only through the army they got Partition.[667]

Of the legacy of empire, a general ignorance prevails. There is, too, a call to 'shed our colonial guilt' and stop 'apologising for the empire', ranging from former Prime Minister Gordon Brown to Monty Python's Michael Palin.[668]

There are occasions, more rarely, when both newspapers reported the words and actions of British politicians outside the template of British reasonableness and neutrality. Consider the following six extracts.[669] There was government 'glee at the death of subversives', 'mild regret that more Provisionals were not killed' and 'uproar in the Commons at the suggestion of a United Ireland.' When a motion

---

665   Equivocal statements from students' organisations regarding the army in Ireland can be found in the *Guardian*, 23 April 1971, 2 February, 3, 4 April 1972. All of these quotations in the text (and more like them) including the events surrounding them can be found in the *Guardian*, 8 February, 6 August 1971, 2 August, 31 October 1972, 30 November, 6 December 1973, and in the *Observer*, 5 July 1970, 28 February 1971, 6 February, 12 March 1972, 25 March 1973.

666   *Observer*, 20 June 1971.

667   Interview with David Astor, London, 22 July 1998.

668   *Daily Telegraph*, 2 October 2009, Daily Mail, 15 January 2005, http://www.dailymail.co.uk/news/article-334208/Its-time-celebrate-Empire-says-Brown.html

669   The six quotations cited in the text and more can be found in the *Guardian*, 8 February, 6 August 1971, 3 August, 3 October 1972, 30 November, 6 December 1973, and in the *Observer*, 5 July 1970, 28 February 1971, 6 February, 12 March 1972, 25 March 1973.

debating the reunification of Ireland was defeated at a Conservative conference, '1,200 delegates stood and cheered.' Following the army killing of four civilians during the Falls curfew, a Home Office spokesman thought 'the introduction of the gun might mark a turn for the better.' Home Secretary Maudling intended to 'deprive the Catholics of every bloody grievance they've got.' Anthony Howard summed up the mood of the governing Conservative Party. There were any number of Tory MPs:

> to whom it is quite simply anathema to grant any political concessions until the government had got on top of the gunmen. They had swallowed Cyprus only because it was the Labour Party doing it and finally gulped down Aden but on Ulster they are betraying every sign of being ready to gag. The Orange card may have lost its former potency but there is still an inherited patriotic bloodline that ties Tories to Unionists at Stormont.[670]

This summation, although accurate, is untypical.

Conclusion

Algeria produced deep divisions in France. Senior officers clashed publicly over torture and were contemptuous of politicians and citizens who professed ignorance. Intellectuals and celebrities actively opposed government policy, as did significant parts of the French Catholic Church. In Britain, political and military elites were not as divided. There was little social division on the Irish question. Political parties pursued an 'all-party' approach. The government, judiciary and officer class were largely united. There was a virtual silence from the British left.

The comparison of the reportages demonstrates an informed and engaged France and an uninterested and unknowing Britain. Algeria was France. Ireland was 'a faraway country about which we know nothing.' The press pitied the French public for their intimidated media. Yet somehow the manacled French media produced enough awareness that Paris 'swarmed with armchair moralists.' There was active opposition to government policy among the French public and in the army. Criticisms from the intellectual and artistic classes generated

---

670   *Observer*, 12 March 1972.

much public debate. French students, professors and teachers protested loudly. Trade unionists organised general strikes. Although the British liberal press proclaimed its freedoms, it did little to explain Ireland.[671] Senior British soldiers and politicians supported a vigorous military option, acknowledged no wrong, and produced false accounts for internal and public consumption. Too often, army killings of civilians were justified by members of the judiciary. Few in Britain seemed to notice. There were no protests from students, academia, organised labour or the left. The Troops Out Movement was made up largely of the Irish in Britain, ex-soldiers and tiny groups of left-wing activists. The liberal press routinely reported British policy as reasonable and the only way forward. The army (implementing Kitson's prescriptions), the Conservative government (identifying Catholics as the problem) and the liberal press (appalled at the perversity of the Irish) were all singing from the same hymn sheet. Britain was holding back Irish barbarism.

The unionist community, used to a regular diet of British boys 'doing no wrong', now rails against growing criticism of the security forces. The liberal press has not prepared them for the emerging challenges to this narrative. This is not new. Unlike Camus and Sartre on Algeria, there had been little British response to their contemporaneous atrocities in Kenya. Liberal Britain now regards army atrocities in Kenya as shameful and puzzling. One *Guardian* editorial, at the height of the Battle of Algiers, may help: 'All the same there is a special fine mercilessness about the French conscience; it can bring to light acts which here tend to remain muffled.'[672] The evidence presented here confirms that the actions of the British army did indeed 'remain muffled'. Huw Bennett examined legal cases of killing and brutality brought against the army and concluded that legal authorities (at times, ex-soldiers) bent the rules. Bennett concludes: 'The evidence released from the National Archives so far gives cause to believe there was more fire [than smoke] than many in the army admitted.'[673] The reality of the killings and abuse was kept from the public.

During his testimony at the Saville Inquiry, the *Guardian*'s Simon Winchester admitted: 'in retrospect I was a useful mouthpiece for the army.'[674] Winchester puzzled over why Kitson selected the *Guardian*,

---

671 There were exceptions, of course, like the *Sunday Times* Insight Team early in the conflict and broadcasters like Keith Kyle, Roger Bolton and Alex Thomson.

672 *Guardian*, 18 March 1957 (editorial).

673 H. Bennett, Smoke without Fire? Allegations Against the British Army in Northern Ireland, 1972–5, *Twentieth Century History,* Volume 24, Issue 2, June 2012, p. 304.

674 *Irish Times*, 21 May 2001.

supposedly a critic, for 'scoops'. He now feels his reporting was 'tainted ... Much later I came to realise his [Kitson's] deeper motives.'[675] This resonates with Sir Basil Clarke's propaganda prescriptions going back to 1920s Ireland. To make their creations more credible they should be dissolved in some liquid that the reader could readily assimilate. Victims' families, using official archives, are now re-writing the 'Troubles', that is, rebalancing the official narrative.

675   S. Winchester, My Tainted Days, *Guardian,* 22 May 2001.

PART THREE

CHAPTER EIGHT

Brothers-in-Faith or Politically Motivated Insurgents

This chapter investigates the motives of those who took up arms against the state. IRA motives have been recorded in multiple interviews and personal memoirs. Their words contrast repeatedly with the motives attributed to them by journalists and academics. An evaluation of IRA interviewees and their critics is included. There is a well-documented reticence by ALN members to speak of their motives. Generally, only the views of FLN leaders are known. However, in 1997 Derradji gained access to the official archives in Algiers and their motives are clear. These testimonies permit an exploration of any similarities and differences between the Algerian and Irish insurgents/terrorists. The comparative coverages, held up against these testimonies and the record, are evaluated for patterns, slants and/or differences.

Algerian Insurgents
Too many humiliations suffered for too long

The source of the Algerian insurrection begins with the memory of dispossession from the land and in the brutal suppression of the rebellions of Abd el Kader[676] and Mohamed el Mokrani.[677] Muslims held communal memories of indignities endured under the *Code d'Indigénat* (1874 to WWII). Councillor Ali Khodja remembered they resented France's failure to push through reforms: 'too many

---

676   In mid-19th century, Abd el Kader prosecuted a jihad. He won praise for his respect for human rights, including saving thousands of Christian lives during the Damascus massacre of 1860.

677   Between 1871-72 Mokrani led Algerians in an uprising against the erosion of political autonomy and the proselytising of the Catholic Church.

humiliations suffered by Muslims for too long.'[678] Rabah Bitat, one of the FLN's 'historic nine', explained: 'We were not allowed to speak Arabic, our maternal tongue, even during recess hours.'[679] A taxi driver complained he could only get dangerous night-time work: 'They give it to a Frenchman first always ... they won't give us work. That is the cause of ... all the troubles.'[680] In 1959 Henry Tanner (*New York Times*) interviewed residents of the Kasbah. They despaired that *pieds-noirs* would deny them dignity unless forced at gunpoint. The metropolitan French were alright, the local French caused all the trouble. The soldiers, too, were only doing a job, most of them. There were deep grievances over electoral fraud. 'They vote for us thus we don't have to inconvenience ourselves.'[681] Muslims were particularly offended by *pieds-noirs* indifference to OAS bombs.

For many, the turning point came with the terrible French reprisals following the events of 8 May 1945 at Setif. Partly frustrated by military intelligence, the day was to have been the start of a general insurrection. Disorganised attacks, accompanied by horrible mutilations, went ahead, leaving 103 Europeans dead. The terrible follow-up resulted in 1,500 to 45,000 Muslim deaths (French vs Algerian figure). Many of the early leaders of the rebellion grew up near Setif. The Algerian writer Katib Yacine remembered: 'There my nationalism was cemented.'[682] But Algerian nationalism was contested. Ferhat Abbas and his party, the *Union Democratique du Manifeste Algérien* (UDMA), had long advocated integration with France: 'Had I discovered the Algerian nation, I would be a nationalist ... However, I will not die for the Algerian nation because it does not exist ... One cannot build on the wind.'[683] Sheik Abelhamid Ben Badis, president of the Association of Algerian Ulema (religious scholars), countered: 'This Muslim Algerian nation is not France, cannot be France and does not want to be France.'[684] The Ulema aimed to re-establish Muslim society, opposed alcohol, tobacco, the emancipation of women and other evils of the West. A third group, Messali Hadj's *Mouvement pour le Triomphe des Libertés Démocratiques* (MTLD), performed well in the 1947 local

---

678 Kettle, *De Gaulle and Algeria, (London, Quarter, 1993)*, p. 359.

679 Heggoy, *Insurgency and Counterinsurgency in Algeria, (Indiana University Press) 1972*, p. 56.

680 Kettle, op. cit., p. 262.

681 Brace, *Ordeal in Algeria*, (Van Nostrum, 1960), p. 74.

682 Kraft, *Struggle for Algeria*, (NY, Doubleday, 1961), p. 64.

683 Entelis, *Algeria: The Revolution*, (Boulder, Westview, 1986), p. 38.

684 Heggoy, *Insurgency, Counterinsurgency in Algeria*, (Indiana University, 1972), p. 15.

elections. Algerian nationalism also had millenarian roots and a widespread belief prevailed that French rule would disappear in a climactic moment. This convinced FLN leaders that the masses were primed for rebellion. Mohammed Boudiaf, the chief architect of the FLN, was contemptuous of the MTLD's reformism. Only the gun could remove the stain of colonial humiliation, and only the FLN, as the engine of the uprising, had the right to represent the nation.

Herb Greer, the American-born journalist who contributed to the *Guardian/Observer*, spent the winters of 1956 and 1957 with the rebels. He found the older men were solid, simple soldiers and French veterans. They liked fighting, had few ideas for sale and of course, they believed in freedom. But few had any idea what *l'Istiqlal* (independence) meant. Idealists and fanatics were in short supply. They were country people, ignorant of most things beyond the necessary facts of survival. The *colons* were a bad lot, and this was a chance for a more exciting life than dusty village existence. The city was different. Ramdane Abane, the FLN's political brain, Mohammed Yazid, the FLN diplomat, and their school friends all admired Michael Collins and the IRA for winning Irish independence. Although the FLN offered French Algerians *'la valise ou le cerceuil'* (the suitcase or the coffin), broadly speaking they did not want a mass expulsion. There was, however, a strong feeling that the departure of a minority would be necessary: *'que les patrons des bistrots s'en aillent.'*[685] This was a reference to *ultras* like café owner Jo Ortiz, an organiser of the counter-terrorists.

Brothers-in-faith before comrades-in-arms
During the night of 1 November 1954, the FLN distributed a tract:

> We call upon you to re-conquer your freedom at the price of your blood. Organize yourself to give aid, comfort and protection to the Forces of Liberation. To take no interest in the struggle is a crime; to oppose it is treason. God is with the fighters of just causes, and no force can stop them now, save glorious death or national liberation.[686]

The FLN aimed to restore the Algerian state, sovereign, democratic and social, within the framework of Islam. They did not publicise the

---

685 Behr, *Algerian Problem,* (London, Hodder, 1961), p. 224.
686 Heggoy, *Insurgency,* p. 104.

insurrection as a jihad but included the Islamic proviso to broaden its appeal. The FLN promised all fundamental freedoms without distinction of race or creed. However, for Muslims there could be no neutrality: 'the spiritual duty of every single man or woman ... [was] fighting against the enemies of God and for the Muslim as well as for the Motherland.'[687] The Islamic imprimatur contrasted with the proclamation's rational Western political concepts. But ALN documents typically began: 'Praise to God alone. The supreme Command ...'[688]

Benjamin Stora explains that within the historical memory of Algerians, 'the notion of an Islamist movement challenging the state in the name of religion is part of a tradition whereby religion is used against the colonial state.'[689] In March 1952, Ben Bella and his co-accused members of *L'Organisation Spéciale* (OS) entered the courtroom in Blida, singing 'We consecrate our efforts to the service of glory and of the jihad.'[690] Demonstrators outside took up the refrain. Those arrested at Setif confessed they had been told to exterminate the French in pursuit of the holy war. Ayache Ben Hanachi Boudria testified that he was on his way to the market when he heard, 'the Holy War has been proclaimed ... The time has come to exterminate them.'[691] The *caid* of the village of Fedj M'Zala testified that a mob attacked the village chanting, 'El jihad fsabil Allah', holy war in God's name.[692] However, FLN leaders were divided over religion as a means or an end. Although the language of jihad was extensively used, Ben Bella would protest to radicals in the leadership: 'You must leave us our Allah.'[693] When captured, Ben Bella was replaced by his deputy Ahmed Tewfik el Madani, secretary general to the Ulema.

Lakhdar Ben Tobbal, leader of *wilaya* 2, has acknowledged the FLN believed they had to rouse fatalistic Muslims. He organised the terrible slaughter of French women and children at Philippeville. The ALN pressed locals into killing Europeans they had known all their lives, and spread rumours that God disguised ALN fighters as sheep.[694] The terrible mutilations led to inevitable French reprisals of between 1,273 (French tally) to 12,000 Muslim dead (FLN figure). This had the desired

687 Derradji, *Algerian Guerrilla Campaign,* (Lampeter, 1977), p. 171.
688 Clark, *Algeria in Turmoil,* (NY, Grosset, 1960), p. 219.
689 B. Stora, *Algeria,* p. 238.
690 Clark, *Algeria in Turmoil,* p. 67.
691 Ibid., p. 32.
692 Ibid., p. 33.
693 Gordon, *Passing of French Algeria,* (OUP, 1966), p. 110.
694 Zohra Drif remembers rumours of ALN supernatural powers, see *Inside the Battle of Algiers,* (Just World, 2017), p. 174.

effect. The ALN were beginning to be viewed as mujahideen. During the Battle of Algiers, people began referring to them as fedayeen, those who redeem themselves through sacrifice to God. The FLN publicised its intentions in its newspaper *El-Moudjahid* (The Holy Warrior): 'Jihad is precisely a dynamic manifestation of self-defence for the preservation and recovery of patrimony of superior values.'[695] *El-Moudjahid* explained that jihad means many things: the ALN soldier, the political militant, the little shepherd who informs, the schoolboy who goes on strike, the saboteur of commerce, the student who joins the *maquis*, the diffuser of tracts, the peasant who suffers and hopes. Abder-Rahmane Derradji reviewed the testimonies of ALN veterans in the archives of the Centre National des Études Historiques in Algiers. They were: 'on the battlefield in their majority, brothers in faith before being comrades in arms.'[696] Zohra Drif was one of Yacef Saadi's all-female bomb units. In her memoirs, she wrote the ALN were mujahideen, volunteers for death who were reserved a place in heaven. They were fulfilling their religious duty, fighting the non-believers.[697]

Sheikh Abd al-Hamid Ben Badis led the Algerian Ulema. He was of the Saudi Arabian Salafi/Wahhabi tradition which sought to resist European colonialism and return Islam to a position of world power. The Sufi brotherhood of the Sanusiya, which originated in the Berber village of Mazouna, was a spectacular manifestation of this religious resistance flowing from the East. In 1902 Captain Lamotte of the Arab Bureau warned: 'It wishes and pursues above all else the expulsion of the infidel from Dar al-Islam [the House of Islam].'[698] In 1932 the Association of Algerian Ulema described itself as oriented to its Arab ancestors and the Arab metropole. They took on the state-sponsored Muslim religious leaders of Algeria. Four years of religious war ended with the 1936 assassination of the official Malikite mufti of Algiers. In 1938 Ben Badis issued a fatwa explaining that the taking up of French citizenship amounted to apostasy. In the spring of 1956 the Ulema came out publicly in support of the FLN. The daily pledge of their *madrasas* (schools) – 'Islam is our religion, Arabic is our language, Algeria is our fatherland' – became the motto of independent Algeria.[699] Official Algerian history proclaims: 'the revolution was essentially a struggle

695   Derradji, *Algerian Guerrilla Campaign*, p. 243.

696   Ibid., p. 243.

697   Drif, *Inside*, p. 121, 124, 130, 164.

698   Cooley, *Baal, Christ and Mohammed*, p. 180.

699   Ben Badis' schools promoted Algerian nationalism, see Entelis, *Algeria*, pp. 44–6, Heggoy, *Insurgency*, pp. 12–15.

to resurrect an Islamic-Arabic past'.[700] The Ulema were suspicious of Western influence on the FLN leadership, but felt they had to support it to Islamicise Algeria from within. After the war they soon fell out.

Irish Insurgents
The nationalist community will not be without an army again
British Intelligence describes the IRA as politically motivated insurgents.[701] In 1969, Irish nationalist rage was directed at Stormont and the RUC for their collusion or passive inaction during the fire-bombings of Catholic neighbourhoods. Catholic rage in Derry was particularly motivated by repeated police assaults. Republicans, in the early 1960s, having abandoned force for political reform, found they were unable to defend nationalist homes. The militarists returned, and the defensive mood changed from anger and despair to an insurgency. An IRA activist remembered: '… it was straight off-the-streets reaction … no way the nationalist community will be without an army again.'[702]

Firebombing of their homes reminded Belfast Catholics of the anti-Catholic pogroms of the 1920s.[703] One elderly couple had suffered three such experiences.[704] The Provisional IRA's improved status was confirmed in July 1970 when the Central Citizens' Defence Committee, including some priests, invited them to tea and thanked them for saving St Matthew's Church which had come under sustained attack by loyalists over a weekend in late June. The army's failure to intervene was never satisfactorily explained. Within days of the IRA's newly improved status, the troops displayed a new energy in the seminal Lower Falls curfew with the army killing four civilians. Sixty civilians and fifteen soldiers also received gunshot wounds. Two unionist politicians – Captain William Long and John Brook, were escorted in military jeeps through the cowed community. 'It's a great day for us,' Captain William Long beamed to accompanying RUC officers.[705] The traditional lines were redrawn. Stormont would suppress the rebellious Catholics. The IRA assumed the title of defender. But MLR Smith (MoD) argues that the IRA sabotaged Army-Catholic relations.

---

700 D. Gordon, *Self Determination and History in the Third World* (Princeton University Press, 1971), p. 32.

701 Coogan, *The Troubles,* (St Martin's, 2002), pp. 212–15.

702 O'Brien, *The Long War,* p. 162.

703 Described as pogroms in English papers at the time, see M. Hopkinson, *The Irish War of Independence* (Montreal: McGill-Queen's University Press, 2013), pp. 153-164 for media and historical neglect of these pogroms. See also Pearse Lawlor, *The Burnings,* (Cork: Mercier, 2009).

704 W. H. Van Voris, *Violence in Ulster,* p. 142.

705 Ibid., p. 179.

To avenge British harassment and 'a crack at the Orangees'
Between 1972 and 1973 anthropologist Frank Burton was researching and living in the Ardoyne neighbourhood of Belfast. One 'particularly politicised' IRA man told him that a 'brave few' (a good number) joined the movement 'to have a crack at the Orangees' (loyalist militants).[706] Harry Murray, a Protestant IRA member, also wanted 'to get back at the Prods.' Married to a Catholic he had been intimidated out of his North Belfast home by loyalists. Fionnuala O'Connor's interviewees confirm 'the fire-bombings, intimidation of thousands of families by loyalists ... the random murders and sadistic mutilations of Catholics propelled many Catholics from defence to revenge.'[707]

The British army's counterinsurgency methods, before any insurgency, transformed the situation into a low-intensity but real war. The saturating of neighbourhoods with CS gas was resented as a collective punishment. One Belfast man, imprisoned for IRA activity, recalled most prisoners were fighting for democracy and Irish reunification. He, himself, was not so politically motivated: 'I was just 100% anti-British because of what they had done to my son.'[708] Sinn Féin's Francie Molloy remembers his Protestant neighbours, in UDR uniform, 'searching your belongings, reading private letters and turning out children's schoolbags.' He rejected the notion of religious war: 'it was the simple arming of one section of the community against the other whilst you deprive that other section of any means of defending themselves.'[709]

IRA leader Brendan Hughes recalled how his early interest in socialism was stirred when, as a merchant sailor, he witnessed the exploitation of black South Africans. Later, on shore leave in Aden, he had been beaten up by British soldiers. The invasions and burnings of Catholic homes completed his alienation from the state. Interestingly, Alan Barker, his Special Branch opponent, had, in his own words, 'an ironically appropriate formative experience' growing up on an RAF base in the Middle East where they 'came under frequent attack from young Arab stone-throwers.'[710] The actions of the police and army also propelled Martin McGuinness into the IRA: 'The Duke Street beatings, the attack on Samuel Devenney and the killings of Cusack and Beattie were the four incidents why I became a republican.'[711] A mid-70s survey

706 F. Burton, *The Politics of Legitimacy* (London: Routledge, 1978), p. 80.
707 O'Connor, *In Search of a State*, p. 116.
708 Parker, *May the Lord in His Mercy*, p. 313.
709 Toolis, *Rebel Hearts, (NY, St Martin's 1995)*, p. 42.
710 Barker, *Shadows*, p. 22.
711 Toolis, *Rebel Hearts*, p. 304.

of IRA prisoners found fully ninety per cent joined to avenge the harassment they had suffered from British forces.[712]

A legitimate war of self-determination
The republican leadership set about explaining the conflict to the newly roused Catholic community. Armed struggle was an unfortunate necessity because the British government had imposed a Northern Ireland lacking democratic credentials. The IRA was fighting for democracy in a legitimate war for self-determination. The Irish government's renouncing of force over the North was an unusual act on the part of a sovereign government regarding a central question of national policy. Meanwhile, the British government imposed its will by force. Thus, any Irish person has the right to take up arms in defence of the nation's sovereignty. Republicans pointed to a 1949 internal British government document: 'Indeed it seems unlikely that Britain would ever agree with this [unity] even if the people of Northern Ireland desired it.'[713] Republicans also noted the 1993 Opsahl Report. Its redefining of democracy in a divided community as something other than majority rule called into question the wisdom of the 1920 'settlement.'[714] While republicans were motivated by self-determination, the injustices of partition and Stormont misrule, the question of self-determination only really began to appear in the media following the 1994 Downing Street Declaration. Stephen Glover wrote that the 'issue of Ulster' concerned Britain's sense of nationhood. 'That is what we have been defending for twenty-five years and that is what the IRA have been attacking.'[715] Danny Morrison, speaking at Sinn Féin's 1987 *Ard Fheis,* stated Irish republicans sought to force the British to surrender control of Ireland.

A hatred of the British?
Eamonn McCann wrote that after Bloody Sunday nationalists 'made a holiday in their hearts at news of dead soldiers.'[716] Imprisoned IRA leader Brendan McFarlane, while conducting a death watch of hunger strikers, congratulated his comrades on their recent ambush of British soldiers: 'Oh, you wonderful people!' He also expressed regret: 'Tis truly a great shame. They kill and die and never think to question.'[717]

---

712   *Independent,* 6 February 1989.
713   K. Kelly, *The Longest War,* (London: Zed, 1982), p. 70.
714   A. Pollak (ed.), *Opsahl Report on Northern Ireland,* (Dublin: Lilliput, 1993).
715   *London Evening Standard,* 16 December 1993.
716   Toolis, *Rebel Hearts,* p. 311.
717   O'Connor, *In Search of a State,* p. 103.

A review of IRA interviews and memoirs, however, does not reveal a commonplace joy at soldiers' deaths.[718] This contrasts with unionist politicians, loyalist paramilitaries and British journalists repeatedly displaying joy at the deaths of republicans. Loyalists rejoiced in killing civilians. Soldiers celebrated killings with parties and champagne. Soldiers and police mocked, sang to and physically abused bereaved Catholic mothers and families.[719]

But Conor Cruise O'Brien cautions us against the Irish. Combining with a pervasive unionist outlook, including journalists, military analysts and politicians, O'Brien held the Irish maintain a public façade but were 'some of the most expert conmen and conwomen in the world.'[720] Lord Peter Mandelson remembered Margaret Thatcher warning him: 'You can't trust the Irish, they are all liars, liars, that's all you have to remember, so don't you forget it.'[721] But the record contains few cases of the 'liars' expressing pleasure over any death. Consider the IRA's Dermot Finucane: 'We would have been delighted in all honesty to hear of Brits getting whacked ... but the anguish and misery that his death will cause his family – no ... I do not wish for the death of any soldier.'[722] Finucane's home was burned down by loyalists and B-Specials. His brother Pat was murdered by combined police/army/UDA killers. His words contradict the dominant media image of bloodthirsty terrorists. Martin McGuinness felt that there was a British indifference to Irish deaths.[723] Sinn Féin's Jim Gibney, at the 1992 Sinn Féin *Ard Fheis*: 'We dared to hope that Peter Brooke would be the first British Secretary of State who would begin the healing process between all the Irish people and ultimately between Ireland and Britain.'[724] The public sentiments of republicans do not reveal a

---

718   See IRA interviewees in Parker, *May the Lord*, Van Voris, *Violence in Ulster*. But O'Rawe, *Blanketmen*, p. 53, remembers the retribution served on the Bloody Sunday and Ballymurphy killers.

719   See Ian Jack, 'Gibraltar', *Granta*, (1989), p. 13, McKay, *Bear in Mind These Dead*, p. 79, P. Pringle and P. Jacobson, *Those Are Real Bullets, Aren't They?*, pp. 256, 275. Gregory Campbell, DUP, was 'delighted at IRA men executed', McKittrick, op. cit. p. 1003, Ken Maginnis, UUP, on IRA deaths: 'two swallows don't make summer', McKay, *Bear in Mind*, p. 231. Further examples of soldiers' joy on IRA deaths see T Geraghty, *The Irish War*, p.149 and K Wharton, *The Long War*, p. 311. See Davis, *Mirror Hate* for loyalists laughing at Catholic civilian deaths.

720   Coogan, *The Troubles*, p. 318. See Journalist Tony Geraghty and Army PR-man Maurice Tugwell, Irish liars, natural propagandists, Hooper, *The Military and the Media*, p. 126.

721   *Belfast Telegraph*, 17April 2013; also K Meagher, *New Statesman*, 19April 2013.

722   Toolis, *Rebel Hearts*, pp. 105–7.

723   Ibid., p. 290. Saadi complained of French indifference to Muslim deaths; Tillion, *France and Algeria*, pp. 24–51.

724   O'Brien, *Long War*, p. 213.

widespread hatred of British people or soldiers.[725]

The distinction was understandably lost on their relatives
Patterson writes of the IRA's banally brutal killings of Irish Protestants in and out of uniform. However, Toolis wrote the IRA did not fight a sectarian war and shot Protestants because they were soldiers in a British regiment: 'But since every member of the UDR was a Protestant, the distinction was understandably lost on their relatives and friends.'[726] This, however, offers no explanation for IRA killings of Catholic RUC officers and UDR members. Archbishop Robin Eames explained that murders of RUC and UDR came to be interpreted as sectarian. This, too, is contradicted by internal RUC views. Detective Ben Forde thought the IRA attacked the police because of the uniform, not out of sectarianism.[727] Gary Armstrong, an evangelical Protestant minister with joint RUC-UVF membership, wrote: 'I never thought that I was a target, because of who I was, but because of what I wore!'[728] Mark Neale, an Ulster Unionist councillor: 'those people weren't killed because they were Protestants but because they wore the uniform of the RUC.'[729] Mervyn Johnson was shot at patrolling the Fermanagh border: 'It wasn't because I was a Protestant. It was because I was a member of the UDR.'[730]

In contrast, M.L.R. Smith, an instructor at a British military college, wrote many IRA members believed because attacks against the security forces 'often resulted in the deaths of Protestants, they were at war with Protestants.'[731] But the IRA did not view the deaths of Catholic soldiers or policemen as operational failures. Further, the religion of regular British soldiers, the largest category killed by the IRA, was seldom recorded. It was of no real interest to anyone. Smith provides a damning quotation: 'One Provisional [Donnelly] admitted that many new recruits joined because they hated Protestants.'[732] The full quotation reads not 'many' but '*some* of Donnelley's intake "joined because they hated

---

725   For similar sentiments, see Joe Austin in Parker, *May the Lord*, p. 137; Kevin Barry McArtt, IRA, in Bishop and Mallie, *Provisional IRA,* p. 75.
726   Toolis, *Rebel Hearts*, p. 59.
727   B. Forde, *Hope in Bomb City,* p. 29. Another RUC officer confirmed: 'nothing against me personally, it's the uniform I wear, what it represents', Van Voris, *Violence in Ulster*, p. 171.
728   G. Armstrong, *From the Palace to Prison,* p. 37.
729   *Newsnight*, BBC 2, May 2000.
730   *Guardian,* 22 November 2017.
731   M.L.R. Smith, *Fighting for Ireland,* p. 98.
732   Ibid.

Protestants", although he says that "this feeling later wore off."' [733]
Further, the original source reveals not hatred but *defence* as a motive.
It also reveals IRA rejuvenation was 'lent force by bitterness at having
suffered at the hands of the B-Specials and Orangemen.' [734] Smith
includes a further dismal IRA motivation: 'Maybe you can't bomb a
million Protestants into a United Ireland but you can have good fun
trying.' [735] However, in the original quotation, the interviewee, Tom,
details his encounter with reporters: 'you could see they wanted
something sectarian, so here's me ... Maybe you can't bomb a million
Protestants ... but you can have fun trying.'[736] Tom's neighbours
described him, not as IRA but, as a Walter Mitty character. Smith's
'evidence' of IRA sectarianism is three distortions of three quotations.

Journalist Eamonn Mallic wrote of IRA targeting: 'whether a private
from England or a Protestant farmer who happened to be a part-time
UDR man.'[737] Mallie's analysis suggests that the farmer's membership
of the British army is coincidental. But these interpretations cannot
explain why the IRA attacked Protestants armed with state-supplied
guns rather than Protestants without them. Bruce's 'evidence' of IRA
sectarianism includes: the IRA bombed Protestant pubs before loyalists
bombed Catholic pubs; the IRA liked killing 'Orangies'; the IRA
preferred to kill Catholic [traitorous] RUC.[738] His evidence for the last
category is, bizarrely, the UDA's killing of John Turnly, not because he
was a republican but, because he was a Protestant republican. For the
other two he offers no evidence at all but finishes with his 'conclusive'
proof: the IRA bomb in Donegall Street that killed seven people (three
municipal employees, one of whom was a UDR member, two RUC
officers and two civilians). Excluding the Catholic RUC member all
victims were Protestant. The IRA placed approximately 19,000 bombs
during the conflict. To cite one atrocious example clearly could not
allow us to draw much of a conclusion. In any event, if Bruce knew his
sectarian geography of Belfast, he would know that Donegall Street
qualifies as Catholic-frequented and a poor choice for the IRA to vent
any anti-Protestantism. Bruce also claims to know IRA thinking. Thus
'security forces' families deserve all they get ... wives, children and
girlfriends of ex-police reservists are not people: they forfeited that

---

733 Bishop and Mallie, *Provisional IRA*, p. 140, emphasis added.
734 F. Burton, *The Politics of Legitimacy* (London: Routledge & Kegan Paul, 1978), p. 80.
735 Smith, *Fighting for Ireland*, p. 119.
736 Burton, *The Politics of Legitimacy*, p. 101.
737 Bishop and Mallie, *Provisional IRA*, p. 159.
738 Bruce, *Edge of the Union*, pp. 124–5.

status when they married or were born to agents of the occupying power.'[739] But General Glover, in his 1978 internal report, specifically noted the IRA did not attack the families of police or soldiers. Bruce's claims are speculation.

Other motivations have been offered. Kevin Myers explained the conflict was due to the 'cycle of psychiatric futility that is Fenianism ... the nationalists of West Belfast ... began their insane war in 1971.'[740] Colm Toibin tells us that for twenty-five years he made a point of asking the schoolfriends of future IRA members about them. One 'speaking for many', described 'the embryonic terrorist as a resentful little cunt.'[741] Journalists Toolis, O'Doherty and Dillon found IRA members who don't speak but grunt or are gruff.[742] O'Doherty could smell stale drink [alcohol] on the IRA.

'We need Protestants in a united Ireland'

IRA leader Seán Mac Stíofáin infamously once said there would be 'no place for those who want their British heritage.'[743] His view was not widely shared. RTÉ's Brendan O'Brien reported a hard IRA man with no regrets over British army deaths: 'No one wants to put them [Protestants] on a boat and ship them out.'[744] Davis points out that in a review of republican papers, there is 'no mention in them of wishing to kill Protestant scum or caricatures of Protestants as dirty, smelly and idle.'[745] In 1993 Gerry Adams appealed to Protestants to help build an Ireland devoid of 'all forms of religious privilege and sectarianism ... This cannot occur without the full involvement of the Protestant people.'[746] An IRA representative speaking to American academics maintained that a united Ireland must not be a Catholic Ireland. 'There must be a clear distinction between church and state to relieve Protestant fears.'[747] O'Connor recorded many IRA men insisting they were not nationalists but socialists, the solution lay in the emancipation of the working classes.[748] IRA leader Tommy McKearney maintained: 'The

---

739   Bruce, *The Red Hand,* (OUP, 1992), p. 186.

740   *Belfast Telegraph*, 23 June 2011.

741   *LRB*, vol 23, no, 23, 29 November 2001, he included loyalists in this study.

742   O'Doherty, *The Troubles*, p. 11; Toolis, *Rebel Hearts*, p. 78; Dillon, *God and the Gun,* (London, Orion, 1997), p. 146.

743   Mulholland, *The Longest War,* p. 104.

744   O'Brien, *Long War*, p. 41.

745   R. Davis, *Mirror Hate,* p. 74.

746   O'Brien, *Long War*, p. 96.

747   Galliher and DeGregory, *Violence in Northern Ireland,* p. 86.

748   O'Connor, *In Search of a State*, p. 371.

world is my country. I'm a republican, not a nationalist.'[749] But republicans admit that, for a period, loyalists drew them into a sectarian exchange. They describe this as their 'darkest hour.'[750]

The Liberal Press
A nationalist insurgency and the most unrepentant form of colonialism

From beginning to end, the liberal press was united in identifying French colonialism as the cause of the war in Algeria. Very early, the *Observer* informed the reader: 'Colonists fear ... the result of free elections.'[751] French policy was designed to undermine democracy: 'The elections which France is offering to hold after a ceasefire would result only in a number of local assemblies so constructed as to be quite unable to express the aspirations of the Muslim majority.' This initiative represented 'the most unrepentant form of colonialism.'[752] In fact, these local assemblies, Swiss-style cantons, were a creative attempt to reconcile the conflicting aspirations of the two communities. A leading article in the *Guardian* noted that the rebel army had strong popular roots, and already represented a rudimentary independent state that 'has, naturally, a much stronger basis in popular loyalty than the decaying French colonial state ... [which] is compelled to depend on terror and extermination.'[753] Hetherington summed up the conflict: 'the war between France and the Algerian Moslem Nationalists is over after 130 years of chequered colonial history.'[754]

The continuous portrayal was of ALN insurgents against a repressive French state, with the *Guardian* reporting: 'France "kidnaps" five Algerian rebels ... the capture of Ben Bella and his colleagues is a major triumph ... against the insurgents.'[755] I found no example of Britain 'kidnapping' IRA leaders. They were captured. The *Guardian* informed the reader: 'The political leaders of the Algerian rebel movement yesterday proclaimed a provisional Algerian Government ... There can, of course, be no recognition from the [British] government.'[756] The

749 *Talkback*, BBC Radio Ulster, April 2000, also McKearney, *The Provisional IRA*, pp. 188–9.
750 Dillon, *God and the Gun*, p. 174.
751 *Observer*, 8 July 1956.
752 Ibid., 8 December 1957.
753 *Guardian*, 31 July 1957.
754 Ibid., 19 March 1962 (editorial).
755 Ibid., 23 October 1956.
756 Ibid., 20 September 1958.

liberal press had no such inhibitions: 'Ferhat Abbas, the Prime Minister of the rebels' provisional Government' was not yet ready to talk to Paris.[757] Clare Hollingworth believed her reporting gave respectability to Algerian nationalists: 'I was sympathetic to the FLN ... an independence movement that was having more trouble than they should have because of the *pieds noirs* ... many correspondents were sympathetic to decolonisation.'[758]

The coverage was unambiguous. France faced an insurgency and a revolution. Its Algerian opponents were insurgents, soldiers and patriots.[759] Consider this *Guardian* report: 'The Algerian High Command arrived here today by air.'[760] High Command hardly conveys the reality of doorstep assassinations, throat-cutting of the recalcitrant, or grenades thrown into schools, buses and cafés. At the height of the Battle of Algiers, the *Guardian* reported the FLN: 'called on its leaders to carry out a census ... Youths should report for duty with the insurgents or face death.'[761] This direct threat to the unenthusiastic brought forward no editorial comment. The *Observer* profiled Claude Gerard, the wartime Resistance heroine, who had 'spent ten days with the Algerian Maquis.'[762] The word *maquis* (WWII French Resistance) equated the ALN with France's liberation heroes. And again: 'The [Paris] police had no fewer than six of their men shot at by members of the Algerian resistance within the past four weeks.'[763] Hetherington could not have been unaware that many in France considered the Resistance analogy an insult. Liberal Britain also rejected the counter-insurgency explanation of the ALN coercing the Muslim population, even as the ALN carried out its threats to assassinate the reluctant: 'Some self-satisfied French officials pretend it is fear alone that persuades workers ... to support and supply the rebels.'[764] The word

---

757 *Guardian*, 14 October 1959. The *Guardian* usually does not use quotations with references to the new Algerian government and Cabinet; see *Guardian*, 20 September, 15 October, 3 November, 9 December 1958, 14, 20 October 1959, 28 January 1960, 6, 25 January, 18, 24 March 1961, and *Observer*, 21 September 1958; for example, 'Ferhat Abbas, the rebel Prime Minister', *Guardian*, 28 January 1960.

758 Interview, Clare Hollingworth, London, 30 July 1998.

759 For rebels and rebellion, see the *Guardian* of: 2 July, 11, 18, 28 August, 7, 8 September, 17, 23 October, 10, 14, 21 November 1956; 1, 4, 5 January, 3, 20 April, 1, 5, 10 June, 7, 9, 13, 28 August, 30 September, 23 October 1957; 9 April, 8 July, 12, 16, 20 August, 9, 15, 23, 26 September, 14 October, 3 November 1958; 6, 8, 12 January, 3, 24 February, 2, 17, 24 March, 27, 29 April, 5, 12 May, 3 June, 18 August, 28 September, 27 October 1959; 14 June 1960; 13 February, 10 April, 10, 31 July, 29 August, 19 September, 9 October 1961; 22 March 1962.

760 *Guardian*, 17 June 1958.

761 Ibid., 20 April 1957.

762 *Observer*, 27 May 1956.

763 Ibid., 23 February 1958.

764 *Observer*, 8 July 1956.

'workers' also implies class struggle; a curious choice for a rural-based uprising and a religiously conservative society.

Hetherington considered the issue of an Algerian national past, and wondered whether 'the guerrilla movement contrived, however bloodily, to instil the national idea in the Moslem mind.'[765] Liberal Britain maintained the war dead had built up a capital of national respect and France must negotiate a settlement acceptable to the FLN.[766] This matched the FLN's belief that France filling cemeteries with martyrs would inevitably generate an Algerian nation. The *Observer* editor urged the British government to make it absolutely clear it favoured a negotiated peace 'under international guarantees acceptable to the rebels.'[767] This looks remarkably like the eventual GFA. The same editorial offices rejected speaking to Irish republicans or even reporting their declared motivations.

In all this reportage I found only one reference to unemployment and poverty motivating young men into the ranks of the ALN, and one other reference of an FLN activist motivated by 'holy nationalism'. Both were from guest writers.[768] Yet it was hard to miss that Islam sustained the insurgency. The ALN maintained no alcohol, no sex, prayer five times a day, strict adherence to Ramadan, and a rigid separation of male and female. Immediately at independence, the local Imam in Guelma oversaw the destruction of the Roman temple, a hated example of pagan idolatry. This was a forerunner of the Taliban's destruction of ancient Buddhist statues in Afghanistan. Robert Fisk pointed out the 'Islamic context of the 1954–62 independence struggle has long been ignored.'[769] John Cooley remembered: 'Everyone who spent any time in Algeria, during the war years, knows the very large part Islam played in arousing national feeling.'[770] Janet Flanner, the Paris correspondent of *The New Yorker*, described the conflict at the time as a 'fanatical, démodé Arab holy war.'[771]

Ancient religious hatred, unemployment and interference from Dublin
The liberal press concluded religious hatred, unemployment and

765 *Guardian*, 13 September 1956.

766 *Guardian*, 13 September 1956 (editorial), 30 September (editorial), 14 December 1958, 20 February 1962 (editorial), and *Observer*, 26 June 1959, 30 October 1960 (editorial).

767 *Observer*, 30 October 1960 (editorial).

768 Swedish journalist Sven Oste, 20 *Guardian*, May 1958, and Gregory Williamson, ibid., 30 October 1959.

769 Fisk, *Great War for Civilisation,* (Harper-Collins, 2006), p. 641.

770 Cooley, *Baal, Christ and Mohammed,* (London, 1965), p. 301.

771 J. Flanner, *The New Yorker*, 9 June 1956.

interference from Dublin produced Ireland's 'Troubles'. From 1969 to 1971, the *Guardian* maintained 'Ulster's big bogey is work.'[772] Unemployment was 'a far more basic cause of discontent than many of the civil rights demands.'[773] 'A man with a clear stake in his community ... is less likely to go around looking for sectarian differences.'[774] Hetherington-Cole equivocated on 'discrimination against both Catholics and Protestants.'[775] This overlooked the previous year's Cameron Report which confirmed Stormont's institutionalised anti-Catholic discrimination. The *Guardian* viewed complaints of discrimination as a line of whingers: 'Latest minority in Northern Ireland with a sense of persecution is a small band of glider pilots ...'[776] There was more editorial obfuscation: 'poverty and unemployment ... are as near the root of the trouble as religious strife.'[777] The *Guardian* had the solution: 'The British Government should finance widespread public works in Ulster.'[778] Hugh Hanning recommended a civilian conservation corps modelled on Roosevelt's 1933 Tennessee Valley initiative. This would also 'test whether unemployed Catholics were willing to work.'[779] This *Guardian* prejudice was not new. Ireland's entry into the European Economic Community would be difficult as there is 'a national distaste for work ... the demands upon both the Irish character and government will be severe.'[780]

There is however a belief, even within the nationalist community, that the *Guardian* championed the Catholic cause. In fact, Catholic intolerance featured often. With reference to Captain O'Neill: 'the shortsightedness of Catholic voters ... with limited exceptions they have declined to vote for Protestants.'[781] Rather than vote for this aristocratic landowner, master of his Orange Lodge and still addressed by his military rank, the intolerant Catholics had 'inexcusably' voted for a

772   Unemployment is the cause, see *Guardian*, 2, 14 (editorial), 17 February (editorial), 22 (editorial), 23 (editorial) April, 18 (editorial), 23 May (editorial), 15 July (editorial), 21 August, 11, 14 October 1969 (editorial) 2, 25 January, 23 March (editorial), 23, 29 June, 3, 4, 6 July (editorial), 19 November 1970 (editorial), 19 (editorial), 22 (editorial), 25 March, 5 June, 10 (editorial), 13 (editorial), 25 August 1971, and *Observer*, 10 October 1971.

773   *Guardian*, 6 July 1970 (editorial).

774   Ibid., 14 October 1969 (editorial).

775   Ibid., 19 November 1970 (editorial).

776   Ibid., 29 February 1972.

777   Ibid., 10 August 1971 (editorial).

778   Ibid., 22 March 1971 (editorial).

779   Ibid., 25 March 1971.

780   Ibid., 17 September 1962.

781   Ibid., 26 February 1969 (editorial).

young socialist and feminist, Bernadette Devlin. The *Guardian's* many recommendations for Catholics can be found in these editions.[782] Catholics 'should respond to Protestant reforms'; instead, they provoke Protestants through rioting and 'insisting on educational apartheid.' Catholics should join the RUC; instead, they attack the police with 'a hatred they took in with their mothers' milk.' Catholics should support the Northern Ireland state; 'instead they abjure any Catholic who does.' Catholics should not push self-determination too far or they would have to face the wrath of loyalist paramilitaries. 'Sensible Catholics will prefer the army.' Catholics 'should shelve the issue of Partition'; instead, they emphasise it. Thus, they cannot be fully accepted. 'Catholics should discipline their children.' 'Catholics should get the IRA to stop'; instead, they help them. The key to the conflict lay with Catholic volition, apparently. According to Hetherington-Cole, the Catholic community 'can only become equal citizens by their own choice.'[783] 'How can the Catholics expect to be fully accepted when they switch the attack from civil rights to anti-partition policies when it suits them?'[784] Hetherington-Cole opined that Catholics had better set aside all doubts about the troops, Stormont and the Conservative government, and get the guns and gunmen out. In a rare slip on IRA motives: 'Catholics must decide whether they are willing to allow the IRA to lead an attempt to overthrow the state.'[785] Nationalists heaped abuse 'on every Catholic public figure in fifty three years who had tried to play a constructive role.'[786]

782　*Guardian*: 2 January, 1, 1 (ed.), 2 (ed.), 17 (ed.), 25, 26 (ed.) February, 19 (ed.) April 19, 23 (ed.) December 1969; 13, 18 April 13, 18 1970 and the *Observer* of 23 February 1969. The following editorials are all examples of Catholic MPs holding up progress. See the *Guardian*, 11 (ed.), 12 (ed.) August, 27 (ed.) October 1971; 7 (ed.), 8 (ed.), 10 (ed.) February, 11 (ed.) March 1972. The following editorials urged Catholics to shelve the issue of Partition, see the *Guardian* of: 23 (ed.) April, 16 (ed.) August 1969; 20 (ed.) March 1970, 'it is the job of religious leaders to make their followers accept the constitutional position', *Guardian* 21 August 1969. Catholics should join the UDR, the RUC, accept the British army and take the oath of allegiance, *Guardian*, 30(ed.) September, 19 (ed.) November 1969; 1 (ed) August 1972; 6 September 1973. *Guardian* editorials noted the SDLP were not serious about unity 'because they were against violence', 14 (ed.) December 1971; 16 (ed.) June 1973. Catholics should make the IRA stop, see *Guardian* editorials of 11 November 1972; 8 February 1973. The *Guardian* editorial of 10 February 1971 warns Catholics against the IRA undoing partition. 'They (loyalists) undoubtedly think they could do the job better than the army. Sensible Catholics will prefer that the army ...' Catholics should discipline their children, *Guardian* of: 4 April 1970; 12 February 1971 and the *Observer* 7 April 1974.

783　*Guardian*, 2 November 1970 (editorial).

784　Ibid., 15 May 1970 (editorial).

785　Ibid., 6 July 1970 (editorial).

786　Ibid., 3 January 1974.

Cole also attacked Catholic 'insistence' on separate schools.[787] 'Can Cardinal Conway not now seek ways of withdrawing Catholic objections to Protestant and Catholic children going to the same schools?'[788] Historically, however, both Protestant and Catholic Churches favoured separate schools. The Catholic Church was prepared to accept state schooling if priests, like anyone else, could sit on the board of governors. The initiative stumbled when unionists resiled from the position pertaining before 1920 – in which all denominational schools were equally funded by the taxpayer – to a biased system of funding (including placing constraints on Catholics they were unlikely to accept). There was also considerable hostility to Catholics. Catholics were liars, stupid, violent, bigoted, bitter, full of hate, sought martyrdom and were to blame for the conflict.[789] Following the second fire-bombing of Catholic neighbourhoods in Belfast, in the summer of 1969, Home Secretary Jim Callaghan 'called for a peace gesture from the Catholics.' [790] Yet the record shows loyalists holding the initiative and repeated police assaults on Catholic neighbourhoods.[791]

Until 1972, Dublin and the Irish Constitution were to blame. Taoiseach Jack Lynch was wildly nationalist, wrong-headed, mischievous and encouraged violence.[792] However, Lynch's 'direct assault on Westminster' turned out to be criticising the concentration on a military solution before reforms. His criticising the terms of reference, of the Compton torture tribunal as too restrictive, was a further assault.[793] While all his concerns are reasonable, Conor Cruise O'Brien deemed Lynch to be 'unworthy, petty, nagging and propagandist.'[794] The Observer joined in: 'Lynch tossed his own petrol

787 Catholic schools as a source of the conflict, see Guardian, 12 September 1969 (editorial), 16 July 1970, 22 March 1971 (editorial), 15 July, 12 September, 2 October 1972, 13 March, 11 May, 14 September, 4 December 1973 (editorial), 1, 2, May 1974.
788 Guardian, 4 December 1973 (editorial).
789 See Guardian: 2 (ed.) February, 2 August 1969; 10 (ed.) July 1970; 8 (ed.) February, 17 (ed.) August 1971; 'Hatred of the RUC was fed into many Catholics with their mother's milk.' 8 August 1972; 31 (ed.) May 1973 and the Observer 17 August 1969. A contrast between the Observer of 30 May 1971 and the Guardian I June 1971 regarding the killing of a soldier shows the Guardian portraying Catholics in a much poorer light. Guardian letters pages contain examples of Catholics as liars, stupid, intolerant and violent, see: 23 April 1969; 13 September 1970; 16, 25, 27 August 1971 and 13 June 1974.
790 Guardian, 13 September 1969.
791 Mulholland, The Longest War, pp. 68-74.
792 Guardian: 22 (ed.) April 22, 15 (ed.), 16 (ed.) August, 24 September, 14(ed.) December 1969; 11 (ed.), 25 (ed.) May, 31 October 1970; 22, 28 October 1971; 23 (ed.) August, 16, 20 October 1972; 4 August 1973. A friendlier Dublin emerges over time, Guardian: 1 May 1972, 6, 15 August 1973; 14 March 1974. The Observer also came to view Dublin as friendly: 6 February, 26 March 1972; 1 (ed.) February 1973.
793 Guardian, 21 October 1971.
794 Ibid., 22 October 1971.

bomb with his demand for UN troops.'[795] This overlooked its own recent editorial suggesting UN assistance.[796] Two themes dominate: (1) Partition is not the issue, Northern Ireland is fully democratic. (2) Protestant self-determination is inviolable; Catholics self-determination should be shelved. Republicanism can be beaten by renewing Atlee's 1949 guarantee 'the border is not negotiable' and 'by showing Catholics they can have a fair deal inside Ulster.'[797] As long as the 'Catholic [sic] campaign' was about civil rights there was something the government could do but they cannot overturn the ballot-box majority. Ignoring the historical context of partition was compounded by the editor's condescending and racist analysis: 'In so far as the current riots have any rational explanation, they are a demand by Catholics for a withdrawal of the British in the belief that Irishmen will somehow solve their own problems.'[798] Britain must protect Protestants from coercion. Catholics must recognise power-sharing 'is a lot to ask of the Unionists.'[799] Coercion of Catholics was not mentioned.

Over five years of the conflict's greatest intensity, there are thirty-seven *Guardian* editorials rejecting partition as an issue and urging the army to protect democracy and not to abandon any territory. Included in these editorials is a demand for a Protestant right to self-determination but a only recommendation of fair play for Catholics.[800] The editor also pressed the unreliable Labour government: 'No one, not even Mr. George Brown [foreign secretary] ought to pretend that Partition is the issue.'[801] Hetherington-Cole never faltered on this: 'Partition as an issue is as outdated as the dinosaurs',[802] or 'a depressing number of civil rights supporters are now dragging in the issue of Partition.'[803] Simon Hoggart explained: 'the border is more a symptom than a cause.'[804] The creation of Northern Ireland and its colonial legacy

795 *Observer*, 17 August 1969.
796 Ibid., 27 April 1969 (editorial), see too *Guardian* 16 August 1968.
797 *Guardian*, 18 October 1968 (editorial).
798 Ibid., 5 August 1970 (editorial).
799 Ibid., 10 February 1972 (editorial).
800 *Guardian*: 18 (ed.) October 1968; 24 (ed.) February, 12 (ed.), 30 (ed.) September, 14 (ed.) December 1969; 8 (ed.), 14 (ed.) April, 8 (ed.) May 8, 5 (ed.) August 1970; 18 (ed.) February, 12 (ed.) March, 25 (ed.) May, 12, 26 (ed.) July, 2 (ed.) September, 20 (ed.) October, 2 (ed.) November, 1 (ed.), 8 (ed.) December 1971; 3 (ed.), 7 (ed.), 10 (ed.), 21 (ed.) February, 25 (ed.) September, 18, 26, 31 (ed.) October, 13 (ed.) November 1972; 21 (ed.) March, 25 (ed.) June 1973.
801 Ibid., 1 November 1968 (editorial).
802 Ibid., 4 February 1969 (editorial).
803 Ibid., 12 August 1969 (editorial).
804 Ibid., 6 March 1973.

were unmentionable. 'The public debate so far has been unhelpful, for most participants have merely attacked or defended the Irish Settlement of 1920.'[805]

To mention partition was mischievous, promoted violence and civil war.[806] 'Dr. O'Brien's thesis that even to talk of a united Ireland is mischievous ... the evidence supports Dr. O'Brien.'[807] Hetherington-Cole responded to demands for Irish self-determination: 'This is incompatible with British pledges ...'[808] Partition, as a source of the conflict, disappeared. Any suggestion of withdrawing 'as elsewhere in the Empire ... is encouraging some psychopath to contemplate further murders ...'[809] This slip pointed to a colonial context. The *Observer* had initially blamed partition.[810] The root of the conflict was: 'four centuries of oppression by English and Scottish settlers.'[811] This would change. Conor Cruise O'Brien explained it was not a legacy of British imperialism but resulted from Irish imperial ambitions.[812] *Observer* editorials reversed: 'It is inconceivable that self-determination for Protestants would not be recognized.'[813] This was quickly followed by two articles denying Protestants were descendants of plantation settlers. Further, the IRA between 1919 and 1921 had not forced Britain to leave Southern Ireland.[814] This points to the influence of O'Brien who wished to expunge any respect accorded to the historic IRA for winning Irish independence for twenty-six of the country's thirty-two counties. The problem, said O'Brien, was the fascist IRA.[815]

Other editorials explained Britain's difficulty: 'Logic and common-sense point to a United Ireland but there's little likelihood of Protestant Ulstermen even considering such a course.'[816] Astor explained: 'The English never thought Ulster was English. They didn't arrange the

---

805   Ibid., 23 August 1971 (editorial).

806   *Guardian* editorials: 15 (ed.) August 1969; 9 (ed.) March, 13 (ed.) August 1970; 2 1(ed.), 23 (ed.) August, 24 (ed.) September 1971; 12 (ed.) July, 11 (ed.) October 1972. One editorial questions NI's political system, 17 July 1971. A second almost permits debate on the Partition issue, 18 February 1972.

807   Ibid., 11 October 1972 (editorial).

800   Ibid., 20 July 1972 (editorial).

809   Ibid., 12 March 1971 (editorial).

810   *Observer,* 17 November 1968, 5 (editorial), 12 January, 10 (editorial), 17 (editorial), 31 August 1969, 5 April 1970 (editorial), 14 March (editorial), 15 August 1971 (editorial).

811   Ibid., 12 January 1969 (editorial).

812   Ibid., 24 October 1971.

813   Ibid., 6 February 1972 (editorial).

814   Ibid., 26 March 1972.

815   *Observer*, 10 October 1971.

816   Ibid., 25 June 1972 (editorial).

plantation ... Sinn Féin would produce a massacre of Catholics because Protestants were brutal and frightened.'[817] Both newspapers sprinkled other explanations: like 'mods and rockers', a 'Rangers–Celtic match', a 'tribal feud' or due to 'IRA romanticism' or 'an Irish failure to embrace openness.'[818] The British liberal press habitually referred to Irish backwardness, supposedly proved by their insisting on Catholic schools. Any discrimination was exaggerated.[819]

Conclusion

The motives of the respective insurgents were both reported incorrectly, but in opposite directions. The FLN-ALN were revolutionaries fighting the most unrepentant form of colonialism, the French variety. But ideas of imperialism, nationalism and socialism were largely unknown to Algeria's rebels. Mostly rural recruits, they believed they were fighting a jihad. This was largely ignored in the reportage. In contrast, IRA testimony and interviews do not reveal a religious motivation. However, republicans were overwhelmingly portrayed as religious sectarians. Their declared motives of fighting against the injustices of partition and for self-determination were dismissed. Partition was unworthy of reporting. But the GFA involved a great deal of constitutional wrangling, resulting in Britain repealing the Government of Ireland Act (1920) and the Republic of Ireland amending Articles 2 and 3 of the 1937 Constitution. The rejection of the colonial explanation affirmed the unionist narrative. But boosted by Brexit, reunification of Ireland is now in the public arena. A border poll inevitably recalls the colonial legacy.

817 Interview, David Astor, London, 22 July 1998.

818 *Guardian:* 12 August 1960 (editorial), 3 April 1970 (editorial), 5 April 1974 (editorial).

819 *Observer* 4 (ed.) December 1955; 17 February 1957; 18 September 1960. *Guardian* analyses of Ireland during the Algerian war included: 'unemployment', 'IRA romantics', 13 December 1956; 'the border is wrong', 'Protestants must not be coerced', 12 (ed.) October 1958; 'Catholics should shelve Partition', 'modern appliances will overcome border feud', 12 (ed.) October and 19 October 1959; 'Nationalists have only themselves to blame', 'unemployment, romance of IRA, senseless violence', 30 (ed.) March, 29 (ed.) May 1962. *Observer* explanations: 'unemployment', 'the romance of the IRA', 'the failure of Irish churches.' Partition was due to Irish nationalism's 'failure to embrace openness'.

CHAPTER NINE

Fearless Masquisards and Psychotic Terrorists

The methods used by those who take up arms against an injustice can result in a rejection of the legitimacy of the cause and an obstacle to understanding it. The record shows the ALN targeted civilians, Muslim and French, as policy. The IRA did not target civilians. However, a large minority of their victims were civilians. Against this record the liberal-press coverage was compared for dominant patterns, themes or consistent portraits.

ALN Tactics
What can we do? Our own people kill us
Twenty-two men met secretly in Algiers in June 1954. They were convinced Muslims could never gain independence through constitutional means. Direct action was their only option. On 1 November 1954 coordinated violence erupted throughout Algeria. Many joined the ALN because of French repression. *Pour encourager les autres* the ALN ordered extreme violence against collaborators which they widely defined. Ben Bella's written orders condemned the lowest civil servants: 'Take their children and kill them. Kill all those who pay taxes and those who collect them. Burn the houses of Muslim NCOs away on active service.'[820] On 7 December 1955, in anticipation of the National Assembly elections, the FLN, 'assuming its responsibilities before God', issued a handbill decreeing incessant violence to ensure abstentionism. This included executing all candidates

---

820 Horne, *Savage War of Peace,* (London, Macmillan, 1977), p. 135, see too Jackson, *The FLN in Algeria,* (Westport, Greenwood, 1977), p. 25.

and cutting the throats of their electoral agents. 'Each patriot will consider it his duty to kill a traitor.'[821] The FLN explained: 'When we've shot him, the head will be cut off and a tag clipped on his ear. Then we'll leave the head on the main road. That way the people can see what happens to traitors.'[822]

A farmer in the village of Rivet despaired: 'What can we do? … The French kill us, our own people kill us.'[823] Feraoun recorded in his journal: 'they [FLN] feel much disdain for the "civilians" that we are, and that, when the time comes, we, "the spineless" or "the slaves" will have to throw ourselves at the feet of them, the saviours.'[824] Muslims were warned not to use French courts. Land reforms should be boycotted, and beneficiaries were habitually found, in their new fields, with a severed throat. The school boycott in the autumn of 1956 was stiffened by grenades into classrooms in Algiers, Setif, Batna and Biskra. Yet in May 1958, even after three years of terrible violence, there were public demonstrations of harmony between the two communities at the Algiers Forum. The FLN were rattled. In the run-up to September's referendum, the ALN destroyed identity cards, threatened and inflicted dire penalties on anyone who voted: 'On 17 August 1958 in a small village on the Moroccan frontier two women had their throats ritually slit in front of the mosque, twenty others were kidnapped and murdered.'[825] Women who had removed their veils at the forum in May faced summary justice. Si Allal, the leader of *wilaya* 5, warned women's freedom ends at their door.

The FLN banned smoking and alcohol for religious reasons and to damage the wine and tobacco industries. The penalty for a first offence was slicing off the nose or lips. For a second offence the penalty was *égorgement*, the 'Kabyle smile' (slitting the throat). At independence, an unmarried couple walking together were likely to be thrown in jail, if not shot.[826] Feraoun remembers a village girl with a reputation for promiscuity. The ALN killed her. 'It was especially important not to suppose that these particular young men had all been, more or less and each in his turn, the lovers of this girl of easy virtue.'[827] Recordings of Western music were prohibited as discs of dishonesty. There was, again,

821 Clark, *Algeria in Turmoil,* (NY, Grosset, 1960), p. 239.
822 Ibid., p. 55.
823 Greer, *A Scattering of Dust,* (London, Hutchinson, 1962), p. 17.
824 Feraoun, *Journal, 1955–1962,* (University of Nebraska Press, 200), p. 162.
825 Kettle, *De Gaulle and Algeria,* (London, Quartet, 1993), p. 275.
826 Humbaraci, *Algeria: A Revolution that Failed,* (London, Pall Mall, 1966), p. 51.
827 Feraoun, *Journal,* p. 131.

a religious dimension to the cinema ban. Grenades were thrown into European bars frequented by Muslims, and bombs exploded in cinemas specialising in Egyptian films. In eastern Algeria, all real-estate transactions with *pieds noirs* were forbidden on pain of death. The wearing of the brimless *chechis* was prescribed over the French beret to accentuate a separate identity.

On 29 May 1957, in Melouza, 300 villagers were massacred for identifying with the MNA (*Mouvement National Algérien*), the FLN's nationalist rivals. Every male over fifteen was herded into the mosque and slaughtered with rifles, pickaxes and knives. Horribly mutilated, they were left on public display to show 'our determination to finish off those who do not want to march with the glorious ALN.'[828] This was an extreme example of a process present from the start: the violent imposition of the FLN as sole representatives of the people. In an earlier massacre, Colonel Amirouche, the legendary but controversial leader of *wilaya* 3, ordered more than two thousand Muslim deaths in a village near Bougie. The ALN was no less ruthless with its own recruits. In one concerted period of trying to breach the Morice Line, they flung thousands at the electrified and heavily mined barrier. The ten-kilometre-wide defences could not be crossed in one night. Thousands died in a six-month attempt.

ALN confidence in its own ranks was proportional to the hopelessness of each case. You could be sure of the new man when he could no longer go back into the colonial system. This initiation was dramatised in Pontecorvo's *Battle of Algiers* when new recruit Ali la Pointe was ordered to shoot down a *gendarme* while unknowingly being shadowed. Any hesitation and he would be shot instead.

In one extraordinary coup, French intelligence convinced Colonel Amirouche his *wilaya* had been infiltrated. His closest lieutenants had their throats cut, and hundreds of young people and students from the city who had taken to the mountains to join the ALN suffered the same fate. To defeat this 'plot', 2,000 Algerians died. After independence, the intra-ALN killings were so terrible that people took to the streets to stand between rivals: 15,000 died before their leaders resolved their differences. When the war was officially over, between 30,000 to 150,000 discharged *harkis* were ritually slaughtered for their service to France.[829] They died clearing minefields or were shot out of hand. They were tortured, made to swallow their decorations and dig their own

---

828   Evans, *Algeria, France's Undeclared War,* (OUP, 2012), p. 217.
829   Evans, *Algeria*, p. 337, Stora, *Algeria*, (Cornell University Press, 2001), p. 111.

graves. They were burned alive, castrated, cut up and fed to dogs. Their families, including children, were put to death.[830] ALN ruthlessness is not disputed.

A fact making the label of 'civilian' inapplicable
On 10 November 1954 *Algerois* awoke to walls daubed with the slogan: *la valise ou le cerceuil*, the suitcase or the coffin. The following catalogue illustrates the ALN policy of deliberately targeting civilians.[831] Following de Gaulle's September 1959 invitation to participate in elections to decide Algeria's future, two bombs exploded without warning in a department store in Algiers, killing three *pieds noirs*. Four more were killed in an attack on a pub. Between 1 December 1959 and 12 January 1960, twenty-two farmers were killed near Algiers. In June, a grenade was thrown into a French wedding in Oran, injuring forty-three. In August, the ALN attacked a beach at Chinoua near Algiers, killing twelve *pieds noirs* and seriously wounding seven more. In September, a bus exploded in Algiers. In November, in Boufarik, bombs exploded in a dance hall, and at the pharmacy treating the victims. Seven *pieds noirs* were killed and fifty-six wounded. Early in 1961 grenades were thrown into wedding receptions, among soccer fans, into buses, among schoolchildren and French civilians. During three weeks of France's unilateral ceasefire between May and June 1961, thirty-one *pieds noirs* civilians were killed and ninety-five injured. In August 1961, the ALN shot up a café terrace in a popular holiday spot, killing six and wounding seven. A grenade was thrown on the beach near Bône, wounding twelve. Zohra Drif recalls she and Djamila Bouhired placed their bombs at peak traffic seeking maximum casualties.[832]

The ALN repeatedly attacked highway traffic. An FLN statement reads: 'January 22, 1957, the Algiers–Koléa bus was attacked. The European passengers were executed.'[833] The leadership took the decision to target French civilians at the Soummam Conference in August 1956. In June 1956 Abane had already ordered attacks against French civilians in response to the execution of ALN members. The French residents of Algiers had demanded their executions for their mutilation-murders, including that of a child. The *pieds noirs*, perceived

---

830   Horne, *Savage War,* pp. 537–8.
831   Hutchinson, *Revolutionary Terrorism,* (Hoover Institute 1978), pp. 69-70.
832   Drif, *Inside the Battle of Algiers*, (Just World, 2017), p. 112.
833   Ibid., p. 58 for ALN attacking civilians see also, Clark, *Algeria in Turmoil* (NY, Grossett, 1960), pp. 194-5.

as enthusiastic supporters of army repression, were not accorded civilian status. Between 21-24 June, Saadi's squads roamed Algiers targeting Europeans, killing ten and wounding thirty-nine. Victims had a note pinned to the body: 'Zabane, Ferradji, you are avenged.'[834] On the eve of Yom Kippur 1959, the ALN attacked the synagogue of Bou-Saada, killing the rabbi's six-year-old daughter. In December 1960 they sacked the Great Synagogue of the Kasbah.

For a year, from 1956 to 1957, the ALN exploded no-warning bombs in dance halls, schools, cafés, playgrounds, department stores, inside buses and metal lamp posts, timed to explode at rush hour. Hundreds of civilians died in the explosions, hundreds more died in shootings.[835] The bombs were small packet-sized devices. The intention was civilian blood, not economic destruction. Hundreds suffered amputations as these small bombs shattered cast-iron tables, decorative mirrors and lamp posts. They deliberately targeted the young. The attack on the Milk Bar, frequented by mothers with children, was designed for maximum effect. Zohra Drif personally selected the Milk Bar as a symbol of 'offensive carefree attitudes, their shameful indifference to our woes and the arrogance of the colonial regime ...'[836] ALN leader Mohamed Lebjaoui acknowledged the ALN targeted civilians, but insisted the attacks were a 'tardy reply to European terrorism, legal or illegal.'[837]

Derradji explains that terrorism, in counterinsurgency terminology, is a strategy of the weak for political motives. But this differs from 'the necessity of a religious terror as a self-defence means to deter the enemy of God and of the colonized.'[838] Derradji consulted the archived testimony of ALN fighters. They were obliged, according to the Holy Koran, *not* to attack civilians. The majority however saw the *pieds noirs* of the city and the *colons* in the countryside as supporters of colonialism. They were all directly and indirectly involved in the war against the FLN and its supporters, 'the fact which had consequently made their label of "civilians" inapplicable.'[839] In her old age, Zohra Drif had no regrets over civilian deaths nor 'would she ever' as they were accomplices in colonialism.[840] She and her comrades were 'happy and proud to have participated in delivering justice.'[841] Clare

834 A. Derradji, *Algerian Guerrilla Campaign,* (Edwin Mellen 1997), p. 275.
835 Clark, *Algeria in Turmoil*, pp. 325–6.
836 Drif, *Inside*, p. 110.
837 Hutchinson, *Revolutionary Terrorism*, p. 57.
838 Derradji, op. cit., p. 228, my emphasis.
839 Ibid., p. 244.
840 Drif, *Inside*, pp. 106, 108, 186.
841 Ibid., p. 128.

Hollingworth recalled: 'It's true they were terribly brutal, but correspondents were sympathetic to them anyway, for de-colonisation. I was.'[842]

IRA Tactics
From defence and retaliation to the bombing campaign

On 11 January 1992, the *Times* published a leaked army presentation, widely understood to be General John Wiley, General Officer Commanding NI, which read: 'the IRA is thought to be better resourced, better led, bolder and more secure against our penetration than at any time before. They are an absolutely formidable enemy ... Some of their operations are brilliant ...' Another internal army paper, released under a freedom of information request in 2007, 'conceded, for the first time, it did not win the battle against the IRA.'[843] Many believe the Downing St Declaration of 1993, which launched the peace process, would not have been signed by British Prime Minister John Major without massive IRA bombs in England.[844]

But this is at the latter end of the conflict. Republicans, initially engaged in political reforms, did not fire an offensive shot until two years after the first civil rights march.[845] In 1969, following the loyalist attack at Burntollet, Major Michael Mates, assessed the situation as: 'civil disobedience rather than resumption of an IRA campaign ... the Protestants, the B-Specials were overreacting.'[846] Initially, the IRA leadership pursued electoral, housing and employment reforms. Gerry Adams later called for a mass unarmed political movement to work for national self-determination. In the years between, the IRA attacked British forces, believing soldiers' deaths would push the British people to demand withdrawal. Bombings would tie down large numbers of soldiers and the economic loss resulting would render the 'six-county state' ungovernable and force Britain to the table.

Republicans maintain they did their utmost to avoid civilian casualties. IRA leader Seán Mac Stíofáin: 'In spite of all precautions civilians were accidentally killed ... we regretted each one of them.'[847]

---

842 Interview, Clare Hollingworth (London), 30 July 1998.
843 Army Paper says IRA not Defeated, http://news.bbc.co.uk/1/hi/northern_ireland/6276416.stm accessed 5 June 2018.
844 Geraghty, *Irish War*, (London, Harper-Collins, 1998), p.237, *Belfast Telegraph*, 6 February 2016.
845 Sunday Times Insight, *Ulster,* (Penguin, 1972), p. 209.
846 Geraghty, *Irish War*, p. 24.
847 S. Mac Stíofáin, *Memoirs of a Revolutionary,* (Edinburgh, Gordon, 1975), p. vii.

IRA leader Dáithí Ó Conaill claimed: 'There is no known case where Provisional volunteers have recklessly endangered lives.'[848] Clearly, he has an inflated view of his recruits. IRA critics acknowledge they routinely gave warnings, with one senior bomb-disposal officer adding: 'now and again they don't ...'[849] Colonel Evelegh explained that republicans seeking publicity 'rather than actual casualties ... [led to] the practice of the Provisional IRA ... giving warning of their bombs to avoid casualties.'[850] Bowyer Bell concluded it was IRA policy to give warnings 'so that not too many innocent civilians will involuntarily have to pay a price for Irish freedom.'[851] Toolis wrote it is generally accepted that Martin McGuinness's 'soldiers were extraordinarily successful in avoiding killing the wrong type of people.'[852] The IRA did not always avoid killing the 'wrong type.'

'There is nothing we can offer in mitigation'
Bloody Friday
In Belfast on 21 July 1972 twenty-two IRA bombs exploded between 2.15pm and 3.30pm. They were placed at: five railway stations, four bridges, two bus stations, a ferry terminal, a haulage depot, an electricity substation, a gas station, taxi depot, bank, utility office, hotel, and a shopping strip.[853] Nine people were killed: five civilians (three Protestants, two Catholics), two soldiers, one RUC officer and one UDA member. One hundred and thirty were wounded, some terribly. It became known as Bloody Friday. Cochrane wrote: 'There were no effective warnings ... the bombs were planted with the intention of killing as many people as possible.'[854] In fact, all came with warnings, most areas were evacuated, two were defused and two remaining bombs did all the killing. The army claimed it received no warnings for these. But the Samaritans and the Public Protection Agency confirmed these deadly explosions were preceded by two warnings of seventy-three minutes and thirty minutes.[855] The IRA maintained it was an attack on infrastructure gone wrong. IRA leader Malachy McNally stated: 'The explosion at the bus station nearly destroyed our morale ...'[856]

848   Kelley, *The Longest War,* (London, Zed, 1982), p. 200.

849   Van Voris, *Violence in Ulster,* (Massachusetts, 1975), p. 243.

850   Evelegh, *Peacekeeping in a Democratic Society,* (London, Hurst 1978), p. 39.

851   Bowyer Bell, *The Gun in Irish Politics,* (Routledge, 1987), p. 161.

852   Toolis, *Rebel Hearts,* p. 305.

853   Oppenheimer, *IRA: The Bombs and the Bullets,* (Irish Academic Press 2009), p. 67.

854   Cochrane, *Northern Ireland, The Uneasy Peace,* (Yale, 2013), p. 77.

855   Pringle, Bloody Friday's Lost Warnings, *Sunday Times,* 30 July 1972.

856   O'Brien, *The Long War* (Poolbeg, 1993), p. 38.

Brendan Hughes, Belfast IRA commander, thought the 'disaster' resulted from 'overestimating the army's ability to clear the area ... they gave warnings ... there was never any attempt, at any time, to kill people with the car bomb.'[857]

Colonel Evelegh believed that 'The Bloody Friday killings had the effect of swinging public opinion away from the republican cause which it had supported since Bloody Sunday ... [Operation Motorman] only became possible after this shift in public opinion, particularly international public opinion.'[858] General Carver immediately labelled the day: 'Bloody Friday. He wanted this name to stick in people's minds, a perfect propaganda reply to Bloody Sunday.'[859]

Just days before the bombings, the *Observer's* Colin Smith noticed: 'an expectant air in Belfast ... Senior officers were saying *earlier in the week* that they could well imagine being asked to give the IRA a bloody nose if they did something sufficiently horrific to produce a public outcry.'[860] Republicans claimed the army deliberately ignored the warnings for propaganda advantage. The army has been exposed as perpetrating mysterious bombings and shootings civilians and there is yet the mystery of the missed or unheeded warnings.[861] But Gerry Adams thought it a moot point: 'Civilians were killed who should not have been killed. This was the IRA's responsibility and a matter of deep regret.'[862]

La Mon Hotel

On 17 February 1978, the IRA bombed the La Mon Hotel a few miles from Belfast. Twelve civilians, all Protestant, were killed, horribly burned. This is often cited as proof of the IRA deliberately targeting Protestants. RTE's Brendan O'Brien put it to IRA leader Malachy McNally. He outlined a catalogue of vandalised telephone-boxes, army checkpoints with the IRA warning dwindling to nine minutes: 'The Republican Movement ... never went out to harm Protestants because they were Protestants.'[863] An IRA army council member informed

857   McKittrick et al, *Lost Lives,* p. 231.
858   Evelegh, *Peacekeeping*, p. 39.
859   Hamill, *Pig in the Middle*, (London, Metheun, 1985), p. 112.
860   *Observer*, 23 July 1972 – my italics.
861   David Blundy detailed army false flag bombings and shooting civilians with captured IRA weapons, *Sunday Times, 1*3 March 197. See too Fisk, *The Point of No Return*, pp. 87, 101, 105, 149n for army black-propaganda operations and Coogan, *Troubles*, 1995, pp. 250-4. A Unionist politician also documented army 'dirty tricks', K Lindsay, *Ambush at Tully West*, (Dundrod Press, 1979).
862   McKittrick et al., *Lost Lives*, p. 231.
863   O'Brien, *Long War*, p. 38.

journalist Eamonn Mallie that the deaths provoked an intense internal debate: 'Guidelines were laid down to each unit. They were to cut out high-risk bombings.'[864] Whatever of the internal debate, many were convinced of a sectarian intent.

Enniskillen bomb
On 8 November 1987, at a Remembrance Day ceremony, an IRA bomb exploded without warning killing eleven Protestant civilians. The IRA said that the bomb had failed to detonate earlier against parading soldiers. However, its claim that the British army detonated the bomb using electronic scanning equipment was untrue. Sinn Féin's Joe Austin despaired: 'The reaction amongst all the republicans I knew was enormous ... a deep sense of shame.'[865] Irish government archives recorded 'unprecedented criticism of the atrocity from within republican ranks.'[866] Guards at Long Kesh/Maze prison camp, often ex-servicemen and Orangemen, confirmed: 'Enniskillen came nearer to breaking them than anything else.'[867] Denzil McDaniel, editor of the local unionist-leaning *Impartial Reporter*, wrote: 'I don't believe the IRA set out to specifically kill civilians ... I think they made mistakes ... the IRA was reckless about civilian life.' He later wrote: '... we cannot easily rule out the dreadful thought agents of the British State knew what was going to happen and let it go ahead. In all honesty, in my opinion that is not only possible but indeed, likely.'[868] In December 2018, under the 30-year rule the Irish government released state papers. An anonymous letter, reputed to be from a disaffected MI5 agent, claimed they were monitoring the IRA unit: 'Our section decided to change the timing device and let the explosion take place so that the IRA would score an own goal ...'[869] Once again, a spectre has been raised. Did state agents murder civilians with the IRA making it possible? All part of the dirty war, perhaps, although the Irish government considered it important enough to preserve it and publish later.

864   Bishop and Mallie, *Provisional IRA*, (Corgi, 1988), p. 268.
865   Parker, *May the Lord in His Mercy,* (Jonathan Cape, 1993), p. 136.
866   Department of Foreign Affairs 2017/ 4/ 70, *Irish News,* 29 December 2017.
867   O'Connor, *In Search of a State,* (Blackstaff, 1993), p. 139.
868   *Sunday Tribune,* 28 October 2007, and D. McDaniel, *Enniskillen, Remembrance Bombing,* (Wolfhound, 1997) pp. 103-9.
869   *Irish Times,* 29 December 2018.

Shankill bomb

On 23 October 1993 an IRA bomb exploded in Frizzell's fish shop on Belfast's Shankill Road. It was an open secret in Belfast that the UDA ran its murder campaign from premises above this shop. [870] David McKittrick observed of Belfast then: 'No one thought it strange to have a terrorist group's headquarters above the local fish shop.'[871] In an attempt to wipe out the UDA leadership it was 'one of the IRA's most disastrous mistakes'. [872] Nine Protestants and one IRA member were killed. A surviving IRA member declared: 'I deeply regret the loss of innocent life.'[873] Gerry Adams, acknowledging it was little comfort to the bereaved, pointed out it was a premature explosion: 'Their intention was to attack the leaders of the death squads …'[874] Once again claims have emerged of British agents who 'set the device to explode prematurely.'[875] It was intended to weaken the position of IRA hawks opposing an impending ceasefire. It joins a list, including the Omagh bomb, with suspected army involvement.

There were other murderous bombs: Birmingham (twenty-one dead) and Claudy (nine), Newry (nine), Teebane (eight), Coleraine (six). After a long silence, the Birmingham bombing has recently received media attention. Among the contested issues now are security forces' advance knowledge, failure to evacuate even with the delayed warnings received and evidence of subsequent falsifying of times when emergency services arrived. The state has long impeded the families in their search for justice.[876] Claudy did not maintain a similarly high profile. There have been suggestions the state colluded to suppress coverage because of the alleged involvement of a Fr James Chesney, fearing this would fan the conflict.[877] The Coleraine atrocity also received much less media attention. The Newry Customs post bomb killed six civilians (five Catholic, one Protestant) and three IRA members. This has almost completely disappeared from the public memory. The Teebane roadside bomb killed seven Protestant workers and one soldier building an army

---

870 McDonald & Cusack, *UDA*, (Penguin, 2005), pp. 187, 207, McKay, *Bear in Mind These Dead*, (Faber, 2008), p. 138.

871 McKittrick, *Independent*, 26 October 1993.

872 McKittrick, *Independent*, 25 October 1993.

873 McKittrick et al., *Lost Lives*, p. 1329.

874 Sharrock and Davenport, *Man of War, Man of Peace*, p. 308.

875 *Independent*, 25 January 2016.

876 *46 Guardian*, 10 February 2016, https://www.theguardian.com/uk-news/2016/feb/10/birmingham-pub-bombings-informer-ira-unit-court-told, *Guardian*, 20 November, 2016, http://justice4the21.co.uk/, and http://www.birminghammail.co.uk/all-about/birmingham-pub-bombings.

877 *Guardian* 24 August 2010.

base. The IRA killed twenty-three (Protestants and Catholics) for working on military installations.[878]

The IRA admits to killing civilians during attacks on the army, police, loyalist paramilitaries or against commercial property. Republicans viewed these as bungled operations or as technical mistakes resulting from faulty equipment. With the growing list of atrocities, the Sinn Féin position evolved to condemning operations with high risk to civilians as conceptually flawed.

If not intentional then certainly forseeable
The IRA placed between 16-19,000 bombs killing hundreds of civilians and wounding thousands, from minor cuts to loss of limbs. Warnings with agreed code words resulted in the British army defusing 5,000. Bew records that twenty-nine commercial bombs killed 118 civilians. This included five without warning, six ignored warnings, seven premature explosions, and eleven inadequate warnings. Of the numerous bombings on security forces, forty-six killed 184 civilians. There were also six sectarian pub bombings and eleven explosions in preparation. These horrendous figures – a glaring censure of an IRA supposedly working to the republican ideal of Catholic, Protestant and Dissenter – do not support the media template of every bomb targeted to kill civilians. Bew's total of ninety two killer-bombs amounts to 0.6% of total IRA bombings.[879] I counted 136 IRA bombs taking civilian lives, 0.7% of IRA bombs (Appendix 1). But just one deadly explosion is an obscenity, and if, as republicans claim, the deaths were not intentional, they were foreseeable.[880]

The UN defines terrorism as targeting civilians and Fintan O'Toole points out that reconciliation requires honest accounting: 'By far the biggest single category of IRA victims is made up of civilians.'[881] But the IRA does meet the UN definition as O'Toole's 'honest accounting' divides state forces deaths into separate categories of army, UDR and

---

878   O'Brien, *Long War*, pp. 219-221.

879   P. Bew et al, *Northern Ireland: Chronology of the Troubles, 1968-1993* (Dublin: Gill. 1993), and Deutsch & Magowan, *Northern Ireland: Chronology,* (Blackstaff, 1973–75). Oppenheimer, citing 19,000 IRA bombs, concluded the IRA 'avoided civilian casualties as far as possible', Oppenheimer, *IRA: The Bombs and Bullets,* p. 10.

880   An inquest into IRA victim Yvonne Dunlop concluded: 'death was not intended or probable [but] a real possibility', McKittrick et al., *Lost Lives*, p. 680.

881   *Irish Times,* 5 December 2020, English, *Armed Struggle*, p. 380, also separates security forces into categories. O'Toole repeatedly cites IRA killings incorrectly, 'a majority of their victims were civilians', *Guardian* 20 July 2007; 'almost 500 Catholics killed by IRA and INLA', *Irish Times* 19 July 1996. The Cain Index records 158 Catholics killed by the IRA, less than half attributed by O'Toole. Less than punctilious, O'Toole writes of 'Bloody Sunday, the ten-minute massacre', *Irish Times*, 21 January 2022, whereas Saville records paratroopers firing for 45 minutes.

RUC. The record shows that civilian dead amount to a terrible twenty-nine percent of IRA victims and state forces amount to fifty-eight percent of IRA killings. Loyalists and security forces do meet the terrorist definition. Civilians amount to a staggering ninety percent of loyalist killings and civilians amount to fifty-two percent of state killings.[882] These are official figures. There is, however, little doubt the army and police colluded with loyalists. The argument is only over the extent. Patterson considered that possibly 'fifty percent of those killed by loyalists [be] added to the security forces figure.'[883] This produces an army-loyalist killing of 627 civilians to the IRA's 508. Bruce's categories of pro-state or anti-state killings yields another accounting. The army, police and loyalists killed 1064 civilians to the IRA's 508.[884]

Depending on the accounting, Protestant civilian dead amount to between 14% and 20% of IRA victims.[885] Some IRA units engaged in a round of reciprocal killings with loyalist paramilitaries made up of UDA, UVF, RUC, UDR and British army.[886] Sutton records 130 republican sectarian murders.[887] The Kingsmill massacre is an example of an IRA unit responding to a joint RUC-UDR-UVF killing of two Catholic families by killing ten Protestant workers. Alan Black, the lone Kingsmill survivor, believes the unit involved were British agents.[888] IRA actions do not betray republicans as inherently anti-Protestant.[889] You can say they misunderstood Protestants and never really believed in their Britishness.[890] Republican claims of a heroic guerrilla struggle are confronted by this callous risking, and taking of civilian lives. The Cain index records a total IRA killing of 1,771 including 255 Protestant

---

882   http://cain.ulst.ac.uk/sutton/selecttabs.html, see also McKittrick et al., *Lost Lives.*

883   *Irish Times*, 30 May 2006.

884   https://cain.ulster.ac.uk/sutton/book/ - Sutton in his introduction to the Cain Index explains he counted prison officers as state forces but does not count 45 loyalist paramilitaries and 59 informers killed by the IRA as state actors, nor were builders erecting security installations. Protestant civilians mistakenly killed by loyalists as Catholics were *not* added to loyalists' *sectarian* tally.

885   http://cain.ulst.ac.uk/cgi-bin/tab3.pl and McKittrick, *Lost Lives*, Table 20, p. 1484.

886   Republicans maintain sectarian motivations were weeded out; White, 'The IRA: An Assessment of Sectarianism', *Terrorism and Political Violence*, vol. 9, no. 1 (spring 1997), pp. 28–31.

887   https://cain.ulster.ac.uk/sutton/book/

888   https://www.bbc.co.uk/news/uk-northern-ireland-26219935 State agents involved, retrieved 18 January 2022.

889   See the debate between Robert White, Steve Bruce and James Dingley in *Terrorism and Political Violence*, vol. 9, no. 1 (spring 1997), vol. 9, no. 2 (summer 1997), vol. 10, no. 2 (summer 1998), and vol. 10, no. 4 (winter 1998). IRA tactics are generally non-sectarian, consistent with their ideology. See also O'Duffy, Brendan. (1985) "Violence in Northern Ireland 1969-1994: Sectarian or Ethno-national?" *Ethnic and Racial Studies* 18, no. 4: 740-72.

890   Smith, *Fighting for Ireland,* (Routledge, 1975), p. 118.

and 162 Catholic civilians.[891] Civilians are a minority of IRA killings but it is a large one.

The Liberal Press
Disciplined rebels with a moral code

The ALN were portrayed as soldiers and patriots. They did not 'murder' French soldiers, they 'ambushed' and 'executed' them. These *maquisards* were disciplined and tough, fearless and elusive idealists, acting to a moral code. They were offering the French generous terms. Although they threw grenades into schools, weddings, synagogues, Sunday-afternoon strollers, cafés and casinos, ALN members were insurgents and rebels, and sometimes just grenade throwers, culprits or simply Muslims. Occasionally, they were classified as terrorists, but infrequently and usually only if the actions took place in France. Consider the following eight extracts,[892] where the *Guardian* described civilians killed by rebels or insurgents: '200 rebels killed twelve people, after holding up a line of cars on a highway outside Mostaganem'; 'Two civilians including the *cure* of the village of Rabbalais were killed. The rebel band were well armed'; 'insurgents killed and mutilated six Europeans including children'; 'six Moslems had their throats cut by insurgents;' 'a massacre by the rebels of 22 Moslems, including 8 women and 2 children'; 'Insurgents kidnapped a European family of ten as they ate their evening meal'; 'rebels threw a grenade into a travelling fun fair, killing a child of 8'; 'insurgents in Oran knocked a European off his bicycle, shot him in the head and set the body on fire after soaking it in petrol'.

This continued even after independence. The murder of an isolated French farmer and his wife was 'the work of guerrillas.'[893]

The *Observer* also portrayed the ALN positively. Consider the following examples.[894] ALN fighters were 'fearless and elusive outlaws',

---

891   https://cain.ulster.ac.uk/cgi-bin/tab3.pl

892   For positive portrayals of the ALN, including examples in the text (identified with an asterisk), see *Guardian*, 14 August, 10*, 12, 29 September, 1, 9, 29 October, 14* November 1956, 1*, 4* January, 19 February, 1, 2 March, 31 July, 28* August 1957, 17 June, 20* August, 20, 26, 30 September, 4 October, 13 December 1958, 1, 10, 17 January, 14 February, 2*, 17 March, 21 April, 22 May, 16 June, 7 July, 14, 20 October, 22 December 1959, 16 February, 6 June, 1, 12, 13, 19, 29 August, 17 September, 11 November 1960, 1 January, 1, 18, 28 March, 4, 7 April, 10*, 31* July, 30 September, 9* October, 7 November 1961, 2 January, 20 February, 21* September 1962.

893   Ibid., September 1962.

894   See the *Observer* (including examples in the text, identified with an asterix) 19* June 1955; 27* May, 8 July 1956; 17* February, 2 June, 10 November 1957; 23 February, 2, 11* November 1958; 4* January, 27 September 1959; 31 January, 26 June 1960. For example, the ALN were the 'Army of Liberation', 8 July 1956 or the description of captured ALN as 'political prisoners', 11 January 1959. Examples of ALN cruelty and terror can be found in the *Guardian* of 30 October, 7 July 1956; 26 May, 17 September 1958; 1, 26 May, 26 September, 12 December 12, 1959; 2, 14 June 1960; 12 July 1962. And the *Observer* of: 26 January 1958; 27 December 1959; 10 January 1960.

'very tough and disciplined'. 'The hungry and often illiterate band proved to be not only formidable fighters but remarkable organizers.' The *Observer* criticised Prime Minister Mollet for calling the ALN 'armed gangs'; rather they were 'ALN combatants.' Killing an oil-company executive was the 'opening of the ALN's new front.' France should recognise ALN captives as 'political prisoners'. Ben Tobbal directed the groups 'that the French call terrorists.' He did, in fact, organise the Philippeville massacre. The *Observer*'s Nora Beloff understood their methods: 'even though they too often did so with cruelty. But do not weakness, misery and despair inevitably lead to cruelty?' Neal Ascherson recalled: 'I spent time with them in the Casbah. I admired them. They were disciplined, ascetic, good at their job. They defended the Casbah, engaged any French troops that might come in. It's likely they had participated with Yacef Saadi in the Battle of Algiers.'[895]

The *Guardian* would report 'yet another successful ambush' even if the dead included civilians.[896] 'The rebels have carried out a successful ambush … killing 23 soldiers and 9 civilians.'[897] The *Guardian* also demanded political status for ALN hunger strikers.[898] The Hunger Strike Committee of Britain's House of Commons (Barbara Castle, Tony Benn, John Baird and Konni Zilliacus) sympathised with ALN demands for political status. ALN death threats against Muslims participating in French elections, even as they were carried out, were described as 'advice', 'instructions' or 'recommendations.'[899] During the spring 1959 municipal elections, the ALN reinforced its advice with the killing of twenty Muslims and the wounding of sixty-four more. The editor described this atrocity as 'a determined effort by the fellaghas to make a demonstration of strength in order to force abstention on the Moslem population.'[900] The killings were also deemed successful.

The killing and mutilating of French civilians and lukewarm Muslims at Philippeville was not reported at all by the *Guardian*. The *Observer* reported it as if it were an attack on the military: '44 soldiers and civilians were killed … The rebels hurled bombs at security force

---

895   Interview, Neal Ascherson (at the *Observer*, London), 28 July 1998.

896   Successful ALN ambushes including dead civilians, see *Guardian*, 14 August, 29 October 1956, 2 March 1957, 16 February 1960.

897   Ibid., 29 October 1956.

898   For articles critical of ALN criminal status, see *Guardian*, 29 October 1956, 'political offenders', 25 August 1961, 24 August 1962, and *Observer*, 'political prisoners', 11 January 1959.

899   ALN methods were 'instructions and recommendations' about elections rather than threats, *Guardian*, 31 May 1960, 6 January and *Observer*, 8 January 1961.

900   *Guardian*, 21 April 1959 (editorial).

encampments.[901] The real figure for the dead was ninety-two civilians and thirty-one soldiers and police.[902] The reporting of the Melouza massacre of 300 Muslims of the rival MNA is especially instructive. The *Guardian* reported three different slaughters of Muslim civilians by the ALN, including the one in the village at Melouza.[903] The 'rebels rounded up the male inhabitants ... They killed all the men over 15.' Its editorial response was not to condemn the ALN atrocity but to criticise the French for failing to protect civilians from 'the wildest of the rebels.'[904] An article in the same edition and again in relation to Melouza cautioned against the idea that 'all Algerian nationalism should be associated ... with criminality.'[905] Its next editorial on the massacre recommended the French negotiate with the rebels no matter how much blood was on their hands or how much it would antagonise 'the settlers.'[906] In the following months, the *Guardian* declared the Melouza massacre was against the ALN's moral outlook, and even suggested it was the work of the French army.

The *Observer* reported the Melouza killings without a hint of reproach: 'the likeliest explanation is that the killings were perpetrated by an isolated FLN band operating on its own ... [and] provided the French with a Heaven-sent opportunity to discredit the FLN.'[907] The *Observer* even found something positive. Although the FLN had lost something in world opinion, they had gained something in the eyes of the hitherto uncommitted Muslim population because the 'French were unable to prevent wholesale slaughter.'[908] The editorial comment of the same edition criticised France's refusal to talk with the FLN: 'that would merely prolong the slaughter.'[909] In the following months, the *Observer* cast doubt on the French version, also suggesting Melouza was the work of the French army.[910] However, it became recognised as the ALN's work, although it denied it for a long time and even called on the pope to investigate. In 1991 French and Algerian television broadcast a remarkable documentary *Les Années Algériennes*. ALN

901 *Observer*, 21 August 1955.
902 Evans, *Algeria*, p. 141.
903 *Guardian*, 1 June 1957.
904 Ibid., 3 June 1957 (editorial).
905 Ibid., 3 June 1957.
906 Ibid., 5 June 1957 (editorial).
907 *Observer*, 2 June 1957.
908 Ibid.
909 Ibid. (editorial).
910 French involvement in Melouza, see *Guardian*, 31 July, 5, 8 August 1957, and *Observer*, 24 March, 2, 9, 23 June, 18 August 1957.

leader Mohamedi Said admitted the Melouza massacre: 'Our first enemy was not the French soldiers it was the traitors among us.'[911] In 1958 the ALN took its campaign to France, attacking isolated police stations and bombing commercial targets. The result was eighty-two police and civilian deaths. There was not one *Guardian* editorial condemnation. There were muted editorials that offered advice to the FLN. This new campaign 'will do the cause of Algerian nationalists no good in the eyes of world opinion.'[912] Another editorial offered more advice: 'The extension of a terrorist campaign to France itself will cause immense suffering to their fellow countrymen.'[913] A year later, *Guardian* editorials were still offering advice without condemnation: 'The French police were the object of a peculiarly ill-conceived campaign.'[914] No mention of the civilian dead. In addition, a leading article on page one, of the same issue, rejected 'the French propaganda line' of portraying the ALN's campaign in France as desperate and fearful of defeat. Rather, ALN attacks can from a 'grim tactical point of view be given more sense than the French radio commentators (and semi-official comment) will admit.'[915] The *Guardian* carried an interview with 'Prime Minister' Ferhat Abbas, who dissociated himself from the campaign in France 'in the presence of the Algerian "Minister of War" Mr Krim Belkacem'. Abbas was the public face of a self-appointed group of insurgents whose political party and military elite continue yet to deny Algerians democracy. To assign 'Prime Minister' to Abbas and to describe Krim Belkacem as the 'Minister of War' would be inconceivable in a post-9/11 world. Abbas explained that 'the [FLN] Government had agreed' to the campaign on condition the attacks were limited to economic or military targets. But in the 'excitement of battle, orders are often transgressed, the Algerian Government was at the moment reconsidering its instructions on terrorism.'[916] This spokesman for an organisation that killed civilians as policy was, in the view of the *Guardian*, a 'head of government.' In fact, Abbas was just a figurehead. Men like Krim were directing the ALN. Martha Hutchinson, who reported the war for the *Guardian*, remembers it differently: 'Abbas was interrupted by Krim ... the GPRA had not yet resolved that

---

911   B. Stora, P. Alfonsi, B. Favre, P. Pesnot, *Les Annés Algériennes* (documentary) Ina/France 2, Nouvel Observateur, 1991.

912   *Guardian*, 26 August (editorial).

913   Ibid., 20 September (editorial).

914   Ibid., 24 June 1959 (editorial).

915   Ibid. (article).

916   Ibid., 15 October 1958.

question [targeting civilians].'[917] Despite this, the *Guardian* gave the last word to Abbas. At the close of the Battle of Algiers, the *Observer* reproached the British government for criticising ALN methods at the UN: 'Unfortunately', the British government had, 'trotted out the hoary old legend that no "true" national movement ever used terrorism ... such hypocrisy only discredits Britain by aligning her with the most unrepentant form of colonialism.'[918]

Sectarian murderers and psychos who kill for pleasure
The liberal press reported the IRA as a gang of psychotic terrorists and sectarian gunmen who took joy in killing. They were gutless, mindless brutes, thugs, mystical romantics and criminals.[919] A *Guardian* editorial explained their 'orgy of blood-letting has become the main purpose of their lives. They are bombing for the sake of bombing and killing for the sake of killing.'[920] It was 'mindless terrorism', only 'sane people can put a stop to it.' The IRA's real weapon was its 'criminal keenness'; its members 'would kill you with sticks if that's all they had.'[921] IRA members were cowards who organised riots and shot from behind women and children.[922] It sent out children with 'medieval weapons like the crossbow, not to speak of biblical ones like the stone.'[923] Hetherington-Cole were particularly keen on an archaic religious slant.

For the *Observer*, the IRA was/were a death machine, a mafia, butchers, hoodlums, cowards, drunks, lunatics, baboons, irrational fascists and crazy fascists.[924] Astor explained the IRA's 'fascist behaviour' and warned against 'the Irish people as a whole thinking in the crazy terms of the IRA' and its 'atavistic fights.'[925] British soldiers were not successfully ambushed, they were murdered.[926] A *Guardian*

---

917 Hutchinson, *Revolutionary Terrorism*, p. 97.
918 *Observer*'s 'Comment' column, 8 December 1957.
919 IRA psychos and filled with bloodlust, see *Guardian*, 2 February, 9, 14 (editorial), 29 September 1971, 4 January (editorial), 18 February (editorial), 11 March (editorial), 11 April, 12 May, 8 July, 3 August 1972, 10 June 1973.
920 Ibid., 11 April 1972 (editorial).
921 Ibid., 29 September 1971.
922 IRA hiding behind women and children, see *Guardian*, 19 (editorial), 25 January, 9 February 1971, 20 April (editorial), 12 May, 7 August 1972, 31 May 1973.
923 Ibid. (editorial), 19 January 1971.
924 For the IRA as irrational fascists, hoodlums, etc., see *Observer*, 10, 17 October, 11 November 1971, 23 April, 25 June, 16, 30 July, 5 November 1972, 17 June, 2 September 1973.
925 Ibid., 2 September 1973 (editorial).
926 See *Guardian*, 13 August 1970 (editorial), 12 March (editorial), 24 May (editorial), 2 December 1971, 18 February (editorial), 3 June 1972, 24 March, 23 November 1973, and *Observer*, 14 March (editorial) 1971 and 17 March 1974.

editorial captured the tone: 'a soldier was seriously wounded by a gun attack that re-created the methods of Chicago gangsters in the thirties.'[927] Attacks on army barracks and elite undercover soldiers were carried out by terrorists, not by insurgent bands or rebels.[928] A typical example reads: 'Two soldiers were killed and four injured in terrorist ambushes in Belfast ... as they lay injured another terrorist hurled a blast bomb ... a dastardly piece of work ... [and] not satisfied with the gun attack – they had to throw a bomb among the men.'[929] These 'cowardly terrorist attacks' on soldiers differed from the ALN's 'successful insurgent ambushes' of bus passengers or from the actions of ALN soldiers who threw grenades at childrens' funfairs. IRA methods were also sectarian. The religion of regular British army casualties was rarely recorded, but Hetherington-Cole explained the significance of the murder of a UDR member: it differed from the 'maquis or other wartime resistance groups. His murder is a contribution to continuing sectarianism in Ireland.'[930]

The following five extracts from an *Observer* article show the continuing sectarian explanation.[931] Under the headline of 'Mau Mau warfare on Irish border', the newspaper painted a picture of Fermanagh's 'frontier war.' This rural struggle, 'the direct descendant of Ulster's colonial pedigree', resembled the experience of 'white farmers in Kenya during Mau Mau'. Most IRA attacks were reported to occur on isolated Protestant farms: 'farmers have been burnt out, ambushed, and on one occasion blown to pieces with a 500 lbs. mine intended for the army.' The record, in County Fermanagh at the time of this article, in addition to this tragic farmer, shows one other civilian had been killed during IRA attacks on the army. Seven others, all UDR soldiers, were killed. Three on patrol or at army barracks, one at his government office and three at their farms.[932]

An IRA attack on the army was also portrayed as an attack on the innocent. When paratrooper Michael Willets was killed in an attack on a Belfast barracks, the *Guardian* editorial explained the bombers 'do not care who they kill as long as they kill someone ... they meant to

927   *Guardian*, 24 May 1971 (editorial).
928   IRA terrorists, see *Guardian*, 26 March, 11 June, 1 November 1971, 18 March, 3 October 1972, 21, 28 February 1973, 21 January, 5, 9 February, 14 June 1974, and *Observer*, 18 November 1973.
929   *Guardian*, 21 February 1973.
930   Ibid., 18 February 1972 (editorial).
931   *Observer*, 5 November 1972.
932   McKittrick et al., *Lost Lives*, pp. 158, 163, 245, 255, 257, 267, 285.

kill innocent people.'[933] There were indeed many innocent civilians, Catholic and Protestant, killed during IRA attacks on soldiers or on commercial bombings. These deaths were intentional due to false or short warnings, or the intention was to provoke Protestants. When the IRA killed a member of a loyalist death squad, this, too, was deemed to be a sectarian killing. Andrew Wilson, in the *Observer,* explained 'the IRA continues to enjoy high prestige in the Catholic ghettoes, [and] its attacks on Protestant civilian targets could be maintained with impunity for a long time.'[934] According to this, the IRA killed Protestants to gain prestige among Catholics, an evaluation ominously coincident with loyalist justifications for the random murders of Catholic civilians. I did also find three reports of the IRA either bombing an army barracks with a warning or releasing captured soldiers, surprising acts on the part of mindless terrorists. I found one report of no-warning bombs described as 'not fitting the IRA pattern', and one other report where the warnings meant that 'deaths were not intended.'[935]

The Bloody Friday bombs also reveal a discrepancy between reporters in Belfast and the editor's office. Simon Winchester and Simon Hoggart reported on the two deadly bombings: 'warnings were given well in advance.' The first warning was 'heard over the military radio net[work]' at 2:10 pm' and the second warning 'an hour before the explosion.'[936] The editorial two days later described 'the wanton killing of non-combatant men, women and children as the inevitable consequences of exploding so many bombs without adequate warning.'[937] Both the *Guardian* and the *Observer* ignored the warnings and even their own earlier coverage when they blamed the IRA for the breakdown of the summer 1972 truce in Belfast. The 'Troubles' were the 'IRA troubles' or were due to the 'IRA campaign of violence', or

---

933   *Guardian*, 27 May 1971 (editorial).

934   *Observer*, 6 February 1972.

935   For targeting civilians, sectarian attacks and provocation of Protestants, see *Guardian*, 15 April, 3, 24 September (editorial), 10 November 1971, 4 January, 24 July, 23 August 1972, 9 September 1973, 14 May 1974, and *Observer*, 5 July 1970, 6 February 1972. A bomb with no warning 'did not fit the IRA pattern' (*Guardian*, 6 December 1971), and a warning meant the IRA 'did not intend death' (*Guardian*, 13 June 1973). For IRA attacks on army barracks with warnings and releasing captured soldiers, see *Guardian*, 8 July 1972, 19 August 1973, 8 March 1974.

936   Ibid., 22 July 1972.

937   Ibid., 24 July (editorial).

the IRA was 'responsible for almost all the violence.'[938]

There was also a general misrepresentation of the casualty figures. Thus, IRA leader Dáithí Ó Conaill 'remains an unscrupulous planner of operations which have led to the deaths of 700 people.'[939] At the time, the IRA was responsible for 378 deaths out of a total of 826. This 378 included 65 of their own members, almost all killed in premature explosions.[940] Kevin Myers' *Observer* article, marking the one-thousandth death, portrayed the IRA as responsible for virtually all the killings. Myers managed to fit in the 214 soldiers killed by the IRA, a Catholic boy's 'war dance of victory' over a dead soldier, and 'all the innocent victims of IRA bombs.' [941] He mentioned two British army killings of IRA members, no army killings of civilians, and none of the loyalist killings of Catholic civilians. The documented figures, at the time of this article, are 465 republican killings (72 self-inflicted) and 499 killings by loyalists and security forces, (285 and 214 respectively).[942]

Citing a UN definition, Colin Legum of the *Observer* pondered the legitimacy of political violence.[943] First, can the grievance be redressed by other means? Second, does the movement seeking change encourage indiscriminate killing of innocent civilians? He denied legitimacy to the IRA on both counts. But the evidence does not reveal a majority of IRA victims as civilians. Further, IRA conditions for a ceasefire, on 10 March 1972, were: withdrawal of the British army from the streets, acknowledgement of the Irish people's right to self-determination, abolition of Stormont regime, amnesty for political prisoners.[944] They are remarkably close to the eventual 1998 GFA. At the time of this IRA offer, the *Guardian* editorial urged the government not to negotiate

---

938 See *Guardian*, 10 (editorial), 11 (editorial), 13 July 1972. Again, there was a divergence between the editorials and the reporters. By 13 July 1972 Simon Hoggart was sympathetic to the IRA version of the breakdown. The *Observer* editorial of 16 July 1972 echoed the *Guardian* editorials, blaming the breakdown on the IRA. On 26 October 1972 the *Guardian* editorial returned to blaming the IRA for the breakdown. Interestingly, the *Guardian* had already reported three offers of a ceasefire from the IRA on 9 September, 29 November 1971 and 11 March 1972. To this last offer the *Guardian* urged *no talks*. Conor Cruise O'Brien also urged no 'talking with the IRA'; see *Guardian*, 19 July 1972. The 'Troubles' were the IRA trouble (see *Guardian*, 10 July 1971, 23 June 1972, 24 April 1973 (editorial)); 'since the IRA troubles began five years ago' *Guardian*, 21 February 1974 (editorial); *Observer*, 21 April 1974).

939 *Guardian*, 24 April 1973 (editorial).

940 See McKittrick et al., *Lost Lives*.

941 *Observer*, 21 April 1974.

942 See McKittrick et al., *Lost Lives.*

943 *Observer*, 26 November 1972.

944 Alan O'Day, *Political Violence,* p. 23.

because the demands were 'too extreme' and because of 'the way they have been presented.'[945]

The Rebel Leaders

Algeria: eloquent, charming and skilled 'invincibles'

Yacef Saadi was the chief organiser of no-warning bomb attacks on Algiers civilians. He was portrayed as a Scarlet Pimpernel figure leading French paratroopers on a merry dance.[946] The *Guardian* stressed 'the difficulty of morally assessing the men engaged in this grim struggle.'[947] Hetherington's editorial sympathised with the fundamental greatness and generosity of Saadi and 'the despair of this modern patriot' who would 'never be free.' He hoped 'this beautiful narrative bears witness, not only for Yacef Saadi, but for the spirit of man with its fundamental greatness.'[948] Another *Guardian* editorial explained ALN savagery: 'some of them appear to have been NCOs in the French Army, with all the limitations that that implies.'[949] Colonel Amirouche was a 'renowned field commander, invincible and invaluable.'[950] At his death, the *Guardian* editorial on Amirouche, is almost a eulogy: 'one of the most ruthless and efficient of the fellagha leaders ... the skill of the professional soldier was judiciously mingled with the terrorism of the revolutionary ... he nevertheless showed himself readier to spare European civilians than some of his fellows ... he will be much missed by the Algerian rebels.'[951] In fact, Amirouche gave the order at Melouza to exterminate 'the vermin'.

Ben Bella was a moderate, a fighter in the field, a decisive and intelligent socialist leader and the best speaker in the country. The *Observer* considered Algeria fortunate to have Ben Bella, who combined 'collegiate leadership with a long-standing dislike for dictatorship ... he has an exceptional political brain ... a practising Muslim who believes in a republic ... the countless dead weigh heavily on him.'[952] Ben Bella was undoubtedly an inspiration to Algerians, but he, himself, was embarrassed that he could only speak French, not

---

945   *Guardian*, 11 March 1972 (editorial).

946   Sympathetic coverage of Yacef Saadi, see *Guardian*, 25 September, 12 October 1957, 26 June, 29 August, 8 December 1958, 27 August 1962, and *Observer*, 21 September 1958.

947   *Guardian*, 29 August 1958.

948   Ibid., 8 December 1958 (editorial).

949   Ibid., 23 (editorial), 24 September 1958.

950   Ibid., 30 March, 1 April 1959.

951   Ibid., 1 April 1959 (editorial).

952   *Observer*, 18 March 1962.

Arabic. He preferred the military to dominate the politicians and accused his rivals of side-lining Islam and Nasser in favour of Europeans and Jews. He and his rivals for power generated 15,000 intra-ALN dead.

Other ALN leaders were impressive, generous, responsible, disciplined and restrained. They were not responsible for reprisals against Europeans and pro-French Algerians following independence.[953] Abbas was 'a Western minded bourgeois ... noble, respectable, lively and loquacious.'[954] The *Observer* agreed.[955] Ahmed Boumendjel was 'an eloquent, engaging man ... one of the best political brains.' Mohammed Ben Yahia 'might be a brilliant Sorbonne student.' Mohammed Yazid 'can disguise unwillingness to divulge information under a charming cloak of bonhomie ... A moderate man.'[956] However, his view of army chaplains and female medics as legitimate targets was hardly moderate.[957] Both newspapers painted a nicer picture of the Algerian nationalist leaders than they did themselves. A veteran CRUA (*Comité Révolutionnaire d'Unité et d'Action*) member acknowledged: 'we were young ... perhaps we were a shade ruthless.'[958]

Ireland: unpleasant, inarticulate and not very bright bigots

It is possible to find a positive portrayal of republicans. Thus, Gerry Adams was intelligent and possessed 'a remarkable organizational ability.'[959] Sean Keenan's claim, of always issuing bomb warnings, was 'almost plausible.'[960] Martin McGuinness achieved his leadership position 'through an abundance of physical courage rather than any great tactical sense.'[961] This is somewhat positive. But mostly, republican leaders were unpleasant, frightening, notorious, inarticulate and not very bright bigots. They were reportedly scandalised at young socialists engaging in sex orgies.[962] They were 'men of narrow but

---

953 For sympathetic coverage of Ben Bella, see *Guardian*, 22 May (editorial) 1959, 22 May 1961, 6 June, 18 August 1962 (editorial), and *Observer*, 18 March 1962. For positive portrayals of FLN/ALN leaders, see *Guardian*, 1 January (editorial), 13 March 1959, 3 November 1961, 5 May (editorial), 6, 28, 29, 30 June 1962, and *Observer*, 27 May 1962.

954 *Observer*, 11 December 1960.

955 Ibid., 3 July 1960, 21 May 1961.

956 *Guardian*, 4 May 1962.

957 Ibid., 25 January 1961.

958 Behr, *The Algerian Problem*, p. 63. The CRUA evolved into the FLN.

959 *Guardian*, 29 November 1972.

960 Ibid., 16 July 1973.

961 *Observer*, 30 July 1972.

962 See *Guardian*, 12 July 1971, 3 February (editorial), 11 March, 4, 15 September, 27 November 1972, and *Observer*, 17 October 1971, 16, 30 July, 3, 10 September, 1 October, 3 December 1972.

determined vision.'[963] Most had the rough hands of manual workers, with 'several wearing cloth caps' – a sure sign of the lower orders. None was especially articulate, nor displayed any theoretical understanding of revolutionary movements, nor exuded any of the charismatic charm of revolutionaries. They were hard, bitter men 'who evoked Popeye, William Faulkner's plastic killer in *Sanctuary*', criminals who lived in their own private world devoid of any morals. One local commander 'spoke in slurred tones from the side of his mouth … not expecting to be believed'.[964] Seamus Twomey 'was not very bright.'[965] Seán Mac Stíofáin was 'really a very, very unpleasant man … a political clodhopper suited only for organizing back-street brutality.'[966] He defended the killing of Protestants: 'they're all bigots anyway.'[967] This widely reported statement was, in fact, an alleged statement.[968] Mac Stíofáin was 'Mack the knife', he was the 'cause of the troubles', 'a Franco', and, (supposedly) worst of all, he 'was baptized a Protestant.' Perhaps inevitably, for the British press, he 'sported a Hitlerian moustache.'[969] The portrayal amounted to a campaign so consistently derogatory that army officers complained it undervalued the difficulty of their task. The 'not very bright' republicans emerged from the conflict with a surprising number of PhDs, lawyers, teachers, authors, Hollywood screenwriters, playwrights, novelists, newspaper columnists, trade union leaders, bankers, successful businessmen, property developers, journalists, politicians, government ministers, university lecturers and university graduates.

Conclusion

The ALN was ruthless with its own members and with reluctant Muslims. The *pieds noirs* were not accorded the status of civilians. For the press, the ALN's worst atrocities, aimed at civilians, were difficult to assess morally. Typically, they were portrayed as soldiers conducting successful ambushes. While they targeted civilians as policy, they were guided yet by a moral outlook. Attacking civilians even made grim tactical sense. The IRA did not have a similar policy of targeting

963   *Observer*, 16 July 1972.

964   *Guardian*, 3 February 1972.

965   Ibid., 4 September 1972.

966   *Guardian*, 15 September 1972.

967   *Observer*, 10 September 1972.

968   See R. White, 'The IRA and Sectarianism', *Terrorism and Political Violence*, vol. 9, no. 2 (1997). He concluded it was 'highly questionable'.

969   For descriptions of MacStíofáin, see *Guardian*, 4, 15 September, 27 November 1972, and *Observer*, 3, 10 September, 1 October, 3 December 1972.

civilians. But the liberal press had no difficulty in morally assessing IRA tactics. They were bloodthirsty psychos whose purpose in life was killing for the sake of killing. IRA attacks on the British army were reported as attacks on the innocent or as sectarian attacks carried out by religious psychopaths. The coverage was so consistently misleading that even British army officers rejected it.

CHAPTER TEN

A Muslim Algeria! A Catholic Ireland?

This chapter investigates the reporting of support for the insurgencies with a focus on the political, community and religious leaders of the respective Irish and Algerian communities. Support changed over time, depending on the actions of the IRA or ALN. Atrocities could increase cooperation with the security forces. Army methods, too, could harden support for the insurgents. The words of the religious leaders are particularly important, as Catholics, for the period under study, were regular and large churchgoers. And in Algeria, the Ulema had generated a re-awakening of Islam. The record of community leaders and the response of the respective communities provides the context for evaluating the corresponding reportages.

Algeria's Muslims: Hedging Their Bets
'How can I betray France? But I am a Moslem'
French culture had penetrated deeply into Muslim consciousness and there was a civil war element to the conflict. Many rebel leaders were more at ease in French than Arabic. Communication between the different *wilayas* was only possible in French, in spite of the obvious security considerations. Indeed, the large number of Muslims who fought for France, as many as 250,000, motivated some senior officers to oppose government overtures to the FLN. A French captain, writing of the May 1958 demonstrations, rejected charges of army manipulation: 'There were barely fifteen of us in all and none of us even carried side arms. It was truly spontaneous.'[970] Muslims viewed the

---

970   Clark, *Algeria in Turmoil,* (NY, Grosset, 1960), p. 394.

metropolitan French differently from the local French. At the December 1960 demonstrations, cries of 'Vive L'Algérie Musulmane' were preceded by 'Vive de Gaulle'. A Muslim veteran, in the village of Rivet, despaired: 'I was wounded in the army. How can I betray France? But I am a Moslem. I can't fight against my own people.'[971] Others remembered that the WWI sacrifices had not been repaid (echoing similar complaints from nationals throughout the British empire, including Ireland, India and Arab peoples formerly under Ottoman rule, including the Palestinians) with promised reforms. In addition, the image of an all-powerful France disappeared in 1940 with Hitler widely regarded as God's revenge on France. Germaine Tillion questioned an officer: 'Are they all against us?' He replied: 'You can't say they don't like us. Only they prefer the FLN.'[972] Mary Motley's memories include a wedding postponed until the ceasefire to allow one ALN brother and another in the army to both attend the ceremony. Algerian writer Mouloud Feraoun (who was to die at the hands of the OAS) remembers the FLN executing so many 'traitors' that it left the villagers in terror. 'One wonders, if all those who fall are traitors … if this continues everyone will accuse themselves of treason.'[973] Some were genuinely committed to France. The Bachaga Boualam was a local leader whose family had fought in every French war going back to the Crimea. He provided many recruits to the *harkis*. He feared the FLN as communists who would expropriate the property of traditional landowners.

The surprising readiness of captured ALN members to fight for France
Philip Williams, Oxford University, was in Algeria in 1961. He believed Muslim politicians went over to the FLN out of expediency. One French officer informed him that if just one ALN member could walk through the village with his gun, then 'most of them will decide the FLN have won, and they'll go over as one man.'[974] Likewise, when General Challe's 1958 offensive demoralised the ALN, the number of Muslims signing up for the French army rose by thousands and desertions to the ALN fell. In addition, the number of ALN deserting to the French was undoubtedly large. Captured ALN members were frequently and easily incorporated, with threat and/or encouragement, into the army. Captain Léger claimed: 'you only had to say the war was a civil war, and it was

---

971   Greer, *Scattering of Dust,* (London, Hutchinson, 1962), p. 17.
972   Tillion, *France and Algeria, Complimentary Enemies,* (NY, Knopf, 1960), p. 175.
973   Feraoun, *Journal,* (University of Nebraska, 200), p.184.
974   Williams, *Wars, Plots and Scandals,* (Cambridge University Press, 1970), p. 185.

Frenchmen fighting Frenchmen.'[975] Mabrouk Kouara, a GPRA member, confirmed at an April 1960 press conference that 2,500 to 3,000 former ALN now fought as French auxiliaries in the Chambi mountains. Another ALN dissident, Si Cherif, brought 500 men over to the French side.[976] These incredible desertions were partly due to the intrigues of French intelligence, but also to the real divisions within Algerian nationalism. In November 1957 Mohammed Bellounis, a military leader of the rival MNA, went over to the French with 2,000 men. At no time, from 1954 to 1962, did the number of Muslims fighting with the ALN match the number fighting on the French side.

Security and protection before ideological commitment
It was only in 1956 that the small bands of isolated rebels merged, and members of the MTLD and UDMA and the Ulema came over to the FLN. But the people of the Aures and Djurajura mountains were very slow to come over. The many Muslims working for France undermined FLN claims to be representative, and uncommitted Muslims were killed at the rate of ten per day throughout 1958–60. It is true that Trinquier's intelligence department played a part in the demonstrations of Franco-Muslim solidarity in Algiers in May 1958, but only a part. The Committees of Public Safety that sprang up throughout the country featured significant Muslim participation. The FLN's relentless attack on the May demonstrations, in print and clandestine radio, indicates that it did not believe it had all been managed.

The actions of *pieds noirs* and legionnaires however, ensured many Muslims turned towards the FLN. Lebjaoui believed that French torture was not just for intelligence gathering but was meant to humiliate the wider community, to make the cost of helping the rebels greater than refusing to do so. When the new (and liberal) governor, General Catroux, arrived in Algiers on 6 February 1956, Paris had him withdrawn in the face of the violent *pieds noirs* reaction. This capitulation provoked grave anxiety among the Muslims. When the *pieds noirs* demanded and achieved the executions of ALN members while killings by soldiers and vigilantes went unpunished, Muslims increasingly felt abandoned by France. Feraoun's journal reveals French-Algerian indifference to Muslim deaths was a constant source of dismay. Although many Muslims rallied to France, it was not always due to ideological commitment. Often they were fed up with the

975   Faligot and Krop, *La Piscine,* (Oxford, Blackwell, 1989), p. 124.
976   Derradji, *Algerian Guerrilla Campaign,* (Lampeter, 1977), pp. 115–16, and Horne, *Savage War of Peace,* (London, Macmillan, 1977), p. 255.

rebellion and FLN extortions. With no ideological commitment they could easily switch sides if they felt unprotected. During the strike of 1957 the population was caught between the FLN and the army. Initial support for the strike ebbed following Massu's overwhelming response. This brought FLN reprisals. On 29 January in Boghni, Kabylia, a woman was found hanging from a tree with a notice: 'traitor to the sister *patrie*'. A shopkeeper who continued trading had his head shaved, notably in the shape of a cross.[977]

The stupid bastards are winning the war for us

For Muslims the Battle of Algiers began not with the September Milk Bar bomb but with the earlier 'counterterrorist' bomb in rue de Thébes on 10 August 1956. Newspapers in Algiers barely mentioned this terrible loss of life but found space for the official (and false) version: 'It is thought the incident features in the struggle between members of the FLN and the Messalists.'[978] This hierarchy of victims was common in the local press, and people cheered when Saadi's no-warning bombs started exploding downtown. A disgusted French officer revealed to *Des Rappelés Témoignent* that reprisals, initially rare, later became massive operations. The killing of two soldiers led to the burnings of village huts, stacks of hay and the entire winter food supply. The local police were only prevented from mortaring the village by the army. Herb Greer's FLN guide brought him to another village reprisal: '*Voilà,* The stupid bastards are winning our war for us.'[979]

Conor Cruise O'Brien argued that the ALN, fighting the full power of the French coloniser-state, was justified in using its poorer resources with fewer moral restrictions. He explained ALN atrocities were a reaction and the colonised correctly refuse to allow their conquerors to instruct them on what forms of violence are legitimate. This included frequent mutilation-murders of French farmers, their wives and children, and even death by stoning of a ten-year-old girl just outside Algiers in the summer of 1961. But O'Brien cautions us: 'before we cry out in horror we might do well to remember ... we do not call it murder when it is done from the air.'[980] Fanon maintained that the conflict derived from the crime of a rule imposed and maintained by violence and inaccessible to any appeal save that of violence. O'Brien concluded: 'Fanon is right.'[981]

977   Evans, *Algeria, France's Undeclared War*, (OUP, 2012), p. 207.
978   Tillion, *Complementary Enemies*, p. 147.
979   Greer, *Scattering of Dust*, (London, Hutchinson, 1962), p. 102.
980   O'Brien, 'Review of *The Wretched of the Earth*', *Nation*, 200 (21 June 1965), p. 674.
981   Ibid.

Companions of the Prophet returned to earth
Feraoun's journal records that many Muslims experienced the war as a jihad, and in some areas was conceived in overtly millenarian terms.[982] After the rue de Thébes bombing the FLN immediately began a search for 'volunteers for death.'[983] People called them 'fedayeen', those who sacrifice themselves. ALN couriers and combatants were all depicted in religious terms. The *moussebbilin,* literally 'those whom the caravan abandons on the road', went to the baths and perfumed themselves, to be ready to appear before God.[984] Djamila Bouhired spoke: 'the profession of faith, clutched the bomb tighter against her chest and waited for the explosion.'[985] Zohra Drif recalled: 'our fate as fidayate was desired and designed by God.'[986] As a youngster she relished her time with the older women in the *hammam,* the traditional space where women enjoyed inviolable sovereignty temporarily free from men and the French. She learned of Algeria's heroes, the 'souhaba ... companions of our Prophet Mohammed.' They were all tall, handsome, invincible mujihadeen 'cloaked in a divine aura.'[987] She learned that 'all good Muslims had an obligation to fight to liberate their land, from its illegitimate occupiers especially when they were non-believers.'[988] People began referring to the bombers as 'companions of the Prophet returned to earth.'[989] The Kasbah cheered their sacred missions. Before WWII, Germaine Tillion had spent six years in ethnographic study in the Aurés mountains. Returning in December 1954, old friends from all the tribes told her: 'People wonder what they [ALN] want.' Initially, everyone called them *imounafqen* (outlaws) but later started to call them companions of the Prophet who had returned to earth.[990] This was not new but drew from a deep well of Algerian culture. Travelling in Algeria in 1847, Alexandre Dumas had noted: 'The Moors ... firmly believed that very soon the Prophet would answer their prayers and drive the French from Algeria.'[991]

982   Feraoun, *Journal,* pp. 40, 69, 169, 216, 242, 262, 278.
983   Drif, *Inside the Battle of Algiers,* (Just World, 2017) p. 155.
984   Tillion, *Complementary Enemies,* p. 145.
985   Drif, *Inside the Battle,* p.164.
986   Ibid., p. 109.
987   Ibid., p.41.
988   Ibid., pp. 124, 130.
989   Quandt, *Revolution and Political Leadership,* (MIT 1969), p. 94.
990   Tillion, *Complementary Enemies,* p. 139.
991   A Dumas, *Adventures in Algeria,* (Philadelphia, Chilton, 1959), p. 185.

The Vatican, the UN, the Jews, US trade unions and British MPs
In his 1954 Christmas message, the pope noted 'explosions of nationalism' in Algeria are 'at least, in part, the fruits of Europe's bad example.'[992] Throughout the war, progressive Catholics assisted the FLN. One famous supporter was Abbé Jean Scotto, the parish priest of Bab-el-Oued, the poor, French neighbourhood of Algiers (and an OAS stronghold). For his activism, the French-Algeria priest Alfred Berenguer, from Oran (another OAS stronghold), was expelled from Algeria. He supplied medicine and clothes to the ALN and supported Muslim families whose sons and fathers had taken to the *bled*. Fr Berenguer was an advisor to the FLN in Tunisia and later a parliamentary deputy in the new Algerian independent state, this time advocating for the *pieds-noirs*. Catholic social-services mission in Algiers, Oran and Souk Ahras sheltered ALN and FLN, leading to the April 1956 expulsion of Fathers Augros, Marot and Kerlan. In July 1957, Fr Barthez and eleven other progressive Catholics were imprisoned for activities harmful to France. Fr Davezies received ten years' for endangering state security. Catholic student organisations and Catholic trade unions called for negotiations. The archbishop of Algiers, Léon-Étienne Duval, championed Algerian independence.

The FLN also received support from the Muslim and socialist worlds. Canada, Ireland and Norway added support at the UN. The FLN was supported by the American Federation of Labor and Congress of Industrial Organizations (AFL-CIO). Irving Brown of the AFL-CIO so enraged French authorities that he was expelled from Algeria. Brown was later exposed as a CIA agent, advocating anti-communism alongside anti-colonialism. The FLN had an office at 150 East 56th Street, New York and at 45 Chandos Place, London. British MPs demonstrated outside the French embassy. Barbara Castle and Tony Benn supported ALN hunger strikes for political status.

Army Repression and the Triumphalism of the Orange State
It is sinful to join or support organisations committed to violence
Unionists complained of the Catholic Church's ambivalence towards IRA violence. Fundamentalists declared the IRA was a Vatican conspiracy. Malachi O'Doherty sourced the conflict to the teaching of Christian Brothers, arguing Catholicism and republicanism share the same template.[993] But the briefest acquaintance with Irish history shows

992   Cooley, *Baal, Christ and Mohammed,* (London. Murray, 1965), p. 309.
993   O'Doherty, *The Trouble with Guns,* (Blackstaff, 1998), pp. 20-1

the Catholic Church opposing Irish nationalism and revolutionary republicans. In nineteenth-century Ireland, the Church was even willing to accept a British veto over episcopal appointments. Britain also funded the Catholic seminary. 'Are not lectures at Maynooth cheaper than state prosecutions?' asked Richard Shiel MP in 1845.[994] He convinced the British government to fund a seminary preaching loyalty. It was cheaper than a standing army and prevented priests picking up revolutionary ideas during continental training. In modern times priests voted overwhelmingly for the SDLP, a party opposed to violent republicanism.[995]

Parish priests had their congregations pray for soldiers, killed or injured; denied the sacraments to republicans; distributed anti-IRA bulletins, and urged Catholics to assist the authorities. The IRA's 'tea-invitation' following their defence of St Matthew's Church was a brief departure from public condemnation. Coffins with IRA regalia were not admitted into churches, and non-compliant priests were disciplined by their superiors.[996] Parishioners praying for the 1981 IRA hunger strikers were locked out of churches. In the 1980s, the Catholic hierarchy ordered a statement to be read out at every Mass throughout Ireland: 'It is sinful to join organizations committed to violence or to remain in them. It is sinful to support such organizations or to call on others to support them.'[997] Previously, the hierarchy deemed it a mortal sin to be in the IRA. The hierarchy refused to condemn internment without trial. Bishop Philbin instructed his priests: 'anything you can do to counteract the IRA, do it.'[999] The Church become part of Britain's counterinsurgency strategy. Following the 1981 hunger strikes, both sides sought to re-establish 'law and order' in republican areas. There were disturbing signs that part of the Catholic population was alienated from the Church as well as the state.

'You know if the army came and wrecked your home'
Saturating Catholic neighbourhoods with CS gas, repeated arrests and harassment were steadily eroding British Army-Catholic relations. An RUC officer admitted that pressures of the job made his colleagues 'hit back before they've been hit ... they start taking exception just to the expression on someone's face and wade into them right away.' [1000] RUC

994 Ryan, *War and Peace in Ireland,* (Pluto, 1994), p. 88.
995 McElroy, *The Catholic Church,* (Dublin, Gill, 1991), p. 176.
996 O'Connor, *In Search of a State,* (Belfast, Blackstaff, 1993), p. 108.
997 O'Brien, *The Long War,* (Dublin, Poolbeg, 1993), p. 143.
999 Dillon, *God and the Gun,* p. 121.
1000 Parker, *May the Lord in His Mercy,* (Jonathan Cape, 1993), p. 202.

Sergeant/UVF killer Gary Armstrong recalled his Special Patrol Group, conducted a 'vendetta against Roman Catholics and used every chance to book, batter or break them ... James and I would go "mickey hunting".'[1001] Hillyard estimates that between 1971-86, twenty-five per cent of Catholic males (aged 16-44) in Northern Ireland were arrested.[1002] But O'Doherty rejected the idea, of early-morning raids and ransacking homes as pushing people towards the IRA, as naive.[1003] In contrast, British officers came to view these tactics as 'turning those on the periphery of the IRA into IRA or at least into their supporters.'[1004] The MoD's *Operation Banner* agreed.

An 1972-73 anthropological study of nationalist Ardoyne found a see-saw relationship between the IRA and the community.[1005] Sluka found support in Divis (Belfast) depended on the activities of the British army, loyalist death squads and the IRA. Most felt they needed the IRA for defence, they didn't feel intimidated but were concerned about crossfire.[1006] Support was not uncritical: 'I don't believe in bombs because sometimes innocent people are killed, but I support the armed struggle against the police and army.'[1007] Parker recorded similar support for the IRA as defenders and avengers, and again, bombings with civilian casualties were rejected.[1008]

The authorities 'confidential telephone', to overcome IRA intimidation, was a complete failure. Catholics felt they had been wronged. A district nurse, visiting homes throughout Belfast, and witnessing many examples of army destruction, explained: 'You know if the army came and wrecked your house ...'[1009] Catholics felt humiliated and resented being policed by their Protestant neighbours. They took exception to the triumphalism of the Orange state that used every opportunity to remind them of a Protestant state for a Protestant people. Catholics were made to feel inferior: 'Uniformed neighbours stopping you on the way to mass and asking your name, holding up

---

1001 Armstrong, *From the Palace to Prison,* (New Wine, 1991), p. 36.

1002 P. Hillyard, in A. Jennings (ed.), *Justice Under Fire* (London: Pluto, 1988), p. 197. Emergency legislation, internment, torture, mass arrests and Diplock courts led to increased violence.

1003 O'Doherty, *Trouble with Guns,* pp. 4, 34–5, 40–1.

1004 Taylor, *Brits,* p. 141. M Mulholland, *Longest War*, p.113, see too Ken Wharton's books of soldier-interviews, many saw these tactics as turning youngsters towards the IRA.

1005 Burton, *The Politics of Legitimacy,* (Routledge, 1978), p. 85.

1006 Sluka, *Hearts and Minds,* (London, JAI, 1989), p. 144.

1007 Ibid., p. 150.

1008 Parker, *May the Lord,* p. 307.

1009 Van Voris, *Violence in Ulster,* p. 220.

your rosary beads for their friends to laugh at.'[1010] An RUC officer conceded it was 'the record of Stormont that led to support for the IRA.'[1011] Everyday experience convinced many Catholics that, though they may not agree with the IRA, they felt they may need them, at least in reserve. The republican newspaper *An Phoblacht* put it this way: 'We remember Orange rule, August 1969, the Falls curfew, internment, loyalist assassinations, Brit murders. We remember ... last week.'[1012] A Derry nationalist, and IRA critic, would say 'there's many like me ... that can't one hundred per cent come out and just say, in black and white, they're wrong, they have no justification.'[1013] The long popularity of the Fianna Fáil party in the Republic of Ireland helped legitimise the armed struggle in the North. From 1932 to the mid-1960s, the Irish government was dominated by former IRA members, including Éamon de Valera, Seán Lemass and Frank Aiken. The IRA claimed revolutionary republicanism was responsible for any gains made in Ireland. It has only recently been denied.

The Liberal Press
Muslims are morally behind the FLN

The ALN were portrayed as enjoying more support than was really the case.[1014] The *Guardian* explained: 'the crumbling away of political bridges through years of war seems to have left no other body besides the ALN to which Algerian Moslems can give their active allegiance.'[1015] Prior to de Gaulle's December 1960 visit, large numbers of green-and-white flags sprang up in the Kasbah. The 'flags and banners of the FLN prove ... that at least 80% of the population is morally behind the FLN.'[1016] But during these demonstrations, youths also yelled: 'Yahia [long live] de Gaulle'. The FLN were surprised by the flags. Just two weeks later, the polls revealed a majority of Muslims had ignored ALN death threats, somewhat obscured by the *Observer*'s curious headline choice: '41% abstained.'[1017] The very courageous fifty-nine per cent, who had voted, were not headline material. One week

---

1010 O'Connor, *In Search of a State*, p. 181.

1011 Ibid., p. 154.

1012 Dunigan, *Deep Rooted Conflict*, (University Press of America, 1995), p. 39.

1013 O'Connor, *In Search of a State*, p. 98.

1014 For ALN support from the masses, see *Guardian*, 1 May 1958, 13, 21 December 1960, 1 January 1961, and *Observer*, 19 June 1955, 8 July 1956, 5 October 1958, 15 January 1961.

1015 *Guardian*, 1 May 1958.

1016 Ibid., 13 December 1960.

1017 *Observer*, 1 January 1961.

later, a *Guardian* headline maintained the same focus: 'Massive Moslem abstentions.'[1018] This headline diverts the reader from its own report of a sixty-per-cent Muslim turnout just weeks earlier, where the reader would learn that while ninety-five per cent of the Kasbah abstained, thirty per cent voted in Maison-Carrée, a suburb of Algiers. Risking death, this bold decision pointed to a determined resistance to ALN 'advice'.

There is coverage of ALN ruthlessness. *Guardian* guest writer Sven Oste noted that the definition of a traitor was wide. Joseph Kraft also pointed out ALN cruelty in the *Observer*.[1019] At the war's end, Darsie Gillie wrote that Ben Bella 'indignantly recognized that torture has been used to make Algerians in France pay their dues.' [1020] It does not point to wholehearted support. In fact, the ALN killed Muslims even for non-payment of the revolutionary levy, failing to obey strike orders, or for not turning out for a demonstration and destroyed schools and infrastructure improvements of De Gaulle's massive Constantine Plan. The press was unimpressed by French reforms and maintained that Algerian idealism could not be bought off with social and economic advances. The ALN itself was more uncertain of its support than both newspapers portrayed. It acknowledged its severe penalties and cruel treatment towards even those using French health clinics.

Clare Hollingworth wrote of 'the strongly held belief that the ALN has already won the war in the field.'[1021] She recalled: 'I was considered pro-Algerian by the French, by the Algerians, by everybody ... I went out on several missions with them.'[1022] In reality, crushing French success was demoralising the ALN, and the FLN was riven with divisions. The reader might find post-independence reportage quite puzzling: 'The reception given to Colonel Boumendienne and his 5,000 men by the Algerians was hardly enthusiastic, although it can scarcely be described as hostile.'[1023] A liberating army entered the capital city and the newly freed population did not embrace it; what was going on? There were soon protests in the Kasbah against the FLN, declaring they preferred work to the status of heroes. Some even waved the French

---

1018 *Guardian*, 9 January 1961.

1019 For examples of ALN iron discipline, see *Guardian*, 30 October 1956, 7 February 1957, 26 May 1958, 27 October 1961, 15 January, 11 September 1962, and *Observer*, 30 November 1958, 11 October 1959.

1020 *Guardian*, 11 September 1962.

1021 Ibid., 19 May 1961.

1022 Interview, Clare Hollingworth, London, 30 July 1998.

1023 *Guardian*, 11 September 1962.

flag and the Kabyles threatened to break away. At war's end, the *Guardian* reported serious fighting between the rival factions of FLN and MNA: 'Some Moslems may wish to pay off personal scores against the FLN or register their strong disapproval of the, sometimes, dictatorial methods used by the local leaders and tax collectors of the FLN.'[1024] In fact, Muslims had nowhere else to go. The French had imprisoned even moderate Algerian nationalists, and the FLN had ruthlessly cleared everybody else from the field. Within the FLN, fighting the French existed alongside a merciless internal power-struggle. They were not a tightly organised vanguard. Fratricidal conflict plagued them from start to finish.[1025]

The reader can also find evidence of Muslim support for France.[1026] Many women were attracted by de Gaulle's plans for their emancipation. Darsie Gillie wrote: 'the savage severity of the maintenance of discipline in the rebel organization has certainly created a bitter desire for revenge to which the French owe the support of the Moslem territorial units.'[1027] The *Guardian* also reported 'an increased willingness of Algerian Moslems to work and serve with them [French army].'[1028] Consider this *Guardian* report during the May 1960 county-council elections referring to 'one of Babette's bill stickers,' an ex-rebel who had come over to the French side some years ago.'[1029] Babette was the wife of Pierre Lagaillarde. It is one thing to go over to the French army, but to leave the FLN and work for OAS-founder Lagaillarde is another. The *harkis* were often as unreliable as ALN members. Villages switched back and forth between France and the FLN depending on which side they thought brought them most security. There was a see-saw effect dependent upon the severity of ALN discipline, the successes of the French army and the perceived political will in Paris. At no time did the numbers in the ALN amount to a nation in arms. The FLN elite were continually trying to forge many disparate groups into a nation. The FLN government is still trying today.

1024 Ibid., 5 April 1962.

1025 Evans, *Algeria: Anger of the Dispossessed,* (Yale, 2007), pp. 63-66.

1026 Muslim support for France, see *Guardian*, 17, 30 May, 9 June, 10 December 1958, 1, 14 May, 13 (editorial), 18 November 1959, 29 June 1960, 20 November 1962, and *Observer*, 6 July 1958, 18 December 1960.

1027 *Guardian*, 1 May 1959.

1028 Ibid., 18 November 1959.

1029 Ibid., 30 May 1960.

A sad people whose deficiencies resulted in support for ancient feuds
There is a curious dualism in the *Guardian*. Although reporting no
support for republicans and IRA intimidation of the Catholic
community, there was also considerable space devoted to the view that
support for republicans was due to deficiencies in the Irish character
and mental processes. Consider Hetherington-Cole's editorial of IRA
intimidation and extorting money: 'The evidence here is widespread ...
a standing instruction that no doors must be barred during a riot in case
a gunman, fleeing the army, needs sanctuary.'[1030] Even IRA members
were intimidated: 'Not everyone who places a firebomb wants to. When
the lawful authority is unable to protect them, people make their own
compromises.'[1031] This editorial goes on to conflate IRA and loyalist
actions. It was all just irrational Irish violence. This was a consistent
portrait conflating IRA violence against the state with loyalist violence
in support of the state. An *Observer* editorial takes up the counter-
insurgency line: 'there was no hope of an end to violence so long as
political control in Belfast was in the hands of one of Ulster's
communities, while the other had been cowed into sympathy with the
aims of the gunmen.'[1032] The *Guardian* once again was more
enthusiastic in portraying this view.[1033]

The *Guardian* identified many deficiencies in the Irish Catholic
character including: a predilection for, and a fascination with, the gun;
an inability to live harmoniously with their neighbours; drunkenness; a
lack of Christian education; a sickness that needs treatment; hypocrisy;
bigotry; labyrinthine ways; inbred brutality; hatred; murdering hatred;
blood feuding; and violence. The Irish were wicked and baleful.[1034] A
few examples from the many will illustrate: 'The Irish, according to
their sad tradition, have always carried their vendettas to the
graveside.'[1035] But this editorial followed an attack on a republican
funeral by loyalists acting to secure their British identity, not an Irish

---

1030 Ibid., 22 March 1971 (editorial).

1031 Ibid., 11 April 1974 (editorial).

1032 Ibid., 26 March 1972 (editorial).

1033 For the counter-insurgency argument of the IRA cowing the Catholic community, see
Guardian, 16 January (editorial), 22 March (editorial), 7 May, 12 July, 28 August, 8
December (editorial) 1971, 14 March (editorial) 1972, 11 April (editorial) 1974, and
Observer, 9 April 1972.

1034 For deficiencies in the Irish character and mental processes, see *Guardian*, 22 January
(editorial), 28 April (editorial), 2 May, 18, 19 August (editorial), 14 October (editorial),
4 November 1969, 15 May, 13 July (editorial), 5 (editorial), 12 August (editorial) 1970,
10 February, 7 May (editorial), 19 June, 12, 24 August, 12 (editorial), 15
(editorial), 20 November, 24 December (editorial) 1971, 1 January (editorial), 5
February, 2 May, 23 June, 18, 21 March (editorial), 2 May, 23 June, 30 August 1972,
6, 9 March (editorial), 13 April, 31 May, 6 June (editorial), 31 July 1973.

1035 Ibid., 10 February 1971 (editorial).

one. In addition, the record shows not the Irish but the British of Northern Ireland (police and loyalists) as particularly prone to attacking funerals. Loyalists murdered mourners at republican funerals. The RUC attacked IRA funerals and knocked coffins to the ground.[1036] Regular British soldiers had initially respected IRA funerals, even saluting IRA dead, but came under pressure from the unionist government. At the funeral of Jim Saunders, IRA, 'one Stormont minister screamed down the telephone to senior army officers "instructing" them to break up the funerals, charge the crowd and arrest the priest for subversion.'[1037] The army and RUC attacked, even shot mourners at republican funerals. Loyalists exploded a bomb during a republican funeral in Ardoyne, killing two teenagers, and fired on republican funerals. The UDA's Michael Stone killed three mourners at another. The IRA exploded a bomb at the entrance of Rosslawn cemetery thirty minutes before the arrival of an RUC funeral as a warning that all funerals should be left in peace. Susan McKay's many reports, of police and UDR soldiers mocking, jeering, singing to and even physically assaulting grieving Catholic parents, points to a disturbing inhumanity.[1038] Pringle and Jacobson reported some RUC officers respected the Bloody Sunday dead while others smirked, whistled and sang 'It's a Beautiful Day' to families who had just found a relative, often a teenager, in the morgue.[1039] A *Guardian* editorial, 'Towards perpetual hatred', informed the reader of this Irish predilection: 'the hate, the murdering hate.' Accordingly, any Catholic who joined the RUC could expect no mercy for joining the 'black bastards'. Irish society was 'permanently split by blood feuds'.[1040] Robin Armstrong elaborated: 'They love it, need it, feed on it, embrace it. Hatred, any kind of hatred is as Irish as a long day's rain … Chatter about the community's desire for peace is so much cant.'[1041] The newly appointed head of the RUC, Sir Arthur Young, compared Ireland to his colonial experiences: 'I'm just beginning to realize how reasonable the Kikuyu [Mau Mau] were.'[1042] The *Observer* explained how reasonable and impartial this former Kenyan police chief really was, and how far he would go to impartially enforce the law. As

1036 McVeigh, *Taking a Stand,* (Mercier, 2004), p. 217.

1037 *Sunday Times* Insight Team, *Ulster,* p. 246. see also S. McKay, *Bear in Mind These Dead* (London: Faber, 2008) for RUC and loyalist attacks on Francis Hughes' IRA funeral and disturbing inhumanity towards grieving families.

1038 McKay, *Bear in Mind These Dead*, pp. 79, 214, 269, 335.

1039 P. Pringle and P. Jacobson, *Those Are Real Bullets, Aren't They?* pp. 256, 275-6.

1040 *Guardian*, 12 November 19771 (editorial).

1041 Ibid., 19 June 1971.

1044 *Observer*, 23 August 1970.

it turned out, not far at all. He did not even interview the eleven RUC inspectors on duty the day police beat Samuel Devenney so badly, in his own home, that he died. The Kenyans might have a different view of a colonial policeman deciding what is reasonable.[1043]

The *Guardian* also identified many deficiencies in Irish mental processes, including: insanity, confusion, irrationality, lack of lucidity and an inability to distinguish myth from reality.[1044] A representative example from the many editorials devoted to this Irish flaw reads: 'Across the Irish Sea ... effects precede their causes and the laws of logic have for so long been disregarded that they have fallen into contempt.'[1045] Journalists were continually mystified by the bizarre behaviour of these strange people: 'You just have to go on reminding yourself that this is Ireland and what matters is not the facts.'[1046] Harold Jackson explained: 'Whatever the present conflict in Ulster betokens, no one could accuse it of lacking Irishness.'[1047] His category of 'Irishness' rested on two sources: 1. Catholics demanding the army fulfil the role of protecting them; 2. A leading unionist calling for the severance of the English connection. The first is a reasonable request any citizen might ask of its government. The second is typical of unionist alternating between super-patriotism and rebellion. It went unexplained, it was just 'Irishness'. The Irish mind was also obsessed with the past and dwelt on myths: 'In Ireland, history tends to repeat itself, not once but many times.'[1048] The Irish love of violence was attributed to a tribal and barbarous nature.[1049] The editor believed these Irish deficiencies could spread violence even to a most reasonable Britain, which was now experiencing difficulties with the 'tribesmen of the North West frontier'.[1050] This depiction of the Irish (on Britain's 'North West frontier') as 'tribesmen' and the British as most reasonable follows the long, damaging distinction of (Irish) barbarism versus (British) civilisation.

1043 'Our police are wonderful', *The Times*, 18 August 1954.

1044 For deficiencies in the Irish character and mental processes, see *Guardian*, 30 (editorial), January, 13, 24 February (editorial), 23 April, 18 August, 13 September 1969, 27 October (editorial), 4 (editorial), 22 March (editorial), 18 June, 3 November (editorial) 1971, 26 October (editorial) 1972, 31 May (editorial), 18 May 1974.

1045 Ibid., 3 November 1974 (editorial).

1046 Ibid., 13 September 1969.

1047 Ibid., 10 January 1969.

1048 Ibid., 21 June 1969 (editorial).

1049 For the Irish love of violence, see *Guardian*, 21 June (editorial), 18 October (editorial) 1969, 9, (editorial), 15 May, 13 July (editorial), 7 December (editorial) 1970, 26 November 1971, 11 November 1972, 15 April (editorial) 1974.

1050 Ibid., 18 October (editorial) 1969.

The *Guardian* offered no evidence for these Irish deficiencies but continued to assert them. The assertions may, of course, be a manifestation of an anti-Irish prejudice or racist culture prevailing in the *Guardian*. For this, there is evidence.[1051] Peter Jenkins resolved to refrain from writing on the 'unrewarding and distasteful subject' of the Irish. Regrettably, the illogical Irish would not go away. 'They insist upon remaining a public nuisance ... On our nice white doorstep.'[1052] Terry Coleman wondered:

> Was the situation possible for an Englishman to comprehend at all? ... it shouldn't be offensive to say Ireland was infinitely removed from the civilised world. Without the presence of an English power able to keep some sort of peace, the sects left to themselves would have to face reality and see reason.[1053]

Harold Jackson despaired: 'The English don't understand ... If only the Irish were black.'[1054] These bizarre people mystified the editor. 'If they [the protests] have any rational explanation, they are a demand by Catholics for a withdrawal of the British in the belief that Irishmen will somehow solve their own problems.'[1055] There were so many anti-Irish references that a word was needed to cover it: an 'Irishism', meaning confused, irrational, bizarre, beyond (English) reason.[1056] The *Observer* could even print these words: 'Lord Scarman can bring himself to feel sorry, even for the Irish.' [1057]

1051 For examples of anti-Irish prejudice, see *Guardian*, 15 October 1968, 18, 22 August, 13 May, 2 October 1969, 2 January, 29 May (editorial), July, 21 April (editorial), 6 May (editorial), 18 June, 5 (editorial) ,10, 13 July, 14 August, 9 September, 26 October, 11 November 1971, 3 January, 1, 18 March, 19, 24 April (editorial), 26 October 1972, 8 January, 9 March, 31 July, 11 December (editorial) 1973, 13 April, 5 May, 7 June 1974. Peter Jenkins on 18 March 1972 depicted the Irish as drunks and ignorant of history. See also Alistair Cooke, 18 August 1969. See also 'Irishness at its most bizarre', ibid., 2 October 1969, and the heading 'Paddy in an IQ stew', ibid., 18 June 1971. See also 'The Irish are green wogs now', ibid., 1 March 1972. During the Algerian War, there are many examples of anti-Irish prejudice, see *Guardian,* 2 September 1961, see Alistair Cooke, ibid., 8 July 1957 and James Morris, ibid., 5 September 1959. See also *Guardian* 22 September 1960, 16, 18, 27 September 1961. For examples of a 'subtle dig' in the *Observe,* see 'the comical Irish' (11 November 1959), 'the ignorant Irish' (31 January 1960), and 'the immature Irish' (17 September 1961). See also Pendennis' column, 'Irish diplomacy, once a contradiction in terms', ibid., 22 October 1961.

1052 Ibid., 7 June 1974.

1053 Ibid., 31 July 1973.

1054 Ibid., 8 September 1969.

1055 Ibid., 5 August 1970 (editorial).

1056 For example, the *Guardian* editorial of 11 December 1973: 'if the Irishism may be excused'. On 9 February 1958 an *Observer* article begins: 'It may sound rather an Irishism but ...' Consider the *Guardian* editorial of 24 February 1969: 'The reason is less "Irish" than some visiting commentators might imagine.'

1057 *Observer,* 9 April 1972.

The press maintained any support for the IRA came from backward-looking madmen whose brutality was bred in them by their religion, family and schools. In fact, the IRA received a variable and critical support from the residents of nationalist neighbourhoods depending on their avoiding civilian casualties, the random killings by loyalist paramilitaries, and the harassment and killings by security forces.

Conclusion

The liberal press exaggerated support for the ALN beyond what was measurable at the time. For the first two years of the war, the counter-insurgency analysis, of the ALN terrorising the Muslim population, is largely correct. The scale of the ALN's mutilations and killings of reluctant Muslims and a tradition of service to France meant that many Muslims volunteered for the French army. But French repression also resulted in the ALN receiving a large, although undependable, degree of support, including the Ulema. ALN ruthlessness and French military successes meant that support for the rebellion was unreliable. Remarkably, more Algerians served as French auxiliaries than in the ALN. Neal Ascherson, who reported from the Kasbah, pointed out that one 'glaring omission of Pontecorvo's famous docudrama *Battle of Algiers* is the absence of the great many Algerians in French uniform.'[1058] They could be unreliable too. The coverage portrayed the number of Algerian martyred dead as inevitably resulting in an Algerian national consciousness. But the ALN never represented a nation in arms. Most were hedging their bets.

The liberal press portrayed support for the IRA as resulting from Irish mental deficiencies, inadequate Irish morality and religious backwardness. This religious explanation contrasts with the Catholic Church publicly opposing the IRA, and for the most part siding with the state. Still, Catholic participation in state forces, the UDR and the RUC, was minimal. Britain's counter-insurgency methods meant republicans could rely on enough support to continue. Many Catholics regarded the IRA as the avenger of army harassment and killings. The IRA also provided assurance there would be no more loyalist invasions. There was an unshakeable support from a core within the working class and others whose support fluctuated if the IRA caused civilian casualties. In Algeria the colonial explanation was promoted over the obvious religious dimension. In Ireland the colonial legacy was denied and a religious explanation promoted. While there were frequent calls for a Muslim Algeria, there were no calls for a Catholic Ireland.

1058 Interview, Neal Ascherson (at the *Observer*, London), 28 July 1998.

PART FOUR

CHAPTER ELEVEN

More French, More British than their Metropolitan Compatriots

This chapter explores the motives of the 'counter-terrorists'. The interviews and testimonies of OAS and loyalist paramilitaries reveal many similarities. Both were obsessed with betrayal at the hands of metropolitan politicians who did not prosecute the war with sufficient vigour. Both claimed to take revenge on terrorists or were defending the values and religion the mother country no longer held dear. They were more French or British than their compatriots of more secure tenure. French-Algerian patriotism was directed more towards the indivisible French Republic than any government in Paris. Unionist loyalty was more to the Protestant Crown than Westminster. Many understood the world according to an ideology that dehumanised the 'other' community. This chapter identifies significant matched pairs. The comparative portrayals of these opérateurs/death squads are evaluated against the record.

French Algerian Ultras
La valise ou le cerceuil

The OAS grew out of many spontaneous vigilante groups and it would be 1961 before the many loosely connected gangs were fully organised under the OAS. The referendum on self-determination spurred them towards cooperation. The *pieds noirs* were ripe for vigilantism as they lived in a perpetual fear of betrayal by Paris. The attacks of 1954 were just an intensification of an eternal siege.[1059] When the new governor general, Marcel-Edmond Naegelen, arrived in February 1948, he found

---

1059 Kraft, *Struggle for Algeria,* (Doubleday, 1961), pp. 31–6.

them in the grip of a psychology of insecurity. The *Parti du Peuple Algérien* (Algerian People's Party) slogan/threat of 'la valise ou le cerceuil', the suitcase or the coffin, was very real to them. They believed change could only mean transformation from privilege to persecution. When de Gaulle referred to them as 'Algerians of French' origin, they felt they were being turned over to a new country they rejected and cut off from the mother country. They wondered how de Gaulle could talk with killers of French soldiers and were enraged by prisoner releases, especially Yacef Saadi, the organiser of the civilian bombings. OAS leader Pierre Lagaillarde denounced '[Prime Minister] Debré who keeps in prison honest men they encouraged in counter terrorism.'[1060] Loyalists made the same claim against unionist politicians.[1061] François Leca, OAS, claimed he acted because French justice released ALN terrorists to assault his community. The Delta death squads were often former soldiers recruited by army deserter Lt Roger Degueldre. Eduoard Slama, another paratrooper, had married a local girl. De Gaulle's self-determination speech so unnerved him, he joined Degueldre's Deltas. French-Algerians played no part in the Evian agreement. The OAS maintained its guarantees would be repudiated. Pierre Nora captured their insecurity: 'the Europeans do not want to be protected by France, they want to be loved.'[1062] Unionists understand this.

Many were motivated by straightforward revenge. Joseph Rizza remembered a hunting trip where he came upon murdered French civilians. Moving on to his sister's farm he found her with a slit throat. OAS leader Jean-Claude Perez maintained every operation was against selective targets and a cooperative effort with police intelligence. Bomb attacks against *café maures* (traditional African cafés) were portrayed in local newspapers as internal ALN killings. Gabriel Anglade spoke of patriotic motives, the Deltas were not killers but 'good people called upon to do things that they should not have been ...'[1063] The OAS was, in fact, 'an uncooked pudding of conflicting ideas, aspirations and principles.'[1064] Operating from a base in Franco's Spain, the many groups of the OAS were all of far-right political persuasion. Its principal political brain, Jean-Jacques Susini, acknowledged he was 'both racist

1060 Kettle, *De Gaulle and Algeria,* (London, Quartet, 1993), p. 601.
1061 Cusack and McDonald, *UVF,* (Poolbeg, 1997), p. 252-3, Garland, *Gusty,* (Blackstaff, 2001), pp. 10, 44-5, 262.
1062 Behr, *Algerian Problem,* (London, Hodder, 1961), p. 221.
1063 Ibid., p. 148.
1064 Henissart, *Wolves in the City*, (London, Rupert-Hart, 1970), p. 244.

and fascist.'[1065] Robert Martel, one of the few real *colons*, led the *Union Française Nord-Africaine*, another rightist organisation serving as a front for counterterror. They aimed to preserve Christianity and the West.[1066] Former Governor General Jacques Soustelle declared it was a fight to save the Christian West in this 'first phase of the coming European civil war.'[1067]

We've done nothing to be ashamed of, each man has his due
Their political intransigence resulted in many lost opportunities. When they rejected the 1936 reforms, Minister of State Maurice Violette despaired: 'When they [Muslims] protest against abuses, you are indignant; when they applaud, you are suspicious and when they are silent, you are afraid.'[1068] Arriving in 1955, the new Governor General, Jacques Soustelle, found that the reform law of 1947 had not been implemented. Instead, repression was a constant theme. In February 1956, when Paris proposed the scrapping of Algeria's double electoral college in favour of a common electoral roll, Colonel Astier responded: 'By the law of numbers it makes the French, who bring civilization, submit to ... the Muslims who receive it.'[1069] But in 1958 French Algerians suddenly voiced support for full integration with France, something they had long opposed. Fearing that single-college elections would ensure Muslim dominance in any Algerian legislative body, they now proposed the abolition of Algeria's institutions. Thus, the Muslim vote would then be outnumbered by votes in metropolitan France. Similar calculations had swirled around the 1800 Act of Union between Britain and Ireland. Fanon captured the mood of French Algeria. The symbols of social order were their symbols, the police were their police and the flag was their flag. The bugle calls, the profusion of flags, the numerous marches and military parades were all 'a reflection of the settlers' *hauteur* and anxiety to test the strength of the colonial system ...'[1070]

Inspector Vitalis Cros, of the Algiers police, once came upon a wounded Muslim, but the owner of the nearest café refused him a

---

1065 Bocca, *Secret Army,* (Prentice-Hall 1968), p. 45.

1066 Ibid., p. 73.

1067 Henissart, *Wolves,* p. 282.

1068 Gordon, *The Passing of French Algeria,* (OUP 1966), p. 39.

1069 Kettle, *De Gaulle and Algeria,* p. 78, Unionists expressed a similar view, McIntosh, *The Force of Culture,* p. 30.

1070 Fanon, *The Wretched of the Earth,* (Penguin, 1965), p. 41.

telephone token to call an ambulance with *'un melon de moins'*, one nigger less. [1071] Jules Roy grew up in Algeria where he learned: *'they are not like us'*, *'they* are lazy', *'they* weren't very intelligent ... [but] now the *ratons* are buying farms.' [1072] Similar concerns led to the Orange Order secretly running a 'land fund' to ensure farms did not fall into Catholic hands. [1073] Camus captured their disdain in *l'Etranger* where the Muslim was anonymous or absent. Pierre Nora wrote of a trial in Algiers: "'Any other witnesses?" "Yes, five; two men and three Arabs."[1074] This blindness was pervasive. There were no wrongs to be righted. 'We've done nothing to be ashamed of, each man has his due.'[1075]

We are not colonial exploiters but ordinary workers

French Algerians were enraged by the description of settlers. Such a representation in *Paris Match* set off a heated correspondence: 'We are not "unspeakable colonialists". I am a third generation *pied-noir*, and a "colonialist" who does not have 10,000 old francs [$20] in his bank account.'[1076] In fact, only two per cent of the European population could be classed as wealthy landowners. Figures for 1950–51 show 7,432 Europeans with farms of ten hectares, meaning subsistence farmers. There were 300 *gros colon*, a dozen of whom held very large estates.[1077] During the general elections of January 1956, PM Guy Mollet asked: 'Do you want our boys to die for the millions of colonial exploiters?'[1078] After being pelted with rotten vegetables during the infamous *journée des tomates,* Mollet looked again. This time he found everyday people: shopkeepers, skilled workers and civil servants, the stuff of trade unions like those who elected him. They were socialists, they told him, *and* they supported *Algérie Française*. Mollet replaced the liberal General Catroux with Robert Lacoste, 'a bread and butter' trade unionist incapable of understanding Algeria in its colonial context. On 9 February, Lacoste changed course: 'You have been depicted as colonialists. I do not share that view.'[1079] Jacques Soustelle responded

1071 Henissart, *Wolves,* p. 389.

1072 Roy, *War in Algeria,* (NY, Grove, 1961), pp. 17–27.

1073 *The Times,* 28 March 2003, *Belfast Telegraph,* 25 September 2013.

1074 Horne, *Savage War of Peace,* p. 55.

1075 Roy, *War in Algeria,* p. 41.

1076 Bocca, *Secret Army,* p. 103.

1077 Brace, *Ordeal in Algeria,* (Van Nostrand, 1960), p. 18.

1078 Kraft, *Struggle for Algeria,* (Doubleday, 1961), p. 147.

1079 Behr, *Algerian Problem,* p. 91.

to Anglo-American charges of outdated colonialism: 'In French Algeria, Arab and Kabyle children have always gone to French schools along with French.'[1080] The US consulate was painted with: 'Algiers proposes self-determination for the Indians of Oklahoma, the Negroes of Little Rock.'[1081] Defenders of French Algeria rejected the coloniser label, and glorified the French pioneer who, like the Roman legionnaire, was the vanguard of Western civilisation in a region of oriental despotism. Latin civilisation had been planted in the Maghreb long before the Islamic invasions. The French were not interlopers but were returning. Ian Adamson sought a similar unionist legitimacy in his (widely disparaged) depiction of Scottish settlers as the Cruithin returning to Ireland.

Ulster's Last Line of Defence

'If we weren't smacking Taigs, they'd have won long ago'

Ulster loyalists were/are surrounded by many enemies: the IRA and liberal unionists, an imperial Dublin, an inconstant London, the international Roman Catholic conspiracy, and the former international communist conspiracy out of Moscow, now replaced by the 'imperial' European Union. Arthur Aughey wrote loyalists justified their 'military' activity on the grounds of forcing 'Catholic withdrawal of support for the IRA ... [and] keeping Britain up to the mark.'[1082] Many became vigilantes to do what the law forbade the security forces. UDA leader Jackie MacDonald was motivated by the deaths of one-year-old Colin Nichol and two-year-old Tracey Munn, killed in an IRA bombing. Their paramilitary tag is accurate. They served as adjuncts, officially or otherwise, to the forces of the state. Republicans were the terrorists. Courtroom testimonies reveal loyalist paramilitaries wanted to punish Catholics for supporting the IRA or to show that the IRA could not protect them. 'You can't trust them [Catholics], they are all the enemy ... Doing nothing, tolerating the IRA wasn't enough.'[1083]

The loyalist *WDA News* justified the December 1971 UVF murders of thirteen Catholics: 'it should be noted that these people never once condemned the IRA.'[1084] This was not new. Historically, Catholics had to prove their loyalty. During a 1935 murder trial, the attorney general of Northern Ireland, Anthony Babington, remarked: 'the victim was a

---

1080 Pickles, *Algeria and France,* (Westwood, 1963), p. 9.
1081 Kettle, *De Gaulle and Algeria,* p. 595.
1082 Aughey, *Under Siege,* (Blackstaff, 1989), p. 87.
1083 M. Dillon, *God and the Gun,* p. 69.
1084 S. Bruce, *Red Hand,* (OUP 1992), p. 52.

Roman Catholic and therefore liable for assassination.'[1085] In 1972, David Burnside, a senior unionist politician, revealed little had changed: 'It is all very well for Catholics, in private conversation, to say they don't support the IRA. I say prove it.'[1086] Proving it was not easy. Service in the British army wasn't always enough to stop loyalists torturing Catholics to death.[1087]

In 1991, Roy Gillespie, DUP, explained: 'the Roman Catholic Church is the problem ... Rome's aim is to destroy Protestantism, our children, way of life ...'[1088] Brian Faulkner, speaking in 1960, explained: 'When we in the Unionist Party defend ourselves against the attacks of the Nationalist Party, we are perforce defending ourselves against the Roman Catholic hierarchy.'[1089] At its birth, almost every unionist MP depicted the new Northern state as a rampart against encroaching Roman Catholicism.[1090] Paisley's *Protestant Telegraph* maintained the IRA was the military arm of the Vatican. Archbishop Robin Eames wrote that the sadism of loyalist torture-murders was difficult to explain. The most popular theory he found was that the future of the Protestant community was at stake, without it their case would be ignored and Partition would be undone.[1091] In 1969, UVF leader Gusty Spence summarised the UVF's objectives: defiance of British direct rule, terrorising Catholics, and attacking the Irish Republic.[1092] Loyalist paramilitaries were the last line of defence in the face of eventual (certain) British betrayal. A senior UDA man despaired: 'My only hope is that when they do pull out, we are still in a position to defend ourselves.'[1093] A rank-and-file UDA man was more forthright: 'if we weren't smacking Taigs [Catholics], they would have won years ago'.[1094]

The UDA, UVF, Tara and the Orange Order all took a strong anti-communist line.[1095] Loyalist paramilitaries were made up of community defenders, evangelicals, trade unionists, and many who just hated

1085 Brewer and Higgins, *Anti-Catholicism in Northern Ireland,* (Macmillan, 1998), p. 99.

1086 Van Voris, *Violence in Ulster,* (Massachusetts 1975), p. 309.

1087 McKittrick et al., *Lost Lives,* victims 459, 577, 641.

1088 Walker, *Dancing to History's Tune,* (Irish Studies, 1996), p. 37.

1089 Bell, *The Protestants of Ulster,* (Pluto, 1976), p. 105.

1090 Nelson, *Ulster's Uncertain Defenders,* (Appletree, 1984), p. 28.

1091 Eames, *Chains,* pp. 30-34.

1092 Cusack and McDonald, *UVF,* p. 87.

1093 Bruce, *Edge of the Union,* (OUP 1994), p. 108.

1094 Ibid., p. 109.

1095 Tara leader William McGrath worked with British Intelligence very early, seemingly he 'knew the conflict was coming', C. Moore *The Kincora Scandal,* p. 231.

Catholics. They knew what they were against but were less sure what they were for. A senior UVF leader admitted they would take down some book, take out a few sentences, 'jumble them up and give it to him [journalist] as our policy.'[1096] But since they felt threatened by international communism and the international Catholic conspiracy, and the IRA was both communist and Catholic, then the IRA was twice the Antichrist.[1097] Political reforms were more feared than IRA violence. For the UDA, the ceasefire was 'the last straw.'[1099]

Hardened soldiers but on a precarious ledge

Loyalist paramilitaries portray themselves as soldiers fighting the IRA.[1100] UVF leader Gusty Spence considered himself a 'hardened soldier.'[1101] UVF men, pouring indiscriminate rifle fire into Catholic homes in Springhill, Belfast, professed to be engaged in 'real soldiering.'[1102] The headstone of Lenny Murphy, leader of the UVF's Shankill Butchers, reads: 'Here lies a soldier.'[1103] Courtroom testimonies are replete with loyalist killing squads claiming to be soldiers. There was also a religious dimension. Spence's boyhood memories were crowded with the belief that Ulster Protestants were God's chosen people.[1104] The inaugural statement of the UDA declared 'the enemies of Faith and Freedom are determined to destroy Northern Ireland and thereby enslave the people of God.' Paisley believed that the conflict was between the Whore of Babylon (Rome) and the Lamb of God (the Protestant people).[1105]

Loyalist paramilitaries frequently complained of being used by unionist politicians. Their disorientation came with the realisation that the state would not publicly support them. Kenny McClinton, UDA, advocated the public displaying of beheaded Catholics. He simply could not believe he was to be imprisoned. The officer who arrested UDA leader Johnny Adair recalled Adair did not believe the police were

---

1096 Bruce advises us not to take UVF politics too seriously, see *Red Hand*, p. 123.

1097 Nelson, *Ulster's Uncertain Defenders*, pp. 58, 158. McGrath had been fighting international communism since 1964. One member stated: 'Tara was effectively the property of MI5', Moore, *Kincora*, p. 232.

1099 Smith, *Fighting for Ireland*, (Routledge, 1995), p. 117.

1100 O'Malley, *The Uncivil Wars*, (Blackstaff, 1983), p. 318; Beattie, *We Are the People*, pp. 31, 217, 225.

1101 Cusack and McDonald, *UVF*, p. 88.

1102 Ibid., p. 100.

1103 Bruce, *Red Hand*, p. 114.

1104 Garland, *Gusty Spence*, pp. 5-16.

1105 Nelson, *Ulster's Uncertain Defenders*, p. 63.

serious and could not physically rise from his chair. When charged with the murder of a Catholic teenager, Gusty Spence protested: 'Is this what you get for being a Protestant?'[1106] Despite their bravado, a certain inferiority was often present. The UVF boasted of the 1991 Cappagh killings, an almost unique occasion when they did kill IRA members: 'we proved we could take the war to the Provos.' And on the Dublin bombs: 'we are not afraid to go to Dublin.'[1107] A loyalist prisoner admitted to a sneaking admiration for IRA hunger strikers: 'We had lots of guys who were happy talking to God but nobody wanted to be that close.'[1108]

Unionist politicians played to the worst fears of Protestants. Reverend William McCrea (DUP) and David Burnside (UUP) claimed that 'Ulster's police and soldiers' were tortured by the IRA.[1109] The Opsahl Report concluded that Protestants believe they are being scapegoated for the actions of the Protestant ruling class.[1110] There is a feeling that Catholics are now getting everything, that Northern Ireland is no longer their country. The UVF threatened to kill more Catholics to halt this encroachment. UDA leader Tommy Lyttle admitted: 'In the end, we'll lose. It's their country. They want it back.'[1111] The Ulster poet John Hewitt despaired of the gathering storm in his poem 'The Colony'. He had hoped to find this nation his own but it was a faulted ledge. In another poem 'Coasters' he condemned unionism's refusal to admit any wrong: 'when the noisy preacher started ... admit, you said in the club "you know there is something in what he says" ... you coasted along.'

Nobody expects that America should be given back to the Indians
British Ulstermen, like French Algerians, bristled at the settler label. However, Buckley's fieldwork among 'evangelicals and innumerable Orangemen' demonstrates the resilience of the colonial mentality: 'Nobody expects that America should be given back to the Indians ... the Protestants brought Christianity and civilization.'[1112] A UDA leader compared Protestant fears to settlers in Kenya and warned: 'if it ever

---

1106 Dillon, *God and the Gun*, pp. 32, 187.

1107 Cusack and McDonald, *UVF*, pp. 256, 270, 276, 324.

1108 Dillon, *God and the Gun*, p. 92.

1109 See Van Voris, *Violence in Ulster*, pp. 203, 307.

1110 See Bruce, *Edge of the Union*, pp. 63–4, and Nelson, *Ulster's Uncertain Defenders*, p. 16.

1111 Rolston, *Children of the Revolution*, (Guildhall, 2011), p. 28.

1112 Buckley, 'We're Trying to Find Our Identity', in Elizabeth Tonkin et al, *History and Ethnicity*, p. 187.

gets like the Mau Mau ...'[1113] A Tyrone farmer worried: 'The ordinary Catholic tolerates the IRA and votes for the IRA because they want us out of our country.'[1114] Senior unionist John Taylor was vigilant to Margaret Thatcher selling-out: 'Our family has been here more than 300 years, and we'll be here when she's gone.'[1115] Ian Paisley attributed his constituents' business acumen to their descent from good settler stock. Sammy Wilson's fears are revealing: '1641 [rising] is very real to us.'[1116] Reverend John Dunlop wondered whether 'the Plantation will yet be reversed and we will, however reluctantly, return to the place whence we came 350 years ago and Ireland shall know us no more.'[1117]

This insecurity is a constant of the Protestant unionist experience. In 1942 W.R. Rodgers wrote: 'It is impossible to convince an Ulster Protestant farmer that, in the event of an all-Ireland ... his farm will not be taken away from him and given to his Catholic neighbour.'[1118] Prime Minister Brookeborough believed: '... in the three and a half centuries since his family had come. It was all one long war.'[1119] He descended from a long line of military adventurers who served the British Empire: 'That's when it paid to be a soldier, you could loot.'[1120] To protect his country estate, he had slept in hedges with his gun. Sarah Nelson recalled a repeated question on the Shankill Road: 'Will you Scots take us in when they drive us out?'[1121] Walter Ellis despaired: 'The Catholics, who, after all, bred the IRA and vote regularly for secession, are, by contrast, loveable rascals ... and better company. The Prods (I am one) are used to being shunned. Nobody likes us.'[1122] This resembles a recurring *pieds-noirs* lament. At home, only in Algeria he desperately craved love and understanding from the mother country. 'It was not enough for France to sympathise ... total involvement in his predicament was required ... anything short of this was equated with treason.'[1123] Ben Lowry complained about Britain's response to the growing acceptance of the republican narrative: 'one of the biggest

1113 Bruce, *Red Hand*, p. 290.
1114 Bruce, *Edge of the Union*, p. 42.
1115 Taylor, *Loyalists*, (Bloomsbury, 200), p. 181.
1116 Parker, *May the Lord in His Mercy*, p. 139.
1117 Dunlop, *A Precarious Belonging*, (Blackstaff, 1995), p. 144.
1118 McIntosh, *The Force of Culture*, p. 215.
1119 Van Voris, *Violence in Ulster*, p. 10.
1120 Ibid.
1121 Nelson, *Ulster's Uncertain Defenders*, p. 30.
1122 *Sunday Times*, 26 June 1994.
1123 Behr, *The Algerian Problem*, p. 221.

scandals since WW2 ... a mixture of moral collapse and near insanity.'[1124] Ulstermen often expressed more ferocious anti-English sentiments than Irish republicans. Brookeborough would tell this story: 'A man said to me ... I'm a Welshman and I hate the English. Since I've become an Ulsterman, I hate them even more.'[1125] Unionists know that if their vigilance is relaxed, Britain would abandon them. UDA leader John McMichael admitted: 'Deep down, we know the British don't want us.'[1126] UDA leader Roy Smallwoods agreed: 'we would not be welcomed in mainland UK.'[1127] In 1973 the UDA justified their killing: 'Our backs are to the wall. We have more in common with the state of Israel ... [a] battle for survival.'[1128]

Bryonie Reid elaborates on Protestant frustrations with Northern Ireland described as colonial. She believes Protestants should be able to acknowledge the colonialism but insist it is inappropriate today: 'I am not certain of the point at which colonists become natives, I am certain it happens.'[1129] The historian Lord Ernest Hamilton reminded the British about the plantation: 'if the title was faulty, then the immorality of transfer lies at the door of the government, not the unhappy *transferees.*'[1130] But unionist historians Hamilton, Phillips and Falls actively represented Ulster Protestants as colonial settlers in the modernising, civilising, pioneer mode. However, since WWII colonial settlers came in for general criticism. The representation changed. Ian Adamson's 'Cruithins returning home' is a direct challenge to Irish nationalist history and transformed a conquest by an imperial power into a return of a previously expelled people. The argument was/is very popular with the UDA and the UUP. The settler colonial mentality is very much alive.

Neither to talk nor walk with ... or to have any dealings at all with them
Racism typically accompanies colonialism. It is a habit, of mind and will, that exploits religion as it exploits pigmentation. For the disadvantaged Catholic community there are striking similarities between the lived experience of racism and sectarianism. There is much

1124 *News Letter*, 18 July 2018.

1125 Van Voris, *Violence in Ulster*, p. 4.

1126 O'Malley, *Uncivil Wars*, p. 332.

1127 Geraghty, *Irish War*, (Harper-Collins, 1998), p. 235.

1128 Wood, *Crimes of Loyalty*, (Edinburgh, 2012), p. 23.

1129 Bryonie Reid 'The Elephant in the Room: Colonialism, *Historical Geography*, vol.42, 2014, pp. 229–241.

1130 E.W. Hamilton, *The Soul of Ulster* (1917), cited in McIntosh, *Force of Culture*, p. 25.

in unionism where any label other than racist appears inadequate. During WWII unionists opposed American Catholic soldiers attending mass in a former Orange Hall. They were placated with an explanation: 'we can have the place fumigated.'[1131] A UVF leader declared: 'all the Taigs [Catholics] look the same.'[1132] Paisley frequently disparaged Catholics: 'these people breed like rabbits and multiply like vermin.'[1133] In 1931 the United Protestant League advised its members: 'neither to talk nor walk with nor to buy nor sell, borrow nor lend, take nor give, or to have any dealings at all with them, or for employers to employ them, nor employees to work with them.'[1134] In 1992, Paisley reassured his supporters that in talks with nationalists, his party took care never to 'sit with these people or sup with them and nor did we enter their habitations.'[1135] David McMillan, speaking for the Evangelical Contribution to the Dublin Forum for Peace and Reconciliation in 1995, explained that: 'to accommodate, even fraternize with, Catholics was to sign your own death warrant [in the spiritual sense].'[1136] One Oxford professor concluded: 'A deep and persistent intolerance, hatred is not too strong a word, of Catholicism, is the very touchstone of the Northern Ireland Protestant identity.'[1137] The Harryville Catholic church in Ballymena had been a scene of protests, rioting and sectarian abuse since it opened in 1968. It was continuously picketed from 1996 to 1998 as was a Catholic cemetery in Glengormley until 2006. St Patrick's Roman Catholic Church, in Belfast, was subjected to the abuse of circling Orange bands, including in 2015 a band playing an anti-Irish/Catholic song about the famine. Many UVF and UDA killers exhibited 'a paranoid hatred of Catholics.'[1138] Motives for murdering Catholics include: 'he was a Fenian bastard', 'they [three women] were only Fenians' and 'We didn't think in terms of them being people.'[1139]

John Morrison explained that the high Roman Catholic birth rate 'encourages violence and aggression' that is turned against 'Protestant neighbours who seem to manage their lives more successfully.'

1131 Rafferty, *Catholicism in Ulster*, 1603-1983, (University of South Carolina, 1994), p. 243.

1132 Cusack and McDonald, *UVF*, p. 245.

1133 D. Boulton, *UVF*, (Dublin, Gill 1973), p. 126.

1134 Kelley, *The Longest War*, (London, Zed, 1982), p. 65.

1135 O'Connor, *In Search of a State*, p. 177.

1136 Walker, *Dancing to History's Tune*, p. 37.

1137 Rafferty, *Catholicism in Ulster*, p. 283.

1138 William Smith, UVF, stated loyalist murder was 'pure sectarianism and bigotry', see also Taylor, *Loyalists*, p, 112.

1139 For these and many more, see McKittrick et al., *Lost Lives*, pp. 288, 442, 628, see also Wood, *Crimes of Loyalty*, p. 100.

Protestant concerns include the 'muddled and disorganized' lives of Catholic unplanned families and 'the roaming gangs of children and the fact that a high proportion of Roman Catholic children are killed in road accidents' with the drain on public expenditure disproportionately borne by those in employment. Catholic propensity to kill Protestants resulted from their 'confused hearts, muddled minds ... and dogmatic verities.' Catholics are given over to dreams fuelled by alcohol, 'practical achievement evades them.'[1140] This dismaying portrait is a 1993 UUP publication. Prime Minister O'Neill, now a paragon of liberal unionism, once advertised for domestic staff: 'Protestant girl required for housework. Apply to ...'[1141] The Fair Employment Commission documented a continued will to discriminate extending even to Queen's University. Discrimination was only the tip of a very persistent and solid iceberg of social exclusion and domination. Dehumanising Catholics was a prime mover in the conflict.[1142]

The Liberal Press
Racist settlers seeking to maintain their privileges
The *Guardian* held French Algerians to be racist settlers seeking to maintain 'indefensible privileges.'[1143] 'These vain and arrogant people equipped with a colonial mentality benefit from the prestige and economic advantages accompanying a colonial power.'[1144] The *pieds-noirs* rationalised their privileges with 'good works paid for by their taxes.' However, these intransigent diehards 'are heading for the Mediterranean as the lemmings.'[1145] 'French settlers' customarily use violence 'to preserve their privileges for ever.'[1146] 'So long as the settlers retain their privileged position they will continue to infect France with Fascism.'[1147] This portrait of unattractive settlers continued right to the end of the war. The settlers wanted 'more than legitimate minority rights, they want to preserve their privileged position.'[1148] But Pierre

1140 Morrison, *Ulster Cover-up,* pp. 52, 140.

1141 *Belfast Telegraph,* 14 November 1958.

1142 See O'Malley, *Uncivil Wars,* p. 316, Nelson, *Ulster's Uncertain Defenders,* p. 64.

1143 For settlers and their privileges as the problem, see *Guardian,* 31 October 1956, 7 June 1958, 21 June, 13 December 1960 (editorial), 28 June, 21 December 1961, 6, 19 February, 5 June 1962 (editorial).

1144 Ibid., 31 October 1956.

1145 Ibid., 13 December 1960 (editorial).

1146 *Observer,* 25 May 1958 (editorial).

1147 Ibid., 1 June 1958 (editorial).

1148 Ibid., 18 February 1962 (editorial).

Laffont, National Assembly representative for Oran and editor of *L'Echo d'Oran*, demonstrates a different picture. His newspaper was popular with French Algerians, took a liberal position and was highly critical of army and OAS extremists. Laffont used the editorials to argue for reforms, power-sharing and fraternisation between the two communities. The 29 April 1959 edition famously declared: *'L'Algerie du Papa est morte.'* Even before the war Jacques Chevallier won the mayoralty of Algiers in May 1953 on a platform of anti-racism and the implementation of the 1947 reform law. Five MTLD municipal councillors held positions in his administration. This might be contrasted with unionist majority councils which refuse yet to nominate a nationalist to the chair, only a symbolic position.

The *Guardian* repeatedly portrayed the *pieds noirs* as: lacking emotional control, not level-headed, hysterically patriotic, dogmatic in their victimhood, vain, bitter, nostalgic, cowardly, ostrich-like, possessed of a blind racist passion, and knowing their privileges were indefensible. They were not civilised, enjoyed an easy life, did not bother to think, loved to make noise, were liars and bad-tempered, provoked the Muslims, possessed an unreasoning and enduring sense of their own victimhood, believed France owed them a debt, and were guilty usurpers.[1149] Darsie Gillie summed up their despairing hatred, they were 'accustomed from their youth to electoral fraud and gross police abuses at the expense of the Moslems ... [and remember ALN outrages] to the total exclusion of the much more numerous outrages suffered by the other community.'[1150] In France, 'the returned settlers are embittered and many are extremists' characterised by 'arrogance, ebullience and pretensions.'[1151] All French Algerians were settlers. When the ALN threw a grenade into a bus carrying workers home during Algiers' rush hour, the slain passenger was 'a young French settler.'[1152] Even the poorest *petits blancs,* residents of Bab el Oued, were settlers. The *Guardian* even described them as middle class.[1153] In fact, they worked as casual labours alongside poor Muslims.

1149 For the *Guardian*'s critical portrayal of the *pieds noirs*, see 7 July, 31 October 1956, 4, 8 January, 17 February, 24, 25 April 1957, 25 July, 13, 30 August 1958, 28 April, 12 November 1959, 22 January, 18 February, 21 (editorial), 23 June, 7, 29 November, 12, 13 December 1960 (editorial), 17 January, 17 March, 1 April, 1 May, 28 June, 14, 26 September, 21 December 1961, 25 January, 6 (editorial), 7, 19, 22, 26 February, 9, 28, 30 March, 27 April, 24 May, 6, 8 June, 12 July, 1 August, 15 October 1962.

1150 Ibid., 25 January 1962.

1151 Ibid.

1152 Ibid., 4 January 1957.

1153 For descriptions of *Bab el Oued* residents as middle class and/or in a negative light, see *Guardian*, 5, 12 December 1960, 9 January 1961, 21, 30 March, 27 April, 28 June 1962.

Strident bedevillers of Algerian settlement
For the *Observer*, the *pieds noirs* were settlers and France had surrendered to 'the settlers' lobby with its barren policy of endless repression.'[1154] They were portrayed as ruthless, self-seeking, hateful, disgruntled, insane settlers. They were counterrevolutionary racists, nascent fascists and mutinous settler mobs. They blamed everybody but themselves; they did not see how they had contributed to it all.[1155] Sartre, in a featured article, explained two complementary and inseparable truths: French-Algerians 'have a divine right and the natives are sub-human.'[1156] Anthony Nutting, a British MP, described them as 'strident bedevillers of any Algerian settlement, the French "colons."'[1157] Philippe Hernandez wrote: 'the settlers deny even the slightest responsibility for what is happening in Algeria ... why should things change? ... they are convinced they stand for all that is best in Western civilization.'[1158] But the *Observer*'s Neal Ascherson remembered: 'The *Observer* and the *Guardian* were well-aware the French community was quite disparate. To compare them to the white Highlanders in Kenya was misleading. Algeria ranged from the "Kenya set" to the "Botany Bay set".'[1159]

Both newspapers recommended Paris should put it up to them. There should be no self-determination for the *pieds noirs*, no partition of Algeria, no integration with metropolitan France and they should be helped to leave.[1160] French-Algerians were endangering the Western world. Hetherington urged de Gaulle to make 'a decisive move to restore control over the Army, and through the Army, over the

1154 *Observer*, 26 May 1957 (editorial).

1155 For the *Observer*'s portrayal of the base motives of the *pieds noirs*, see 1 January, 26 May 1957 (editorial), 16 February, 9 March, 18, 25 May (editorial), 1 (editorial), 8, 16 June 1958, 15 February 1959, 30 October, 11, 18 December 1960, 19 March, 30 April 1961, 21 January, 2 February (editorial), 1, 8 April 1962.

1156 Ibid., 9 March 1958.

1157 Ibid., 15 February 1959.

1158 Ibid., 18 February 1962.

1159 Interview, Neal Ascherson (*Observer*, London), 28 July 1998.

1160 De Gaulle should negotiate; safeguards but no self-determination; see *Guardian*, 17 February, 5 June 1957, 12 September 1959, 6, 9, 31 October 1960, and *Observer*, 26 May 1957 (editorial), 27 April 1958, 30 October, 13 November 1960 (editorial). On 27 April 1958, in an *Observer* article, Robert Lacoste (resident minister of Algeria) asked, 'surely the principle of self-determination applied to the pieds-noirs as well?' But the *Guardian* and *Observer* thought they should be helped to leave; see *Guardian*, 21 May, 10 June 1959, 31 May (editorial), 24 October 1960. Partition would lead to an ugly chapter in French history: see *Guardian*, 1 January, 1 March 1960, 29 June, 3, 6, 7, 18 July, 3 August, 10 October 1961, 22 January, 20 February 1962. Paris should put it up to the *pieds noirs*: see *Guardian*, 15 (editorial), 17 (editorial), 20 (editorial), 23 May 1958 (editorial), 18 September 1959 (editorial), 21 June (editorial), 16 December 1960, 4 May 1961 (editorial), 6 February 1962 (editorial); *Observer*, 6 February 1956, 1, 22 June 1958, 31 January, 30 October 1960 (editorial).

Europeans of Algiers.'[1161] John Gale wondered: 'will the French army put them in their place?'[1162] Integration was not an option either: 'the integrationists are rarely denounced outside of private conversation.'[1163] Algiers was a problem city where the integrationists 'still have a fast hold on European loyalties.'[1164] Partition would be ugly. The ALN 'controls the Algiers mob ... a very strong argument ... against partition which would leave Algiers on the French side.'[1165] Another 'Israel' was unlikely 'because the European Algerians are better at tearing down than at building up.'[1166] The *Observer* rejected the idea of '*a pieds-noirs* government in Algiers as ominous', and recommended Paris help them leave.[1167]

Bill Millinship recalled: 'I didn't really like them ... journalists looked down on them like they looked down on the Arabs.'[1168] Clare Hollingworth was sympathetic to the 'pleasant French who had settled there and built all the infrastructure, but the people who called themselves *pieds noirs* ... It was hard to have sympathy for them.'[1169] Tom Pocock was of the same view: 'We called them settlers. The working-class *colons* ... we had no love for them.'[1170] Ronnie Payne was of the same opinion: 'We used to call them "settlers"; it always irritated them ... It's somewhat similar to your Ulstermen.'[1171]

Moderate democrats ready for any reasonable reform
On Ireland, the *Guardian* was certain: British Ulstermen 'were not settlers.'[1172] Describing people as settlers when their families have been in Ireland 'since before the Mayflower left for America reveals the type of hypocrisy in terminology which clouds the issue.'[1173] Anticolonialism was not a useful basis for discussion. It would require Bostonians to hand back their city to native Americans. The *Observer*,

1161 *Guardian*, 20 May 1958 (editorial).
1162 *Observer*, 22 June 1958.
1163 *Guardian*, 10 June 1959.
1164 Ibid., 31 May 1960 (editorial).
1165 Ibid., 3 July 1961.
1166 Ibid., 20 February 1962 (editorial).
1167 Ibid., 13 November 1960, weekly review column.
1168 Interview, Bill Millinship (London), 18 July 1998.
1169 Interview, Clare Hollingworth (London), 30 July 1998.
1170 Interview, Tom Pocock (London), 29 July 1998.
1171 Interview, Ronnie Payne (London), 22 July 1998.
1172 Northern Ireland was not a settler state. See Chapter Eight for 37 editorials on self-determination for Protestants and fair play for Catholics.
1173 *Guardian*, 23 August 1971 (editorial).

too, was sympathetic. Following the critical Cameron Report, it explained that Ulster Protestants had been asked to accept a burden 'of the same quality which the German people were asked to accept after the war ... their leaders encouraged them to expect privilege.'[1174] With remarkable *inaccuracy*, a leading *Observer* article explained: 'One favourite myth is that the present majority community stems from the Plantation of Ulster.'[1175] Astor outlined a change which occurred: 'There was a general sentiment in liberal progressive circles that unionists were reactionary people and wrong in every way ... The British don't have a real sympathy with the unionist position but learned to take it seriously ... It gradually became apparent they wouldn't go quietly.'[1176]

Hetherington-Cole described unionists as democrats, moderates, reformers, decent, hurt and restrained. They have suffered immense loss, have been provoked, are sorely tried and abhor lawlessness. They don't just want to clobber the Catholics. They were definitely not fascists, bigots or oppressors.[1177] Terence Prittle, in the following extracts, clears up some misconceptions.[1178] The first was that Northern Ireland was ruled by bigots. The 'plain truth' is that they are 'middle-of-the-road men who realize that certain reforms are needed but intend to put them into effect at a measured pace.' The second is that the B-Specials have not been let loose: 'only nine people died in disturbances.' And since virtually all opposition members 'disbelieve in the constitutional order ... How could they serve effectively?' There are not, he explained, two factions of 'oppressors and oppressed'; it is more a balance of fears: 'The Protestant majority has been obsessed ... by the fear of being abandoned by Britain.' Catholic fears were not cited. This is curious, as just two weeks earlier, the RUC had conducted a brutal assault on the nationalist community in Derry, and loyalists had firebombed hundreds of Catholic homes in Belfast with police collusion and/or acquiescence.

Peter Jenkins, in another featured article, bizarrely explained: 'The Catholics themselves do not help by their insistence on churches and schools for each community.'[1179] Although unionist politicians openly

1174 *Observer*, 12 October 1969.

1175 Ibid., 26 March 1972.

1176 Interview, David Astor (London), 22 July 1998.

1177 For sympathetic portrayal of unionism, see *Guardian*, 1 January (editorial), 5 (editorial), 20 February, 20 May (editorial), 2, 8 September (editorial), 11 November 1969 (editorial), 12 February, 21 May (editorial), 4 (editorial), 6, 10 July, 19 August 1970 (editorial),22 March 1971 (editorial), 1, 8 May, 11 December 1972 (editorial).

1178 Ibid., 2 September 1969.

1179 Ibid., 10 July 1970.

admitted patronage was their first concern, this was understandable. 'The men I met were moved not by ideology, still less bigotry, but by purely practical considerations of political power.'[1180] Indeed, there was reason to hope. Stormont ministers Norman Porter and Brian Faulkner were 'good and competent men, convinced moderates.' This 'moderation' was undermined by his own summation: 'No concession to the Catholics, whatever its intrinsic merit, was worth the price of dividing the Unionist party.'[1181] Brian Faulkner's 'moderation' included resigning from the Cabinet to protest the British government appointing the Cameron Commission to investigate police violence; not its conclusions, just the appointment. In 1964, 'moderate' Norman Porter warned against getting too close to the Roman Catholic Church. 'It's alright to feed the lion in its cage but to get too close and start patting its head is inviting serious trouble.'[1182] In 2017, DUP leader Arlene Foster responded to demands for an Irish Language Act: 'If you feed a crocodile, it will keep coming back for more.'[1183] These attitudes prevail yet.

A few early editorials in the *Guardian* had chided unionist politicians for their slow pace of reform. This, too, would soon change.[1184] Three years after the first civil rights protests, Hetherington-Cole wrote: 'Chichester-Clark has genuinely tried for reform.'[1185] However, in April 1969, the 'genuine reformer' Major Chichester-Clark had resigned from Cabinet because the time was not right for 'one man, one vote.' Harold Jackson was irritated by the air of 'complete unreality behind Catholic complaints' of unionist lethargy. 'The Catholic community expected Utopia yesterday ... it would be a lovely world for all of us if our troubles could be put right overnight.' Jackson appraised Catholics of 'an unwelcome truth' to which 'the Irish block their minds ... there is virtually no point at which nationalist aspirations and economic reality touch.'[1186] The *Guardian* was expert on the limitations of the Irish mind.

1180 Ibid.

1181 Ibid.

1182 *Belfast Telegraph*, 13 July 1964.

1183 *Irish Times*, 4 September 2017.

1184 There are a few *Guardian* editorials mildly critical of the pace of reform; see 10 December (editorial), 1 February (editorial), 29 April 1969. See *Observer*, 20 November 1968 (editorial) and 10 May 1970. However, the *Guardian* felt unionists were picking up the pace: 4 December 1968, 17 September 1969 (editorial), 5 February (editorial), 14 August, 22 November 1971 (editorial), 10 February 1972 (editorial), 2 July 1973 (editorial).

1185 *Guardian*, 5 February 1971 (editorial).

1186 Ibid., 14 August 1971.

If there was any resistance to reform, it was 'based on human fears about consequent loss of jobs.'[1187] Simon Winchester explained that Protestants had suffered huge losses, including 'an immense number of people killed or maimed, an incalculable reduction in their prosperity, reputation and future.'[1188] The *Guardian* held the Northern Ireland Civil Rights Association to be as bad as the Orange Order.[1189] Harold Jackson reported on an Eleventh Night annual celebration of a 300-year-old Protestant victory over Catholics. He concluded that the message was: '"We are the people" ... It is just the same in the Catholic ghetto ... They just take it in with their mother's milk.'[1190] It is difficult to understand how the *Guardian* could get this centrepiece of exclusive Protestant identity so wrong. If there is one thing Catholics knew, and were frequently reminded of, it was that they were *not* 'the people'. This was at the heart of the conflict, the almost total exclusion of the disadvantaged community by the advantaged one.

Understandable retaliation due to security failures
The *Guardian* frequently warned Catholics they would surely suffer, as Protestant restraint in the face of Catholic provocation must inevitably break down.[1191] One example is the explosion at Kelly's bar in Catholic Ballymurphy which was described as a provocation to Protestants. The Secretary of State William Whitelaw informed Parliament that further terrorist actions, since the weekend explosion at Kelly's, suggested that 'the IRA were now desperately trying to provoke a Protestant reaction.'[1192] Hetherington-Cole agreed: 'Can anyone doubt his belief that the IRA's latest acts are designed only to provoke a Protestant reaction? ... the continuation of Protestant restraint is essential.'[1193] This resembles misleading *pieds-noirs* press coverage of the rue de Thebes bomb in Algiers. The bomb at Kelly's was the UVF's in coordination with murderous gunfire from Springmartin heights on to the Catholics below. One UVF participant remembered the British army 'winked' at

1187 Ibid., 12 February 1970.
1188 Ibid., 1 May 1972.
1189 *Guardian* editorials 9 January, 23 April, 5 May 1969 and a cartoon equating civil rights demonstrators with Paisleyite counter demonstrators, 23 April 1969.
1190 Ibid., 14 July 1970.
1191 For provocation of Protestants and restraint, see *Guardian*, 29 June 1970, 15 April (editorial), 2, 22, 29 July (editorial), 1 October, 3, 9 November 1971, 17, 18 January, 19 (editorial), 26 May (editorial), 20 July (editorial), 28 August, 11 December 1972 (editorial).
1192 Ibid., 19 May 1972.
1193 Ibid., (editorial).

this example of their 'real soldiering.'[1194] In fact, the recorded deaths since that weekend were: seven Catholic civilians (six killed by loyalists, one by the army), three soldiers (killed by the IRA), two IRA members (one killed by the army and one self-inflicted), two Protestant civilians (one killed by the army, the other by republicans).[1195] The *Guardian* never corrected this, nor explained how a supposed IRA bomb which killed two Catholic civilians might provoke Protestants. The 'Battle of Springmartin' looms large in loyalist mythology and is remembered as 'the UVF taking on the IRA.'[1196] The record shows the 'continuation of Protestant restraint' at this point amounted to an average of one sectarian murder per week for the previous eight months.[1197] This is part of a pattern of deflection where Catholic civilians killed by loyalist bombs in their homes or at the pub and where the RUC stated the victims were themselves responsible or the IRA was responsible. Or there was no political motive or the Catholic victim of loyalists 'may have been mistaken for a policeman', suggesting republicans were responsible.[1198]

The *Observer*, too, felt that the unionist community had been 'remarkably patient in the teeth of violence ... the Protestant people will never again accept a situation where they feel unable to defend themselves.'[1199] This does not bear much scrutiny. In 1924, the new state had 40,000 B-Specials.[1200] This excludes the RUC and the A and C Specials. Interestingly, Northern Ireland's first Prime Minister James Craig felt secure enough to warn even the British government about tampering with the border. In 1926, Northern Ireland's population included 608,396 males.[1201] We can safely assume one third, 200,000, were Catholic, of which approximately 80,000 would be between 16-44 years. That amounts to one B-Special to every two adult Catholic males, without including the RUC, A and C Specials. This may explain Craig's confidence. The apartheid regime in South Africa could hardly have been better defended. Additionally, there were more than 100,000 privately held guns, almost exclusively in Protestant hands.

1194 Cusack and McDonald, *UVF*, pp. 98–100; Bruce, *Red Hand*, p. 210.

1195 McKittrick et al., *Lost Lives*, pp. 182–8.

1196 Cusack and McDonald, UVF, pp. 98-9, 152.

1197 My calculation from McKittrick's et al's compilation.

1198 McKittrick et al, *Lost Lives*, victims 192-206, 352-6, 349, 538, 1764-65, 1791,1793, 1989-90, 2158, 2730, 2770, 2898, pp. 66, 674-75, 1102.

1199 For Protestant restraint, see *Observer*, 12 October 1969, 12 September 1971, 6 February, 26 March, 22 October, 5 November 1972.

1200 M. Farrell, *Northern Ireland: The Orange State*, London, Pluto, 1992, p. 76.

1201 Census of Northern Ireland, General Report, HMSO, 1929.

However, the day-to-day reporting undermines the editorial portrait. The diligent reader could find evidence of typical settler behaviour: anti-London, anti-Catholic, and calling for increased repression. One British correspondent was appalled at the Apprentice Boys' repeated description of Derry's (Catholic) Bogside: 'They are all animals down there.'[1202] PM Brian Faulkner warned London about handing Protestants over to Dublin: 'the overwhelming majority of the people would come out fighting.' He reminded Westminster of the 1912 UVF: 'when that generation of loyalists was faced with the ultimate betrayal of its right to be British citizens'.[1203]

The *Observer* had earlier cautioned about the prospect of direct rule: 'Unionist MPs are already warning of civil war.'[1204] Billy Hull, of the Loyalist Association of Workers, explained Protestant anger at the army's 'kid gloves' approach to Catholic protesters: 'The army should be given the power immediately to clear the streets and if it doesn't happen in three minutes they should be allowed to open fire.' In the same article his words demonstrate the settlers' conditional loyalty. 'Loyalists' would not hesitate to take on 'even the British if they attempt to sell our country.'[1205] In 2022 Orange Grand Secretary Mervyn Gibson again invoked UVF gunrunning of 1921.[1206] Consider this startling example of the frontier outlook: 'Protestant extremists regard the new Public Order Bill prohibiting the carrying of offensive weapons in public places (till now a hair-raising departure from English law) as surrender to Catholic intimidation.'[1207] The reader could also find people who hated Catholics and found them pathologically incapable of the truth. One employer explained: 'We've had a good dozen Catholics working for us ... Frankly, I wouldn't trust a single one. Would you?'[1208] Under the heading of 'There's a Catholic – kill him', Andrew Wilson

---

1202 For examples of anti-London outlook, see *Guardian*, 12 October 1969, 11 November 1971, 18 January, 28 March, 14 August, 28 October 1972, 4 June 1973, 22, 27 April 1974, and *Observer*, 28 March 1971. For examples of anti-Catholic bigotry, see *Guardian*, 26 February, 23 (editorial), 26, 28 April, 21 May, 8, 9 September 1969, 2 April, 6 June 1970, 11 May, 11 August, 25 October, 24 December 1971, 20 March, 9 June, 11 September 1973, and *Observer*, 3 November, 15 December 1968, 16 February, 27 April, 17 August 1969, 4 July 1971, 26 March, 5, 12 November 1972. For examples of unionist calls for further repression, see *Guardian*, 1 July 1970, 6, 7, 14 September, 26 October 1971, 8, 26 January 1972, 22 January, 30 April, 8 June 1973, and *Observer*, 21 March (editorial), 12 September 1971, 27 February 1972, 19 May 1974.

1203 *Guardian*, 28 October 1972.

1204 *Observer*, 28 March 1971.

1205 *Guardian*, 6 September 1971.

1206 *News Letter* 22 April 2022.

1207 Ibid., 3 February 1970.

1208 Ibid., 25 October 1971.

explained: 'with the first blow on my head I had what can only be described as a blinding insight into the predicament of a Belfast Catholic.'[1209] The accusation of 'being Catholic' had been noted from the inception of the state: 'it became an offence simply to be born a Catholic in Northern Ireland.'[1210] The *Observer* elaborated on Ivan Cooper, a young Protestant whose Christian ethos spurred him to work for civil rights. 'He has been struck off the board of elders of his church, his parents' shop has been boycotted, he has been called a traitor and a Judas in the local press.'[1211] Although *Guardian* and *Observer* reports often revealed a settler outlook, there was little space allocated to putting it up to British Ulster.[1212] Editorials explained that any reasonable civil rights demand could be met, but not 'the unacceptable attacks on Northern Ireland's constitutional position.'[1213]

Conclusion

French Algerians feared betrayal and abandonment. Some *opérateurs* wanted revenge. Others were fighting to save Christianity or against international communism. These bringers of civilisation were not going to submit to its recipients. Ulster unionists, too, were civilisers and equally obsessed with eventual abandonment. Fearing and opposing any inclusion into Ireland, they fought for their reformed faith against an inconstant London and an imperial Rome. They claimed to be misled by their politicians. This chapter identified a remarkable similarity. French-Algerians and Ulstermen were very sensitive to the usurper charge and sought to portray themselves as the original inhabitants returning after an earlier expulsion. The comparative coverages displayed two distinct patterns. French Algerians were self-seeking extremists and fascists, reactionary settlers seeking to maintain indefensible privileges. Their intransigence and blind racist passion provoked Muslims to rebellion. British Ulstermen, on the other hand, had been provoked. They were restrained, moderate and reforming democrats despite having suffered immense loss at the hands of deluded Irish terrorists. Self-determination should be denied French Algerians.

1209 Ibid., 4 July 1971.

1210 *Manchester Guardian* 21 May 1921.

1211 *Guardian*, 6 October 1968, See also McKay, *Northern Protestants*, pp. 31-318.

1212 The *Guardian* recommended support: 6 January (editorial), 20 May (editorial), 20 June (editorial), 8 September 1969 (editorial), 21 May (editorial), 19 August 1970 (editorial). The editorial of 19 August 1970 specifically rejects the idea of any major injustice.

1213 ibid., 6 January 1969 (editorial).

Self-determination for British Ulstermen was inviolate. Ulstermen, like French Algerians, bristled at the label 'settler' although the Orange Order's self-description is of 'unconquerable colonists.'[1214] Unionism is offended now by reference to colonialism and rejects its use in explaining or re-writing the Troubles.

1214 Revd M Dewar, *Why Orangeism* (undated late 1950s), in O'Brien, *The Long War*, (O'Brien Press, 1999), p. 82.

CHAPTER TWELVE

OAS Provocateurs and Loyalist Backlash

Counter-terrorists' claims of taking the war to the terrorists are evaluated against the record including the compilations by McKittrick et al and the Cain website. There is also an evaluation of their actions as either revenge or designed to oppose political reforms. Their relationship with state forces is examined for collusion. Both super-patriots rebelled against a government to which they loudly professed loyalty. This chapter includes a focus on this apparent contradiction. The actions of these counter-terrorists or super patriots/loyalists/death squads are compared to identify any patterns in the corresponding reportages.

OAS Counter-Terrorists
Police files and selective operations
French Algerians were used to getting their own way. They frustrated the 1936 Blum-Violette Bill that proposed extending full citizenship to the native elite and refused to implement the 1947 Statute of Algeria which permitted Muslims full French citizenship while retaining their position under Shariah law. The 1956 *journée des tomates* riots forced a dramatic reversal of government policy, and their May 1958 mobilisation brought down the Fourth Republic. Every time they massed at the Algiers Forum, their will had prevailed. When political lobbying and mass demonstrations did not work, a proliferation of 'counterterrorist' networks sought to roll back reforms.

There were several different phases. The initial phase of 1954–56 was a period of 'artisan style' replies to ALN attacks. Information came from *Renseignements Généraux* (Special Branch). By 1956 these working-class death squads were supplemented by the *Union Française Nord-Africaine*, a front for many disparate groups. There was a lull in 1958 when General Challe was inflicting heavy casualties on the ALN, and Massu had rid Algiers of bomb attacks. By the end of 1959 ALN bomb attacks were once again visited upon Algiers, and by January 1960 the *pieds noirs* were painfully aware they faced a government determined on change. The many loosely affiliated groups began to combine under the OAS. Counterterror was mostly confined to Algiers. The failure of the Generals' Putsch in 1961 brought it to Oran. Although ALN bombs started exploding in Algiers on 30 September 1956, so-called counter-terrorists had already bombed the *Union Générale des Travailleurs Algériens* on 30 June, the communist newspaper office on 17 July, and rue de Thébes on 10 August. This last bombing resulted from *ultras* learning the address of a slain ALN member and decided to punish the whole neighbourhood. Seventy Muslims died. The *Écho d'Alger*, devoted a meagre nine lines in its report, omitted the number of dead but included the official (and false) version: 'It is thought the incident figures in the struggle between members of the FLN and the Messalists.'[1215] Following the September ALN bombings, Algiers' papers were filled with the horror for four days.

The OAS, like Ulster loyalists, claimed they acted as soldiers. OAS *opérateur* Jo Rizza insisted: 'I conducted these operations as a soldier … precise operations.'[1216] Jean-Pierre Ramos explained: 'We always had a "b.r." [*bulletin de renseignements*, a police file] and a photo of FLN terrorists.'[1217] Their killings were *opérations ponctuelles* (necessary interventions). Josue Giner, a notorious gunman, showed a 'b.r.' to Ben Walles of the *New York Times*. The police and army provided information. The method was left to the Delta squads.

The Arab hunt

The Evian ceasefire reputedly prompted the OAS to change from selective to indiscriminate attacks. A better description would be an earlier phase of selective killings by former soldiers, accompanied by indiscriminate, opportunistic killings by loosely organised gunmen. The totally indiscriminate killings were justified by deeming all Muslims assisting or acquiescing in ALN attacks. On 10 May 1962, the OAS, in seven separate attacks, murdered seven female cleaners, as 'spies'. They

1215 Tillion, *France and Algeria,* (NY, Knopf, 1960), p. 147.
1216 Harrison, *Challenging De Gaulle,* (NY, Praeger, 1989), p. 72.
1217 Ibid., p. 88.

boasted of taking the war to the terrorists but their victims were mostly civilians. Previous to December 1960, the army and *pieds noirs* were convinced of the loyalty of significant numbers of Muslims. There was some truth to it but as independence approached they were shocked to learn that *harki* loyalty did not match their own. The early more selective counter-terrorists claimed they were helping Muslims who suffered most from the ALN. But the December 1956 attacks against the Kasbah, following the ALN murder of Mayor Amédée Froger shows the indiscriminate killers were always active. Muslim victims included: misdirected taxi drivers, delivery workers in the wrong neighbourhood, market vendors, and Arab neighbourhoods shot up in drive-by shootings. French liberals were regularly gunned down. The intention was always the same: roll back reforms.

Following Evian, the *ratonnade* (Arab hunt) became almost fashionable. OAS slaughter was intended to provoke ALN atrocities. The *ultras* believed the army could not stand by. But the FLN, confident of victory, restrained enraged Muslims, even at gunpoint.

To be an *opérateur* was a source of pride. *Ultras* boasted of their killings. They went about their activities almost openly, distributing weapons and explosives without any great discretion in Bab-el-Oued. The UDA also operated openly from headquarters on Belfast's Newtownards and Shankill Roads; their leader Andy Tyrie even walking free from the premises where police found weapons.[1218] Some journalists said the OAS were cowardly, attacking only the unarmed. OAS leader Ian Ziano acknowledged: 'When you shoot down people who are unarmed, I don't call that courage.'[1219] They just circulated in cars, machine-gunning passers-by on the grounds that 'Any Arab will do.'[1220]

Loyalist Paramilitaries
Any Taig will do

Loyalist paramilitaries pursued similar tactics of: 'any Taig [Catholic] will do.'[1221] One UVF member recalled: 'A lot of it was lads sitting around drinking and then someone would say "let's stiff a Taig". Someone would go and get a weapon and that was that. It wasn't high powered operational stuff.'[1222] Loyalist operations, aimed at random

1218 RUC protected UDA, *Irish Times*, 19 October 2016.
1219 Harrison, *Challenging De Gaulle*, p. 29.
1220 Evans, *Algeria: France's undeclared war,* (OUP, 2012), p. 304.
1221 Bruce, *Red Hand,* (OUP, 1992), p. 276.
1222 Shirlow, *End of Ulster Loyalism,* (Manchester, 2012), p. 77.

Catholic civilians, included: drive-by shootings, petrol bombing Catholic homes, bombing Catholic schools and churches, no-warning pub bombings and roving abduction squads followed by torture-murder.

In 1966, when Spence's UVF could not find suspected IRA member Leo Martin, they settled for killing John Patrick Scullion, a random victim returning home late. Court testimony revealed UVF members understood their instructions 'not to come back without a result' meant they should kill any Catholic if their intended target wasn't available.[1223] Spence offered another portrayal: 'Volunteer violence was not totally indiscriminate. It was directed at male Catholics.'[1224] Even this was not true. When the UVF murdered Sara Larmour in her living room, the UDA condemned them as 'too cowardly to go after known IRA murderers but instead vent their frustration on defenceless people.'[1225] UVF leader David Ervine admitted it was policy 'to murder the easiest targets possible to instil fear and terror in the Catholic community and put pressure on the IRA to stop.'[1226] John White, UDA, confirmed: 'any Roman Catholic would have done.' [1227] UDA Supreme Commander Andy Tyrie argued that killing Catholics were not criminal acts but emotional ones. Roy Garland recalled Tara planned the wholesale murder of Catholic civilians. Republicans were contemptuous of two loyalists (convicted of raping teenage girls) accepted into UVF prison compounds and thereby gaining 'special [political] status.'[1228] The political nature of the rapes was the mistaken belief their victims were Catholic.

Many loyalists were former soldiers who had been schooled in counterterrorism in Cyprus and Kenya. They portrayed their violence as reactive. The press and establishment figures agreed. Lord Chief Justice Robert Lowry presided at the trial of the Glenanne Gang for a gun and bomb in Keady. He explained the motives of this UVF-RUC-UDR gang: 'more than police work was needed and justified to rid the land of pestilence ... So far as I can temper justice with mercy I am resolved to do so ... [on] these misguided but above all unfortunate men.'[1229] The 'unfortunate men' received one and two year suspended sentences for attempting to murder citizens they were employed to

1223 McKittrick et al, *Lost Lives,* p. 799.

1224 Ibid., p. 167.

1225 McKittrick et al., *Lost Lives,* p. 801.

1226 McKay, *Bear in Mind These Dead,* (London, Faber, 2008), p. 247.

1227 McKittrick et al, *Lost Lives,* pp. 371-2.

1228 Toolis, *Rebel Hearts,* (NY, St Martin's, 1995), p. 152.

1229 Cadwallader, *Lethal Allies,* (Mercier, 2013), p. 306.

protect. In 1981, Taoiseach Garret Fitzgerald praised the UDA for its 'restraint in the face of IRA attempts to provoke loyalists into sectarian killings', and in 1985 he explained: 'loyalist violence was reactionary.'[1230] In October 1996, RUC Chief Constable Hugh Annesley, claimed loyalist violence was reactive, complimented loyalists on their ceasefire, but warned: 'If they were pushed back into violence, and they have been severely pushed, then ...'[1231] The record, however, shows the IRA went on the offensive in the summer 1970, whereas the UVF embarked on a campaign of random murder and bombings of Catholic schools, homes, businesses and Dublin's RTÉ in 1966.[1232] Their first act was petrol-bombing Holy Cross girls' primary school in Ardoyne. Unionist politicians and the media maintained this description of counterterrorism. Cusack and McDonald wrote, it is 'worth pointing out' there are UVF members who 'quite genuinely abhor sectarianism.'[1233]

Some journalists and academics portrayed loyalists as becoming more selective: 'By 1992 and 1993 ... unlike so often in the past, many of their victims were republicans.'[1234] But the record, between 1992 and 1993 shows loyalists killed sixty-five Catholic civilians, four Sinn Féin politicians, one former-IRA prisoner and one member of another republican organisation.[1235] Cusack and McDonald argue Johnny Adair, UDA, played a 'major role in forcing the republican movement to find a way out of the armed struggle' and further conclude Adair 'insists (with some justification) that he ... "took the war" to the IRA and forced them into a ceasefire.'[1236] But at the end of their twenty-five-year campaign, loyalists killed possibly twenty-seven IRA members, a selectivity of 2%.[1237]

In contrast, IRA killings of UDR/RIR and RUC were reported as sectarian. A number of journalists and some academics propagating this view have a background in the Official Republican Workers' Party; a competing organisation to what became the mainstream Republican Movement. The Workers' Party became effectively pro-unionist and shared Britain's narrative: 'opposition to the Provo "other" ultimately

---

1230 O'Malley, *Uncivil Wars,* (Blackstaff, 1983), p. 351, and O'Brien, *The Long War,* p. 172.

1231 Sluka, *Death Squad,* (JAI, 1989), p. 146.

1232 Bruce, *Red Hand,* p. 31.

1233 Cusack and McDonald, *UVF,* p. 273.

1234 Taylor, *Loyalists,* p. 210.

1235 McKittrick et al., *Lost Lives.*

1236 McDonald & Cusack, UDA, p. 211, 405.

1237 http://cain.ulst.ac.uk/cgi-bin/tab2.pl *and* McKittrick et al., *Lost Lives.*

defined Official republicanism. Rivalry turned into raison d'etre.'[1238]

Some victims were more deserving than others. Irish President Mary Robinson refused three times to meet the Bloody Sunday relatives: 'the constitutional parameters of the office precluded her involvement ... visiting the Bloody Sunday memorial would privilege nationalist suffering over unionist suffering.'[1239] The parameters had not prevented her laying a wreath for unionist victims of the Enniskillen bombing. Eamon Dunphy, argued Robinson represented a nation 'which reserves the right to discern between those who are victims of the evil they support and those who are ... merely victims.'[1240] Victims of the IRA were just that, they were victims. Victims of the British army or loyalist death squads were explained by Conor Cruise O'Brien who reminded Catholics: 'Ye brought it on yourselves.'[1241] The descripter 'counterterrorist' carries a justificatory element.

Romper Rooms

Loyalist violence includes: torture murders, throat cuttings, frenzied multiple stabbings, pulling teeth, sexual mutilations, burning with blowtorches, branding with hot pokers, hanging victims upside down and dropping them on their head, and beating victims to death with axes and spades or dropping concrete blocks on their heads. UDA gangs, operating from East Belfast and the Shankill Road, conducted 'Romper Rooms' where they would leisurely dispatch their victims, often before an audience of revellers in illicit drinking clubs. Albert Baker, a former British soldier, led the UDA's Baker-McCreery gang. They stabbed, tortured and branded their victims before shooting them to death. One victim had a cross burned in his back, another was stabbed 200 times. Baker turned himself in to English police. He admitted to membership of the Military Reaction Force, one of Brigadier Kitson's counterterror gangs.

The Shankill Butchers was a UVF unit that murdered at least thirty people, usually after unimaginable torture. Victims were repeatedly stabbed, burned with cigarettes and brutally beaten. They usually had their throats cut, some almost beheaded. One victim had all but three of his teeth pulled out. Another was skinned alive. Judge Turlough

---

1238 Review, Lost Revolution, *History Ireland*, Issue 1, January/February 2010.

1239 Campbell, *Setting the Truth Free,* (Liberties, 2012), p.74; Conway, *Commemorating Bloody Sunday,* (Palgrave, 2010), p. 57.

1240 *Irish Voice*, 29 September 1993

1241 Ibid.

1242 Dillon, *Shankill Butchers,* (London, Arrow, 1990), pp. 276–7.

O'Donnell said their killings were 'so cruel and revolting as to be beyond the comprehension of normal human beings.'[1242] The police were commended for eventually capturing part of the gang when, incredibly, one victim survived. Many wondered how the gang could operate from 1972 to 1982 in north Belfast, one of the most militarised parts of the country and little more than two square miles in area. These torture-murders reflect the racial hatred and dehumanising of the natives that is characteristic of the settler mentality. Steve Bruce, a keen observer of loyalism, offered three explanations: the conflict had dehumanised people generally, Catholics were not really viewed as people, and in loyalist communities their activities were rewarded.[1243] A part of the explanation may also be found in the loosely organised nature of loyalist paramilitaries, which permitted recruitment of psychotic elements.[1244] An East Belfast UDA club would even extend its opening hours to serve drinks to those who had brought their girlfriends to watch.

Mysterious bombings and shootings

The early loyalist false flag bombings of electrical and water infrastructure brought down the mildly reforming Terence O'Neill. Their greatest success was the 1974 Ulster Workers' Council strike/rebellion, when they shut down industry, intimidated workers, killed thirty-eight people and destroyed the power-sharing Executive. However, loyalist killings did not receive the same media coverage as IRA killings. There are overlooked patterns in loyalist killings. They perpetrated 119 deadly explosions taking 202 civilian lives.[1245] At times, the army and RUC deflected suspicion from loyalists or wrongly portrayed their victims as republicans or the judge sympathised with or explained their motives. Other patterns include the frequency of

1243 Bruce, *Red Hand*, pp. 185–7.

1244 Dillon, *God and the Gun,* p. 19. For loyalist torture and rape, see ibid., pp. 19, 25–7 and Bruce, *Red Hand*, pp. 183, 276.

1245 See McKittrick et al, *Lost Lives*. The victims are numbered, including 17 Protestant civilians: 3, 71, 139, 591, 592, 631, 949, 958, 1017, 1022, 1048, 1049, 1084, 1700, 1929, 1978, 3568 and 185 Catholic civilians: 192-206, 221, 259, 309, 352, 370, 508-9, 581, 594, 612, 623, 652, 630, 633, 663-4, 688-9, 704, 722-3, 745, 776, 799, 861, 900, 923, 927-8-9, 954, 957, 1016, 1046-7, 1078-9, 1080-1-2, 1092, 1098-1123, 1142, 1639, 1918, 2835, 1141, 1159, 1188, 1212, 1283, 1312, 1326, 1371, 1339-40, 1354-8, 1364, 1361-2, 1377, 1395, 1398, 1417-20, 1440-1, 1445, 1451, 1468, 1470, 1476, 1481-3, 1523, 1547, 1550-4, 1556, 1585-6, 1598-9, 1603, 1636-8, 1646-9, 1665-6, 1673, 1683-5, 1702, 1699-90, 1716, 1764-5, 1793, 1782-3, 1788-9, 1790, 1904, 1914, 1919, 1921, 1989-90, 2618, 2898, 3250-1, 3351-3, 3370, 3462, 3487, 3553, 3594-6, 3632, 3635. There are sixteen UVF: 19, 799, 963, 1072, 1371, 1393, 1394, 1420, 1421, 1484-5-6-7, 1891-2, 3402 and nine UDA: 130, 141, 796, 802, 1930, 1941, 2233, 2244, 3565. The bombs also killed three RUC: 1330, 2619, 3629 and two UDR: 580, 1929.

Catholic civilians, from children to pensioners, shot or stabbed to death in their bedrooms or homes. There is another pattern of abduction and torture-murders of random Catholic civilians.[1246] Protestant civilians, guilty of 'running around with Taigs', were also susceptible to be murdered.[1247] Some atrocities are especially remembered in nationalist communities, including bomb attacks where the army, police and the highest offices of the government deflected suspicion away from loyalists and on to republicans (listed below, not in chronological order):

- UVF, McGurk's Bar bomb, 15 dead, 'P.M. Faulkner helped cover up truth'[1248]
- UVF, Kelly's Bar bomb, 5 dead, SOSNI Whitelaw falsely blamed the IRA[1249]
- UVF, White Fort Inn bomb, 3 dead, IRA 'bomb in transit', said RUC[1250]
- UVF, Dublin-Monaghan bombs, 33 dead, British non-cooperation with Barron inquiry, RUC lost evidence
- UVF, Loughinisland, 6 dead, RUC collusion[1251]
- New Lodge Six, 3 civilians, 3 unarmed IRA dead, suspected MRF-loyalists operation[1252]
- UVF's 'October 2nd Big Push', 12 dead, motivated by IRA-government talks[1253]

1246 These victims are numbered in McKittrick, *Lost Lives*. For examples of police/army deflection, see victims numbered: 192-206, 303, 349, 352, 353, 355, 356, 358, 370, 384, 1454, 1764, 1765, 1793, 2158, 2730, 2770, 2898; for examples of murders by stabbing or gunfire in their bedrooms or simply murdered in their homes, see victims: 451, 1506, 1560, 1561, 1562, 1563, 1564, 1604,1625-26-27, 1697, 1751, 1752, 1762, 1762, 1771, 1783, 1795, 1807, 1837, 1808, 1850, 1856, 1896, 2158, 2378, 2732, 2745, 2900, 3270, 3270, 3341, 3511, 3566; burned to deaths in their bedrooms, see victims numbered: 3, 1788-89-90, 1978, 3250-51, 3594-95-96; killed by bomb attacks on their homes, see victims: 581, 630, 799, 923, 1361-2-3, 2619, 2898, 3635; for torture-murders by Shankill Butchers, see victims: 785, 1615, 1730, 1772, 1829, 1882, 1907, 2471; for torture-murders in UDA romper rooms, see victims: 498, 499, 508, 509, 510, 537, 538, 577, 608, 611, 620, 628, 690, 882, 884, 1165, 2806, 3304, 3464; for abduction and torture-murders by non-specific loyalists, see victims: 743, 744, 748, 792, 878, 1207, 3515. These lists are not exhaustive and contain unfortunate Protestants mistaken for Catholics or who had fallen foul of loyalists.

1247 Ibid., see Mc Kittrick victim numbers: 863, 915, 1173, 1335, 1499, 1707, 2745, again non-exhaustive.

1248 *Irish News*, 4 December 2010 and see http://mcgurksbar.com/.

1249 British army log entries were discovered by Paper Trail's Ciaran Mac Airt, *Irish News*, 30 May 2017. See also McKittrick, *Lost Lives*, pp. 183-4. Gerard Clarke died of his injuries in 1989.

1250 McKittrick et al, Lost Lives, pp.666, 675.

1251 *Irish Times* 29 November 2018.

1252 *Independent*, 23 November 2002 and see http://www.thenewlodge.com/index.php?option=com_content&view=article&id=14&Itemid=140.

1253 McDonald and Cusack, *UVF*, P. 165.

- UVF, Strand Bar, 6 pensioners dead, motivated by IRA-government talks[1254]
- UVF, Ramble Inn, six dead, 5 Protestants but Catholic target[1255]
- UVF, Chlorane Bar, 5 dead by Shankill Butchers, five minutes from their base[1256]
- UDA, Annie's Bar, 5 dead[1257]
- UDA, Greysteel Massacre, 8 dead
- UDA, Graham's Lower Ormeau, 5 dead, RUC collusion[1258]

The Liberal Press
Nazis, gratuitous murderers and reactionary fascists

De Gaulle saw the OAS as a nuisance, and there is much in the reportage that confirms a rather pathetic side. The OAS was partial to issuing leaflets of 'no surrender', hoisting flags, hot-air rhetoric, florid threats against critical priests and journalists, clandestine broadcasts and fabricating hoax treaties between France and Russia.[1259] A case in point was the OAS Committee of Resistance to Surrender issuing this militarist statement: 'all Frenchmen of an age to fight should enlist in political associations and await in disciplined calm for instructions.'[1260] There is something sad in this report of a noisy racket that burst from the kitchens of Algiers clanging out over and over again for half an hour – three shorts and two longs (*Al-gér-ie Fran-çaise*). This demonstration of will peaked with a 'saucepan concert ... public trial of strength.'[1261] French newspapers mocked the progress of this concert, progressing from car horns to frying pans, and pondered what escalation came next. This turned out to be the hoisting of 'flags with the letters OAS ... followed by a traffic halt of 20 minutes. OAS youths let down the tyres of buses and attacked police with stones.'[1262] In the face of an impending rupture with their motherland, this reveals a people floundering before looming independence.

1254 *Irish News*, 9 April 2015, McKittrick, *Lost Lives*, pp. 533-4.
1255 *News Letter*, 8 March 2009.
1256 McKittrick, *Lost Lives*, pp. 652-3.
1257 *Belfast Telegraph*, 20 December 2012.
1258 http://relativesforjustice.com/wp-content/uploads/2016/11/S.Graham-Full-Report-Web.pdf.
1259 For OAS nuisance actions, see *Guardian*, 12 October 1959, 1 May, 22, 23, 26, 29 September, 4, 6 October, 18 November 1961, 3, 7, 23 February, 23, 30 March 1962.
1260 Ibid.,12 October 1959.
1261 Ibid., 23 September 1961.
1262 Ibid., 29 September 1961.

Even the plastic bombings were often sound and fury.[1263] Clare Hollingworth reported from Algiers: '200 violent explosions shook the city this morning ... no loss of life and only twenty have been wounded.'[1264] Sartre's apartment was struck by an 'unusually large' blast, so large it shattered a staircase. Eventually, it became a badge of honour among the left to have received a visit from the *plastiquers*. There was a more deadly side, including the selective killings of European liberals, overeager policemen and alleged FLN members, indiscriminate killing of Muslims, the 'rat hunt' and lynching of Muslim civilians, often after the funeral of a *pieds noirs* victim.[1265] The latter were typically spontaneous teenage attacks that the OAS did not organise but could prevent when it so desired. The *Guardian* provides an example of the selective category with a report of the assassinations carried out by Degueldre's Delta squads: 'their work is probably to be distinguished from that of the provocative murderers ... shooting down any Muslim.'[1266] The selective assassins struck again when 'the Chief Constable of Algiers, Roger Gavoury, was murdered in his flat last night. He was personally in charge of the investigation into the OAS.'[1267] Other reports show OAS units killing suspected ALN members: 'An OAS commando burst into a police station, shooting dead one Moslem prisoner and wounding six others.'[1268] There were also examples of indiscriminate killings: 'Twenty-two Muslims were killed here today ... The day opened disastrously with the discovery of the corpse of a beheaded European in a sack.'[1269] As the conflict progressed, Oran's afternoon 'rat hunts' became increasingly common: 'The day began with four or five murders of European passers-by ...

1263 See *Guardian*, 27 October 1960, 7, 18, 20, 27 January, 3, 6 March, 8 April, 10, 11, 15 May, 13 June, 5, 27 July, 24 August, 7, 25 September, 18, 31 October, 10, 23 November, 7 December 1961, 9, 10 January, 2, 15, 26 February, 6 March 1962. But on 9 February 1962 a bomb at the flat of Andre Malraux, the minister of culture, infamously 'blinded a neighbour's child Delphine Renard'.

1264 *Guardian*, 9 March 1962.

1265 For examples of OAS selective attacks, see *Guardian*, 30 June, 17 July 1956, 26, 27 January, 14 February, 1 April, 2 June, 11 September, 25 October, 2, 11, 14, 22, 25 November, 16 December 1957, 6, 16, 29 January, 5, 7, 8 February, 3, 12, 14, 30 March, 9, 10 April, 17 May, 21 June 1962. For examples of OAS indiscriminate killings, see *Guardian*, 13 August 1956, 28 December 1960, 24 January, 25 October 1961, 27 February, 6, 16 March, 4, 7, 25, 30 April, 5, 9, 11 May 1962. For indiscriminate killings during 'rat-hunts', see *Guardian*, 29, 31 August, 13 September, 18, 19, 26, 27 October, 1 December 1961, 4, 5, 30 January 1962.

1266 Ibid., 9 April 1962.

1267 Ibid., 2 June 1961.

1268 Ibid., 17 May 1962.

1269 Ibid., 27 February 1962.

The necessary impetus was thus given to ... start one of their rat hunts.'[1270] All three categories of 'counter-terror' killings can be found in the reportage.

The *Guardian* evaluated these *opérateurs*. They were Nazis, right-wing extremists and fascist desperadoes, colonial terrorists, right-wing terrorists and mad-dog terrorists, gangsters, armed thugs, ruffians and murder gangs. They were criminal terrorists and political criminals, mad, blind, stupid and insane. They were gratuitous murderers, had no courage and were not soldiers.[1271] Hetherington noted 'how closely the OAS corresponds to the Nazi movement in its early days in wanting not public sympathy for a rational cause but public obedience before a savage one.'[1272] The *Observer* agreed. They were thugs, right-wing gangs, Nazis, reactionaries, the fascist OAS and the settler OAS.[1273] Alan Williams remembers Algeria differently: 'I could see the point of view of the OAS, a workers' alliance, sort of like your Ulstermen's strike ... The officers and *colons* were sophisticated, impressive and educated ...'[1274] The *Observer* reported on the trial of a group of youths accused of lynching a passing Muslim. They claimed their victim had been singing the FLN national anthem.[1275] The Irish national anthem justified the same murderous rage among Ulster loyalists.

Understandable retaliation due to security failures
The *Guardian* correspondent sought to dispel any image of mindless Ulster loyalism. The six young men of the loyalist tartan gang who 'tolerated' his questions were 'impressively disciplined and coherent.'[1276] This is curious. The habitual, inarticulate paranoia displayed by loyalist spokesmen was/is a source of dismay within unionism. The following seven extracts are part of a pattern of similarly

---

1270 Ibid., 5 January 1962.
1271 For descriptions of the OAS, see *Guardian*, 20 October 1959, 4 March, 3 April, 22 May 1961, 24 (ed), 28 February, 5 (ed), 7, 19, 24 (ed), 31 March, 17 (ed) April, 22 June, 7 July 1962.
1272 Ibid., 5 (ed) March 1962.
1273 Descriptions of the OAS as thugs and Nazis can be found in the *Observer* of 10, 24 September, 31 December 1961, 4, 25 February, 25 March, 27 May 1962.
1274 Interview, Alan Williams (London), 19 July 1998.
1275 *Observer*, 25 March 1962.
1276 *Guardian*, 25 May 1972.

wide-eyed portraits.[1277] The UDA were 'well-trained and understandably militant', 'highly disciplined', 'undoubtedly disciplined' and 'formidably well disciplined.' They were 'mostly defensive and unarmed.' They 'kept the peace.' They meant to 'take on the IRA.' This portrait extended to the credulous acceptance of even outrageous loyalist statements. The UDA would protect Catholic families, and the UVF was seeking out and would deal with sectarian killers. The UVF would not tolerate indiscriminate bombings. Both newspapers accepted loyalist statements at face value and in an almost unbelievably naïve fashion. A *Guardian* report of a promised UVF ceasefire opined that 'as the UVF had denied sectarian killings, it is thought the statement relates mainly to the bombing of Catholic pubs and meeting places.' The killings of Catholics by bombing pubs apparently are not sectarian. In similar fashion, the *Observer* reported that 'in spite of many claims to the contrary from Catholics it is by no means certain that the UVF is responsible ... No known UVF man has been charged ... the organization has consistently condemned sectarian killings.'[1278] It is hard to account for such naivety from professionally sceptical journalists. Simon Hoggart explained the UDA's 'inability to prevent' the intimidation of Catholics out of east Belfast: 'They seem lost in a hopeless tangle of non-communication with the army.'[1279] Derek Brown again explained attacks on civilian (Catholic) targets: 'it must be stressed that there is no evidence that the UDA is involved.'[1280] At this point, loyalist paramilitaries had carried out 160 sectarian murders, and the *Guardian* itself already had the evidence of UDA murders and rapes. In addition, the UDA had even claimed responsibility for pub bombings.[1281] One year later, Brown wrote a glowing tribute to the UVF that included the trusting repetition of this outrageous UVF statement: 'Under no circumstances will the indiscriminate shooting or bombing of ordinary civilians or civilian property be tolerated.'[1282] At this point,

---

1277 For a benign portrait of loyalist paramilitaries, see *Guardian*, 26 (ed) July 1971, 20 March, 29 May, 12 (ed), 13, 14 (ed), 30 June, 3, 5, 18, 22, 24 July, 9 September, 17 October 1972, 5, 6, 8, 19, 22, 25, 29 January, 12 (ed), 18 June, 11 September, 19 November 1973, 4 February, 20 March 1974. It is possible to find suspicions and suggestions of loyalist involvement in assassinations; see *Guardian*, 10 March, 4 July, 20, 30 September, 2 October, 4 December 1972, 17 March, 25 August 1973, 16, 22 February, 25 March 1974.

1278 *Observer*, 4 February 1973; *Guardian*, 19 November 1973.

1279 *Guardian*, 17 October 1972.

1280 Ibid., 29 May 1973.

1281 For *Guardian* reports of UDA murder and rape, and the UDA admitting to bombing pubs, see 15 July, 2, 6 November 1972.

1282 Ibid., 20 March 1974.

loyalist paramilitaries had killed 238 Catholic civilians. Within a week of this statement, UVF bombs would kill two more and a further forty-three before two months had passed. Hetherington-Cole's decision to print this, in the prevailing circumstances, requires some explanation. Hetherington-Cole also claimed that any loyalists taking up arms 'would merely be debasing their standards to match the IRA's. They would also be making the army's task harder.'[1283] Not wrong but tactically wrong. The *Observer* reported the case of Albert Baker. His disclosures of indiscriminate killings of Catholics 'could further damage the reputation of the UDA.'[1284] What reputation can this possibly refer to?

The *Guardian* maintained loyalist violence was reactive and an understandable retaliation against 'Catholic provocation.'[1285] Loyalists explained their violence was reaction but the *Guardian* seldom missed an opportunity to portray the conflict as religious. Cole justified loyalist actions as contributing to the defeat of the IRA. It was also the result of the government's breach of its compact with the people to maintain order. Loyalist paramilitaries, said Cole, were the IRA's most obvious creation. There was, however, a limit to their restraint, and they must be furious with all this talk of a united Ireland. Still, their actions had brought Dublin and the Catholics to a new realism. Catholics, although slow to learn, had been brought around to opposing violence: 'These changes coincide with and, if one is to be honest, partly result from the growth of Protestant terrorism in response to that of the IRA.'[1286] During the civil rights phase of the conflict, the *Guardian* had already warned of the danger of 'Protestant extremists launching reprisals.'[1287] These 'reprisals' were a year before the IRA offensive began. Simon Hoggart offered a peculiar explanation: 'it is not entirely perverted to see the [loyalist] assassinations as a cry for help.'[1288]

The *Guardian*'s response to loyalists shooting a Catholic doctor and

1283 Ibid., 26 (ed) July 1971.

1284 *Observer*, 1 July 1973.

1285 For explanations of loyalist violence as reactive and justifications of it, see *Guardian*, 15 July 1969, 10 (ed) February, 12 March, 3, 14, 15 (ed) April, 13 (ed) September, 16 December 1971, 16 (ed), 20 March, 18, 31 (ed) May, 28 (ed) June, 22, 29 (ed) July, 1 (ed) 16, 28 August, 6 (ed) September, 19 (ed) October), 13 (ed), 24, 27 (ed) November, 1 (ed), 4 (ed), 11 (ed), 21 December 1972, 3 (ed), 16 (ed) January, 1 (ed), 8 (ed) February, 23 (ed) March, 11 (ed) April, 29, 31 May, 25 (ed) June, 24 (ed) July, 25 October, 23 (ed) November 1973, 1 February, 30 March, 1 (ed), 11 (ed) April), 20 May 1974, and *Observer*, 12 (ed) September, 17 October, 12 December 1971, 4 June 1972, 25 November 1973, 26 (ed) May 1974.

1286 *Guardian*, 3 (ed) January.

1287 Ibid., 15 July 1969.

1288 Ibid., 25 October 1973.

his two sons, killing one, is representative. The blame lay not with the UVF killers but with the IRA and the British government: 'To any sane man an extreme Protestant reaction was the probable outcome of a sustained IRA campaign.'[1289] The editor pondered: 'how far is the state entitled to go, by way of special measures?' If the government could not maintain order, then 'organizations like the UVF fill the vacuum, meeting terrorism with terrorism.'[1290] Three days later, Hetherington-Cole accused Harold Wilson of an anti-Protestant obsession, and demanded 'a frank acknowledgement that the Protestant violence is a reaction to a long IRA campaign that successive governments, including Mr. Wilson's, have been unable to end.'[1291] Cole repeated that the UVF killing of the doctor's son was due to the IRA. He again endorsed loyalist justifications, explaining that the IRA campaign was being ground down 'principally by the army and police, but also because of anxiety among ordinary Catholics that continued IRA atrocities will bring more Protestant reprisals.'[1292] Hetherington-Cole's editorial spelled it out: 'The horrible antidote to terrorism is counterterrorism which is what the sectarian murders amount to.'[1293] An *Observer* editorial during the UWC strike/rebellion considered the relationship between the 'Protestant irregulars and the army ... after all, both were against the IRA.'[1294]

Random murders: ignored, motiveless and finally mysterious
There are also considerable inaccuracies in the *Guardian*'s reporting of loyalist killings. Initially, they were simply ignored. Cusack and McDonald explained this was because the media were 'overwhelmed by the violence, most of it by the IRA.'[1295] 'Overwhelmed' as they were, they managed to report IRA violence. The first *Guardian* report of loyalist abduction-murders did not appear until 16 August 1972. At this point, the number of bodies was impossible to ignore. In July alone, loyalists perpetrated twenty-two sectarian murders in Belfast, two in Portadown, and are suspected of two more in Belfast. The killings then became 'motiveless murders' and finally a mystery: 'there appears to

1289 Ibid., 27 November 1972.
1290 Ibid., 1 December 1972 (ed).
1291 Ibid., 4 December 1972 (editorial).
1292 Ibid., 12 December 1972.
1293 Ibid., 16 January 1973 (editorial).
1294 *Observer*, 26 May 1974 (editorial).
1295 Cusack and McDonald, *UVF*, p. 113.

have been thirty-seven murders in Belfast since the beginning of July
… The number of Protestants and Catholics killed is roughly equal.'[1296]
The record, for this period, shows loyalists carried out five times as
many sectarian killings as republicans.[1297] This is the sustained pattern
in the *Guardian* reports (and more so in editorials), portraying an
equivalence of sectarian murder. For the period under study, I found
seventeen *Guardian* examples and three *Observer* examples where the
number of victims was directly evaluated. In every case, the number of
killings by loyalists is downgraded, and in most cases the number of
killings by republicans is inflated.[1298] For example, the *Guardian* of 10
July 1972 reported 'only one Catholic shot dead that weekend.' In fact,
six Catholics were shot dead that weekend.[1299] The editorial of the same
issue noted 'the continuing murder of individual Protestants.' At the
time, five Protestants and forty-five Catholics had been victims of
sectarian murder. Hethrington-Cole's editorial the next day (11 July
1972) noted that 'most of the dead of the past two weeks were
Protestant.' The correct figures were fourteen Catholics and seven
Protestant dead.[1300] The *Guardian* assessed the casualties for the year
1972: 'of the civilians, 121 were killed in a series of assassinations …
81 Catholics and 40 Protestants.'[1301] But in 1972 loyalists perpetrated
102 sectarian murders and republicans perpetrated eleven.[1302] These
inaccuracies reproduce the official British narrative of the army
separating two warring tribes. The reality was an IRA overwhelmingly
engaged in attacking security forces with a smaller contingent of
republicans participating in sectarian murder. Loyalists attacked the
community from which the insurgents emerged. Kevin Myers reflected
on the milestone of 1,000 dead without reference to one loyalist
killing.[1303]

1296 *Guardian*, 17 August 1972.

1297 McKittrick et al., *Lost Lives*, pp. 209–48.

1298 See the *Guardian*, 22 (ed) April 1969, 29 (ed) March, 11 (ed) May, 10 (ed), 11 (ed), 29
July, 9, 16, 17 August 1972, 2, 4 January, 1, 5 February 1973, 21 January, 5 (ed) April
1974 and *Observer*, 10 December 1972, 7 (ed), 26 April 1974. The inaccuracies are
always in the same direction, indicating greater republican killings and lesser loyalist
killings.

1299 McKittrick et al., *Lost Lives*, pp. 212–17.

1300 Ibid.

1301 *Guardian*, 2 January 1973.

1302 McKittrick et al., *Lost Lives*.

1303 *Observer*, 21 April 1974.

Inaccuracies like these point to an over-reliance on army and RUC sources.[1304] In the explosions at Catholic-frequented McGurk's and Kelly's bars, the army and police confirmed, without a doubt, that the bombs exploded inside (suggesting IRA bombs in transit) when the forensic evidence showed the bombs exploded outside, pointing, correctly, to loyalists. Following the explosion of a loyalist bomb incredibly stored inside the Crescent Bar, and which killed two Protestant civilians, the RUC distorted in reverse. This time the RUC said the bomb had been thrown in, suggesting republican involvement and diverting attention away from the real culprits, careless loyalists. When loyalist paramilitaries killed Catholic civilian Bernard Rice in a drive-by shooting, the RUC was mystified by this motiveless murder, and suggested he had been killed because he was wearing a Rangers scarf (suggesting republican involvement). When loyalists killed Catholic civilian John Crawford, the RUC blamed it on republicans even though a police agent inside the UVF had participated in this killing. The army added greater, even ludicrous, distortions, stating it had evidence the UFF/UDA was a front for the IRA and that the UVF did not exist.[1305] A credulous (or a naïve and/or supportive) press was portraying the conflict as a sectarian squabble rather than an insurgency confronted by the state and its loyalist paramilitary adjuncts (officially or otherwise).

Patriotic Rebellions
The conspiratorial rabble of Barricades Week
The liberal-press coverage of Barricades Week correctly depicted it as a ramshackle, precipitous move.[1306] French Algerians were devastated by de Gaulle's proclamation of Algerian self-determination. The recall of their champion General Massu foreshadowed their certain abandonment. *Ultras* seized government buildings and the university, blocked downtown Algiers, and demanded de Gaulle's removal and a change in policy. They killed fourteen policemen. Local troops helped

1304 For examples of security force information minimising loyalist sectarianism and amplifying republican sectarianism, see *Guardian*, 11 October, 6, 21 December 1971, 2 March, 21 April, 15, 16 (editorial), 18, 19 May, 1, 3, 6, 29 July, 5 August, 25, 29 September, 13 November, 8, 13 December 1972, 20 January, 5, 9, 15 February, 2 March, 19, 20, 27 June 1973, 15 January, 15, 18 April 1974. On 15 April 1974 the *Guardian* was still reporting McGurk's pub bomb as the work of the IRA. See also *Observer*, 6 February 1970, 14, 21 May, 1 June 1972, 31 March, 1 April 1974.

1305 *Guardian*, 19, 20 March 1973; *Observer*, 6 February 1970.

1306 See *Guardian*, 11, 21, 22, 23 (ed), 25, 26 (ed), 27, 28 (ed), 29 (ed), 30 (ed) January, 1, 2 (ed), 3, 4, 5, 9, 10, 11, 12 February, 9, 10, 19, 25 November, 7, 9, 31 December 1960, and *Observer*, 31 January, 6 March 1960.

enforce the strike. Every ten minutes, at the height of the stand-off, the local state radio warned that the army would do its duty. The *Guardian*, however, was unsure of government resolve: 'The French Cabinet issued a statement reaffirming the [self-determination] policy ... but Algiers extremists have very long experience of getting their own way.'[1307] Algerian parliamentary deputies considered themselves in a 'state of legitimate defence', and were enraged by local police remaining loyal to Paris, describing them as 'mercenaries.'[1308] The *Guardian* repeatedly urged Paris to put it up to the *ultras* and eliminate the conspiratorial rabble from French politics. The government should confront the 'hostile white population.'[1309] At one point Resident Minister Paul Delouvier broadcast an emotional appeal, attempting to talk the *ultras* out from their barricades. Hetherington's editorial denounced his speech as 'more that of a man chained to settler opinion than that of an agent of central power.'[1310] The next day's editorial was unambiguous: 'the time has come for action.'[1311] An *Observer* editorial opined that France could no longer be a partner in the Western alliance 'if de Gaulle should either fail to repress the revolt or should be forced to compromise with it.'[1312] De Gaulle did face down the *ultras*, disbanded the locally recruited regiment, imprisoned its commanding officer, and replaced 'lukewarm' officers of the regular army. The *Guardian* approved: 'The Europeans at large may be shocked into opening their minds to other solutions besides an Algeria forever merged with France.'[1313]

The press opposed the 'fascists of Algiers' throughout the crisis. Thus, when *pied noir* insurgents sent parties into the kasbah 'in the hope of persuading Moslems to take part, the total catch was only 500.'[1314] But 500 would surely be a large number to publicly oppose the FLN, especially in its stronghold and considering the deadly punishments for lesser transgressions. The *Guardian* reminded the French press that 'the prime purpose of de Gaulle's policy is to end the war by gaining the assent of the Moslem rebels.'[1315] Paris, however, did not wish to hand either community over to the FLN, and urged French Algerians to find a new harmony with Muslims.

1307 *Guardian*, 26 January 1960.
1308 Ibid., 19 January 1960.
1309 Ibid., 26 (ed) January 1960.
1310 Ibid., 28 (ed) January 1960.
1311 Ibid., 29 (ed) January 1960.
1312 *Observer*, 31 (ed) January 1960.
1313 *Guardian*, 2 (ed) February 1960
1314 *Guardian*, 29 January 1960.
1315 Ibid., 30 January 1960.

The responsible and moderate Ulster Workers' Council

The Ulster Workers' Council was a front for loyalist paramilitaries. Their strike/rebellion of May 1974 aimed to secure a reversal of power-sharing with Catholics, and the abolition of the Council of Ireland. It achieved both through control of power supplies, skilful intimidation of workers, a servile local BBC, and a wavering British government frustrated by generals who refused to support government policy. The reportage portrayed this loyalist front as a workers' council (no 'Ulster' tag), sympathised with unionist trauma, and understood the army's remarkable lack of response. This was despite both newspapers having reported, two years earlier, the army's awareness of the state's vulnerability over power supplies and, had even *predicted* these tactics. However, editorials in both newspapers blamed the IRA for Britain's reversal, deemed the whole episode to be 'un-bloody', and proposed reconsideration of power-sharing.[1316]

The *Guardian* had first reported unionist power-sharing opponents as a minority in the local assembly: 'the UWC strike call came immediately after the Assembly rejected, by 44 votes to 28, a Loyalist resolution condemning power-sharing.'[1317] There was also a noticeably indefinite tone in the reports of army movements: 'an unspecified number of specialist troops, Royal Engineers, are standing by ... the army is bound to have put other units on alert ... the security forces are for the moment, evidently keeping their heads down.'[1318] There was further uncertainty: 'army and Royal Navy technicians are apparently standing by somewhere in the province.'[1319] Somehow, the army was unprepared: 'Ministers are worried that the skilled technical troops already in Ulster may not be able to handle the different types of power stations.'[1320] The normally bullish defence secretary, Roy Mason, explained the army was 'very unwilling to begin the first strike breaking operation in Northern Ireland since the troubles began.'[1321] This contradicted the *Guardian*'s own reports that Brigadier Kitson's views of proactively dealing with striking workers and internal subversion 'have gained widespread support within the army at every level.'[1322] The army's knowledge of the state's vulnerability over power supplies

1316 Coverage of the UWC strike/rebellion can be found in the *Guardian*, 15, 16, 17, 18 (ed), 20, 21, 22 (ed), 23, 24 (ed), 25, 27 (ed), 28, 29 (ed), 30 (ed), 31(ed) May, 1, 3, 4 (ed) June 1974 and in the *Observer*, 19, 26 (ed) May, 2 (ed), 9 June (ed) 1974.

1317 *Guardian*, 15 May 1974.

1318 Ibid., 21 May 1974.

1319 Ibid., 22 May 1974.

1320 Ibid., 24 May 1974.

1321 Ibid., 25 May 1974.

1322 Ibid., 8 January 1974.

points to a curious gap in military preparations. In addition, Protestant power workers had already threatened to strike two years earlier unless security at power plants was removed from British soldiers and entrusted to the local UDR. Hetherington-Cole's understanding of army inaction was misplaced. Thirty years later, the public learned that army lethargy was part of an MI5 plot (Clockwork Orange) to undermine Harold Wilson. Rumoured for years, in 2006 the plot finally came in from the cold in a BBC documentary.[1323]

Guardian editorials urged Dublin to accede to loyalist demands for greater repression. The Irish government was 'beginning to understand this, and the lesson has been bitterly underlined by the Dublin massacre.'[1324] Dublin must acknowledge its half-hearted repression of the IRA and suspend by three years any ideas about the Council of Ireland so that 'ordinary Protestants will have emerged from their trauma.'[1325] Wilson's frustration and growing awareness of army disloyalty became apparent during a broadcast, where he insulted Protestants as 'spongers.' The next day, a *Guardian* editorial explained: 'the army is understandably reluctant to become involved in a major confrontation.'[1326] The same editorial also recalled IRA misdeeds and urged Wilson to admit his Reunited-Ireland plan was a mistake. A further editorial concluded that the fall of the Executive was a tragedy, 'un-bloody though the prelude to it has been.'[1327] The 'un-bloody' prelude included loyalists murdering thirty-eight civilians.

An initial *Observer* editorial described the strike/rebellion as a 'coup ... Westminster must be willing to recognize ... new and different solutions like repartition.'[1328] But a follow-up editorial reversed this position, and suggested renegotiating a new settlement that retained 'the essence of power sharing while further watering down the powers of the Council of Ireland and further strengthening the safeguards to remain in the United Kingdom ... [then] the generally responsible and moderate character of the new [UWC] leaders, would, with time, begin to show.'[1329] Harold Jackson summarised the portrayal, the logic of

---

1323 For army awareness of state's vulnerability over power and the popularity of Kitson's ideas, see *Guardian:* 9, 12, 13, 14, 16 September 1972, 7 February, 3 November, 11 December 1973, 7, 8 January 1974, and in the *Observer:* 19, 26 March 1972. See 'Enough of the cover-up; the Wilson plot was our Watergate', *Guardian*, 15 March 2006, and *Panorama*, 'The Plot Against Harold Wilson', BBC, 16 March 2006.

1324 *Guardian*, 22 (ed) May.

1325 Ibid., 24 (ed) May.

1326 Ibid., 27 May 1974.

1327 Ibid., 29 (ed) May.

1328 *Observer*, 26 (ed) May 1974.

1329 Ibid., 2 (ed) June 1974.

power-sharing meant inevitable reunification with the Irish Republic, and the earliest unionists had got it right: 'The Catholics had to be treated as a threat because the fact of that threat was the reason for the existence of the Border.'[1330] Further, the reports portrayed the events as the actions of 'workers', not 'Ulster' workers or paramilitaries.[1331] Lastly, the rejection of power-sharing originated with 'harassed Protestant workers who had suffered 18 months of terrorism.'[1332] In the same period, four times as many Catholics had lost their lives.

Conclusion

This chapter showed the respective counter-terrorists were active before any insurgency. They were a *forelash* not a *backlash*. Nor did they attack the terrorists, but typically vented their rage on defenceless civilians randomly chosen from the 'other' community. The OAS sometimes attacked French state forces, particularly those over-eager in their pursuit or when alarmed by government initiatives. Loyalist paramilitaries had no similar occasion to confront British forces. The army largely ignored them. Military intelligence used them. There was no corresponding undercover Barbouze shooting down loyalists. Westminster never pursued a policy in the face of determined unionist opposition. Two distinct patterns of reportage emerged. OAS gunmen were gratuitous fascist murderers. The drive-by shootings of loyalist paramilitaries were 'a cry for help'. The OAS provoked Muslims. Loyalists had been provoked. They were also helping to defeat the IRA. This chapter highlighted the remarkably similar episodes of super-patriots rebelling against government of their supposed devotion. The press made two different recommendations. Paris should suppress the fascists of Algiers and press forward with its policy of self-determination. London should accede to a loyalist front, described as 'moderate workers', whose objection was to power-sharing with Catholics, a proposal a lot less radical than the French proposals of independence. Still, power-sharing was a lot to ask of unionism. Republicans did not re-write this episode. Robert Fisk's account, of a self-selected provisional government of Protestant power workers, armed loyalists and extremist politicians staging a rebellion against the Crown, has already re-written the liberal press account.

1330 *Guardian*, 28 May 1974.
1331 Ibid., 25, 29 May 1974; *Observer*, 9 June 1974.
1332 *Guardian*, 29 May 1974.

CHAPTER THIRTEEN

Isolated Ultras and Friends of Ulster

.

This chapter explores the words and actions of constitutional politicians, religious leaders, the army, police and establishment figures in assessing any support (overt and covert) for the activities of loyalist paramilitaries or French Algerian super-patriots. Their words and actions are examined against their professed adherence to the rule of law and democracy. The term 'counterterrorism', rather than simply terrorism, suggests a justificatory element. The comparative liberal press coverage is evaluated against the record with a focus on editorials in a search for patterns, slants or emphases.

Algérie Française Ultras: Increasing Isolation
'Algeria is worth a meal, I suppose?'

ALN atrocities against French civilians and recalcitrant Muslims pushed many to revenge. There were, perhaps, one thousand French Algerians active in the OAS. At war's end, there were at least fifty Muslims imprisoned for OAS activity. There was also a Jewish branch of the OAS, the *Organisation de L'Armée Secrète Juive*, organised in the wake of ALN attacks on synagogues. The OAS enjoyed the backing of right-wing academics, lawyers and metropolitan politicians, notably former Prime Minister Georges Bidault, who re-established the *Conseil National de la Resistance* (CNR) in 1961, consciously modelled on WWII resistance. Former Prime Minister Antoine Pinay refused even to denounce the OAS, and ALN mutilations also pushed the liberal Jacques Soustelle to *Algérie Française*. But it is important not to reduce the OAS to a fascist caricature. Its ranks included veterans of the

Spanish civil war's international brigade. The Communist Party held the FLN to be 'the conscious or unconscious agents of another imperialism [Islam].'[1333]

But not all supported the OAS. Jean-Jaques Susini, OAS propaganda chief, was compelled to issue warnings against non-cooperation. Businessmen who did not pay their monthly levy had their premises bombed. During the Battle of Bab-el-Oued, the better-off residents of El Bair went to the cinemas and cafés and opined that the working-class militants got what they deserved. OAS leader Paul Mancilla complained that Special Branch received information denouncing them daily and European liberals were a popular OAS target. On the second day of Barricades Week, many drifted from the forum to the beach, went to lunch or watched from boats in the harbour. A furious Susini railed: 'Algeria is worth a meal I suppose?'[1334] Genevieve Salasc, OAS, was tortured by military intelligence, but unlike FLN militant Djamila Boupacha also believed to have been tortured, there was no book by de Beauvoir, nor a portrait by Picasso. When the army massacred the *petits blancs* on the rue d'Isly, there was no inquiry and not one liberal voice called for one.

A subversive Church intent on proving its universality
Soustelle warned Washington this was the first phase in the coming war between the Christian West and the communist East. Robert Martel of the rightist *Union Française Nord-Africaine* also claimed to be defending Christianity. Pierre Chateau-Jobert's *Armée du Christ-Roi*, an organisation more political than violent, wished to take on Islam and undo the 1789 revolution. In Oran, some parish priests feared for religious freedom under Islam. The Oran Catholic Welfare Association defended OAS actions as legitimate self-defence. Fr Georges Grasset, a mystic and a writer of religious tracts in defence of the Christian West, was associated with the OAS Madrid office. The paratoopers' chaplain, Fr Delarue, insisted on a Christian's duty to defend the oppressed, but he was ridiculed for having absorbed more of the paratroopers' outlook than the Church's.[1335]

Archbishop Duval consistently condemned all atrocities. Twenty-five per cent of Algiers university students belonged to the Catholic-left organisation the *Association Générale des Étudiants d'Algérie*, which

1333 *L'Humanité*, June 1945, in Gaucher, *The Terrorists,* (Secker & Warburg. 1968), p. 226n.
1334 Kettle, *De Gaulle and Algeria,* (London, Quartet, 1993), p. 581.
1335 Henissart, *Wolves in the City,* (London, Rupert-Hart, 1970), pp. 348, 421.

supported an independent Algeria. There was also a strong current of anti-colonial opinion in the French Catholic Church. Handbills distributed outside churches relayed soldiers' shame over Algeria. On 29 September 1956, 200 soldiers celebrated Mass for 'peace in Algeria and for the souls of the dead on both sides.'[1336] This might be compared to the public outcry when Fr James Wixted, of Oxfordshire, announced he would celebrate Mass for IRA hunger striker Bobby Sands. Bishop Anthony Emery forbade him to mention Sands' name and Thatcher rebuked him in parliament. With some satisfaction the media reported that only five people showed up. Bishop James Mehaffey, of Derry and Raphoe, rebuked the Reverend Cecil Thornton for attending a prayer vigil for Sands. *The Times* reported that the archbishop of Canterbury, Reverend Robert Runcie, was 'clearly upset by the allegations that he had asked people to pray for the soul of Robert Sands.'[1337] He, himself, prayed for the hunger-strikers which infuriated some Protestant clergy in Ireland.[1338]

French diplomats complained the Catholic Church was 'a subversive force intent on proving its universality, at the expense of the state.'[1339] In a series of *Le Monde* articles in September 1956, Catholic intellectuals François Mauriac and Louis Massignon explained ALN violence was morally no worse than the repression and that Algeria as part of France was an illusion. The French Catholic Church had never been so prominent in radical causes. Traditionally, it had been allied with the right against a republic it viewed as anti-clerical.[1340]

'The army does not fight for racist privileges'

The Cinquième Bureau secretly nursed the 'counter-terrorists' into existence, local police often winked at their activities, and the locally recruited regiment openly colluded during Barricades Week. But army activists did not go over to *Algérie Française*. Their concern was the honour of the army and a duty to France above de Gaulle. Their plans

1336 Clark, *Algeria in Turmoil,* (NY, Grossett, 1960), p. 199.

1337 O'Malley, *Biting at the Grave*, (Boston, Beacon, 1990), p. 201. Lawrence McKeown, IRA, credits Bishop Mahaffey's intervention for facilitating his attending his mother's funeral.

1338 Collins, *Irish Hunger Strike,* (White Island, 1986), p. 342.

1339 Clark, *Algeria in Turmoil,* p. 206.

1340 Cooley, *Ball, Christ and Mohammed,* (London, Murray, 1965), pp. 308-320 for activist clergy.

1341 Gaucher, *Terrorists,* p. 264.

were frustrated by the *Organisation Clandestine du Contingent*, OCC, draftees who supported Algerian independence. Massu was always a faithful Gaullist, Salan favoured a federated Algeria and Challe, while protesting self-determination, vowed to fight *ultras* who sought to maintain their privileges. General Ailleret's order of the day was 'war on the OAS.'[1341] Susini, the political brains of the OAS, remembers they barely escaped disaster during the anti-OAS offensive of 1961. Hundreds were arrested, and 157 Algiers policemen were struck off or suspended. The Gaullist *Barbouze* agents, colluding even with the ALN, bombed OAS hideouts and shot down Delta gunmen in the streets. Colonel Debrosse relentlessly pursued and tortured the OAS. His deputy, Major Allaire, propelled towards understanding the rebellion when his son was killed by the ALN, became an open supporter of *Algérie Algérienne*. Following Barricades Week, the local *Unités Territoriales* were dissolved and not replaced. Their commanding officer, Major Victor Sapin-Lignières, was imprisoned. The psychological-warfare bureau was shut down and rebellious generals were jailed. From his prison cell General Faure warned the OAS to expect no help from the army. The army, newly-disciplined, cooperated even with the FLN against the OAS. The *Algerois* had once considered the 10th paratroopers their own, but many *petits blancs* did not regard the security forces, in general, as friends. The people of Oran detested the 'foreign' soldiers from France and complained about their brutality. While there were sympathisers in the police, the majority remained loyal, especially the metropolitan reinforcements and the CRS. Rebellious companies of the Foreign Legion were disbanded and escorted at gunpoint from their base in Sidi bel Abbes.

Ulster's Super-Protestants: Well-Placed Friends
'Killing Catholics is something which may be helpful'

The Stormont administration has a history of massively arming the Protestant population, to canalise vigilantism in addition to resisting Irish nationalism. This included paying gunmen to shoot Catholic civilians to inhibit Catholic-Protestant working-class solidarity.[1342] The original UVF did not go away in 1914 but was reactivated from time to time in the 1920s and 1930s.[1343] UVF leader Gusty Spence maintained the UVF was reconstituted in the early 1960s by members of the

---

1342 Townsend, *Britain's Civil Wars,* (London, Faber, 1986), p. 207, Brewer and Higgins, *Anti-Catholicism in Northern Ireland,* p. 97.
1343 Garland, *Gusty,* (Blackstaff, 2001), pp 10, 43-4, 53.

Unionist Party. Police suspected three unionist politicians.[1344] Two were caught with explosives but never prosecuted.[1345] Former Stormont minister William Craig counselled: 'we should be prepared to liquidate the enemy.'[1346] Jean Coulter, Vanguard Unionist, demanded RAF bombing raids: 'there are no innocent people in republican ghettoes.'[1347] Another Vanguard unionist admitted: 'One must condemn these things ... But one wouldn't like to say there weren't those who weren't satisfied – deep down.'[1348] A clergyman-politician explained: 'Protestant action (or reaction) was, if not to be welcomed, at least not to be frowned upon.'[1349]

UDA killer John White told the court: 'any Roman Catholic would have done' and claimed he had been misled by speeches of liquidating enemies.[1350] When the IRA shot dead local soldier Jack Donnelly, Harold McCusker MP claimed: 'If his murderer was not a neighbour or a workmate then his neighbour or workmate set him up.'[1351] John Taylor, UUP, referencing the local nationalist vote, declared: 'there are 30,000 potential accomplices of murder.'[1352] When an INLA bomb killed another UDR soldier Andrew Stinson, Ken Maginnis, UUP, repeated McCusker's claim: 'a neighbour helped arrange his murder.'[1353] Loyalist killers understood these sentiments as official confirmation of a general Catholic guilt and acquiescence in any unofficial retribution. In 1972 Craig proclaimed: 'we have avoided any revenge or retaliation against the Roman Catholic community as such.'[1354] PM Brian Faulkner thought it was 'quite remarkable that the majority population here has not indulged in retaliation.'[1355] In fact, during the previous year an average of two Catholics per week had been murdered, often after gruesome torture. Muslims likewise despaired at *pieds-noirs* blindness to their suffering. Faulkner even denied UDA involvement. Some Queen's University Belfast's law lecturers advised the UDA on searches and arrests, others offered them political

1344 Edwards, *UVF*, (Merrion, 2017), p. 21.
1345 Dillon, *Dirty War,* (Arrow, 1990), pp. xxxix-xxxx.
1346 Nelson, *Ulster's Uncertain Defenders,* (Appletree, 1984). pp. 104, 123.
1347 D. McKittrick et al, *Lost Lives,* p. 746.
1348 Nelson, *Ulster's Uncertain Defenders*, p. 124.
1349 Ibid., p. 124.
1350 McKittrick et al., *Lost Lives*, p. 372.
1351 Ibid., p. 855.
1352 Ibid.
1353 Ibid., p. 945.
1354 Van Voris, *Violence in Ulster,* (Massachusetts, 1975), p. 268.
1355 Ibid., p. 304.

advice.[1356] Belfast mayor Ian Adamson, a 'senior advisor to UDA leaders', liked to celebrate the 'Twelfth' at the home of UDA Supreme Commander Andy Tyrie. When B-Specials killed civilian John Gallagher, Stormont Prime Minister Major Chichester-Clark, complained about 'that wretched man supposedly killed by idiotic B-Specials.'[1357] All seventeen 'idiots' had, unjustifiably, fired on the 'wretched man.'

In 1972, a loyalist news sheet reported DUP support: 'victory will be ours through the endeavours of the UDA.'[1358] At this point, they had already perpetrated multiple murders, abduction, rape and secretly buried one of their victims.[1359] Unionist deputy leader John Taylor evaluated Catholic fears of murder by loyalist death squads: 'in a perverse way this is something which may be helpful.'[1360] Trimble's response to the UVF murder of his teenage constituent Dennis Carville was: 'some idiots have gone and taken the law into their own hands.'[1361] Hugh Smyth, Belfast mayor, complained that the imprisoning of the Shankill Butchers' UVF leader Lenny Murphy 'made a mockery of British justice.'[1362] Deputy mayor Fred McCoubrey, called for the release of UDA leader Johnny Adair. At Belfast's City Hall Sammy Wilson proposed: 'would the council be prepared to congratulate all those who have a good job on two sides of the border ... a none too subtle reference to the UFF murder of Sinn Fein councillor Eddie Fullerton'.[1363] For thirty years, senior unionist politicians voiced opinions from which loyalist paramilitaries took encouragement.[1364]

Steve Bruce interviewed fifty-eight loyalists convicted of murder. They were 'old fashioned patriots', some were 'much maligned saints' and a greater number of their victims could be more 'legitimate than the media suggest.' But 'not enough people are persuaded of their

1356 Bruce, *Red Hand*, p. 72, Davis, *Mirror Hate*, (Aldershot, 1994), p. 53, McDonald & Cusack, UDA, pp. 363-4.

1357 Van Voris, *Violence in Ulster*, p. 162, McKittrick et al., *Lost Lives*, pp. 36–8.

1358 *Londonderry Loyalist*, no.12 (August 1972), p. 6, in O'Dochartaigh, *From Civil Rights to Armalites*, (Cork, 1997), p.292. The first UDA killings in L/Derry occurred in December 1972.

1359 McKittrick, pp.165, 176, 178, 181,185, 186, 190, 191, 197 199, 201 205, 209, 210, 217, 219, 225.

1360 *Fortnight Magazine*, #321, pp. 32-33, 1993, see also O'Malley, *The Uncivil Wars*, p. 314, and Dillon, *God and the Gun*, pp. 6, 85, 93.

1361 *Irish News*, 8 October 1990.

1362 McKittrick et al., *Lost Lives*, p. 270.

1363 Ó Muilleoir, *Belfast's Dome of Delight*, (Belfast: Beyond the Pale, 1999), p. 152.

1364 Dillon, *God and the Gun*, (Orion, 1997), p. 193.

usefulness to overlook their defects.'[1365] However, the UDA could point to a *News Letter* poll (6 July 1993), showing forty-two per cent supported random killings of Catholics, rising to fifty per cent under certain circumstances.[1366] Aughey found: 'justification of random Catholic murder, in an effort to break support for the IRA, carried a good deal of force in the Protestant community.'[1367] A UVF spokesman disclosed unionists politicians: 'whispered [support] behind closed doors ...'[1368] UVF leader David Ervine claimed a prominent DUP politician appealed to the UVF to keep killing Catholic civilians, 'There was no point stopping now ... I could tell you the colour of their [the politicians'] wallpaper.'[1369] Ervine would also explain: '... why wouldn't loyalists collude with the security forces. We were all on the same side ...'[1370] During the UWC strike/rebellion, UVF and UDA leaders met at the home of Stormont minister Roy Bradford. Bradford also visited UDA HQ.

'Attack the people who represent the anti-Christ'
Archbishop Robin Eames acknowledged: 'it is striking the length of time the Protestant community denied the random assassinations ...'[1371] Throughout the 1970s there was no concerted condemnation of loyalist murders by Protestant Church leaders. Eames explained that communal uncertainty and unease 'led to an absence of any concerted effort to prevent support for sectarian killings.'[1372] Consider Paisley's sermon sanctifying violence against Catholics:

> Christ was not a man of peace! Christ was a violent man ...
> violent for God's sake! Our battle is not against a system, it
> is against the people who uphold that system! ... Remember
> it is not the system we must attack but the people who
> represent the Anti-Christ in our midst ...[1373]

1365 Bruce, *Red Hand*, pp. 1, 3, 28, 289–90.

1366 McDonald and Cusack, *UDA*, p. 245.

1367 Aughey, *Under Siege*, p. 88.

1368 Shirlow, *End of Ulster Loyalism,* p. 8. See too McAuley, Cuchulainn and an RPG in Hughes (ed.), *Culture and Politics in Northern Ireland* (Buckingham: Open University Press, 1991), pp. 65–6, and Nelson, *Ulster's Uncertain Defenders*, pp. 117–20.

1369 Cusack and McDonald, *UVF,* p. 323, *Independent*, 9 January 2007.

1370 A. Edwards, *UVF*, p. 198.

1371 Eames, *Chains to Be Broken,* (Blackstaff, 1992), p. 37. See also Nelson, *Ulster's Uncertain Defenders*, pp. 14, 122, Bruce, *Red Hand*, pp. 92, 189.

1372 Eames, *Chains*, p. 36. See also Dunlop, *Precarious Belonging,* p. 38.

1373 Galliher and DeGregory, *Violence in Northern Ireland,* (Dublin, Gill, 1985), p. 146.

Following the fire-bombing of Catholic neighbourhoods, Paisley declared:

> Catholic homes caught fire because they were loaded with petrol bombs; Catholic churches were attacked and burned because they were arsenals and priests handed out machine-guns ...[1374]

In 1966, Paisley campaigned for the release of UVF leader Gusty Spence, convicted of murdering a random Catholic teenager. One adviser from Terence O'Neill's office believed Paisley knew all about the early bombings. UVF leader Billy Hutchinson claimed Paisley paid for them. The British were concerned enough to consider locking him up and charging him with conspiracy.[1375] Paisley's associate, the Reverend William McCrea, questioned Catholic innocence and argued peace may require their expulsion.[1376] He called for RAF strikes against the Irish Republic and urged authorities to 'lift the ban on the UVF so they could openly aid the security forces.'[1377] Reverend Ivan Foster, DUP, also called for nuclear strikes against Dublin.[1378] Reverend Martin Smyth MP inspected the assembled ranks of uniformed UDA men. Reverend Robert Bradford, Orangeman and unionist MP, sourced the conflict to Rome, Marxism and ecumenical confusion: 'If the preservation of the UK would involve killing, then that would have to be.'[1379] In 2001 Pastor Clifford Peoples, UVF, was imprisoned for a two-year campaign involving 200 bomb attacks on Catholic homes and churches. On reflection, after thirty years, Paisley felt he should have been more forceful in confronting the civil rights marches.[1380] Of course, there have always been ministers who sought reconciliation. In 1985, for sympathising with a Catholic priest whose church had been bombed, Reverend David Armstrong was snubbed by his own congregation, had his own church picketed and was forced to leave under death threats. A fellow minister, fearing the reaction of RUC members in his own

---

1374 *Belfast Telegraph*, 12 September 2014.

1375 Van Voris, *Violence in Ulster*, p. 121, Hutchinson, *My Life in Loyalism,* (Dublin, Merrion 2020), p. 235, *Guardian*, 29 December 2007.

1376 Van Voris, op. cip., p. 202.

1377 *Belfast Telegraph*, 29 Dec 2014, Boulton, *UVF*, p. 155.

1378 McGarry and O'Leary, *The Politics of Antagonism*, 2nd ed., (Athlone, 1993), p. 275, n. 10.

1379 McKittrick et al., *Lost Lives*, p. 887.

1380 *Sunday Sequence*, BBC Radio Ulster, 3 October 1999.

congregation, refused to accompany him on a visit to the Catholic church. In the 1960s, some Protestant clergy, notably, the Reverend Eric Gallagher reached out to fellow Catholics and stood up to the Orange Order.

Everyone knows the security forces are for us
British officers admit to a benign view of loyalist paramilitaries, especially in the early 1970s.[1381] Initially, the army stated 'the UVF is non-existent' and even claimed 'the UFF were a front for the IRA.' [1382] In 1974, an unnamed officer told the conservative Monday Club that the 'army chose, quite deliberately to give the UDA tacit support.'[1383] General Tuzo designed a ferocious plan encouraging UDA vigilantes, aimed at the extirpation of the IRA.[1384] In 1972, the 6th Earl of Enniskillen UDR Major David Cole called for the RUC to be permitted tactics used in the colonies: 'a total war machine ... such as we had abroad and which proved very efficient.'[1385] The British saw some benefit in loyalist assassinations: 'it would concentrate the minds of Catholics' as when British ambassador, Sir Anthony Galsworthy telegrammed London following the UVF's Dublin bombs: 'I think the Irish have taken the point.'[1386] UDR members considered themselves a citizen army, with local teachers telling pupils: 'come on son, time you were putting the uniform on.'[1387] As early as August 1969, in an RUC barracks, Tara's Roy Garland and Ian Paisley were demanding a People's Militia: 'what is surprising is that [William] McGrath, Paisley, myself and a man called Black ... were talking to the Prime Minister about it.'[1388] On 7 August 1974, the Secretary of State Merlyn Rees met with the UVF, UDA and former B-Specials who demanded security in local hands. The RUC was very soon greatly expanded. The UDR was increased to two full battalions. British and loyalist interests coincided

---

1381 Cusack and McDonald, *UVF*, pp. 128-9, 262-6, and Bruce, *Red Hand*, pp. 47–8, 210, 212–13, 274.

1382 *Observer*, 6 February 1970, *Guardian*, 19, 20 June 1973.

1383 *Irish Times*, 4 September 1974, in Farrell, *The Orange State*, p. 297.

1384 *Irish Times* 19 January 2013, See also *Belfast Telegraph*, 29 January 2016 for Tuzo's ambitions for a large-scale fire fight with the IRA.

1385 Cole was an officer in the Kenyan Police combating the Mau Mau, see his memo to Whitelaw, PRONI, D1702/12/69/1-9, Earl of Enniskillen papers, 6 April 1972, in Burke, *An Army of Tribes*, (OUP, 2018), p. 90.

1386 Bowyer Bell, *Secret Army,* p. 398, Hanley, Who Bombed Dublin? *History Ireland*, no.3, vol. 22 (May/June) 2014, and McKittrick et al., *Lost Lives*, pp. 184, 666.

1387 Arthur, *Northern Ireland,* pp. 222-38.

1388 Moore, *Kincora Scandal*, p. 67.

on 'Ulsterisation', the policy to give the RUC primacy over security. At army checkpoints, the UDR boasted of sectarian killings to their Catholic neighbours. When the victim turned out to be a relative of a republican, he was a 'pig from the same litter.'[1389] Although the UDA remained a legal organisation, incredibly, until August 1992, unionists could never completely trust the British, only their own RUC: 'They've always helped in the past.'[1390]

Not all British soldiers would match this solidarity or subscribe to those views. On Halloween night 1972, a UDA bomb killed Clare Hughes, aged four, and Paula Stronge, aged six. A British Captain was appalled to overhear a UDR soldier: 'They'd only have grown up into the sort of Fenians who produce another ten Fenians.'[1391] In January 1976, a female UDR soldier commented aloud on the joint UVF-RUC-UDR murders of the Reavey and O'Dowd families: 'Good enough for the likes of them.'[1392] The officer who recoiled at this sectarianism wanted her dismissed. Another British officer similarly recoiled from a loyalist kitchen worker commenting on Catholic children burned in bombings: 'Fenians? It's OK then.'[1393] One soldier, Jimmy, was visibly distressed on pulling a young woman's body from the rubble of a loyalist bomb.[1394] A group of middle-aged women offered their own form of comfort: 'Don't worry son, she was only a Catholic. I couldn't handle this. We were supposed to be fighting fucking terrorists! Not Women! Not Catholics!'[1395] *News Letter* editor Cowan Watson advocated firm measures:

> ... the astounded [British] officer understood Watson to suggest that perhaps a few Catholics hostages could be taken and, if necessary, shot. Confirming this to us later, Watson said he thought the context might be that 'by trying to more humane now one was leading to greater inhumanity later.'[1396]

1389 Toolis, *Rebel Hearts,* pp. 62, 68. See also C. Ryder, *The RUC,* pp. 150–85.

1390 Parker, *May the Lord*, (Jonathan Cape 1993), pp. 319–22.

1391 Arthur, *Northern Ireland*, (Sidgwick, 1987), p. 93. See also Cusack and McDonald, *UVF*, p. 248, and Bruce, *Red Hand*, p. 218.

1392 Wharton, *The Long War,* (Solihull, 2010), p. 157.

1393 Wharton, *Wasted Years, Wasted Lives,* (Solihull, 2013), p. 54.

1394 Carmel Knox in McKittrick et al, *Lost Lives*, p. 167.

1395 Lindsay, *Brits Speak Out*, p. 53.

1396 *Sunday Times* Insight, A Perspective on Ulster, 14 November 1971.

Covert action that remains covert

Numerous inquiries have documented a widespread collusion between state forces and their loyalist adjuncts, including: the Stalker Report, Sampson Report, Stevens Inquiry (three), Cory Report, Cassell Report, Barron Report and the O'Loan Report, in addition to the UN's Curamaswamy Report and inquiries by Amnesty International and the ECHR.[1397] One in six UDR soldiers was linked to loyalist killing squads. Since at least 1973 the government knew the UDR was the single biggest source of training and weapons for loyalist paramilitaries, supplying more than 400 rifles in one year alone.[1398] The Irish government's Oireachtas Report was 'fully satisfied' not only that collusion occurred but that it was 'widespread' and highlighted British failure to act decisively against the UDR.[1399] Collusion, initially dismissed, is now explained as the actions of 'rogue elements', and the imprisonment of loyalists is proffered to suggest that the law was rigorous and was working. But these convictions are a tribute to the integrity of police who put the pursuit of justice above political allegiance.[1400] They do not demonstrate the absence of collusion but reflect the calibre of loyalist paramilitaries, ironically often the weakest link in the chain of command. Courtroom evidence reveals examples of loyalist killers dependent on drugs or alcohol, with mental disorders and below average level of education or intelligence, or simply bigots.[1401] Habitually leaving plenty of evidence, the police referred to them as 'Prod jobs.'[1402] Many turned themselves in. Some officers mocked them for attacking defenceless civilians.[1403]

A young unionist seeking to protect the state had many options: the regular army, the UDR, part-time UDR, RUC, RUC-reserve and the prison service. The remainder found their way to the loyalist paramilitaries. Billy McFettridge remembers many of his UDA comrades had been rejected by the RUC. Johnny Adair and Andy Tyrie both wanted to join but the RUC was more selective. UVF leader David Ervine resented an RUC sergeant's: 'We don't need the likes of you.'[1404]

1397 http://cain.ulst.ac.uk/issues/collusion/, accessed 29 April 2021.

1398 *Irish News*, 2 May 2006, and www.patfinucanecentre.org , accessed July 2015).

1399 *Irish Times*, 29 November 2006.

1400 Police officers like Johnston Brown, Alan Simpson and Trevor McIlwrath; see Brown, *Into the Dark*, (Dublin: Gill & Macmillan, 2015).

1401 Bruce, *Red Hand*, pp. 270–6. See also McKittrick et al., *Lost Lives*, pp. 237, 238, 247, 578, 665, 726, 922, 1351.

1402 McKittrick et al., *Lost Lives*, pp. 275, 287–8.

1403 Bruce, *Red Hand*, pp. 280–1. See also McFettridge, *Full Pardon*, p. 76.

1404 Bruce, *Red Hand*, pp. 272–3; McFettridge, *Full Pardon*, p. 51; E. Maloney, *Voices from the Grave*, p. 307.

To the military handlers, however, recruits from the compromised, the malleable or the vulnerable, were easier to manipulate and manage.

Too often, there was little investigation of loyalist killings, as confirmed by the ECHR.[1405] One example is the McGurk's bar massacre. For twenty-seven years, this was the conflict's single greatest atrocity and while the RUC, very early, had a list of five suspects no one was even arrested. Six years after the bombing, Robert Campbell, a name on that list, turned himself in.[1406] The week before the bombing, Belfast city centre had been totally disrupted by IRA bombings. To prevent a repeat, 4,000 soldiers swamped the city centre with a 'ring of steel'.[1407] In addition, Belfast was peppered with multiple army checkpoints designed to re-capture IRA prisoners who, two days earlier, had escaped from a prison, less than a mile from the bomb site. While residents complained of soldiers and checkpoints at every turn, the UVF slipped through and waited patiently for fully ninety minutes with their 50-pound bomb, literally within yards of a major army/police barracks. How could the army have missed them? Former British soldier Aly Renwick remembered soldiers' frequent puzzlement at last-minute OOB (out of bounds) orders. The significance only became apparent when they subsequently learned of loyalist attacks, they could have prevented.[1408] Robert Campbell testified his gang was spirited away by military handlers.[1409] In 2011, the Ombudsman found an RUC investigative bias on McGurk's. PSNI chief constable Matt Baggott refused to accept the findings.

Government responses are also instructive. Albert Baker, UDA and a British soldier, turned himself in and was imprisoned for torture-murders. His claims of complicity with senior members of the RUC were dismissed. Continuing revelations from loyalists Robert Campbell, Lindsay Robb, Bobby Philpott, Stephen MacFerran, John Black and others, were dismissed as self-serving. John Weir, William McCaughey and Gary Armstrong, of the RUC's Special Patrol Group, were all eventually imprisoned for some of their crimes, including murder. All stated their superiors approved of their activities. This, too, was ignored.

1405 Armstrong, *From Palace*, (New Wine, 1991), pp. 40–1, Bruce, *Red Hand*, pp. 273–4.

1406 http://mcgurksbar.com/massacre/ and *Belfast Telegraph*, 9 July 2010, *Irish News*, 4 December 2010.

1407 See David McKittrick, *Independent*, 7 December 1992.

1408 See A. Renwick, *Hidden Wounds,* (London: Barbed Wire, 1999).

1409 J. Black, *Killing for Britain*, (Edinburgh, 2008) confirms this, see too https://policeombudsman.org/getmedia/893d20b0.../McGurk-s-Final-Report.pdf. Police Ombudsman Report p. 16.

William Matchett, former RUC Special Branch, describes 'collusion as the best fake news story in the world, a product of hundreds of Carl Beeches and a deal between a British prime minister and republican terrorists.'[1410] There were, too, interesting responses to whistle-blowers. Captain Colin Wallace, Military Intelligence, spoke out about collusion. He was framed on a murder charge and served six years before his conviction was quashed.[1411] Captain Fred Holroyd, Military Intelligence, also claimed collusion. He was committed to a mental institution but almost thirty years later the Stevens Inquiry corroborated his claims.[1412] For his investigative zeal, John Stalker, deputy chief constable of Manchester, was suspended and smeared with associating with criminals. The case eventually collapsed in court.[1413]

In 2007 the reformed PSNI maintained the Stalker and Sampson reports were still 'top secret', prompting the chief coroner, John Lecky, to complain that he could not do his job properly. The many long-delayed or never-held inquests tell their own story. In similar fashion, the Stevens Inquiries were only partially (minimally) published. Even so, Sir John Stevens wanted to prosecute twenty-five senior RUC officers. After an inordinate four-year delay, the DPP decided not to prosecute. Stevens also sent a file to the DPP on Colonel Gordon Kerr, head of the army's Force Research Unit. Again, there was no prosecution. Kerr was moved to Beijing as a military attaché.[1414] Sir Hugh Orde, an Englishman and former RUC Chief Constable, stated that Gordon Kerr should have been prosecuted.[1415] Canadian Supreme Court Judge Peter Cory, also finding murderous collusion, recommended public inquiries into the murders of the lawyers Pat Finucane and Rosemary Nelson. After long delays, Cory was moved to remind Britain that his recommendations were binding under the Weston Park Agreement. The government rushed through the 2005 Inquiries Act. Cory testified to a US House Foreign Affairs Committee that the Inquiries Act made an independent inquiry impossible.[1416]

1410 *News Letter*, 18 September 2020, 27 November 2019. Matchett's view resembles the settler's distrust of metropolitan politicians. Beech was an exposed fraudster who made false claims of a VIP child abuse ring.

1411 P Foot, *Who Framed Colin Wallace?* (London: Macmillan, 1989).

1412 Holroyd, F. *War Without Honour,* (Hull: Medium Publishing, 1989).

1413 J Stalker, *Stalker,* (London: Harrap, 1988), P. Taylor, *Stalker: The Search for the Truth,* (London, Faber, 1987).

1414 John Ware, *Guardian*, 19 June 2002; Neil McKay, *The Sunday Herald*, 26 November 2000.

1415 *Belfast Telegraph*, 12 June 2015.

1416 US Congressman Chris Smith
https://chrissmith.house.gov/news/documentsingle.aspx?DocumentID=57069, 17 March 2005.

Amnesty International found the very people under investigation would control the information to be made public. Lord Saville would refuse to sit on any such inquiry.[1417]

Taoiseach Bertie Ahern speaking on Pat Finucane's murder said: 'everyone knows the Brits were involved.'[1418] Despite the Supreme Court ruling that the Weston Park Agreement was 'unequivocal' the British government refuses yet to hold a public inquiry. US law professor Douglas Cassel was shocked at the level of collusion and condemned PSNI Chief Constable Hugh Orde: 'We have not received a single scrap of paper.'[1419] The O'Loan Report also found damning evidence of RUC-UVF collusion. But unionist politicians, usually loud defenders of the law, combined to prevent even debate of the report in the Northern Ireland Assembly. First Minister Arlene Foster illegally blocked funding into legacy inquests. Unionists fear that rewriting the past will unfairly focus on 'their' security forces.'[1420]

During the Stevens Inquiry, the operation room mysteriously caught fire inside a secure RUC station. Curiously, the alarms did not sound. Stevens stated 'the fire was a deliberate act of arson.'[1421] RUC officers openly mocked his team and repeatedly selected the Billy Joel song, 'We Didn't Start the Fire' on the canteen's jukebox.[1422] In 1992, a determined Stevens did, eventually, succeed in bringing to trial Brian Nelson, a UDA member/army agent. He was charged with five murders. Solicitor General Sir Patrick Mayhew worked out a deal whereby no evidence would be heard in court. Colonel Gordon Kerr, himself recommended for prosecution, spoke on Nelson's behalf. So, too, did Conservative Cabinet minister Tom King. Nelson served less than half his ten-year sentence and received a new life in Cardiff. None of this is new. In 1972, during a trial for importing guns, a character reference for UDA leader Charles Harding Smith from the RUC Chief Constable was read out in a London courtroom.[1423] Smith, a self-confessed British agent, walked free. So, too, did his co-accused, Robert Lusty, a serving RUC officer, and the UDA's John White, who went on to a career of savage killings.

1417 *Guardian*, 21 April 2005.
1418 *Guardian*, 13 December 2010.
1419 *Irish News*, 7 November 2006, and
      www.cain.ulst.ac.uk/issues/collusion/docs/cassel061106.pdf (accessed 15 July 2015).
1420 *Belfast Telegraph*, 29 January 2018, *News Letter*, 18 July 2018.
1421 *Guardian*, 18 April 2003.
1422 *Sunday Times,* 13 April 2003, see also
      www.patfinucanecentre.org/cases/rosemary/practicalities.html , accessed 4 July 2015.
1423 Coogan, *The Troubles*, p. 143.

Chief Constable Colin Port, of the Avon and Somerset police, investigated RUC collusion in the murder of Rosemary Nelson. He compared the non-cooperation of senior RUC officers to 'wading through treacle while treading on eggshells.'[1424] Judge Cory, finding evidence of collusion in Nelson's murder, also recommended a public inquiry. The Inquiries Act 2005 and MI5 ensured that the pursuit of truth would be conducted within very British limits. Still, the inquiry found the police had 'legitimised Rosemary Nelson as a trophy target for loyalists and failed to protect her.'[1425] In 2011, Secretary of State Owen Patterson, concluded that this did not amount to collusion. The [Justice Henry] Barron Report 2003 investigated the 1974 Dublin and Monaghan bombings. The British government refused to cooperate. The DUP refused to ask for their cooperation. The forensic evidence held by the RUC mysteriously disappeared. Barron found the case against the security forces not proven but their involvement was 'neither fanciful nor absurd given the number of instances in which similar illegal activity has been proven.'[1426] He also concluded that members of the RUC and UDR had highly likely participated in, or were aware of, preparations for the bombs, and that a high-level cover-up cannot be ruled out. Lieutenant Colonel Nigel Wylde, former British Army Commander Ordnance Disposal, testified loyalists did not have the skills to undertake this operation in 1974. They never demonstrated the same level of sophistication again.

The words of Sir Michael Howard, Britain's foremost military historian, may help. Drawing on Britain's long experience in counter-insurgency, he recommended the 'qualities needed in a serious campaign against terrorists: secrecy, intelligence, quiet ruthlessness and covert actions that remain covert.'[1428] Strong indications have now emerged that the Dublin and Monaghan bombs were part of a British military-intelligence plan to force the collapse of the 1974 power-sharing Executive as part of a wider plot to undermine Prime Minister Harold Wilson through operation 'Clockwork Orange'. The evidence points to the Glenanne Gang, a combination of UVF, RUC and British soldiers already proven to have carried out many sectarian killings. Their final tally is estimated to be more than 120 murders.[1429] A major

---

1424 *Guardian*, 4 July 2009.

1425 *Belfast Telegraph*, 31 May 2011.

1426 *Irish Times*, 26 December 2003.

1428 See Sir Michael Howard, 'Mistake to Declare this a War', *RUSI* [Royal United Services Institute], vol. 146, no. 6 (December 2001), p. 1.

1429 Cadwallader, *Lethal Allies*, p. 16.

suspect is Robin Jackson, a UVF member and UDR soldier. He is also suspected of murdering William Strathearn, for which two RUC members and one UVF member were convicted. During the trial, the judge asked why Jackson was not before the court. 'Operational strategy', said the police.[1430] As an explanation, one senior Special Branch officer proffered: 'Jackson always refused to talk.'[1431]

Sometimes, covert operations are forced out on to the public. A temporary fall-out in August 1989 between army intelligence and loyalist paramilitaries permitted the public a rare glimpse into this murky world. To justify their murder of republican Loughlin Maginn, loyalists pasted hundreds of army photomontages of suspects on street walls. They were quickly punished. Brian Robinson, UVF, was killed by undercover soldiers, minutes after murdering random Catholic civilian, Patrick McKenna. The UVF complained bitterly its 'soldier' had been killed by 'former friends.'[1432] They had reason to remonstrate. The only other occasion when the army killed a member of a UVF death squad had been fourteen years earlier, in April 1975, following a hapless gun and bomb attack on a Catholic-frequented pub. Robinson's death was such a departure that loyalists have, ever since, held an annual parade to commemorate his sacrifice 'to make the army look good.'[1433] Loyalists might turn themselves in following an attack of conscience or get caught by a diligent detective, but when they set out to kill Catholic civilians, they faced an almost zero possibility of police or army bullets. For the UDA, the risk of death was literally zero. Friendly forces might run the risk of the justice system, albeit a Kitson-constrained version, but the death rate, two UVF and zero UDA, points strongly to military intelligence ensuring their safe passage.[1434] These extraordinary numbers for a twenty-five-year campaign of murder cannot be explained by rogue elements.

In June 2022 the British government proposed an Independent Commission for Reconciliation and Information Recovery, ICRIR, to replace the Stormont House Agreement Legacy Bill and the Statute of

1430 McKay, *Bear in Mind These Dead,* p. 182.

1431 Ex-RUC officers dismay, *News Letter,* 17 September 2020.

1432 Cusack and McDonald, *UVF,* p. 363.

1433 *Belfast Telegraph,* 9 September 2013.

1434 Six UDA members were killed by the army: four shot and two run over by army vehicles, all during street disturbances, McKittrick et al., *Lost Lives,* pp. 207, 281-2, 327, 422, 425. Two UVF men, perpetrating murderous attacks against Catholics, were killed by the army; April 1975 and March 1983, pp. 533, 1177. The RUC shot dead two UVF members, one during a riot, the other in disputed circumstances and, two UDA members, both during robberies, pp. 263, 264, 654, 940.

Limitations or amnesty which had suddenly replaced it. The government backed off from the proposed amnesty which would have included their IRA opponents. The ICRIR would conduct reviews rather than investigations and dispensed with Troubles inquests such as the recent Ballymurphy Massacre inquest which overturned the long standing false version propagated by government and media. It would put an end to civil actions, police ombudsman inquiries and formal trials. It is a shield to avoid pursuing justice. It does not comply with human rights law requiring thorough murder investigations and fails to meet the criteria of the Stormont House Agreement which all parties and the Irish and British governments signed up to. It gives supervisory powers exclusively to the secretary of state. These proposals would protect the state from investigations into collusion and veterans from prosecution.

The Liberal Press
The hysterical European supporters of the OAS
The liberal press portrayed French authorities as soft on *pieds-noirs* ultras. The OAS enjoyed a strange protection, and the army was unwilling to pursue it.[1435] They could not 'carry out their crimes ... without the tolerance accorded so long to fanatics whose hearts were in the right place.'[1436] Clare Hollingworth describes a 'pantomime' that often took place on the streets of Algiers: '"Are you Colonel G?" ... "Yes, I am, and I hope you, too, are a patriotic Frenchman." Colonel G is allowed to pass.'[1437] But the FLN only accused the army of negligence and of occasional complicity with the OAS. In addition, the diligent reader can find many short reports of army arrests, soldiers shooting OAS gunmen, bomb attacks on OAS-frequented cafés carried out by Gaullist agents, the *Barbouze* (counter counter-terrorists?), and other actions against the *ultras*.[1438] For example, during disturbances in Oran, the police made: '72 arrests of young European rioters to a mere 9 Moslems.'[1439] A corresponding ratio of loyalists-nationalists rioters arrested by the RUC cannot be found. Nor were the arrests a recent

---

1435 See *Guardian:* 17 February 1957, 17 October, 6 December 1959, 6, 7 April 1961, 20 February, 16 March 1962.

1436 Darsie Gillie, *Guardian*, 6 April 1961.

1437 Ibid., 20 February 1962.

1438 See *Guardian*, 6 March 1957, 14 February, 12, 15, 18 May, 31 July, 9 September, 2, 20 October, 1, 4 December 1961, 2, 22, 29, 31 January, 1 February, 17, 30 April, May 1962.

1439 Ibid., 20 October 1961.

development. At the height of the Battle of Algiers, the *Guardian* reported: 'The 22 counter-terrorists cannot understand why they have been arrested.'[1440] Disorientation came with the realisation that the state would not openly support them. Their dismay would be echoed by loyalist paramilitaries Johnny Adair, Kenny McClinton and Gusty Spence. In contrast to the editorial portrait of racist *colons*, a close reading of the day-to-day reportage does not reveal a massive support for the OAS; in fact, often the opposite, with many *pieds noirs* prepared to follow de Gaulle.[1441] When *ultras* organised strikes against his December 1960 visit, the dockworkers' and transport workers' unions refused to participate. However, in January 1962 the doctors and shopkeepers did strike in sympathy with OAS aims. One month later, there was again a class difference in responses, when the unions representing railwaymen, dockworkers, civil servants, and oil workers all participated in a strike, *opposing* the OAS. And this when the OAS was at the peak of its power. Henri Alleg, anti-colonial activist and editor of Algeria's most popular paper, the left-wing *Alger républicain*, counted fifteen to twenty per cent of French Algerians opposed colonialism and voted for progressive policies of full equality and independence.[1442]

There were times when the OAS called for public demonstrations of support. It did not happen. The *petits blancs* eagerly beat out the three short and two long notes (*Al-gér-ie Fran-çaise*) on pots and pans but displayed the tricolour of the republic instead of the required OAS flag. When the OAS then demanded the *pieds noirs* show their support by displaying a tricoloured ribbon in their buttonholes, it was a complete failure. The *Guardian* had an explanation for these lukewarm displays: 'These demonstrations have become less and less successful as they required more and more personal courage.'[1443] However, just a few months after this report, French Algerians launched a new organisation, *Je Suis Français*. Members publicly proclaimed their support for *Algérie Française* but deplored the activities of the OAS. An airline pilot, Auguste Arnould, chaired the public meeting made up of ex-

---

1440 Ibid., 6 March 1957.

1441 See *Guardian:* 29 December 1956, 5 December 1960, 28 April, 28 December 1961, 10, 17, 19 February, 11 June 1962. For lukewarm support or opposition, see *Guardian*, 2 January 1957, 8 December 1960, 25 April, 26 September, 10, 23 October, 12, 16, 19 December 1961, 9 January, 5, 8, 10, 17, 19 February, 23 March 1962. For *pieds noirs* assisting the FLN, see *Guardian*, 2 February, 26 March, 31 July 1957, 29 June, 11 July 1959.

1442 Alleg, 'Political Violence in Algeria', in Darby et al, *Political Violence: Ireland in a comparative perspective,* p. 137.

servicemen's associations, student associations, trade unions, civil servants and professional associations. Signatories had to declare they were neither fascists nor candidates for office, pledged to defend France and denounced *all* terrorism. The *Guardian* reported that 450,000 had signed up to the new organisation.[1444] Yet a few months earlier, its editorial had condemned 'the hold the OAS had on the hysterical Europeans.'[1445] The editorials and commentary are again at odds with their own reports.

There was further evidence of a *pieds noirs* first loyalty to Paris. When the police asked for the handing in of legal weapons, the *Guardian* reported long queues outside police stations: 'Yesterday 5,000 weapons, the majority of them revolvers, were handed over ...'[1446] This is hardly the behaviour of vigilant *colons* suspicious of fickle, metropolitan politicians. The RUC and Brian Faulkner refused to pursue a similar scheme. The *Observer* reported on Barricades Weeks where 'a crowd of about 3,000 had assembled.'[1447] This was hardly an endorsement. The *Observer*'s own short reports contradict their editorials of hateful settlers.

Additional armed security forces with a different responsibility
A close reading of the reportage shows that there was considerable community support for the loyalist campaign. Unionist political conferences, for example, included unionist parties, the Orange Order and representatives from the UVF and UDA.[1448] The heads of all Protestant Churches, while condemning the attack on civil rights activists at Burntollet, nevertheless felt 'many who took offensive action may have done so out of a conviction and a concern for the defence of their faith.'[1449] John Brown, clergyman and B-Special commander, had 'observed' the attack. This model of a frontiersman had not felt it necessary to intervene to restore the peace. Senior unionist politician Captain Austin Ardill proffered a revealing criticism of Craig's infamous 'prepared to kill' speech: 'There are several people who think as he does. But we are not ready to say it.'[1450] The outcome of this

1443 *Guardian*, 10 October 1961.

1444 Ibid., 19 February 1962.

1445 Ibid., 28 September (editorial).

1446 Ibid., 28 April 1961.

1447 *Observer*, 31 January 1960.

1448 For community and politicians' support for loyalist paramilitaries, see *Guardian*, 1 January 1969, 26 June (editorial), 21 (editorial), 23 October, 12 November, 18 December 1972, 6 February, 9 May 1973, 18 February, 4 March, 24 April, 10 May 1974.

1449 Ibid., 10 January 1969.

1450 Ibid., 20 October 1972.

internal dispute was that the unionist party censored Ardill (the covert supporter of killing), not Craig (the public proponent).

John Taylor, Stormont Minister of Home Affairs, despairing over UDR efficacy, called for 'an additional armed security force with a different responsibility.'[1451] Loyalist paramilitaries would have their own view of 'different responsibility.' John (later, Lord) Laird declared: 'If the militants decide that they have got to take matters into their own hands I am not going to condemn them or go out to tell them to stop.'[1452] It is no surprise, then, to learn the attorney general's reason for abolishing the jury system: it had worked well until loyalists started to appear in court. A pattern then emerged of 'UDA men who had been acquitted in spite of overwhelming evidence against them.'[1453] Most jurors were unionist because of the then property qualifications as a panellist. Support for a force with 'different responsibilities' extended to the *News Letter*'s editorial office: 'the guerrilla war is too serious to be left to the politicians.'[1454] The *Guardian* held that: 'Not too many *News Letter* readers would agree with the leader writer's rather chilling conclusion.'[1455] But this was overly generous as revealed by the *News Letter's* 1993 poll cited earlier; forty-two per cent supported random killings of Catholics, rising to fifty per cent under certain circumstances.[1456] Reverened Martin Smyth voiced similar support: 'those who defend the Constitution cannot be castigated in the same terms as those who oppose it.'[1457] John Taylor 'who expressed his personal sorrow [on Dublin bombs] said he had encountered a great deal of satisfaction among his constituents that the South had got some of its own medicine.'[1458] Neal Ascherson remembers a lot of journalists met 'Ulster Protestants and became aware of skewed perceptions and appalling attitudes ... the British are always looking to like the unionists, but they can't because they have no likeable leaders ... nobody liked the *pieds noirs*.'[1459]

1451 Ibid., 14 September 1971.

1452 Ibid., 1 December 1973. Laird endorsed army brutal interrogations and commended them on Bloody Sunday.

1453 Ibid., 9 May 1973.

1454 Ibid., 13 February 1974.

1455 *Guardian* 18 February 1974.

1456 *Belfast News Letter*, 6 July 1993.

1457 *Observer*, 4 February 1973.

1458 *Observer,* 19 May 1974, *see also* reports of support for the loyalist paramilitaries: 19 March, 22 October 1972, 4 February 1973, 12, 19 May 1974.

1459 Interview, Neal Ascherson (London), 28 July 1998.

Both newspapers reported considerably cordial relations between the army, police and loyalists.[1460] After an unusual exchange of shots between the British army and the UDA, Colonel Derek Wilford declared: 'I personally feel a sense of betrayal. We have done all we can to accommodate the UDA.'[1461] When UDA leader Tommy Herron was murdered, the *Guardian* reported that while 'UDA officers' questioned people from inside and outside the organisation: 'two RUC detectives from the Special Squad conducted their investigation *in another room of the UDA headquarters.*'[1462] At this point, illegal UDA guns had already been found and the UDA/UVF had already committed 176 sectarian killings, including some with RUC-supplied guns.[1463] In addition, the police, while conducting a murder inquiry, required UDA permission to conduct interviews with 'senior UDA officers.' The UDA had a public address, and the location of its 'headquarters' was public knowledge. The OAS telephone number was in the Algiers' phone book.

Following the McGurk's bar bomb, the army quickly deflected suspicion, explaining that an IRA bomb 'in transit' had definitely exploded prematurely inside. John Taylor, minister in the Stormont administration, responded to suggestions of collusion from Patrick Kennedy MP: 'I would solemnly request Roman Catholics throughout the province to think twice before they accept the type of propaganda that is being fed to them about this incident.'[1464] The *Guardian* presented the most extravagant summation: 'five men were standing around the bomb when it went off inside the bar.'[1465] The *Guardian* also urged its readers to believe the army version. Following many years of dogged investigation and revelations unearthed by Ciaran MacAirt (grandson of one of those killed in the bombing), the British government apologised to the families for its misleading account. Taylor maintains he has nothing to apologise for.[1466]

The *Observer* reported this revealing encounter at a barricade where an army officer asked for the local UDA leader by name: 'They greet

1460 For examples of cordial relations between the security forces and loyalists, see the *Guardian*, 27 September, 11 October 1971, 20, 27 March, 10 April, 24 May, 14, 15, 18 July, 8, 9 September, 13, 16, 19 October, 7, 8 November, 12 December 1972, 8, 9 February, 9, 12 March, 4 June, 17, 18 September, 24 November 1973, and the *Observer*, 4 June, 20 August, 10 September, 12 November 1972, 18 February, 22 July 1973.

1461 *Guardian*, 9 September 1972.

1462 Ibid., 18 September 1973, my emphasis.

1463 McKittrick et al., *Lost Lives*, pp. 122-392.

1464 Stormont parliamentary record, 7 December 1971, pp 890-1.

1465 *Guardian*, 9 December 1971.

1466 *Sunday Life,* 27 July 2008.

each other in a friendly fashion.'[1467] A group of loyalists had hijacked one of the army's land rovers: 'Its four-man crew walked away rather than open fire, and the army want it back, please.'[1468] The officer also wanted another of his vehicles returned, this one an unmarked car. These undercover soldiers had also been relieved of their covert transport. To resolve the situation, 'the young UDA commander goes to see the local army commander.'[1469] The journalist Colin Smith noticed: 'His pistol is still under his anorak but nobody searches him.'[1470] In the spring and summer of 1972, in spite of roving undercover soldiers, the bodies of twenty-three Catholics, tortured and shot, were found behind these very barricades.[1471] While elite soldiers were relieved of their unmarked cars by UDA gunmen in the loyalist Shankill, on the nationalist Glen Road at the same time, undercover soldiers Captain Alistair MacGregor and Sergeant Clive Williams were shooting Catholic civilians, at random, from their unmarked car.[1472] Colin Smith also noticed a UDR land rover flying the flag of loyalist paramilitaries: 'Here were the soldiers meant to guarantee Catholics' safety flying the flag waved by the very people who wanted to burn them out.'[1473]

Since both newspapers knew of these cordial relations, were journalists simply gullible when dealing with official and security-force sources? Or was there a willingness to accept stories damaging to the official republican enemy and a private recognition of loyalists as unofficial last-ditch defenders of the state? There is evidence to support this, and the *Guardian* was again more partisan than the *Observer*.

The reporting of the murderous attack on Kelly's bar, in a nationalist neighbourhood, is again instructive.[1474] There were two conflicting accounts: first, the army claimed to have witnessed the bombers drive up in the bomb car and go inside and insisted the UVF was not firing into this Catholic neighbourhood; second, the nationalist residents' version at odds with every point of the army's. The *Observer* printed the residents' version of loyalist responsibility, now accepted as the

---

1467 *Observer*, 11 June 1972.

1468 Ibid.

1469 Ibid.

1470 Ibid.

1471 McKittrick et al., *Lost Lives*, pp. 165–256.

1472 P. Taylor, *Brits,* p. 130. Ciaran MacAirt unearthed previously undisclosed information that undercover soldiers opened fire the night Jean Smith was killed, *Belfast Telegraph,* 8 September 2016.

1473 *Observer*, 12 November 1972.

1474 Reports of the bomb at Kelly's pub can be found in the *Guardian*, 15, 16 (editorial),

correct account.[1475] But the *Guardian* repeated the army version for four days, with Hetherington-Cole's unwavering editorial line of IRA responsibility rather than the UVF. Simon Winchester reported the army's 'numerous reasons' for stating the bomb was an IRA one: the army pointed to 'the timing (Saturday night is a popular time for Provisional bomb planting operations) to the fact that the car in which the bomb was left had been stolen earlier in the day, to the observation made of Kelly's Bar, and so on.'[1476] The army's 'observation' does not match the record. Winchester's reasons for accepting it are unknowable. But to describe two innocuous details (Saturday nights favoured by the IRA and a car stolen earlier in the day) as 'numerous reasons' indicates an overeager acceptance of army sources. The appendage 'and so on' indicates an effort to bolster a position already known to be weak. The most naïve would question why republicans would attack the very people they were supposedly defending. In addition, the army already knew the car had been stolen on the loyalist Shankill Road.[1477]

The reporting of the Dublin bombings provides further evidence of a definite partiality in the editor's office. Page one of the *Guardian* carried a report of a man calling himself Captain Craig telephoning to say 'there were two bombs in Dublin. He added that the campaign would be escalated until something was done about Sunningdale.'[1478] The editorial on page ten reads: 'Some loyalist extremists carried out the raid presumably in retaliation against IRA activities and as another assault on Sunningdale.'[1479] The editor shifted the caller's stated rejection of power-sharing towards retaliation against the IRA. His choice of the word 'raid' to describe that day's indiscriminate slaughter of thirty-three civilians is particularly revealing. Kevin Myers confirmed in the next day's *Observer* that loyalists believed the bombs were their best tactics against power-sharing.[1480]

There is considerable evidence in the reporting, and more so in the editor's office, of a downplaying of loyalist violence, and an

---

18, 19 May 1972. There is a divergence between the editorials and the reporting in the *Guardian*, 16 May 1972. The *Observer*, 14 May 1972, printed the residents' (and correct) version.

1475 McKittrick et al., *Lost Lives*, pp. 182–5.

1476 *Guardian*, 16 May 1972.

1477 C. de Baroid, *Ballymurphy and the Irish War,* pp. 154–61.

1478 *Guardian*, 18 May 1974.

1479 Ibid. (editorial).

1480 *Observer*, 19 May 1974.

understanding of militant loyalism.[1481] A *Guardian* report of a week of 'sectarian slaughter' leaving eleven Catholic dead and five Protestant dead is illustrative.[1482] The five Protestant dead were: two soldiers, one police officer, one member of the Police Authority, and the fifth victim was a Protestant civilian mistakenly killed by loyalists targeting Catholics.[1483] The full picture, then, was of twelve loyalist killings targeting Catholics, and three republican killings of state forces and one civilian police official (Protestant). The *Guardian* portrait of an inter-communal sectarian conflict followed the official narrative. There was no suggestion of insurgent attacks and collective-punishment reprisals. This was the consistent pattern of the *Guardian*'s inaccuracies. In the *Observer*, Kevin Myers wrote of the UVF's 'major offensive against Republican targets', the IRA and UVF as 'respective enemies', and the UVF's determination to fight until 'their enemies were vanquished.'[1484] This points to the UVF as fighting the IRA rather than killing random Catholic civilians. It is, perhaps, no surprise to learn that the UVF leadership 'had come to admire and trust Kevin Myers.'[1485]

Myers' writing would later evolve to include British direction in this slaughter. Jim Hanna, a leading UVF man, 'so trusted Myers that he gave him photographs of himself with two British army intelligence officers taken in his own home ... show[ing] Hanna holding one of the officer's rifles.'[1486] Tommy 'Tucker' Lyttle, a leader of the Shankill UDA killers, liked to throw parties after killing Catholics. Myers described Lyttle as 'a killer whom I liked though he had killed the wonderful Rose McCartney.'[1487] Rose was a popular local singer who

---

1481 The following are all accounts where the *Guardian* reports obscure the reality, downplaying loyalist killings (editorials marked with an asterisk claim that loyalists have not really started or are on the brink of killing, when in reality the killings were well under way): 12, 20 (editorial) June, 13, 31 July, 23, 28 August, 11 (editorial)* October, 6, 21 November, 21 (editorial), 22 December 1972, 1 (editorial), 8 (editorial)*, 9 February, 9 March, 16 April, 18, 19 May, 12 June (editorial), 6, 24 (editorial)* July, 10, 11, 30 August (editorial), 3 October, 12 November (editorial). To take the 24 July 1973 example, the loyalists on the 'brink of killing' had already carried out 173 sectarian killings (McKittrick et al., *Lost Lives*). Or take the editorial of 1 February 1973, which equates the UDA's random killing of a fifteen-year-old Catholic civilian with the IRA's almost immediate retribution against his UDA killer. Cruise O'Brien continued the obfuscation in the *Observer*, 4 February 1973.

1482 *Guardian*, 22 December 1972.

1483 McKittrick et al., *Lost Lives*, pp. 305–10.

1484 For misleading accounts of loyalist killings see *Observer*, 11*, 25, November 1973, 7* April, 23*June 1974. The dates highlighted with an asterisk are Kevin Myers' portrayals of the UVF as fighting republicans rather than randomly murdering and torturing Catholic civilians.

1485 Cusack and McDonald, *UVF*, p. 146.

1486 Ibid.

1487 Myers, *Watching the Door*, p. 268.

had been shot six times in the head and face. Her companion, Patrick O'Neill, had been tortured before his murder.[1488] Myers acknowledged later: 'The security policies of the British and Stormont Governments of the time, 1971-72, in effect allowed Davy Payne [Rose McCartney's killer] to roam free North and West Belfast, finding his victims; and he found them in large numbers.'[1489] State papers from 1971 indicate that Payne was a British asset. He certainly did the MRF a great favour a few weeks before he killed Rose McCartney.[1490]

Conclusion

Some French politicians refused to condemn the OAS but support was mostly confined to right-wing organisations and activist army officers. The French Catholic hierarchy opposed them, as did Gaullist agents, trade unions, elements of civil society and, eventually, the army. *Guardian* and *Observer* editorials portraying French-Algerians as hysterical supporters, do not match even their own reports. Unionist politicians and fundamentalist clergymen encouraged or acquiesced in loyalist violence. Elements of the security forces colluded with them. Multiple attempts to delay or frustrate investigations reveal a well-placed support for loyalist paramilitaries. The reports of community support for loyalists contrasts with the editorial portrait of moderate, law-abiding, unionist democrats ready to reform. While the OAS faced more opposition than their loyalist counterparts, French army collusion with patriotic vigilantes was reported as routine. No hint of British military collusion with 'friendly forces' shattered the fictitious orthodoxy of a neutral Britain maintaining the peace. The daily reportage of both conflicts conforms fairly well to the historical record. The editorials and featured analyses do not, but in the opposite directions.

Collusion in Ireland is the most contentious issue frustrating attempts to deal with the past. The liberal press coverage affirmed the official view of state forces standing in the middle of a sectarian squabble. This portrait is increasingly contested by emerging evidence and supranational bodies. Unionists fear the 'collusion lie' rewrites the

---

1488 McKittrick p. 234.

1489 An Irishman's Diary, *Irish Times*, 25 March 2003.

1490 See James Kinchin-White and Ed Moloney, Is This Botched MRF Operation Evidence That Downing Street Endorsed Collusion with Loyalists? https://thebrokenelbow.com/2018/09/24/the-mrf-file-part-five-is-this-botched-mrf-operation-evidence-that-downing-street-endorsed-collusion-with-loyalists/ (accessed 13 January 2018).

past, unfairly focuses on their security forces and reinforces the 'IRA narrative'.[1491]

1491 *News Letter*, 18 July 2018.

CHAPTER FOURTEEN

Rewriting the Troubles?

This study rests on the proposition that the media's unquestioned premises, choice of topics, range of opinions expressed, highlighting of issues and general framework of interpretation lends itself to a portrait of the world useful to power. In 2012, Lord Justice Leveson's public inquiry into British media culture found the relationship between politicians and the press was too close and not in the public interest. Much of the British press is politically conservative, loudly patriotic and often jingoistic. Early in the conflict in Ireland, both public broadcasters, BBC and ITV, declared there would be no impartiality between [IRA] gunmen and the government. The liberal press, then, was the only outlet on a national scale, where an alternative voice might find space, in the era before social media. The comparison of the coverage of Northern Ireland and Algeria reveals an almost complete dichotomy. In Algeria, legitimacy rested with the insurgents. The 'bad guys' were the French army and the French Algerians. In Ireland, the insurgents were criminal terrorists. The 'good guys' were the British army, with decreasing degrees of merit attributed to the unionist community (constitutionalists) and the loyalist paramilitaries (helping fight IRA 'bad guys').

A conspicuous dichotomy

From the plentiful space devoted to it, the reader learns of the French tradition of torture. For this, there could be no justification, not even a 'ticking bomb' scenario where swift intelligence might save lives. Nor was it an excuse to claim the other side (ALN) was worse. There was a healthy scepticism of official French sources, and prominent space devoted to critics of the French army, especially liberal French intellectuals and the French Catholic clergy. This brave stand has been vindicated.

The brutality of British army interrogations, however, was deemed justified and effective. 'In-depth' interrogations were necessary to save lives even though the British army did not use the 'ticking bomb' scenario as justification. Indeed, 'internment and systematic interrogation are powerful and legitimate weapons where a military victory is obtainable'.[1492] In any event, accusations of British brutality were dismissed as less than schoolyard bullying. There was, too, a repeated emphasis on the other side (IRA) being so much worse. A willing acceptance of official British denials contrasted with the hostility towards the accusers, this time because they were Catholic.[1493] This timid and credulous stand was subsequently undermined by the European Court of Human Rights. The damning indictment of the court, 'the methods were an administrative practice' was immediately side-lined for an attack on the motives of the accusers, the Irish government.

Little space was given to the indiscriminate harassment and widespread abuses practised by the British army in Irish neighbourhoods. Rather, the troops conducted themselves with a 'superhuman restraint'. Accusations to the contrary were so much cant. This portrait of a restrained British army, 'unbelievable leniency' according to the *Guardian,* does not match the evidence then available.[1494] Hetherington already knew different. In December 1971 he delivered a lecture at the army Staff College at Camberley where he informed the 'embanked tiers of colonels, majors and captains' of a case where army actions inflamed the situation rather than calming things and he 'could produce more than a dozen other such cases in the past few months …'[1495] The record shows the British army killed civilians more often than they killed insurgents, while the French killed

---

1492 Peter Jenkins, *Guardian*, 25 October 1971.
1493 ibid.,18 August 1971.
1494 Ibid., 27 May 1971.
1495 Hetherington, *Guardian Years*, (London, Chatto, 1981), p. 305.

insurgents more often than civilians.[1496] Despite this, the prevailing portrait was of British restraint and French ruthlessness.

The unquestioned truth of indiscriminate IRA bombing was proof of their terrorist status.[1497] They were psychopaths perpetrating irrational violence. IRA attacks on army patrols and barracks were acts of terrorism. The ALN's policy of killing thousands of civilians was somehow less heinous. Attacks on French forces resulting in the deaths of civilians were still successful ambushes. The ritualistic slaughter of Muslim civilians even made sense from a 'grim tactical point of view'.[1498] When ALN civilian slaughter became too excessive, it was explained as typical of anti-colonial struggles. The excesses of the 'wilder men' of the ALN were not to be equated with Algerian nationalism generally.[1499] These wild men were, after all, 'products of the French army with all its limitations.'[1500] ALN bombs directed at civilians were considered difficult to assess morally. In a post 9-11 world this equivocal position is no longer unacceptable. Yacef Saadi, prolific bomber of civilians, was a patriot and an example of the unquenchable spirit of man. Patriotism, in the Irish context, was the preserve of a sad and backward people.

While the ALN's targeting of civilians made grim sense, the fascist OAS conducted a gratuitous murder campaign against Muslim civilians. 'Gratuitous murder' did not extend to the portrayal of UVF-UDA random slaughter of Catholic civilians. Initially ignored, they progressed to a mystery, and were finally explained as resulting from tremendous provocation, including 'all the current talk of the eventual

---

1496 French state killing of civilians amounts to 20% of the total, Evans, *Algeria*, p. 337-8 while civilians make up 51% of total British state killings, http://cain.ulst.ac.uk/cgi-bin/tab2.plSutton. If we include the paramilitary adjuncts of OAS and UDA-UVF, civilians make up between 21% and 23% of French killings, Evans, *Algeria*, p. 337-8 and 77% of British killings, see Status summary by Organisation summary, http://cain.ulst.ac.uk/cgi-bin/tab2.plSutton

1497 Civilians killed by British/NATO bombings in Kosovo and Serbia produced a different evaluation, they were 'regrettable' see *The Herald*, 25 March 1999, or 'inadvertent civilian deaths' or there was 'no other option', see http://news.bbc.co.uk/1/hi/uk_politics/321188.stm. https://www.theguardian.com/world/1999/apr/28/balkans11 Senior Conservative Norman Tebbitt rowed for two years with the BBC over its reports of 1986 US-led bombing raids on Tripoli, the planes flying from British bases. He accused the BBC of 'stressing' civilians casualties and an 'uncritical carriage of Libyan propaganda', M Holmes, *Thatcherism; Scope and Limits, 1983-87*, (Palgrave Macmillan, 1989), pp. 131-2, see also http://www.bbc.co.uk/historyofthebbc/research/culture/bbc-and-gov/libyan-bombing

1498 *Guardian*, 30 September 1958.

1499 Ibid., 3 June 1957.

1500 Ibid., 24 September 1958 (editorial).

reunification of Ireland.'[1501] Loyalist torture killings were explained as a 'cry for help'.[1502] Hetherington-Cole demanded that Harold Wilson acknowledge loyalist murders were reactive and a result of the government's failure to defeat the IRA. In addition to defeating the IRA, killing Catholics made them see sense. Hetherington and Cole only ever had one editorial difference, Cole's continuing support for internment.

Space was found in the opinion columns for the views of unionist politicians and academic critics of Irish nationalism.[1503] This might be compared with the lack of contributions from nationalists and republicans. The Civil Rights leader Bernadette Devlin was not allocated space, rather she attracted the particular animus of John Cole, describing her as with 'murderous hate', 'Ireland's greatest catastrophe', 'never wrong', a 'relentless' and 'angry schoolgirl' and even a cartoon as a witch.[1504] According to liberal Britain, the problem was a religious one and an Irish one. It was most definitely not a colonial one. Any explanation of the conflict as a legacy of colonialism was deemed hypocritical. The partition of Ireland or the history of its creation should not even be mentioned. It would be a provocation towards unionists. In both papers, however, Conor Cruise O'Brien received ample space to deny the colonial legacy and to elaborate his explanation of religious extremism, an Irish, not a British phenomenon. Responsibility for the conflict could really be laid at many doors: London, Stormont, Dublin, British forces, the IRA and loyalist paramilitaries. The focus was on the IRA, followed by the irredentism of Dublin. British violence was legitimate and unionist violence was understandable. Any analysis of the violence that pointed to a British-unionist source, current or historic, was beyond the bounds of the expressible.

Republicans were religious sectarians or irrational fascists. Their declared motives, of fighting for self-determination and against injustice, were dismissed as articles of faith. The ALN, in contrast, was portrayed as having fought a legitimate war of liberation against the most unrepentant form of colonialism, the French variety. Unionists

---

1501 Ibid., 6 December 1971.
1502 Ibid., 25 October 1973.
1503 The contributors between 1968 and 1974, with featured articles, included unionist politicians Terence O'Neill, Robin Baillie, David Blakeley, evangelical businessman Fred Catherwood, and Conor Cruise O'Brien.
1504 See Cole's 'Fatal flaws in the mirror', 29 June 1970 and 'Never in the wrong', 21 November 1969. The *Guardian's* own Harold Jackson was moved to write a letter condemning her portrayal. See the cartoon of Devlin as a witch, 3 November 1969, as 'Ireland greatest catastrophe', 23 October 1969 editorial, 'relentless Bernadette', 23 November 1973 and 'angry schoolgirl', 23 March 1971.

were moderate democrats prepared to make reasonable reforms. The unionist right to self-determination was inviolate, and the British government was regularly reminded of its historical commitment. French Algerians were racist settlers seeking to maintain indefensible privileges. These unrepentant *colons* had no right to self-determination, nor should Algeria be partitioned. Rather, Paris should put it up to these fascists and push on with independence. London, however, should accede to the demands of the Ulster Workers' Council and downgrade the power-sharing dimension of the Sunningdale Agreement. In addition, this front, for loyalist paramilitaries and unionist parties, was portrayed as moderate trade unionists. On the other hand, if Paris would only initiate reforms and negotiations, peace would inevitably follow. But in Ireland, the army should first 'get on top of the [IRA] gunmen'. Only then can there be talks about reform but excluding partition. 'Security first ... this must never be forgotten.'[1505]

The general framework was replete with unquestioned premises: the IRA was indiscriminate, loyalist violence was reactive, the French were ruthless, the British army was a peacekeeping force and lagged behind sophisticated IRA propagandists. There were worthy and unworthy victims: Catholics brought it on themselves, British soldiers were not soldiers but musicians, cooks, dog-handlers and school-crossing guards. They were also innocent. Unattributed sources were permitted expressions of outrage depicting the IRA reputedly shooting informers through the mouth and unnamed victims burnt with hot pokers. The UVF's murder of thirty-three civilians was 'a raid on Dublin'.[1506] The comparative reportage exceeded even the predictions of the propaganda model. Some quotations warrant repeating. On Algeria, the *Observer* rejected 'the hoary old legend that no "true" nationalist movement ever used terrorism.'[1507] The *Guardian* ridiculed the idea that a nationalist movement (Algeria's) that had endured a bloody colonial war would ever agree 'to surrender its arms and submit its dispute with the colonial ruler to a popular verdict organised under the latter's auspices and in the presence of his whole army.'[1508]

1505 *Guardian*, 2 July 1973 (editorial).
1506 Ibid., 18 May 1974 (editorial).
1507 *Observer*, 8 December 1957.
1508 *Guardian*, 17 March 1957.

A critical press?

A widespread view prevailed that a critical press helped sap the morale of 'our boys doing a dirty job' while risking a bullet in the back. David Astor found the controversy over the killings of IRA members in Gibraltar to be 'incredible … the British [press] attitude was anti-the British … that you mustn't hit back, that's rather perverse … much more astonishing is the violence [of the reaction] over Gibraltar'.[1509] Astor was a paragon of British liberalism. It is his recollections that are incredible. The tabloids were jubilant over the killings. Journalists sported SAS ties, re-enacted the shootings with water pistols, and sang songs of the prowess of 'Maggie's SAS'.[1510] The headline in the *Sun* was 'Why the dogs had to die.'[1511] Carmen Proetta, an eyewitness who contradicted the official British version, was smeared as a prostitute and her family described as drug dealers. She successfully sued five newspapers, including the *Sunday Times*. The media coverage was so partisan and jingoistic that Enoch Powell, arch-Conservative and no friend of Irish republicans, was moved to ask, 'Where have all the journalists gone?'[1512]

The *Guardian* shared Astor's view of a critical British media, especially compared to the tamed French media that treated Algeria as the 'centre of the sacrosanct zone.'[1513] The British people were doubly fortunate. They enjoyed an independent BBC protected by charter and the *Guardian* itself, singled out for its honesty by none other than George Orwell. Yet this uninformed France somehow produced the Jeanson Network that actively resisted government policy, and public figures called on soldiers to disobey orders. The fortunate British, however, were moved to protest more over US actions in Vietnam than any actions of the British army in their own backyard. From academia, religious leaders, public intellectuals, students and the left, there was barely a murmur, with the exception of the Troops Out Movement. A small number of politicians and human rights lawyers stood out from the general apathy.

This study also reveals an enduring self-deception. Astor voiced a familiar challenge: 'Find me another army anywhere who would behave with such restraint.'[1514] One month after Bloody Sunday, Alun Chalfont

1509 Interview, David Astor, London, 22 July 1998.
1510 I. Jack, 'Gibraltar', *Granta*, no. 25 (1989), pp. 13–36.
1511 *Sun*, 12 September 1988.
1512 Miller, cited in Rolston, *The Media and Northern Ireland* (Basingstoke: Macmillan, 1991), p. 94.
1513 *Guardian*, 23 March 1957.
1514 Interview, David Astor, London, 22 July 1998.

could write that stone-throwing children are 'reasonably safe in the knowledge that, as they are in Londonderry and not in Prague or Birmingham, Alabama, it is unlikely that anyone will get his head blown off.'[1515] This deception runs deep. Simon Winchester wrote the British army had only been accused of the killings at Amritsar. Journalists were noticeably keen to point out the French were distinguished from the British by their ruthlessness, frequently and mistakenly pointing to the rue d'Isly killings as confirmation.[1516] 'Nor do we have a de Gaulle to shoot them down with impunity.'[1517] In the weeks following Bloody Sunday, Secretary of State William Whitelaw informed IRA negotiator Martin McGuinness: 'We don't shoot civilians.'[1518] In reality, the Bloody Sunday killings were a much more sinister affair, and reached much higher, politically and militarily, than the killings on rue d'Isly.[1519] This widespread belief in British benevolence precludes the possibility of 'our boys doing any wrong'.

This belief of British restraint was pierced more often by serving soldiers than journalists. Contradicting the justifications of brutal interrogations producing much-needed intelligence, one British officer maintained: 'there was very little gain whatever anyone says.'[1520] Col. Robin Evelegh thought it was stupid to justify brutality 'with the idea that the suspect comes to no real harm and that lives might be saved by the information.'[1521] The British army's own manual (*Land Operations, Vol III – Counter-Revolutionary Operations*) reveals the soldiers, were not on peacekeeping operations but, on 'Setting 4'. This means a counterinsurgency campaign verging on limited war where the security forces had lost control of certain areas.[1522] Roy Hattersley, journalist and Labour politician, explained away the killings and flagrant excesses of the army during the Falls Curfew, 'had General Freeland been St. Michael and his soldiers been angels or archangels someone would have complained that Lucifer was ejected from heaven with more force than was necessary.'[1523] The positing of the soldiers as angels and the

1515 *Guardian*, 6 March 1972.
1516 Ibid., 12 March 1971.
1517 *Observer*, 19 April 1970 (editorial).
1518 Toolis, *Rebel Hearts,* (NY, St Martin's, 1995), p. 362.
1519 Saville Report, June 2010. See also McKittrick et al, *Lost Lives*, pp. 143-149 and Evans, *Algeria,* pp. 313–16.
1520 D. Hamill, *Pig in the Middle,* (London: Methuen, 1985), p. 64.
1521 R. Evelegh, *Peacekeeping in a Democratic Society* (London: Hurst, 1978), p. 136.
1522 Urban, *Big Boys*, (London, Faber, 1992), pp. 19, 161-2.
1523 *Guardian*, 11 July 1970.

corralled and frightened residents as the devil, reveals a determined template. The residents had just witnessed the army killing four civilians and wounding many more. But a paratrooper was more honest: 'you are there to kill people ... after every shooting incident we would order 1,500 house searches, 1,500, it really makes people think.'[1524] In fact, the army's coercive counter-insurgency methods so radicalised a dormant Irish nationalism that it sustained the republican insurgency for thirty years.

Colonel Styles, Commander, Explosive Ordnance and Disposal Team, cited IRA bomb warnings as evidence they seldom intended to kill. Officers complained, too, that the media portrayal of the IRA as mindless thugs undervalued their work. Rather than victims of clever republican propaganda, the study reveals a media-savvy army with a well-staffed and frequently successful PR department. While *Observer* editorials thought the British public would never accept the ruthless French methods, opinion polls revealed 'many people back the army to the hilt and have little or no sympathy for the 13 people killed in Derry on Bloody Sunday.'[1525] The *Guardian* described glider pilots who complained over the loss of their runway to the MoD as 'the latest minority in Northern Ireland with a sense of grievance.'[1526] This hardly indicates a crusading newspaper; rather, one that framed political protest as a procession of unsubstantiated whingers. According to the *Guardian*, the solution lay with Catholic volition. Loyalty to the Northern Ireland state would result in better treatment for Catholics. This analysis was turned on its head by the Good Friday Agreement. The reformed state is charged with winning the support and consent of the people, this time, including Catholics: an idea that has even started to filter into unionist policy consideration. In contrast to the recommendations of the liberal press, the AIA and the GFA revealed the British government does not consider the Northern Ireland state to be inviolate. The 'critical' press was more resolute in following the official narrative than soldiers.

No debate with the enemies of the state
The *Guardian* was so convinced of its liberal credentials that Hetherington felt free to lecture the Indian press reporting of India's response to a local Naga insurgency, contemporaneous with the

1524 Ibid., 13 July 1973.
1525 *Observer*, 6 February 1972.
1526 *Guardian*, 29 February 1972.

Algerian struggle.[1527] One editorial ridiculed familiar phrases:

> that grated on the ears of anti-colonialists ... there can be no
> compromise with terrorism ... To restore law and order,
> without which no constitutional progress is possible, a certain
> inevitable minimum of force has to be employed ... The
> armed forces have done a very good job and have behaved
> with exemplary forbearance.[1528]

These familiar phrases, which grated the ears of anti-colonialists, could
be a template for the *Guardian*'s own reporting of Ireland. This template
rested on a central axiom, provided by Conor Cruise O'Brien: the force
used by the state is legitimate, while the violence of the terrorist is not.
In this framing, O'Brien overturned his own criticism of Camus as
justifying French repression in Algeria.[1529] The British government,
according to O'Brien, was rationally seeking a political solution, and
the IRA, being violent, is quintessentially irrational. The recent
publication of an internal British government memo dated 10 July 1972
and marked 'secret' has the government urging the army to 'carry the
war to the IRA with utmost vigour.'[1530] In the context of a British-IRA
ceasefire, this rather undermines O'Brien's central axiom. It is also
immediately obvious that any analysis of the historical context of the
conflict would have opened a debate on British army and IRA violence.

Significantly, the voice of liberal Britain remained free of any
diversity of opinions on the creation of Northern Ireland or its
democratic credentials. To even mention it was anathema. The coverage
was informed by O'Brien's recommendation that political debate with
the terrorist should be refused, for 'though he can argue fluently from
his own peculiar premises, he is not accessible to rational argument on
premises other than his own.'[1531] De Gaulle had a different view.
Speaking during the peak violence of the Battle of Algiers, he
maintained that 'to deal with men and not believe in their humanity, in
their reason is a wicked position and a stupid one for it excludes the
possibility of agreement ... one must talk, negotiate, *prendre langue*.

1527 The Naga have fought a barely reported struggle for independence from India since the
1950s.

1528 *Guardian*, 7 October 1957 (editorial).

1529 O'Brien was wrong. Camus condemned French repression and ALN violence while
O'Brien endorsed ALN violence.

1530 C.C. O'Brien, 'Liberty and terror' *Encounter*, vol. 49, no. (October 1977), pp. 34–41.

1531 Cole complained journalists gave a harder time to constitutional politicians than to IRA
spokesmen, *Let's Talk*, BBC Northern Ireland, 3 May 2001.

One cannot abandon a people, whoever they may be, in quarantine!'[1532]

Liberal Britain missed this lesson, and the press quarantined the constitutional question. It also denied any possibility of large-scale British army brutality or the possibility of army repression promoting violence. There was no explanation left except the racist explanation of some inherent Irish disposition or the ludicrous one of the irrational Irish fighting because they liked it. This absurd idea can be found even in official British government publications: 'The history of Northern Ireland where ... *a habitual belief in the concept of violence as a first rather than a last resort in political and social conflict and the corresponding failure of political settlement* ...'[1533] That these absurdities were considered important enough in briefing civil servants and government ministers may help explain Britain's approach. Rejecting O'Brien's framework, media analyst Philip Schlesinger argued that 'a general presumption of political rationality would seem to be an important precondition for analysing a "terrorist problem".'[1534] O'Brien's rigorous drawing of conceptual lines had attendant dangers. By criminalising political violence and dehumanising the state's enemies, negotiations were precluded in favour of the military option. Moreover, the 'liberal' press recommended a reduction in civil liberties and, further, let there be no squeamishness about it. The appalling and inevitable miscarriages of justice duly followed.[1535]

Remarkably similar dramas

The Battle of Algiers and IRA bombings generated respective media dramas around army torture. Père Delarue, chaplain to Massu's 10th Paratroopers, justified torture in Algiers, and Lord Compton repeating

---

1532 G. Tillion, *France and Algeria,* (NY, Knopf, 1960), p. 144.

1533 Claire Marson, *History of Northern Ireland from 1650,* NIO publication, see Geoffrey Bell, The Irish are violent – official (secret), in *History Ireland*, Issue 6 (November/December 2014), Volume 22. The one author she quotes directly is Conor Cruise O'Brien's States of Ireland.

1534 P. Schlesinger, *Media, State and Nation* (London: Sage, 1991), p. 19.

1535 Following the Birmingham bombs, the *Guardian* editorial advocated: 'From now on anyone who complains that he is being harassed by the police bomb squad, will find a less sympathetic audience'; 23 November 1974. The *Guardian* held: 'The police bomb squad must be allowed to be less fastidious in its inquiries among those suspected of guilty knowledge ... The IRA must be defeated even at a cost in civil liberties ...'; 24 November 1974. Six Irishmen were subsequently wrongly convicted, received life sentences and exonerated seventeen years later. The *Guardian*'s prescription harmonises with Sir Michael Howard's instructions: 'Once isolated, they [terrorists] should be referred to as criminals and murderers and can be hunted down with popular support. They can only be destroyed if public opinion at home and abroad supports the authorities in regarding them as criminals rather than heroes.' RUSI, vol 146, no. 6, December 2001.

Delarue's words, almost verbatim, justified torture in Belfast. The super-patriots of French Algeria and the staunchly loyal Ulstermen both managed to rebel against the motherland they professed to hold dear. The settler rebellion of Barricades Week in Algiers in January 1960 was replayed during the May 1974 Ulster Workers' Council strike/rebellion. Both armies conducted infamous civilian massacres (Bloody Sunday and rue d'Isly). Both refused to comply with the policies of their political masters. While the mutinous French generals have received widespread attention, the dubious loyalty of senior British officers has received little. Algerian rebels claimed they were inspired by Irish republicans, and Brigadier Frank Kitson adapted the methods of Col. Roger Trinquier who openly advocated torture. British army collusion with counter-terrorists in Ireland was a repeat of its performance in Kenya, and followed a prescription elaborated by French intelligence in Algeria.

Loyalist paramilitaries, like *pieds noirs opérateurs*, were plausibly deniable 'friendly forces'. Ulster loyalists and French Algerian *ultras* exhibited striking similarities: his flag flew, his culture dominated, his police kept order, he did no wrong. The innumerable patriotic parades of the French Algerian find a parallel in the Orange Order's 3,500 annual marches. But Ulstermen bristle at any comparison with French settlers. They claimed to be earlier natives returning to their original home after a previous dispossession. French Algerians also rejected the settler label and claimed a similar return following an earlier expulsion from North Africa. Politicians in Paris warned that Algeria was turning into 'France's Ireland', and Harold Wilson's Cabinet secretly discussed withdrawal from Ireland under the code word 'Algeria.'[1536] The weekly *Témoignage Chrétien* recognised the Algeria-Ireland analogy on many levels, including torture and the colonial background. This 'Christian witness' held Britain responsible for the conflict in Ireland and criticised the British people for their unquestioning indifference.[1537] The Algerian analogy, frequently denied, is actually too close for comfort.

The denial, often a pained but unexplained denial, of this historic match meant Algeria's war was portrayed as a progressive, anti-colonial struggle against an unjust France, while Ireland's 'Troubles' were a backward religious squabble contained by a British umpire. In fact, the religious dimension of the Algerian War has been much overlooked,

---

1536 P. Dixon, *The British Approach to Counterinsurgency,* (Basingstoke, Palgrave Macmillan, 2012), p. 269.

1537 See P. Brennan et al, 'The Northern Ireland Conflict in the French Press', in Darby et al, *Political Violence: Ireland in a Comparative Perspective* (Belfast: Appletree, 1990).

while the insurgency in Northern Ireland was motivated more by the desire to remove a remnant of the colonial legacy than by religion. The liberal press sympathised with the Algerian insurgency against an intransigent colonialism but rejected any explanation of an insurgency in Britain's backyard. Paris was urged to negotiate with rebels. London was urged to 'get on top of the gunmen' before any talks.

What was it all about?

The Belfast (Good Friday) Agreement was signed in 1998, but 'Truth and Reconciliation' have floundered on differing interpretations of the conflict. Since the political compromise, the British narrative has been increasingly challenged. Repeated official inquiries and supranational bodies such as the European Court have revealed the security forces as participants rather than peacekeepers. Counter-insurgency methods in Algeria have been held to have prolonged the conflict, fostered its murderous intensity, and to have left an enduring enmity between Paris and Algiers. This enmity is mirrored in the slow reconciliation between London and Dublin and between the two communities in the North, and by the large numbers of Catholics alienated from the British state. Britain and France now seek to overcome the legacy of history. In 2011, Queen Elizabeth laid a wreath at a memorial to an earlier IRA, previously held to be murder gangs, now lauded as the 'good old IRA'. President Hollande, speaking in Algiers in December 2012, departed from his predecessors' silence and acknowledged the unjust and brutal nature of colonial rule. Ulster unionists, like their French Algerian counterparts, expressed much reserve about these new departures. But Hollande's words, that nothing can be built on secrets, forgetting or denial, resonate in Ireland.

The British liberal press was not always so accommodating to the government. The British public first became aware of British army atrocities in Ireland through the efforts of the liberal English press from 1918 to 1922. In the *Guardian*, C.P. Scott's denunciations of reprisals, such as the sacking of Balbriggan in 1920, stand in stark contrast to the liberal-press response to Bloody Sunday in 1972. The constitutional writer A.V. Dicey had warned if:

> the only means by which it [the union] is found maintainable
> are measures clearly repugnant to the humanity or the justice
> or the democratic principles of the English people then ... the
> union must for the sake of England, no less than of Ireland,
> come to an end. [1538]

The liberal press has come a long way. The *Guardian*'s advocating a reduction in civil liberties, to defeat the IRA, indicates the distance travelled. The bending of the law to counter-insurgency requirements has opened Britain up to a long procession of appearances and embarrassments before international tribunals. By the time of the latest conflict in Ireland, the press had already been disciplined by the government and the market. Journalists policed themselves. A reliance on official sources and approved experts accounts for much of the ideological closure. The views of editors Cole and O'Brien coincided with, and were recommended by, army counter-insurgency writers. In 1992, in his Ian Gow lecture and long after the British government had recognised the folly of repression, O'Brien was still advocating a military solution with no undue squeamishness.

The extent of anti-Irish prejudice was perhaps the greatest surprise. Lord Arran proclaimed: 'I hate the Irish. I always have hated the Irish. I always will ... I loathe and detest the miserable bastards. They are savage murderous thugs. All of them.'[1539] He believed he spoke for most people in Britain and had no fear of prosecution. The depth of anti-Irish prejudice and its pervasive but unrecognised background in British culture contributed to the prolonged dichotomous treatment. This pervasive prejudice has been pointed up by American counter-insurgency writer J. Bowyer Bell. The Canadian essayist and philosopher John Ralston Saul remarked that Ireland could not be discussed socially in London. Since the peace process, anti-Irish prejudice has abated, but during the conflict it was extremely vicious. It is hardly conceivable that this prejudice, expressed by columnists and in the letter pages of the British liberal press, would find any media space today if aimed at another minority. It hasn't gone away. Brexit had one Tory grandee declare: 'The Irish really should know their place.'[1540]

1538 A.V. Dicey, *England's Case against Home Rule,* (London: J Murray, 1886), cited in D. G. Boyce, *Englishmen and Irish Troubles,* (London: Jonathan Cape, 1972), p. 23.

1539 *Guardian*, 31 May 1974. See also M. Hollingsworth, *The Press and Political Dissent* (London: Pluto, 1986), pp. 92-93 for legal and Press Council inaction against similar anti-Irish racism.

1540 *Belfast Telegraph*, 17 November 2021.

In 1969, long before the Leveson Inquiry, Lord Devlin, chairman of the Press Council, stated that real freedom of the press could not be written into a constitution but depended on the men in power recognising that 'however irritating at times they find it to be, its freedom is necessary to a good society.' Happily, in Britain 'This belief really exists. It is not lip service.'[1541] Mark Curtis found this same cosy relationship between British journalists and power, and an intrinsic belief in Britain's basic benevolence.[1542] In addition, the significance of British ignorance of Ireland has been much underestimated. It exists at the highest levels of government and among journalists who do not question the political consensus. The longevity and the lack of challenge to this consensus benefitted from this lacuna. John Pilger, prominent war correspondent and investigative journalist, wrote in Philip Knightley's celebrated book on propaganda: 'the most important issue addressed in this book, [is] the virulence of unrecognised censorship, often concealed behind false principles of objectivity.'[1543] In this book, written to address *unrecognised* censorship, the reader can find correspondents working in Algeria, Vietnam, the Falklands and stretching back to the Crimea, but on Ireland, not a word. The propaganda model predicts that the media will reflect the elite consensus generally, including any divisions. The British government viewed Algeria as a colonial problem and a war. That is how the liberal press portrayed it. Officially, the British were not at war with the IRA but were invoking the law against mindless criminals even as they attacked military barracks and 10 Downing Street. Withholding recognition of war denied the existence of a competing political claim. And that is how the liberal press portrayed it. Of course, the French government had done the same to the FLN, and the French Algerian press described the ALN as the pathological expression of an unrepresentative minority.

There is now a general regret that the conflict in Ireland went on so

---

1541 *Observer*, 5 October 1969.

1542 M Curtis, *Web of Deceit, Britain's Real Role in the World* (London, Vintage, 200). Alistair Hetherington wrote that Prime Minister Jim Callaghan, Home Secretary Reginald Maudling and Northern Ireland Secretaries William Whitelaw and Merlyn Rees all consulted and trusted John Cole. He also acknowledged Cole 's 'powerful influence on me and on Guardian policy', see his *Guardian Years*, (London, Chatto and Windus), 1981, pp. 294-322.

1543 P Knightley, *The First Casualty: The War Correspondent as Propagandist and Myth-maker* (London: Prion, 2000). Knightley wrote a famous article following the death of IRA hunger striker Bobby Sands: 'Is Britain Losing the Propaganda Battle?', *Sunday Times*, 31 May 1981.

long, and there is no doubt it could have ended sooner if all sides, Britain, the IRA and unionism, had not all believed in outright defeat of the other. The meta-conflict, the conflict about the meaning of the conflict, has now been transferred into a clash of narratives about who was to blame.[1544] The battle is now one for truth and competition over the legitimacy of motives and actions. Collective remembrance involves the status of the victims: soldiers are commemorated, criminals and terrorists are not. The Eames-Bradley Report, designed to deal with the legacy of the past, was rejected by unionists for referring to all the dead as victims. Unionist victims' groups are generally hostile to nationalist victims' groups and see them as representing the perpetrators. Unionist opposition to the Saville Inquiry was vociferous.[1545] The opposition took the form of 'I have done no wrong' and 'We do not need to apologise for the past.' These phrases echo the sentiments of Memmi's eternally vigilant French Algerian settlers. Church of Ireland bishop, the Reverend Harold Miller, was accused of giving in to the IRA when he suggested: 'We Protestants ... are still inclined to see ourselves, as a community, as entirely the victims in the Troubles.'[1546] The record, however, shows that Catholic civilian dead was almost twice that of Protestant civilians. Considering the relative size of the two communities, Catholics civilians were almost three times as likely to suffer death than Protestant civilians.[1547] The balance of dead across the communities moves closer when you add police, UDR and republican dead but Catholics, however coded, died more often, proportionately and absolutely.

It is important to note that the self-image of all sides has been publicly dented. Unionists are angered by Sinn Féin members calling for a truth commission while the previous role of some of them in the IRA remains hidden or denied. Nationalist anger is reserved for unionism's resolve in denying the army and loyalist paramilitaries acted in collusion. Unionists are angered by London's insufficient challenge to a republican narrative, spread by 'embittered propagandists who are backed in their distortions by fools.'[1548] A News Letter editorial warned

---

1544 L. Kennedy, *Who Was to Blame for the Troubles?* (McGill-Queen's University Press 2020), blames the IRA and argues there is little evidence for collusion.

1545 See G. Dawson, *Making Peace with the Past*, (Manchester University Press 2007), pp. 202, 262, 285.

1546 *Belfast News Letter*, 24 June 2005.

1547 http://cain.ulst.ac.uk/cgi-bin/tab3.pl ... 1097 Catholic and 569 Protestant, using a population ratio of 40:60, for the period.

1548 Ben Lowry, *News Letter*, 18 July 2018.

that nationalists' rewriting of history must be urgently challenged, and accused 'even the most moderate nationalists' of promoting the narrative of a 'murderous British state to which the only response was IRA violence.'[1549] Unionists are outraged at any equating of IRA members with members of the police and army. Progress towards a truth-and-reconciliation commission has been especially inhibited by unionist fears of blame shifting onto their security forces. In the unionist narrative, the IRA conducted a sectarian campaign of murder against the law-abiding people of Ulster. The same *News Letter* editorial repeated an alarming narrative focusing on 'serial killer republican thugs known to be guilty to the communities that harboured them.' This 2013 editorial, repeating the loyalist justification for the random murder of Catholics, points up the real danger in not resolving the issues of the past.[1550] Unionists are correct to point out that republicans were the biggest killers but the liberal press affirmation of the unionist narrative of 'terror versus democracy' has left unionism unprepared for the new world of political compromise. The *News Letter* laments the disastrous PR attempts by unionists and the government intended to challenge 'the lie of a gangster state resisted by a heroic band of freedom fighters.'[1551] But each succeeding revelation – through long campaigns and research by victims' families and, by human rights activists, supranational bodies and including official Britain – of the state force's dirty war adds support to the republican narrative. Supposed British restraint is refuted by American military academies teaching that the restrained 'British method' is a myth.[1552] Rather, the intensity and longevity of the conflict resulted from the radicalisation and alienation of Catholic communities generated by a brutally systemic counter-insurgency policy implemented by an army shaped by long experience of putting down anti-colonial movements. British officers, too, admit now many years later, that their methods were counterproductive: 'we were turning those on the periphery of the IRA into the IRA or, at least, their active supporters.'[1553]

This directly challenges unionist academics who argue the violence resulted from 'softly softly' British security policies that ignored

1549 *Belfast News Letter* editorial, 29 October 2001.

1550 Ibid.

1551 Ibid.

1552 See D. Porch, *Counterinsurgency: Exposing the New Ways of War*, (Cambridge University Press, 2013). See too M. Punch, *State Violence, Collusion and the Troubles*, (London: Pluto 2012) for documentation of British government using desperate illegal methods.

1553 Taylor, *Brits,* p. 141.

unionist fears and the recurring unionist narrative of a reforming Stormont regime undermined by a clever IRA/Roman Catholic conspiracy. But how could it be otherwise in a political compromise? With no clear victor like the FLN – which, since 1962, has held a monopoly on truth and falsely propagated its heroic war of liberation to the exclusion of all other narratives – the contrasting narratives in Ireland must compete in the public arena, now increasingly accessible to republicans. While unionists complain of 'rewriting history', republicans are engaged in excavating their narrative from journalism's first (propaganda) version of history.

Contrary to unionist complaints, republicans do not seek to be equated with the security forces. In the republican narrative, they are morally superior. The IRA is the only organisation that can correctly claim civilians make up a minority of its victims. The IRA did not abduct soldiers, policemen or Protestant civilians to torture them. Critics of republicanism acknowledge the IRA did not have squads roaming Protestant neighbourhoods seeking to pick up Protestants for torture. There was no IRA equivalent to roaming loyalist death squads.[1554] The police, the army, the UVF and the UDA all tortured Catholic civilians and for a long time. The record shows the IRA did not attack civilians as policy. They do admit to a 'dark period' when some members reciprocated in sectarian killings. Some part of British Intelligence and pro-state loyalist paramilitaries, acting in tandem, deliberately targeted Catholic civilians. Forces acting in support of the state killed more civilians than did the IRA; a ratio of two to one or a ratio of five to three, depending on the differing compilations.[1555] Nor did the IRA habitually label Protestant civilian dead as gunmen or loyalist death squads. The army and the loyalist paramilitaries routinely and unjustifiably labelled Catholic civilian dead as IRA members or gunmen. Republicans have acknowledged their worst deeds and apologised, while accepting it offers little comfort to the bereaved. In contrast, the British have yet to come clean on their role, routinely blocking inquiries into collusion and civilians killed by the army. The Bloody Sunday and Pat Finucane admissions had to be wrestled from

---

1554 'There is no republican equivalent of the romper room of the UDA one side is not as bad as the other', K Myers, *Irish Independent*, 23 June 2011.

1555 The IRA killed 508 civilians while the state and loyalists killed 1064 civilians (186 and 878 respectively) http://cain.ulst.ac.uk/cgi-bin/tab3.pl, McKittrick at al., *Lost Lives,* record 636 civilians killed by the IRA which would generate a 5:3 ratio rather than 2:1. Republicans, in total, killed 722 civilians, a ratio of 3:2 of 'British' killings of civilians to republican killings of civilians, http://cain.ulst.ac.uk/cgi-bin/tab3.pl. By all accounts the state and pro-state actors killed civilians more often.

them. There is a British pattern: denial, followed by impeding the inquiry, finally an apology, extracted not proffered. The British steadfastly maintain the lie of an honest broker. Yet the verdicts of the European Commission and Court regarding brutality, torture, collusion and the use of lethal force have revealed Britain was engaged in a dirty war rather than invoking the law against deluded criminals.

The republican self-image has also been dented. While civilians are a minority of their victims, republicans need to recognise it is a large one. Whether during attacks on state forces or commercial bombings the IRA risked civilian lives, with atrocious and foreseeable consequences. Recklessly endangering civilian lives is a war crime. In addition, between 1975 and 1976 some republicans engaged in reciprocal sectarian killings with loyalist paramilitaries. This falls far short of the republican ideal of Protestant, Catholic and Dissenter and the narrative of a heroic war.

The more powerful British always had greater scope for initiative and have been accused of squandering these opportunities in attempting to weaken republicans militarily. As noted previously, Secretary of State Merlyn Rees writing of an IRA-British truce, said: 'we set out to con them and we succeeded.'[1556] Perfidious Albion was not negotiating in good faith: 'my aim was to weaken the IRA. The longer the ceasefire lasted the more difficult for the IRA to re-start.'[1557] The truce did weaken the IRA but trying to trap republicans was a tactical mistake for it only resulted in the emergence of a new and younger leadership. Hopes raised of constitutional concessions (not made) could have allowed the IRA to call off its campaign. Sir Patrick Mayhew, a later Secretary of State, was aware of the damage and of IRA mistrust of Britain rooted in this.[1558] IRA individuals have acknowledged the prolonged ceasefire around 1975 as the closest it came to defeat, at a time when it lost its way. After regrouping it responded with the 'long war', with continued resistance to British repression being equated with an ongoing moral victory. The Anglo-Irish Agreement of 1985 was a turning point, with Britain recognising that defeat of the IRA was not possible.

The hunger strike had shown the republican struggle could not be criminalised, and the belated search for a comprehensive political solution began. Journalist Ed Moloney and William Matchett, ex-RUC Special Branch, argue that spies halted the IRA. But the IRA leadership,

1556 Coogan, *The Troubles,* (St Martin's, 2002), p. 260, Ryan, *War and Peace in Ireland*, (London, Pluto, 1994), p. 58.

1557 M Rees, *Northern Ireland, A Personal Perspective*, (Metheun, 1985), p. 223.

1558 Julia Langdon, *Mo Mowlan*, (London: Little, Brown & Co, 2000), p. 273.

already aware of Britain's wish to see a republican-unionist agreement, decided they could pursue their objectives politically. Talking with the IRA not intelligence operatives ended the conflict.[1559] The final GFA differs in two ways from an IRA ceasefire offer as early as 10 March 1972. First, the simultaneous vote, North and South, to endorse the agreement was designed to counter the IRA's demand of Ireland voting on self-determination as one unit. The agreement recognised a qualified self-determination but is nevertheless a British concession. The institutions of the GFA rest on a joint Irish act of self-determination but, crucially, not on the revisable will of a British government. The second difference is that it does not contain a date for withdrawal of troops; then a key IRA had demand. But IRA leadership had already moved from seeking a declaration of withdrawal to pursuit of self-determination. And with this agreement lodged at the UN, Britain made a binding commitment to withdraw politically.

In the quest for the legitimacy of the competing narratives, the issue of British collusion with loyalist paramilitaries is highly significant. The evidence for it continues to grow. For nationalists, the full story of British-loyalist collusion is the great untold story of the conflict, only gradually emerging into the light. Will it be like Kenya and take sixty years before the public is informed of the army's dirty war in Ireland? The republican communities always knew it, and loyalist paramilitaries always claimed they were assisting the security forces. Unionist politicians, some academics and journalists continue to deny it. But Paul Bew argues collusion and the peace process are linked: 'What if they are parts of one, mutually reinforcing process? What if this is the way we brought our Irish wars to the end in the 20th century?' He continues: 'So is not everybody tacitly saying … it [collusion] was justified? [1560] This also overturns the government's long-standing position of 'never talking to terrorists'. Now the state was killing its own citizens to force the rebellious ones into talks. To admit British collusion would shatter the narrative of a democracy beset by terror. But Britain finds it increasingly difficult to deny.[1561] Loyalists and British army/intelligence

---

1559 See T Leahy, *The Intelligence War Against the IRA,* (Cambridge University Press, 2020). In addition, the PSNI admitted to finding 'agents of the IRA in its staff and the government of NI was riddled with them', *Irish Times,* 27 June 2018. The IRA had their own successes: 'The leak of MI5 documents to the IRA is the biggest security disaster in the 20-year war with the Provos', *New Statesman,* 20 October 1989.

1560 Bew cites the historic evidence of Lloyd George pursuing the same policy of carrot and of 'the stick' in 1920 and suggests a 'not dissimilar process may have reappeared again in the 1990s' *Irish Times,* 2 April 2004, accessed 17 October 2020. See also the Press TV documentary, 13 Sep 2012, https://www.youtube.com/watch?v=swHhb3dF86s, accessed 22 May 2018.

1561 Niall Stanage, *Guardian,* 26 June 2002.

services targeting civilians is also a war crime. The republican community was silenced for so long that the recent space permitted to the alternative narrative has unsettled unionism. The *Guardian* editorial, of 18 March 1957, may help: 'All the same there is a special fine mercilessness about the French conscience; it can bring to light acts which here tend to remain muffled.' This was at the height of the Battle of Algiers. Collusion and army brutality in Ireland did indeed 'remain muffled'. The same revelations about South Africa or South America would bring howls of outrage. On death squads in Ireland, there was a strange silence. This 'muffling' may be the result of what Caroline Elkins condemned, with reference to Kenya, as the 'Old Boys Protection Society'[1562] or UK law restraining liberal impulses or a combination of both. At pivotal moments, liberal editors David Astor (*Observer*) and Harold Evans (*Times*) shrank from exposing Britain's extreme coercive measures; Kenyan atrocities and Bloody Sunday respectively.[1563] *Guardian* editor Alan Rusbridger would quote a definition of a free press coined by veteran US journalist David Broder: 'it's the best we could do, under the circumstances and we will be back tomorrow, with a corrected and updated version.'[1564] For the period under study, this is demonstrably what the British liberal press did not do.

There is now also a new sympathy for the *pieds noirs* in the post-9/11 world. They were wronged when de Gaulle withdrew from Algeria. Mohammed Harbi, a former member of the FLN, rejects the portrait of a heroic anti-colonial struggle in Algeria and of the FLN as a revolutionary liberation movement. He maintains that it was not a war of liberation; rather, the conflict allowed a military caste to take power, and it has suppressed democracy ever since. The liberal press got that wrong, too. British 'Ulster' has fared better than French Algeria.

1562 Elkins, C, *Britain's Gulag*, p. 337. Operation Legacy, from the 1950s to 1970s, hid or destroyed files to prevent their falling into the new governments' hands in former colonies, Ian Cobain, *The History Thieves* (Portabello) 2016.

1563 Astor held a letter smuggled from Kenya's Mariira camp detailing atrocities. He immediately offered the Colonial Secretary Lennox-Boyd an opportunity of responding privately, suggesting he might hold off publication. In spite of the mounting evidence elsewhere, including the resignation of the police chief and a parliamentary investigation, Astor accepted Lennox-Boyd's dismissals of all allegations and explaining away 'natural deaths'. He printed neither the internees' letter nor the government's denials, Elkins, *Britain's Gulag*, pp. 337-339. Acutely aware of 'contempt of court' law, Evans decided not to print Murray Sayles and Derek Humphries' immediate report on Bloody Sunday. Their 1972 findings of soldiers' responsibility were eventually confirmed by the Saville Inquiry thirty-eight years later, Evans, *Paper Chase*, (Back Bay, 2002), pp. 471-480. Sayles resigned over non-publication: 'publication might have saved much subsequent bloodshed'.

1564 *Guardian*, 6 October 2011.

Although considered, there has been no British scuttle. In addition, republicans have shifted their focus from an imperial Britain to recognising unionist agency and have emphasised that 'Brits out' never meant the expulsion of Protestants but that Britain should recognise Ireland's right to self-determination. Reconciliation may be possible. Catholics no longer live in an Orange state and unionists need not fear being flung out like the *pieds noirs*. Their interests are secured by the GFA.

It would take thirty painful years and American help before this political compromise was negotiated between IRA representatives, the British and Irish governments and all shades of unionism. Northern Ireland has been portrayed as a democracy beset by religious terrorism. But with a new deal between Britain and her former IRA enemies, the liberal press may remember the role of the 'removed outsider'. Regarding Algeria, the liberal press favoured the colonial explanation and ignored the religious dimension. In Ireland, the colonial legacy was rejected, and a religious explanation promoted. Although misrepresenting in opposite directions, the liberal press habitually propagated the government version on both occasions. This misrepresentation led directly to the new controversy. Unionists view republicans as rewriting the 'Troubles', republicans argue they are excavating their narrative from a previously dominant propaganda.

POSTSCRIPT

The Distorting Mirror of Memory

Commemorative efforts on both sides attempt to rearrange Algeria's past in justificatory terms of heroism, resistance or duty. Official attempts at forgetting have left the field open to rival memories that have encouraged ethnic tensions. The role of the French Communist Party is still contested as is the extent of torture and where responsibility lay. Amnesties have precluded justice. However, Algerian victims took some comfort in the conviction of General Paul Aussaresses for his justifying war crimes. This followed the publication of Louisette Ighilahriz's 2002 book, *L'Algérienne*, detailing her torture at the hands of the army. General Massu, maintaining his reappraisal, helped to validate her account, and repeated that torture had not been necessary.

After the war, official history fused the FLN and the people into one, propagating a simple narrative of unbroken heroic resistance to France since 1830, finally reaching fruition through FLN leadership. The FLN maintained a true culture of forgetting and excluded all others from its official history of resistance to France. Algeria's dominant memory was one of gain, while for France the relinquishing of Algeria meant loss.

Pluralist Irish republicans and Protestants of the liberal tradition can both look on the GFA as a gain. For unionists of the Orange ascendancy tradition, the dominant memory, as with the exiled *pieds-noirs*, is one of loss. For a long time, France could not call it a war because of an inability to formulate a coherent narrative of its Algerian past. Loss resulted in silence, but France cannot forget because of the multidimensional *pied-noir* narrative of dispossession and the alienated children of the betrayed *harkis*. Britain cannot officially state it was a war because it would shatter its narrative of a referee operating within

323

the law. Britain, too, wants to forget but victims' appeals to supranational bodies will not allow it. The Algerian War is inadequately covered in the French curriculum, and students have only a superficial knowledge of it.[1565] The so-called 'Troubles' receive scant attention in the British curriculum. In the Irish Republic, the history of the northern conflict was often squeezed in, if covered at all, at the end of term.

Of course, Northern Ireland cannot move forward unless it produces a reasonably positive image of itself. In France, Benjamin Stora warns of the danger of 'cloistered memories', of a past not forgotten but locked in unchanging, almost mythical constructions.[1566] Unfortunately, Ireland is confirming his fears. While unionists now must accept some responsibility for the conflict, Britain continues, albeit with less success, to claim the status of referee. The French left took up Ighilahriz's book, and French generals and academics once again engaged in a fierce public debate. But the revelations by human rights activists, Amnesty International and multiple official and international inquiries detailing Britain's dirty war have not had the same impact. Unlike senior French soldiers (Massu, Bigeard, Aussaresses), British officers (Kitson, Kerr and Ford) have not had to justify their methods in public.

Now, Noam Chomsky's intellectual authority has cast credible doubt on the state as the upholder of truth and an adherent to human rights and the law. He recommends we develop tools of intellectual self-defence: methods of defending doubts and questions about power. Given that we live in a democracy where government (supposedly) adheres to the law and human rights codes, the people the state kills must, logically, be to blame. Exercising intellectual self-defence would therefore mean learning and automatically raising the historic record to expose this deceit; for example, British Secretary Whitelaw's memo promising a future legal indemnity for army killings or Prime Minister Heath's Cabinet approving torture. Intellectual self-defence would mean questioning why, given Britain's record in Ireland, the response to official spokesmen is not one of automatic scepticism. Westminster portrayed itself as an honest broker. But Douglas Porch, an American military historian, describes this as a self-perception that anyone, with the most superficial knowledge of Britain's historic role in Ireland, should consider delusional.[1567] Once again, a military source is more

---

1565 See Jo McCormack, *Collective Memory: France and the Algerian War,* (Lanham, MD: Lexington, 2007), pp. 57-98, 172-175.

1566 See Patricia M.E. Lorcin (ed.), *Algeria and France, 1800–2000: Identity, Memory and Nostalgia* (Syracuse University Press, 2006), p. 256.

1567 See D. Porch, *Counterinsurgency: Exposing the Myth of the New Way of War* (Cambridge University Press, 2013).

prepared to depart from the prevailing orthodoxy than the 'liberal' press. Porch wonders how anyone at Westminster could harbour the illusion that the British army would respect minimum force and legality. They had not done so in any other campaign (Kenya, Aden, Malaya) and certainly not earlier in Ireland.

The media schooled the public not to understand. In Britain, Ireland is perceived as an incomprehensible place where myth and romance obscure reality. Even, perhaps particularly, among journalism's educated liberal elite we find the selective amnesia Stora warns of in France. Thus, David Astor seemed to genuinely believe: 'the strange thing about this whole story is there has been no anti-Irish feeling or action in this island at all ... not anywhere ... It's astonishing, considering, you know, Irish pubs all painted green and nobody has broken the windows.' Against all the evidence, he also maintained that 'bad army interrogation techniques were a great scandal ... They were stopped.'[1568] Bill Millinship, a brilliant Oxford student, forty years at the *Observer* and with frontline Algiers experience, refused to discuss Ireland: 'I don't know anything about Ireland. I've never really thought about it ... I couldn't begin to compare.'[1569] Ronnie Payne spoke at length about a distant Algeria but could not comment on more recent Irish questions: 'No, Ireland was a long time ago.'[1570] Neal Ascherson remembered how 'people could not believe the police were capable of the turpitude in preparing cases or trying to secure convictions which unfortunately they turned out to be.'[1571] It may be explained by an official British policy of portraying the withdrawal from empire as consensual and largely peaceful; 'a transfer of power over tea.'[1572] It is certainly a pervasive sentiment. Ronnie Payne again recalled Algeria: 'The British were taking a superior attitude at the time. The political class were reconciled to a retreat from empire and were even boasting about it. We've sorted this and it can be done with a lot less bloodshed.'[1573] Tom Pocock displayed the same, perhaps unconscious, selectivity: 'The French wanted to hang on so hard because they had so many settlers, we had not got the same problem.'[1574]

1568 Interview, David Astor, London, 22 July 1998.

1569 Interview, Bill Millinship, London, 18 July 1998.

1570 Interview, Ronnie Payne, London, 22 July 1998.

1571 Interview, Neal Ascherson (the *Observer*, London), 28 July 1998.

1572 J. Hughes, 'State Violence in the Origins of Nationalism: British Counterinsurgency and The Re-birth of Irish Nationalism', in Hall and Malesevic, *Nationalism and War* (Cambridge University Press, 2013), pp. 237-238.

1573 Interview, Ronnie Payne, London, 22 July 1998.

1574 Interview, Tom Pocock, London, 29 July 1998.

To understand the world, the cosmologist Carl Sagan advocated sceptical scientific inquiry: independent confirmation of the 'facts', substantive debate including all points of view, and, if possible, numerical quantification to better discriminate between competing hypotheses. Clearly, the media and, more importantly the liberal media, has failed to comply with all three prescriptions. The conflict in Ireland is now centred on rewriting history and who will uncover the 'truth' about the past? Contestation is as much about who is entitled to speak about the past as it is about contested accounts of what happened. The unionist academic group Arkiv accuses Northern Ireland's Transitional Justice Institute of promoting a republican narrative. It describes its own project as framing the historical narrative by using 'documentary evidence and victims' experiences as an antidote to the attempt by perpetrators of crimes to downplay their historic activities.'[1575] But Arkiv also fails all three of Sagan's prescriptions. It criticises Sinn Féin for not apologising for the 'historic fact' of 'initiating a war against the unionist population of Northern Ireland and the British state.'[1576] Colonel Richard Iron, however, found a different source of the conflict: 'a local government that was itself part of the problem.'[1577] Britain, he believed, was mistaken in supporting it. General Michael Carver, Chief of the General Staff, thought the source of the conflict lay with the injustice of the border in Ireland. As early as 1972 he advised that 'a lasting solution must lie in finding a way in which HM Government can gradually escape the commitment to the border.' He proposed calling a poll, organised 'in such a way that it shows up the iniquity of the existing border.'[1578] Iron further acknowledges that, the army's heavy-handed tactics, in response to unionist pressure: 'sustain[ed] the republican insurgency for much of the following thirty years.'[1579] Arkiv is, however, very much in step with the *pieds-noirs* who, since 1962, have been promoting their narrative of blameless victims. They were/are driven by fear, frustration and especially righteous indignation.

In similar fashion, Kirk Simpson outlines unionist fear of losing out

1575 Maire Braniff and Cillian McGrattan 'Dealing with The Past in Post-conflict Societies', 11 March 2012, www.opendemocracy.net/maire-braniff-cillian-mcgrattan/dealing-with-past-in-post-conflict-societies (accessed 10 July 2015).

1576 Ibid.

1577 R. Iron, 'Britain's Longest War: Northern Ireland, 1967–2007', in Marston and Malik, *Counterinsurgency in Modern Warfare* (Oxford: Osprey, 2008), p. 159.

1578 https://www.bbc.co.uk/news/uk-northern-ireland-49579260 accessed 17 September 2019.

1579 Iron, *Britain's Longest War*, p. 158.

to the republican narrative. Consider the following seven extracts.[1580] Simpson describes a Protestant father's dismay: 'my son comes home from university ... he gives me this version ... it is republican propaganda.' Unionists have other fears of the university experience: 'boys with GAA [Gaelic Athletic Association] shirts ... he [his son] knew them. I was stunned. I nearly went mad.' Simpson lists their frustrations: 'what did we have to do ... IRA atrocities should convince the watching world ... that we are the victims.' For unionists 'the conflict only makes sense in terms of a historical framework in which they, as the innocent, were persecuted by wrong-doers.' Unionists want an apology from an 'immoral collective ... any moral evaluation must focus on republicans.' Simpson endorses the unionist use of the word 'terrorist' to retain the moral high ground 'because it is their natural right as the law-abiding and the innocent.' Unionists want republicans to accept UDR soldiers and RUC policemen as innocent, and they were guilty.

Arkiv members, too, writing from a position of moral certainty, describe their project as a non-partisan engagement in explaining the past 'with an ethical awareness ... harnessed to historical accuracy.'[1581] Patterson endorses his colleague McGrattan's 'frontal assault on the shibboleths of "truth recovery" and academics who reproduce and legitimise the self-justifying narratives of loyalist and republican ex-paramilitaries.'[1582] But loyalist paramilitaries are not addressed in this righteously indignant book, and the index contains no entries for 'UDA', 'UVF' or 'collusion'. McGrattan seeks a foregrounding and centring of victims. By this, he means unionist victims as, in his view, they have been muted while nationalist victims have been foregrounded. He ridicules the 'trope' of state violence and objects to 'the idea that an outside agency must be brought in that serves to allocate responsibility away from Provisional republican extremists.'[1583] This, he maintains, would be a silencing of unionist victims. But of course, any denial of nationalist victims seeking justice beyond the British 'referee' would mean a continued silencing of the nationalist narrative, as perpetrated by British inquiries such as Widgery, Parker, Compton and da Silva. To repeat, victims of the state must, necessarily, be to blame. McGrattan

---

1580 K. Simpson, *Unionist Voices and the Politics of Remembering the Past in Northern Ireland* (Basingstoke: Macmillan, 2009), pp. 20, 28, 98, 107–8, 133, 148.

1581 C. McGrattan *Memory, Politics and Identity: Haunted by History* (Basingstoke: Macmillan, 2013), p. 17.

1582 See Patterson's blurb on the cover of McGrattan, *Memory, Politics and Identity*.

1583 Ibid., p. 16.

explains unionist reluctance to engage in truth recovery: 'a community that repudiated violence and espoused democratic means of resolving conflict is coupled with terrorists.'[1584] But this reliance on memories contrasts with the historic record. McGrattan repeats Simpson's explanation of unionist reluctance to engage in truth recovery: 'it would involve too much ethical and political compromise.'[1585] He also wants no connection between Bloody Sunday and the IRA's armed struggle. It is bad history and 'mealy mouthed equivocation.'[1586] This is contradicted now by counter-insurgency teaching at US graduate military colleges and, indeed, by British officers such as Richard Iron and even the British Prime Minister. McGrattan's Arkiv colleague, Aaron Edwards, also accepts the British army's disproportionate use of force made the conflict worse.[1587] McGrattan uses well-worn media shibboleths of IRA sociopaths and portrays the British army as unfortunately engaged in ill-advised adventures. He describes the Irish Republic as 'utterly misguided and ethically bankrupt, a country where myths have been used and continue to be used to justify horrific acts of slaughter.'[1588] The zeal to dismiss the tropes of state violence displays a dismaying elision of British imperial history. McGrattan laments that Catholics had 'no sure moral foundation', questions the 'personal morality' of John Hume and the ethics of 'Hume aficionados.'[1589] Arkiv's framing of the historical narrative elides the nationalist narrative from a declared position of non-partisanship and morality. Clearly, Stora's warning, of unchanging mythical constructions, has a particular relevance for Northern Ireland.

Unionist fears, of re-writing the past, exhibit all the *pieds-noirs* moral indignation. McGrattan disapproves of the nationalist narrative, nationalist academics, their ethics and their lazy claims, amoral platforms, misguided ethics, bankruptcy, moral repugnance, absurd fatuous scholarship, wilful deception, simplistic notions, perniciousness, absurdity, asininity, clouds of hackneyed banalities, naivety and platitudinous banalities. He wants to foreground Bloody Friday because Bloody Sunday has muted the Protestant/unionist

---

1584 Ibid., p. 136.
1585 Simpson, *Unionist Voices*, pp. 133-134.
1586 Ibid., p. 120.
1587 A. Edwards, 'Misapplying Lessons Learned: Analysis of the Utility of British Counterinsurgency in Northern Ireland 1971–76', *Small Wars and Insurgency*, vol. 21, no. (June 2010), pp. 303-330.
1588 McGrattan, *Memory, Politics and Identity*, p. 55.
1589 Ibid., pp. 158, 162, 164.

experience. But Bloody Friday was not an exclusive Protestant/unionist experience and includes Catholic/nationalist dead. The 'muting' also overlooks the government printing 250,000 copies of a twelve-page pamphlet *The Terror and the Tears* describing that terrible day in gruesome detail. The pamphlet was written by the Ulster Unionist Party. In a further lapse from Sagan's scientific approach, the number of republican killings is frequently inflated and the repeated claims of twenty-two no-warning bombs are simply wrong. The events were bad enough, there is no need for misrepresentation.[1590]

So many authors claiming 'historical accuracy', yet their analyses exaggerate republican sins. This points to the difficulty of shedding 'instinctive bias'.[1591] State violence, however, is only a trope. Patterson's response to Saville's exonerating Bloody Sunday's victims was that it did not prove a Cabinet decision. Citing Peter Hart, Patterson also writes of an IRA campaign of ethnic cleansing of border Protestants which repeats a West Cork ethnic cleansing during the Irish War of Independence.[1592] He, too, neglects Sagan's recommendation to quantify. He provides no figures at all but relies on grieving Protestant memories of dutiful only-sons, bequeathed the family farm, who lost their lives serving in the RUC and UDR. Patterson's 'documentary evidence' of ethnic cleansing also sits uneasily with: the history of repeated burnings of nationalist neighbourhoods, Paisley's call for the 'forced removal' of Catholics, Thatcher's 'Cromwell solution' encouraging Catholics to move south and the continued loyalist petrol bombings of Catholic schools, churches and homes in East Antrim, Ballymena and South Down, to say nothing of the earlier pogroms and burnings, including security forces participation.[1593] When the UVF burned the three Quinn children to death, it was only one of 137 petrol bombings of Catholic homes that week alone.[1594] In addition, there is the British army's own record of ethnic cleansing, uncomfortably

---

1590 See McGrattan, *Memory, Politics and Identity*, p. 64; Edwards, 'Misapplying Lessons Learned', p. 313; Simpson, *Unionist Voices*, p. 82; 'no effective warnings', F Cochrane, Northern Ireland: The Reluctant Peace, p. 77, J. Moran, *From Northern Ireland to Afghanistan*, Ashgate, 2013, p. 155. Forty-six years after the event Kevin Myers was still writing of twenty no-warning bombs, *News Letter*, 6 October 2018. The record is all bombs carried warning. The atrocity centers on the dispute over two bomb warnings the security forces claim they never received.

1591 See *Belfast News Letter*, 29 October 2013.

1592 See H. Patterson, *Ireland's Violent Frontier*, (Basingstoke: Palgrave Macmillan, 2013), p. 42.

1593 Low Level Ethnic Cleansing in Evidence, *Irish Times*, 11 July 1998.

1594 *Belfast Telegraph*, 4 November 2019.

acknowledged by the UDR's commander, no less.[1595] Further, two years before Patterson's account Peter Hart had already denied he ever claimed ethnic cleansing in Cork. This repeated inaccuracy only adds to the pain and fear of grieving relatives.[1596] Patrick Wolfe's highlighting of territoriality as the settler colonists' specific irreducible element may help here. The steadfast unionist position of 'what we have, we hold', 'not an inch', 'no surrender' is definitive of a general outlook.[1597] It is no surprise that colonists, having driven so many of the original inhabitants into the desert, should express an abiding fear of being driven into the sea themselves. Unionist fixation with Catholic family size is not new. Wolfe explains the settler 'destroying to replace' does not necessarily mean liquidation but replacing the earlier culture with a demand of accepting the new one.[1598] 'We have always found the Irish a bit odd. They refuse to be English,' as Churchill said. This may also account for the current unionist disdain for the Irish language and culture and their concerns of the eradication of Britishness in Ireland. Wolfe's analysis also helps explain those alienated Catholics viewing resistance as an end in itself, a guarantee against assimilation into non-Irish identity.

Clearly, history needs to be more than simply 'memory' that reinforces a victims-villains narrative. It is about understanding, whereas memory is too often inspired by the desire to re-live past experiences of victimhood. Mohamed Harbi and Benjamin Stora warn against this in France: '*Les mémoires ... sont à la fois rappel d'événements et miroir déformant. L'historien ne peut ni les dédaigner, ni s'y soumettre*'[1599] – 'memories are at once a reminder of events and

---

1595 UDR commander Charles Ritchie was a lieutenant during Britain's counterinsurgency in Aden, their conduct was 'no less than ethnic cleansing'; Saunders and Wood, *Times of Troubles*, (Edinburgh University Press, 2012), p. 204. See also Margaret Thatcher's 'Cromwell solution', *Guardian* 16 June 2001 and P Lawlor, *The Burnings 1920*, (Mercier 2009) for Catholic neighbourhoods burned down in Banbridge, Dromore and Lisburn. Roslea and Desertmartin were razed by the Special Constabulary, *History Ireland*. https://www.historyireland.com/20th-century-contemporary-history/tit-for-tat-the-war-of-independence-in-the-northern-counties/, accessed 16 June 2018.

1596 On 28 June 2006 Hart wrote in the *Irish Times*: 'I never argued that "ethnic cleansing" took place in Cork or anywhere else in the 1920s, in fact the opposite'. These claims were comprehensively debunked by P O'Ruairc, *Truce: Murder, Myth and the Last Days of the Irish War of Independence*, Cork, Mercier 2016. See also Niall Meehan Ireland's Freedom Struggle and the Foster School of Falsification, *Counterpunch*, 11 November 2006. Discredited claims of ethnic cleansing are still repeated by the Orange Order and unionist academics.

1597 For example, the land fund established by the Orange Order to ensure farms remain in Protestant hands, BBC N. Ireland Spotlight, 18 February 2015.

1598 P Wolfe, Settler Colonialism and the Elimination of the Native, *Journal of Genocide Research*, vol. 8, 2006, issue 4, December, pp. 387-409.

1599 M. Harbi and B. Stora, *La Guerre d'Algérie* (Paris: Robert Laffont, 2004), pp. 10–11.

a distorting mirror. The historian can neither dismiss nor submit to them.' We need a history that challenges simplified accounts.

Colin Sparks believes the propaganda model is still one of the best for understanding media performance.[1600] But if it is to work as a theory on a general level, it must be able to explain the workings of the mass media in societies other than the US, especially where circumstances are similar; for example, in the advanced democracies of Europe. He highlights some differences. There is more competition in European newspapers and often a public broadcaster (which he accepts is limited to the views of the government and the official opposition). In Britain, as we have seen, the remarkable longevity of the all-party consensus ensured few dissenting voices. Spark's second point is that not all journalists are socialised into an elite political culture. But for Britain's thirty-year war in Ireland, he offers only two examples of dissent: the twenty-four-hour news blackout over the non-broadcasting of the *Real Lives* documentary featuring IRA leader Martin McGuinness, and the opposition of BBC journalists to the broadcasting ban on Sinn Féin. But failing to have their opposition endorsed by the National Union of Journalists rather undermines his second example, leaving just the one-day action.

Sparks also argues that source dependence does not guarantee journalistic compliance with the source's perspective. Now, two sources dominate any understanding of Ireland and Algeria: Conor Cruise O'Brien and Albert Camus. O'Brien rewrote history through the prism of contemporary politics and created a political reflex that remains in Ireland to this day. His concern was the democratic legitimacy of the Irish Republic and the mandate of the men and women of 1916. O'Brien wrote that to deal with the IRA in the present, they must be defeated in the past. He intended to deliver a shock to the Irish psyche, and he found his audience. Accordingly, he 'rewrote the history' of the Irish state owing its existence to the IRA. O'Brien disapproved of the focus on the men of 1916 and sought a focus on the 1921 Anglo-Irish Treaty. The existence of the state is due to the demand of the majority of its inhabitants for self-government and, in O'Brien's view, to Britain's recognition of the legitimacy of that demand.[1601] O'Brien belonged intellectually and viscerally to the Redmondite tradition and his critique

1600 C. Sparks, 'Expanding and Refining the Propaganda Model', *Westminster Papers in Communication and Culture*, vol. 4, no. (2000), pp. 69–84.

1601 O'Brien, cited in D. Whelan, 'Conor Cruise O'Brien and the Legitimisation of Violence', *Irish Political Studies*, vol. 21, no. (2006), pp. 223–41.

of Northern Ireland is flawed.[1602] He was only interested in the North when it created problems for the South. He accepted that Catholics of the North were second-class citizens, but their experience was insufficiently oppressive. The removal of their inferior status was not worth the unionist response. He did not question why removing this insufficient oppression would face such violent opposition.

Some evaluation of Camus and O'Brien, then, is necessary. Camus had famously said: 'People are planting bombs in trams in Algiers. My mother might be on one of those trams. If that is justice, I prefer my mother.'[1603] He also rejected negotiations with the FLN, maintaining they were a military elite who would deny rights to *pieds-noirs* and Muslims alike. O'Brien, equally famously, attacked Camus for preferring his mother, which he disingenuously depicted as supporting French repression. In making this claim, he ignored Camus' repeated condemnation of French colonialism since the 1940s, which included a comparison with German methods. He also condemned Camus' *La Peste* as an allegory of struggle against oppression that is opposed to FLN methods. He is correct in this but Camus' essential point was that there must be limits to the methods of fighting against injustice. Any independent Algeria produced by blind terror was not worth it. And any French promise of future justice was not worth state terror and torture. When there are no limits, the form of resistance to one plague becomes the carrier of the next. O'Brien missed that Camus aimed this at France as well as at the FLN, while he levelled this only at the IRA, never at Britain. He supported full British military repression with no undue squeamishness.

O'Brien continued his critique: 'Eight years after the publication of *La Peste* the rats came up to die on the streets of Algeria ... and the eruption came precisely from the quarter where the doctor [Rieux], and by implication Camus, never looked.'[1604] But O'Brien's accusation that Camus did not look (and thus wrote Arabs out of Algeria) is misplaced and can be levelled more accurately towards him. It is O'Brien who did not look. He accused the IRA and Irish nationalism of an Irish Catholic imperialism, but while he was, in his own words, a fanatical supporter of Algeria's nationalists, he overlooked the Islamic imperialist dimension of the FLN. Indeed, the Algerian bloodbath of the 1990s

1602 John Redmond. leader, 1900-18, of the Irish Parliamentary Party, cooperated with Britain in its 'constitutional' rule over Ireland. He encouraged Irishmen to fight for Britain in WW1 expecting to be rewarded with Home Rule.

1603 *Guardian*, 28 February 2010.

1604 C.C. O'Brien, *Camus* (London: Fontana, 1974), p. 51.

erupted when the Islamic Salvation Front (FIS) challenged the FLN government for not completing the true Islamic intent of the 1954 uprising. It is important to recognise that the FIS does not represent a deep cultural cleavage in Algeria. There is a popular wordplay in Algeria today: 'Le FIS est le fils du FLN.'[1605] O'Brien further accused Camus: 'The source of the plague is what we pretend is not there and the preacher himself is already, without knowing it, infected with the plague.'[1606] But it is O'Brien, not Camus, who is infected, maintaining that Britain was a referee and not a participant in the conflict.

O'Brien claims that Camus' true face was that of a partisan colonialist. This is simply inconsistent with Camus' repeated condemnation of French repression: 'Yet the facts are there, the clear and hideous truth: we are doing what we reproached the Germans for doing.'[1607] However, Richard English claims Camus never had O'Brien's courage. But many of Camus' critics have now been forced to make an abrupt reversal. Camus had always been accorded a score of two out of three: correct on Vichy, correct on Stalin, wrong on Algeria. Now he is regarded as especially adept at predicting how the FLN's penchant for authoritarianism would threaten Algerian society.[1608] With Camus in mind, O'Brien wrote: 'if the writer defends, for example, the propaganda of the perpetrators such that the war is being fought for freedom then [that writer] would be lying.'[1609] In the debate over who was right about Algeria, Camus or O'Brien (or Sartre and Fanon), until recently few would have said Camus. But Camus' predictions have come true. Mohammed Harbi, advisor to Ben Bella and a former member of the FLN Cabinet, has exposed the image of the FLN as a national-liberation movement as a mirage. In fact, the eight-year struggle allowed the 'army of the frontiers' to seize power. Harbi's study sent shock waves across France and the Third Worldist left. The official FLN version of a popular uprising has now lost its dominance, and the concept of the people's army is coming to an end.[1610]

1605 See M. Willis, *The Islamist Challenge in Algeria,* (NY University Press, 1996), p. 102.

1606 O'Brien, *Camus*, p. 51.

1607 D. Carroll, *Albert Camus the Algerian* (Columbia University Press, 2007), pp. 52–3.

1608 D. Le Seuer, *Uncivil War: Intellectuals and Identity Politics During the Decolonisation of Algeria* (University of Pennsylvania Press, 2001), p. 88.

1609 See J. Foley, 'A Post-Colonial Fiction', *Irish Review*, nos 36-7 (winter 2007), p. 2.

1610 Harbi and Stora set out to rescue the history of the war from the FLN's official narrative. Harbi subjected the FLN version to a 'withering critique'; A. Shatz, 'The Torture of Algiers'; *NYRB*, November 2002, and B. Stora, *Algeria, 1830–2000,* (Ithaca, NY: Cornell University Press, 2001), pp. 231–41.

Camus always denied the FLN leaders were liberators.[1611] He repeatedly argued that saving lives had to take priority over any cause, even over the cause of justice itself. A French victory by repression and torture would make the continuation of colonial rule unjust, but independence achieved through terror would also be unjust. Camus injected the human dimension. There must be limits even in the pursuit of justice: 'For to defend life itself before justice as a general principle is in fact to defend justice itself.'[1612] In his essay 'Algeria 1958' he supported the Lauriol Plan, an Algeria federated with France, similar but more original than the Swiss model, with different populations overlapping, a federation of communities with different personalities. Camus is now regarded as having argued for justice for both communities, while O'Brien, attempting to explain his contradictions, claimed one consistency: his steadfast opposition to Catholic imperialism (and revealing his previously disguised unionism). O'Brien hoped the Northern peace talks would fail and even impeded peace efforts.[1613]

While Camus has been vindicated, O'Brien's previously dominant analysis is eroding. This may explain the unionist protest of the occluding of their history. Unionist academics correctly note that O'Brien called into question the founding principles of the Irish Republic. Richard English argues O'Brien revealed with 'striking originality' that: 'the IRA were the imperialists, they were trying to annex by force a territory a large majority of whose inhabitants were opposed to them.'[1614] By this reasoning, Ukrainians currently attempting to maintain their national territory are imperialists. O'Brien accused Camus of defending a colonial war by a stylish regurgitation of propaganda. The reader can decide whether O'Brien's analysis, which framed the first history of the 'Troubles', was strikingly original or a stylish regurgitation of propaganda.

1611 Camus' view was shared by Jean Daniel, and the philosopher Jacques Derrida, who was silent during the war, but recent scholarship shows he believed the FLN would be intolerant of minorities, see E. Baring, 'Liberalism and the Algerian War: the case of Jacques Derrida', *Critical Inquiry*, vol. 36, no. 2 (winter 2010). See also Elie Kedourie; see 'The Retreat from Algeria', *Times Literary Supplement*, April 1978.

1612 D. Carroll, *Albert Camus the Algerian* (Columbia University Press, 2008), p. 185.

1613 On 24 April 2005 the *Belfast Telegraph* reported that in 1976 O'Brien had 'scuppered peace talks' between republicans and loyalists. Loyalists had insisted on confidentiality and O'Brien blew their cover when, as an Irish government minister, he discovered it. They were searching for common ground on a federal Ireland following Sinn Féin's Éire Nua proposals.

1614 English and Skelly (eds), *Ideas Matter*, p. 20.

APPENDIX

Civilians Killed in Explosions

The IRA placed up to 19,000 bombs (Oppenheimer 2009), 138 of which (0.7%) took 273 civilian lives. All the victims are numbered chronologically in McKittrick et al's *Lost Lives,* including 151 Protestants, 66 Catholics, 62 civilians in England and 1 Nigerian in Northern Ireland.

There were 5 premature explosions that took 11 civilian lives in Northern Ireland including 8 Catholics, 2 Protestants and one Nigerian. The Catholic dead are in *Lost Lives*: 24-5, 376, 377, 381, 383, 1580-1, the Protestant dead are: 983, 2208 and one Nigerian: 2209.

There were 12 sectarian bombings that took 23 civilian lives including 21 Protestants and 2 Catholics (8 pub bombings, one during a riot, one in a car thought to have been used in a sectarian killing, one [Balmoral] after McGurk's bomb and one in a housing estate, almost all in the year 1975. The Protestant dead are referenced: 91, 133-4, 214-6, 1322, 1341-5, 1428-31 & 1436, 1434, 1606, 1709-10, 1866, 1867. The Catholic dead are: 213, 1489.

There were 46 IRA 'commercial bombings' that took 117 civilian lives: 50 Protestants, 24 Catholics and 43 deaths in England, mostly through inadequate or confused warnings. There were two explosions with no warnings (373, 2411), two explosions where victims tried to move or defuse the device (226, 1493), two explosions where victims ignored the warnings (3392, 3533-4), two explosions while the victim was warning others (263, 947), and two explosions while the victim was investigating (348, 1025&1030). The 50 Protestant dead are: 114, 207, 313, 314, 316, 326, 333, 348, 373 (NO warn) 483, 488, 490, 494, 515, 320, 521, 522, 553, 870, 871, 872, 873, 874, 875, 1030, 1661-2-3,

1695, 1797, 1811, 1898, 1992-3-4-5-6-7-8-9, 2000-1-2-3, 2062, 2130, 2411, 2423-4, 3416. The 24 Catholic dead are: 226, 263, 293, 294, 493, 495, 517, 518, 525, 532, 539, 551, 552, 554, 555, 559, 947, 1025, 1044, 1668, 1669, 1873, 1976, 2058. In England 43 civilians died: 1246-7-8-9, 1250-1-2-3-4-5-6-7-8-9,1260-1-2-3-4-5, 1276, 1281,1284, 1265, 1266, 1493, 1522, 1526, 1527, 1670, 2594 -5-6, 3174, 3183, 3313-4-5, 3383, 3390, 3392, 3533, 3534.

There were 75 IRA explosions attacking British forces, public figures including one on loyalists, that took 122 civilian lives including 71 Protestants, 32 Catholics and 19 in England. The Protestant dead are: 55-6-7-8, 170-1-2, 321-2, 572, 842, 1384, 1610-11, 1622, 1634, 1758, 1988, 2123, 2135, 2385, 2399, 2453, 2477, 2490-1-2-3, 2558, 2559, 2611, 2804, 2883-4-5-6-7-8-9, 2890-1-2-3, 2952-3-4, 2995, 2996, 3077, 3108, 3116-7, 3129, 3277-8-9-, 3280-1-2-3-4, 3379, 3418-3425, &-27. The Catholic dead are: 80, 598, 779, 935, 1025, 1029, 1074, 1136, 1293, 1852, 1853, 2078-9, 2272, 2508, 2696, 2948-9, 2984-5, 3031, 2998, 3000-1, 3018, 3033, 3093, 3125, 3146, 3224, 3274, 3451. The civilian dead in England are: 1054-5-6, 1202, 1227, 1503, 1760, 2134, 2155, 2375, 2377, 2505, 2652-3-4-5, 2611, 2776, 2792 and the establishment figures Christopher Ewart-Biggs 1759, Lord Mountbatten 2133 and Ian Gow 3127.

ACKNOWLEDGEMENTS

I would like to than all who have contributed to this study. The critical reading of Professors Bill Rolston, Patricia Lundy, Paddy Hillyard and David Miller improved this study. Vinny McCormack, co-author with Bowes Egan of *Burntollet*, gave me my first lessons on the Northern Ireland conflict. I would like to thank Conor Kearney, EU, for ongoing discussion of Ireland and the librarians at the University of Ulster.

In Toronto, I would like to thank Sylvia Tessaro, Chris Fullan, Susan and Joe McReynolds and John and Angela McCabe for their hospitality and many discussions on Ireland. For many years Frank Benson, CJMR, allowed me precious radio air time to broadcast about the conflict in Ireland. I would also like to thank the librarians at the University of Toronto. The critical reading of Professor Brendan O'Leary, University of Pennsylvania, greatly improved this study.

In London, veteran correspondents of the Algerian War and Northern Ireland provided valuable material form their frontline experiences: Neal Ascherson, Robert Kee, David Astor, Clare Hollingworth, Ronnie Payne, Alan Williams, Herb Greer, Ian Aitken, Tom Pocock and Bill Millinship. Thanks to Maureen and John Flavin and Clare and Mark Redway whose hospitality facilitated my London research. Thanks also to the librarians at the British Newspaper Archive at Colindale.

Extracts from Steve Bruce's *The Red Hand: Protestant Paramilitaries in Northern Ireland* (1992) are reprinted with kind permission of Oxford University Press. Extracts from Peter Taylor's *Loyalists* (2000) are reprinted with kind permission of Bloomsbury publishing. I would like to thank Danny Morrison, editor at Greenisland Press, who helped clarify many issues; Seán Mistéil for his saintly patience for setting the manuscript; and to Dr Thomas Pago of Greenisland Press and Elsinor Verlag for bringing my book to publication.

The book could not have been written without the love and support of my wife Mary Pat and sons Conall and Rory.

BIBLIOGRAPHY

Abder Rahmane-Derradji, *The Algerian Guerrilla Campaign and Tactics* (Lampeter: Edwin Mellen, 1977)

Ackroyd, C. et al *The Technology of Political Control* (London: Pluto, 1980)

Adamson, I. *The Cruthin* (Newtownards: Colourpoint 2014)

Akenson, D. H. *Conor: A Biography of Conor Cruise O'Brien*, (Cornell University Press, 1994)

Akenson, D. H. *God's Peoples: Covenant and Land in South Africa, Israel, and Ulster,* NY: Cornell University Press, 1992)

Alexander, M. *The Algerian War and the French Army 1954-62: Experiences, Images, Testimonies*, (Palgrave Macmillan 2002)

Alleg, H. *La Question*, (Paris, Edition du Minuit, 1958)

Alleg, H. 'Political Violence in Algeria', in John P. Darby et al (eds), *Political Violence: Ireland in a Comparative Perspective* (Belfast: Appletree, 1987)

Anderson, D. *Histories of the Hanged: Britain's Dirty War in Kenya and the End of Empire* (London: Weidenfeld & Nicolson, 2005)

Andrew, C. *Defence of the Realm: The Authorised History of MI5* (London: Penguin, 2010)

Ardoyne: The Untold Truth, (Belfast: Beyond the Pale, 2002)

Armstrong, D. *A Road Too Wide* (Basingstoke: Marshalls, 1985)

Armstrong, G. *From the Palace to Prison* (Chichester: New Wine Press, 1991)

Arthur, M. *Northern Ireland: Soldiers Talking* (London; Sidgwick & Jackson, 1987)

Ascherson, N, *C.C. O'Brien, The Irascible Angel*, Open Democracy, 22 Dec 2008

Aughey, A. *Under Siege: Ulster Unionism and the Anglo-Irish Agreement* (Belfast: Blackstaff, 1989)

Aussaresses, P. *The Battle of the Casbah* (NY: Enigma, 2006).

Barker, A. *Shadows: Inside Northern Ireland's Special Branch* (Edinburgh: Mainstream, 2006)

Barnet DL and Njama, K. *Mau Mau from Within* (London: MacGibbon & Kee, 1966)

Beattie, G. *We Are the People: Journey to the Heart of Protestant Ulster* (London: Heinemann, 1992)

Beckett, A. *When the Lights went out*, (London: Faber, 2010)

Behr, E. *The Algerian Problem* (London: Hodder & Stoughton, 1961)

Bell, G. *The Protestants of Ulster* (London: Pluto, 1976)

Bell, J. B. *On Revolt: strategies of liberation* (Harvard University Press, 1976)

Bowyer Bell, *The Gun in Irish Politics,* (Routledge, 1987)

Bell, J. B. *The Secret Army: the IRA, 1916-79* (Dublin: Poolbeg, 1989)

Bell, J. B. *The Irish Troubles: A Generation of Violence, 1967-1992* (New York: St Martin's, 1993)

Bennett, H. *Report of the Committee of Inquiry into Police Interrogation in Northern Ireland* (London: HMSO, 1979)

Bennett, H. Smoke without Fire? Allegations Against the British Army in Northern Ireland, 1972–5, *Twentieth Century History,* Volume 24, Issue 2, June 2012

Beran, H. 'Who Should Be Entitled to Vote in Self-Determination Referenda?' in Werner & Crisp, Terrorism, Protest and Power (Aldershot, Edward, 1990)

Bew, P. & Gillespie, G, *Northern Ireland: Chronology of the Troubles, 1968–1993* (Dublin: Gill & Macmillan, 1993)

Bew, P. *Politics of Enmity,* (OUP 2007)

Bishop, P. Maillie, R., *The Provisional IRA*, (Corgi, 1988)

Black, J. *Killing for Britain* (Edinburgh: Frontline Noir, 2008)

Bloch J. and P. Fitzgerald, *British Intelligence and Covert Action* (Dingle: Brandon, 1983)

Bocca, G. *The Secret Army* (New Jersey: Prentice-Hall, 1968)

Bolton, R. *'Death on the Rock'* (London: WH Allen, 1990)

Boyce, D G, *Englishmen and Irish Troubles: British Public Opinion and The Making of Irish policy*, (London: Jonathan Cape, 1972)

Boyce D. G. and O'Day, A. *Defenders of the Union: A Survey of British and Irish unionists since 1801* (London: Routledge, 2000)

Brace, R&J *Ordeal in Algeria* (NJ: Van Nostrand, 1960)

Brady, C. (ed.) *Interpreting Irish History: The Debate on Historical Revisionism*, (Dublin: Irish Academic Press)

Brewer, J. & Higgins, G. *Anti-Catholicism in Northern Ireland, 1600–1998: Mote and Beam* (Basingstoke: MacMillan, 1998)

Briere, C. *Ceux Qu'On Appelle Les Pieds Noirs ou 150 Ans De L'Histoire d'un Peuple*, (Versailles, Editions de l'Atlanthrope, 1984)

Bruce, S. *Edge of the Union* (OUP 1994)

Bruce, S. *The Red Hand* (OUP 1992)

Burke, E. Counterinsurgency against 'Kith and Kin'? The British Army in Northern Ireland, 1970–76, *Journal of Imperial and Commonwealth History*, Vol 43, issue 4, 2015

Burke, E, *An Army of Tribes*, *British Army Cohesion, Deviancy and Murder in Northern Ireland*, (Oxford University Press 2018)

Burton, F. *The Politics of Legitimacy* (London: Routledge & Kegan Paul, 1978)

Byrne, JJ. *Mecca of Revolution: Algeria, Decolonisation and the Third World Order* (OUP 2016)

Cadwallader, A. *Lethal Allies* (Cork: Mercier, 2013)

Campbell, F. *The Orange Card: Racism, Religion and Politics in Northern Ireland* (London: Connolly, 1979)

Campbell, J. *Setting the Truth Free: Inside the Bloody Sunday Justice Campaign (Liberties 2012)*

Carroll, D. *Albert Camus the Algerian* (Columbia UP 2007)

Carver, M. *Out of Step*, (Hutchinson, 1989)

Carver, R. & Handley, L. *Does Torture Work* (OUP 2017)

Charters, D. and Tugwell, M. Armies in Low Intensity Conflicts (London: Brasseys, 1989)

Clark, M. *Algeria in Turmoil* (New York: Grosset & Dunlap, 1960)

Clarke, AFN, *Contact* (London: Secker & Warburg, 1989)

Clayton, A. *Counterinsurgency in Kenya,* (Manhattan, KS: Sunflower University Press, 1984)

Clifford, B. *Against Ulster Nationalism* (Belfast: Athol, 1992)

Clostermann, P. *Leo25 Airborne* (London: Chatto-Windus, 1962)

Cobain, I. *Anatomy of a Killing*, (Granta, 2020)

Cobain, I. *The History Thieves*, (Portobello, 2016)

Cochrane, F. *Northern Ireland, The Uneasy Peace.* (Yale University Press 2013)

Cockett, *David Astor and the Observer* (London, Deutsch, 1991)

Colley, L. *Britons: Forging the Nation, 1707-1837* (Yale University Press, 1992)

Collins, T. *The Irish Hunger Strike* (White Island, 1986)

Conway, B. *Commemorating Bloody Sunday, Pathways of Memory*, (London: Palgrave, 2010)

Coogan, T. P. *The Troubles: Ireland's Ordeal 1966-1995 and The Search for Peace* (St Martin's 2002)

Cooley, JK., *Baal, Christ and Mohammed: Religion and Revolution in North Africa* (London: John Murray, 1965)

Courrière, Y., *La Guerre d'Algerie*, 4 vols (Paris: Fayard, 1968–72)

Crawford, R. *Loyal to King Billy: A Portrait of Ulster Protestants* (Dublin: Gill & Macmillan, 1987)

Curtis, L. Anglo-Saxons and Celts: A Study of Anti-Irish Prejudices in Victorian England, (New York University Press, 1968)

Curtis, L. *Ireland and the Propaganda War*, (London, Pluto, 1984)

Curtis, L, *Nothing but the Same Old Story: The Roots of Anti-Irish Racism, (London, Information on Ireland, 1985)*

Curtis, M. *Web of Deceit: Britain's Real Role in the World* (London: Vintage, 2003)

Cusack, J & MacDonald, H. *UVF* (Dublin: Poolbeg, 1997)

Darby, J. *Conflict in Northern Ireland: The Development of a Polarised Community* (Dublin: Gill & Macmillan, 1976),

Darby, JP et al *Political Violence: Ireland in a Comparative Perspective* (Belfast: Appletree, 1987)

Davis, R. *Mirror Hate: The Convergent Ideologies of Northern Ireland Paramilitaries* (Aldershot: Dartmouth, 1994)

Dawson, G. *Making Peace with the Past*, (Manchester University Press, 2007)

De Bollardiere, J., *Bataille d'Algiers, Bataille de l'Homme* (Paris, 1972)

De la Billière, P. *Looking for Trouble* (London: Harper Collins, 1994)

Deane, S. *Civilians and Barbarians* (Derry: Field Day, 1994),

Deutsch, R. & Magowan, V. 3 vols, *Northern Ireland: Chronology of Events* (Belfast: Blackstaff, 1973–75)

Deveney, P. *Callaghan's Journey to Downing Street*, (Basingstoke: Palgrave Macmillan, 2010)

Dewar, M. *The British Army in Northern Ireland* (London, Armoury Press, 1985)

Dicey, AV. England's Case against Home Rule, (London: J Murray, 1886), in D. G. Boyce, *Englishmen and Irish Troubles: British Public Opinion and the Making of Irish policy*, (London: Jonathan Cape, 1972)

Dillon, M. *The Shankill Butchers* (London, Arrow 1990)

Dillon, M. *Dirty War,* (Arrow 1990)

Dillon, M. *The Enemy Within: the IRA's War against the British* (London: Doubleday, 1994),

Dillon, M. *God and the Gun: The Church and Irish Terrorism* (London: Orion, 1997),

Dixon, P. *The British Approach to Counterinsurgency: From Malaya and Northern Ireland to Iraq and Afghanistan,* (Basingstoke, Palgrave Macmillan, 2012)

Drif, Z. *Inside the Battle of Algiers*, (Just World, 2017)

Dumas, A. *Adventures in Algeria*, (Philadelphia, Chilton, 1959)

Dunigan, JP. *Deep Rooted Conflict and the IRA Ceasefire* (Lanham, University Press of America, 1995)

Dunlop, J. *A Precarious Belonging: Presbyterians and the Conflict in Northern Ireland* (Belfast: Blackstaff, 1995)

Eames, R. *Chains to Be Broken* (Belfast: Blackstaff, 1992)

Edwards, A. 'Misapplying Lessons Learned: British Counterinsurgency in Northern Ireland 1971–76', *Small Wars and Insurgency*, vol. 21, no. (June 2010)

Edwards, A. *UVF: Behind the Mask*, (Merrion, 2017)

Edwards, D. *Burning All Illusions: A Guide to Personal and Political Freedom* (Cambridge: South End Press, 1995)

Edwards, O. D., *Conor Cruise O'Brien Introduces Ireland,* (Harper Collins, 1969)

Elkins, C. *Britain's Gulag: The Brutal End of Empire in Kenya,* (Bodley Head, 2014)

Elstein, D. "Death on the Rock" *Open Democracy,* 23 November 2009.

English, R. & Skelly, JM (eds), *Ideas Matter: Essays in Honour of Conor Cruise O'Brien* (Lanham, MD: University Press of America, 2000).

English, R. *Irish Freedom: The History of Nationalism in Ireland* (London: Macmillan, 2006)

English, R. *Armed Struggle: History of IRA (Pan, 2012)*

Entelis, J.P. *Algeria: the Revolution Institutionalised,* (Boulder, Westview, 1986)

Evans, H. *Paper Chase* (NY, Back Bay, 2002)

Evans, M. *Algeria: Anger of the Dispossessed* (Yale University Press, 2007)

Evans, M. *Algeria: France's Undeclared War* (Oxford University Press, 2012)

Evelegh, R. *Peacekeeping in a Democratic Society* (London: Hurst, 1978)

Faligot, R. & Krop, P. *La Piscine: The French Secret Service* (Oxford: Basil Blackwell, 1989)

Faligot, R. *The Kitson Experiment* (London: Zed, 1983)

Fanning, B *Histories of the Irish Future,* (London, Bloomsbury, 2015

Fanon, F. *A Dying Colonialism* (Harmondsworth: Penguin, 1970

Fanon, F. *The Wretched of the Earth,* Penguin 2001)

Farrell, M. *Northern Ireland: The Orange State* (London: Pluto, 1976)

Feraoun, M. *Journal, 1955–1962: Reflections on the Algerian War* (University of Nebraska Press, 2000)

Fields, RM. *Northern Ireland: Society under Siege* (New Brunswick, Transaction Books, 1980)

Finnan, JP. *John Redmond and Irish Unity* (Syracuse University Press, 2004)

Fisk, R. *The Great War for Civilisation: The Conquest of the Middle East* (London: Harper Collins) 2006

Fisk, R. *The Point of No Return: The Strike Which Broke the British in Ulster* (London: Andre Deutsch, 1975)

Foley, J. 'A Post-Colonial Fiction', *Irish Review,* nos 36-7 (winter 2007)

Foot, P. *Who Framed Colin Wallace?* (London: Macmillan, 1989

Forde, B. *Hope in Bomb City* (London: Lakeland, 1979)

Foster, JW. *Colonial Consequences*, (Lilliput 1989)

Gale, J. *Clean Young Englishman* (Penguin, 1965)

Galliher, JF., and DeGregory, JL., *Violence in Northern Ireland: Understanding Protestant Perspectives* (Dublin: Gill & Macmillan, 1985)

Garland, R. *Gusty Spence*, (Blackstaff, 2001)

Gaucher, R. *The Terrorists: From Tsarist Russia to the OAS* (London: Secker & Warburg, 1968)

Geraghty, T. *The Irish War*, (John Hopkins University Press, 2000)

Gillingham, J. "The Beginnings of English Imperialism", Journal of Historical Sociology 5, no.4

Gillissen, C, 'Ireland, France and the Question of Algeria at the UN, 1955–1962', *Irish Studies in International Affairs*, vol. (2008)

Gordon, D. *Self Determination and History in the Third World* (Princeton UP 1971)

Gordon, D. *The Passing of French Algeria* (OUP 1966)

Gray, J. *Climbing the Army Ladder*, (Xilibris, 2010)

Greer, H. *A Scattering of Dust* (London: Hutchinson, 1962)

Guelke, A. and F. Wright, 'The Option of British Withdrawal from Northern Ireland: An Exploration of its meaning, influence and feasibility', *Conflict Quarterly* (autumn 1990)

Hall, J.A. and S. Malesevic, *Nationalism and War* (Cambridge University Press, 2013)

Hamill, D. *Pig in the Middle* (London, Methuen 1985)

Hanley, JB. Who Bombed Dublin and Monaghan? *History Ireland*, no.3, vol. 22 (May/June)

Harbi, M. & Stora, B. *La Guerre d' Algérie* (Paris: Robert Laffont, 2004)

Harbi, M. *Le FLN, Mirage et Réalité* (Paris: Jeune Afrique, 1986)

Harclerode, P. *PARA: Fifty Years of the Parachute Regiment* (London: Armoury, 1992).

Harnden, T. *Bandit Country,* (London: Coronet, 1999)

Haroun, A., *La 7e Wilaya: La guerre du FLN en France* (Paris: Seuil, 1986)

Harrison, A. *Challenging de Gaulle: The OAS and the Counter-revolution in Algeria* (New York: Praeger, 1989)

Heggoy, A. *Insurgency and Counterinsurgency in Algeria,* (Indiana University Press, 1972)

Henissart, P. *Wolves in the City: The Death of French Algeria* (London: Rupert Hart-Davis, 1970)

Hennings, A. *Justice Under Fire*, Pluto, 1988

Herman, E. 'The Propaganda Model: a Retrospective', *Journalism Studies*, vol. 1, no. 1 (2000)

Herman, E. and Chomsky, N., *Manufacturing Consent: The Political Economy of the Mass Media* (New York: Pantheon, 1988)

Hetherington, A. *Guardian Years* (London, Chatto and Windus, 1981)

Hoggart, S. 'The Army PR Men of Northern Ireland', *New Society*, 11 October 1973

Holroyd, F (with Nick Burbridge), *War Without Honour*. (Hull: Medium Publishing, 1989)

Hooper, A. *The Military and the Media* (Aldershot, Gower, 1982)

Hopkinson, M. *The Irish War of Independence* (Montreal: McGill-Queen's University Press, 2013)

Horgan, JJ. *The Complete Grammar of Anarchy by Members of the War Cabinet and their Friends* (Dublin: Mansel 1918)

Horne, A. *A Savage War of Peace* (London: Macmillan, 1977)

Howard, M. 'Mistake to Declare this a War', *RUSI*, December 2001

Hughes, J. 'State Violence in the Origins of Nationalism: British Counter-insurgency and the Re-birth of Irish nationalism', in J.A. Hall and S. Malesevic, *Nationalism and War* (Cambridge University Press, 2013)

Hughes, J. Frank Kitson and 'British Way' of Counterinsurgency, *History Ireland*, Issue 1, Jan-Feb 2014, Vol 22

Humbaraci, A. *Algeria: A Revolution that Failed* (London: Pall Mall, 1966)

Hutchinson, B. *My Life in Loyalism,* (Dublin, Merrion 2020)

Hutchinson, M.C. *Revolutionary Terrorism: The FLN in Algeria* (Stanford: Hoover Institute, 1978)

Hyndman, M. *Further Afield: Journeys from a Protestant Past* (Dublin: Beyond the Pale, 1996)

Iron, R. 'Britain's Longest War: Northern Ireland, 1967–2007', in D. Marston and C. Malik, *Counterinsurgency in Modern Warfare* (Oxford: Osprey, 2008)

Jack, I. 'Gibraltar', (*Granta*, 1989)

Jackson, HF. *The FLN in Algeria* (Westport: Greenwood 1977)

Jackson, M. *Soldier: The Autobiography of General Sir Mike Jackson* (Transworld, 2007)

Joannon, P. *DeGaulle and Ireland*, (Dublin: Institute of Public Administration, 1991)

Joesten, J, *The Red Hand* (London: Robert Hale, 1962)

Johnson, P. *Ireland* (London: Granada, 1981)

Kamiya, G. 'Bush's Favorite Historian', *Salon*, 8 May 2007

Kedourie, E., *Verities Sur la Revolution Algerienne,* (Paris: Gallimard, 1970)

Keesings Contemporary Archives, vol. xiii (1962–63)

Kelley, K. *The Longest War: Northern Ireland and the IRA* (London: Zed, 1982)

Kennedy, L. *Who was to Blame for the Troubles?* (McGill Queen's University Press, 2020)

Kennedy, PM. *Soldier 'I' SAS* (London: Bloomsbury, 1989)

Kenny, I. *Talking to Ourselves* (Galway: Kenny's, 1994)

Kettle, M. *DeGaulle and Algeria, 1940-60* (London: Quartet, 1993)

Kitson, F. *'Gangs and Countergangs'*, (London: Barrie and Rockliff, 1960)

Kitson, F. *Low Intensity Operations* (London: Faber, 1971)

Kraft, J. *The Struggle for Algeria* (New York: Doubleday, 1961)

Langdon, J. *Mo Mowlan*, (London: Little, Brown & Co., 2000)

Larkin, P. *A Very British Jihad: Collusion, Conspiracy and Cover-up in Northern Ireland* (Belfast: Beyond the Pale, 2004)

Lartéguy, J. *The Centurions* (London: Heinemann, 1961)

Lawlor, P. *The Burnings,* (Cork: Mercier, 2009)

Le Seuer, D. *Uncivil War: Intellectuals and Identity Politics During the Decolonisation of Algeria* (University of Pennsylvania Press, 2001)

Lebow, N. 'British Historians and Irish History', *Éire-Ireland*, vol. 8, no. 4 (1973)

Lebjaoui, M., *Bataille d'Alger, ou Bataille d'Algerie* (Paris: Gallimard, 1972)

Lentin, A., *Historia Magazine*, (November 1972)

Leulliette, P. *St Michael and the Dragon: Memoirs of a Paratrooper* (London: Heinemann, 1964)

Lewis, B. *Semites and Anti-Semites* (New York: Norton, 1986)

Lindsay, J. *Brits Speak Out*, (Derry: Guildhall, 1998)

Lindsay, K. *Ambush at Tully West* (Dundrod Press, 1979)

Lloyd, D. *Irish Culture and Colonial Modernity*, (Cambridge U P 2011)

Loesch, A., *La Valise et le Cerceuil* (Paris: Plon, 1963)

Lorcin, Patricia (ed.), *Algeria and France, 1800–2000: Identity, Memory and Nostalgia* (Syracuse University Press, 2006)

Lustick, I. *State Building Failures in British Ireland and French Algeria* (University of California Press, 1985)

Lustick, I. *Unsettled States, Disputed Lands: Britain and Ireland, France and Algeria, and the West Bank-Gaza* (Ithaca, NY: Cornell University Press, 1993).

Asher, M. *Shoot to Kill* (London: Viking, 1990)

Mac Bride, O. *Family, Friends and Neighbours, An Irish Photobiography* (Belfast: Beyond the Pale, 2001)

Mac Stíofáin, S. *Memoirs of a Revolutionary* (Edinburgh: Gordon Cremonesi, 1975)

Madden, P (ed.), *The British Media and Ireland* (London: Campaign for Free Speech on Ireland, 1979)

Maran, R. *Torture* (New York: Prager, 1989)

Massu, J., *La Vrai Bataille d'Alger* (Paris: Plon, 1971)

Massu, J., *Le Torrent et la Digue* (Paris: Plon, 1972)

May, A and K. Rowan, *Inside Information: British Government and the Media* (London: Constable, 1982)

McCormack, Jo, *Collective Memory: France and the Algerian War, 1954-62* (Lanham, MD: Lexington, 2007)

MacDonald, M. *Children of Wrath* (Cambridge: Polity, 1986)

McDonald, H. & Cusack, J. *UDA* (Penguin, 2005)

McElroy, G. *The Catholic Church and the Northern Ireland Question* (Dublin: Gill & Macmillan, 1991)

McGarry, J. and O'Leary, B, *Explaining Northern Ireland* (Oxford: Basil Blackwell, 1995),

McGrattan, C. *Memory, Politics and Identity: Haunted by History* (Basingstoke: Macmillan, 2013)

McGuffin, *The Guineapigs,* (Penguin, 1974)

McIntosh, G. *The Force of Culture: Unionist Identities in Twentieth Century Ireland* (Cork University Press, 1999)

McKay, S. *Northern Protestants, An Unsettled People*, (Belfast, Blackstaff, 2000)

McKay, S. *Bear in Mind These Dead* (London: Faber, 2008)

McKay, S. *Northern Protestants on Shifting Ground*, (Belfast, Blackstaff, 2021)

McKittrick D et al, *Lost Lives: The Stories of the Men, Women and Children who Died as a Result of the Northern Ireland Troubles* (Edinburgh: Mainstream Publishing, 1999)

McLaughlin, P.J. *John Hume and the Revision of Irish Nationalism*, (Manchester University Press, 2013)

McNair, B. *The Sociology of Journalism* (London: Arnold, 1998)

McPhilemy, S. *The Committee: Political Assassination in Northern Ireland* (Boulder: Roberts Rinehart, 1998)

McVeigh, J. *A Wounded Church: Religion, Politics and Justice in Ireland* (U Michigan Press, 1989)

McVeigh, J. *Taking a Stand: Memoires of an Irish Priest*, (Cork: Mercier, 2004)

Meehan, N. Conor Cruise O'Brien, *Counterpunch*, 22 December 2008

Memmi, A. *The Coloniser and the Colonised* (Boston: Beacon, 2016)

Miller, D, *Queen's Rebels: Ulster Loyalists in Historical Perspective* (Dublin: Gill & Macmillan, 1978)

Miller, D. 'The Media and the Rock', in B. Rolston (ed.), *The Media and Northern Ireland* (Basingstoke: Macmillan, 1991)

Miller, D. *Don't Mention the War: Northern Ireland, Propaganda and the Media* (London: Pluto 1994)

Miller, D. *Re-thinking Northern Ireland: Culture, Ideology and Colonialism* (New York: Longmans, 1998)

Miller, R. *Britain, Palestine and Empire: The Mandate Years*, (New York: Routledge, 2016)

Moody, TW. and Martin, FX *A New History of Ireland* (Oxford: Clarendon, 1976)

Moore, C. *The Kincora Scandal* (Marino, 1996)

Moran, J. *From Northern Ireland to Afghanistan*, (Ashgate, 2013)

Morgan, T. *My Battle of Algiers* (New York: Harper Collins 2005)

Morrison, J. *The Ulster Cover-up* (Lurgan, Ulster Society, 1993)

Morton, P. *Emergency Tour: Para in South Armagh* (Northamptonshire: William Kimber, 1989)

Motley, M. *Home to Numidia* (London: Longmans, 1964)

Mulholland, M. *Longest War*, (OUP, 2002)

Murphy, B. *The Origins and Organisation of British Propaganda in Ireland, 1920* (Cork: Aubane Historical Society, 2006)

Murray, R. *The SAS in Ireland*, (Cork: Mercier, 2004)

Murray, S. *Legionnaire* (London: Sidgwick & Jackson, 1978)

Nelson, S. *Ulster's Uncertain Defenders: Loyalists and the Northern Ireland Conflict* (Belfast: Appletree, 1984)

Newsinger J. *British Counterinsurgency: From Palestine to Northern Ireland* (Palgrave, 2015)

Norman, E.R., *Anti-Catholicism in Victorian England* (London: Allen & Unwin, 1968)

Ó Muilleoir, M. *Belfast's Dome of Delight: City Hall politics, 1981– 2000,* (Belfast: Beyond the Pale, 1999)

O'Ballance, E. *The Algerian Insurrection* (London: Faber, 1967)

O'Brien, B. *The Long War: the IRA and Sinn Féin, to Today* (Dublin: Poolbeg, 1993)

O'Brien, C. C. *Memoir: My Life and Themes* (Dublin: Poolbeg) 1999

O'Brien, C. C. 'Violence in Ireland: another Algeria?' *New York Review of Books*, September 1971

O'Brien, C. C. *States of Ireland*, (London: Faber 1972)

O'Brien, C. C. 'Review of *The Wretched of the Earth* by Frantz Fanon', *Nation*, 200 (21 June 1965)

O'Brien, J. *Killing Finucane: Murder in Defence of the Realm* (Dublin: Gill & Macmillan, 2005)

O'Connor, F. *In Search of a State: Catholics in Northern Ireland* (Belfast: Blackstaff, 1993)

O'Day, A. *Political Violence in NI: Conflict and Conflict Resolution*, Greenwood, 1997

O'Doherty, M. *The Trouble with Guns: Republican Strategy and the Provisional IRA* (Belfast: Blackstaff, 1998),

O'Doherty, S. P. *The Volunteer*, (Harper Collins, 1993)

O'Dochartaigh, N. *From Civil Rights to Armalites*, (Cork University Press, 1997)

O'Leary, B. 'Lost Nun and Closet Extremist', *Times Higher Education*, 9 April 1999

O'Leary, B. 'A Long March', *Dublin Review of Books,* no. 5 (spring 2008)

O'Leary, B. 'Cuttlefish, Cholesterol and Saoirse', *Field Day Review*, no. 3 (March–April 2007)

O'Mahony, B. *Soldier of the Queen* (Dingle: Brandon, 2000)

O'Malley, P. *Biting at the Grave: The Irish Hunger Strikes and the Politics of Despair* (Boston: Beacon, 1990)

O'Malley, P. *The Uncivil Wars: Ireland Today* (Belfast: Blackstaff, 1983)

O'Neill, T. *Ulster at the Crossroads*, (London: Faber, 1969)

O'Rawe, R. *Blanketmen: An Untold Story of the H-Block Hunger Strike* (Dublin: New Island, 2005)

Operation Banner: An analysis of military operations in Northern Ireland (London: MoD 2006)

Oppenheimer, AR., *IRA: The Bombs and Bullets*, (Dublin: Irish Academic Press, 2009)

Parker, T. *May the Lord in His Mercy be Kind to Belfast* (London: Jonathan Cape, 1993)

Parkinson, AF. *Ulster Loyalism and the British Media* (Dublin: Four Courts, 1998)

Patterson, H. *Ireland's Violent Frontier: The Border and Anglo-Irish Relations during the Troubles* (Palgrave Macmillan, 2016)

Patterson, H. *War of National Liberation or Ethnic Cleansing: IRA Violence in Fermanagh during the Troubles,* 6th international conference, Spanish Association for Irish Studies, University of Valladolid, May 2006

Paulin, T. *Ireland and the English Crisis*, (Newcastle: Bloodaxe, 1984)

Pickles, D. *Algeria and France: Colonialism to Co-operation* (Westport: Greenwood, 1963)

Porch, D. *Counterinsurgency: Exposing the New Ways of War*, Cambridge University Press, 2013

Porter, B. 'How Did They Get Away with It?', *LRB,* vol. 25, no. 5 (3 March 2003)

Porter, *Lies, Damned Lies and Some Exclusives* (London: Chatto & Windus, 1984)

Porter, S and D. O'Hearn, 'New Left Podsnappery', *New Left Review*, no. 212 (July–August 1995)

Pringle, P. & Jacobson, P. *Those Are Real Bullets, Aren't They? Bloody Sunday, Derry, January* (London: Fourth Estate, 2000)

Punch, M. *State Violence, Collusion and the Troubles*, (London: Pluto 2012)

Quandt, W. *Revolution and Political Leadership, Algeria, 1954-62* (Cambridge, MA: MIT Press, 1969)

Rafferty, O.P. *Catholicism in Ulster, 1603–1983: An Interpretive History* (Dublin: Gill & Macmillan, 1994)

Reed, D. *Ireland: The Key to the British Revolution* (London: Larkin, 1984)

Rees, M. *Northern Ireland: A Personal Perspective* (Metheun 1985)

Reid, B. 'The Elephant in the Room: Colonialism, Postcolonialism and Northern Ireland', *Historical Geography*, vol.42, 2014

Rejali, D. *Torture and Democracy* (Princeton University Press, 2007)

Renwick, A. *Hidden Wounds: The Problems of Northern Ireland Veterans in Civvy Street* (London: Barbed Wire, 1999)

Reynolds, D. *The Paras: Years of Courage* (London, Express Newspapers, 1990)

Roberts, H. *Northern Ireland and Algeria: A Suitable Case for Gaullism?* (Belfast: Athol, 1986)

Roberts, H. *The Battlefield: Algeria, 1988–2002: Studies in a Broken Polity* (London: Verso, 2003)

Rolston, B. *Children of the Revolution* (Derry: Guildhall, 2011)

Rolston, B.& D. Miller (eds), *War and Words: The Northern Ireland Media Reader* (Belfast: Beyond the Pale, 1996)

Ross, FS. *Smashing H-Block* (Liverpool University Press, 2011)

Roy, J. *The War in Algeria* (New York: Grove Press, 1961)

Ruairc, P.O., *Truce: Murder, Myth and the Last Days of the Irish War of Independence,* (Cork, Mercier 2016)

Ryan, M. *War and Peace in Ireland, Britain and the IRA*, (London, Pluto, 1994)

Sanders, A & Woods, I.S. *Times of Troubles, Britain's War* (Edinburgh University Press 2012)

Schmidt A. P. and J. de Graaf, *Violence as Communication: Insurgent Terrorism and the Western News Media* (London: Sage, 1982)

Servan-Schreiber, JJ. *Lieutenant in Algeria* (Westport: Greenwood, 1977)

Sharrock, D. & Davenport, M. *Man of War, Man of Peace: The Unauthorised Biography of Gerry Adams* (London: Macmillan, 1997)

Shirlow, P. *The End of Ulster Loyalism* (Manchester University Press, 2012)

Simpson, K. *Unionist Voices and the Politics of Remembering the Past in Northern Ireland* (Basingstoke: Macmillan, 2009)

Si Azzedine, *On Nous Appelait Fellaghas* (Paris, 1976)

Sluka, JA, *Hearts and Minds, Water and Fish: Support for the IRA and INLA in a Northern Irish Ghetto* (London: JAI Press, 1989)

Smith, A. *The British Press Since World War Two* (Vancouver: David & Charles, 1974)

Smith, MLR. *Fighting for Ireland: The Military Strategy of the Irish Republican Movement* (London: Routledge, 1995)

Snoddy, R. *The Good, the Bad and the Unacceptable* (London: Faber, 1992)

Sparks, C. 'Expanding and Refining the Propaganda Model', *Westminster Papers in Communication and Culture*, vol. 4, no. (2000)

Stalker, J. *Stalker,* (London: Harrap, 1988)

Stora, B. *Algeria, 1830–2000: A Short History* (Cornell University Press, 2001)

Sunday Times Insight Team, *Ulster* (Harmondsworth: Penguin, 1972)

Sutton, M. *Bear in Mind These Dead: An Index of Deaths from the Conflict in Ireland, 1969-1993* (Belfast: Beyond the Pale, 1994)

Talbott, J., 'French Public Opinion and the Algerian War', *French Historical Studies*, no. 9 (fall, 1975)

Taylor, P. *Brits: The War Against the IRA,* (London: Bloomsbury, 2002)

Taylor, P. *Loyalists* (London: Bloomsbury, 2000)

Taylor, P. *Stalker: The Search for the Truth.* (London: Faber, 1987)

Thomas, J. 'Bloody Ireland', *Columbia Journalism Review*, vol. 27, no. 1 (May–June 1988)

Tillion, G. *France and Algeria: Complementary Enemies* (New York: Knopf, 1960)

Todd, J. and Ruane, J. *The Dynamics of the Conflict in Northern Ireland* (Cambridge University Press, 1996)

Todd, O. *Camus: A life* (Da Capo Press, 2010)

Tonkin, E. et al (eds), *History and Ethnicity* (NY: Routledge, 1989)

Toolis, K. *Rebel Hearts: Journey within the IRA's Soul* (New York: St Martin's Press, 1995)

Townsend, C., *Britain's Civil Wars* (London, Faber, 1986)

Trinquier, R., *Modern Warfare: A French View of Counterinsurgency* (London: Pall Mall, 1964)

Unwin, M. *A State in Denial British Collaboration with Loyalist Paramilitaries*, Mercier 2016

Urban, M. *Big Boys Rules, The Secret Struggle Against the IRA*, (London, Faber, 1992)

Van Voris, WH., *Violence in Ulster (University Massachusetts, 1975)*

Vidal-Naquet, P. *Torture: Cancer of Democracy* (Harmondsworth: Penguin, 1974)

Walker, B. *Dancing to History's Tune* (Belfast: Institute of Irish Studies, 1996)

Walsh, J, *The Falling Angels: An Irish Romance*, (London: Flamingo, 1999)

Watts, D. *The Constitution of Northern Ireland*, (London: Heineman, 1981)

Weitzer, RJ. *Transforming Settler States: Conflict and Security, Northern Ireland and Zimbabwe* (University of California Press 1992)

Wharton, K. *A Long Long War: Voices from the British Army in Northern Ireland 1969-98* (Solihull: Helion, 2010)

Wharton, K. *Wasted Years, Wasted Lives, The British Army in Northern Ireland, 1975-77*, (Solihull: Hellion, 2013

Whelan, D. 'Conor Cruise O'Brien and the Legitimisation of Violence', *Irish Political Studies*, vol. 21, no. (2006)

White, R. 'The IRA: An Assessment of Sectarianism', *Terrorism and Political Violence*, vol. 9, no. 1 (spring 1997)

Wilkinson, P. *Terrorism and the Liberal State*, (London: Macmillan 1977)

Williams, A. *Barbouze* (London: Panther, 1965)

Williams, P. *Wars, Plots and Scandals in Post War France* (Cambridge University Press, 1970)

Willis, M. *The Islamist Challenge in Algeria: A Political History* (New York University Press, 1996)

Wolfe, P. Settler Colonialism and the Elimination of the Native, *Journal of Genocide Research*, vol. 8, 2006, issue 4, December,

Woodies, J. *Armies and Politics* (London: Lawrence & Wishart, 1977)

Wright, F. *Northern Ireland: A Comparative Analysis* (Dublin: Gill & Macmillan, 1992)

INDEX